STATES OF LIBERATION

GERMAN AND EUROPEAN STUDIES

General Editor: Jennifer L. Jenkins

SAMUEL CLOWES HUNEKE

STATES OF LIBERATION

GAY MEN BETWEEN DICTATORSHIP AND
DEMOCRACY IN COLD WAR GERMANY

UNIVERSITY OF TORONTO PRESS
Toronto Buffalo London

© University of Toronto Press 2022
Toronto Buffalo London
utorontopress.com

ISBN 978-1-4875-4210-8 (cloth)   ISBN 978-1-4875-4213-9 (EPUB)
ISBN 978-1-4875-4214-6 (paper)   ISBN 978-1-4875-4212-2 (PDF)

Library and Archives Canada Cataloguing in Publication

Title: States of liberation : gay men between dictatorship and democracy
    in Cold War Germany / Samuel Clowes Huneke.
Names: Huneke, Samuel Clowes, author.
Description: Includes bibliographical references and index.
Identifiers: Canadiana (print) 20210339551 | Canadiana (ebook) 20210339675 |
    ISBN 9781487542108 (cloth) | ISBN 9781487542146 (paper) |
    ISBN 9781487542139 (EPUB) | ISBN 9781487542122 (PDF)
Subjects: LCSH: Male homosexuality – Germany – History – 20th century. |
    LCSH: Gay men – Germany – History – 20th century. | LCSH: Gay
    men – Political activity – Germany – History – 20th century. | LCSH: Gay
    rights – Germany – History – 20th century. | LCSH: Cold War.
Classification: LCC HQ76.2.G4 H86 2022 | DDC 306.76/62094309045–dc23

The German and European Studies series is funded by the DAAD with funds
from the German Federal Foreign Office

 DAAD **Deutscher Akademischer Austauschdienst
German Academic Exchange Service**

We wish to acknowledge the land on which the University of Toronto Press
operates. This land is the traditional territory of the Wendat, the Anishnaabeg,
the Haudenosaunee, the Métis, and the Mississaugas of the Credit First Nation.

University of Toronto Press acknowledges the financial support of the
Government of Canada, the Canada Council for the Arts, and the Ontario Arts
Council, an agency of the Government of Ontario, for its publishing activities.

 Canada Council   Conseil des Arts
for the Arts   du Canada

ONTARIO ARTS COUNCIL
CONSEIL DES ARTS DE L'ONTARIO
an Ontario government agency
un organisme du gouvernement de l'Ontario

Funded by the   Financé par le
Government   gouvernement
of Canada   du Canada    Canada

For Mom and Dad

The growing good of the world is partly dependent on unhistoric acts; and that things are not so ill with you and me as they might have been, is half owing to the number who lived faithfully a hidden life, and rest in unvisited tombs.

– George Eliot, *Middlemarch*

Contents

Figures

Acknowledgments

I remember clearly that sunny spring day at Stanford University. It was 2015, and I was walking to the History Department when I received an email from my doctoral adviser, Edith Sheffer. She wanted to know what had happened to queer Germans during the Cold War. That seemingly simple question launched me on the research that eventually became this book. In the years since, Edith has been an unwavering friend and mentor. She has read too many drafts of this work to count and has never ceased to offer incisive, generous critiques of it, for which I am profoundly grateful. It would not be the book it is without her.

Over the last several years, J.P. Daughton, Adrian Daub, Pieter Judson, and Matthew Sommer also read numerous drafts of this manuscript. Their feedback shaped the book's arguments and helped me to think expansively about the stakes of this work. I am indebted to them for their guidance and their friendship.

In graduate school I was lucky to find a tight-knit cohort of German historians. Ian Beacock, Benjamin Hein, and Michelle Kahn were always happy to peruse new chapters or think through fresh ideas. We became fast friends during my six years in the Bay Area, and I cherish my relationships with them.

During my California years, I was also fortunate to befriend Paul Robinson, who has been both a generous mentor and a forgiving bridge partner.

In 2019 I came to George Mason University's Department of History and Art History, and I consider myself lucky to have joined such a congenial and intellectually stimulating group of colleagues. This book has profited immensely from their engagement with and support of it.

In May 2020, in the early weeks of the COVID-19 pandemic, an international group of scholars logged onto Zoom for a workshop dedicated to discussing this manuscript. I am incredibly grateful to Monica Black,

Anna von der Goltz, Dan Healey, Steve Barnes, Alison Landsberg, and Sam Lebovic for the care they took in reading it, especially in the midst of a global health emergency. Their critiques and suggestions made it a far more compelling book. My thanks also go to Joan Bristol, who generously took notes during the workshop.

As I researched, wrote, and rewrote this book, my work benefited from conference panels, workshop presentations, and conversations with colleagues around the world. For their help, encouragement, and faith in this project, I thank Scott Arcenas, Josh Armstrong, Keith Baker, Robert Beachy, Maria Borowski, Robert DeCaroli, Jeremy DeWaal, Rowan Dorin, Jennifer Evans, Christopher Ewing, Kyle Frackman, Estelle Freedman, Geoffrey Giles, David Halperin, Dagmar Herzog, Erik Huneke, Mills Kelly, Matthew Karush, Rüdiger Lautmann, Martin Lücke, Norman Naimark, Marti Lybeck, Sun-Young Park, Brian Platt, Andrew Port, Steven Press, Andrea Rottmann, Londa Schiebinger, Zachary Schrag, Randolph Scully, James Sheehan, Suzanne Smith, David Spreen, Veronika Springmann, Peter Stansky, Philipp Stelzel, Lauren Stokes, Katie Sutton, Carolyn Taratko, and Richard Wetzell.

Stephen Shapiro at University of Toronto Press has been a joy to work with, demystifying the often-stressful process of publishing my first book. Kate Blackmer produced two beautiful maps for this project, for which I thank her. I am also grateful to the three anonymous reviewers, whose suggestions substantially improved the final copy.

The research presented here would have been impossible without a legion of archivists who helped me along the way. My thanks go to Carsten Repke at the Stasi Archive; Martin Luchterhandt and Lydia Kiesling at the Berlin Regional Archive; Jean McElwee Cannon at the Hoover Institution Library and Archives; Kristine Schmidt at the Berlin Gay Museum Archive; Roland Pfirschke, Karin Schorsch, Michael Merchel, Petra Sprenger, and Ragna Petrak at the Saxony Main State Archive in Dresden; Michelle Bleidt at the Federal Archive in Koblenz; Martin Stingl and Sandra Schleinitz at the Karlsruhe General Regional Archive; and Johann Zilien at the Hessian Main Archive in Wiesbaden.

To my oral history partners, thank you. I hope I have done justice to your stories.

A number of institutions supported me while I researched, wrote, and revised. This work was funded by a Silas Palmer Fellowship from the Hoover Institution Library and Archives, two Lane Summer Research Grants from the Stanford Program in the History and Philosophy of Science, a G.J. Pigott Fellowship from the Stanford School of Humanities and Sciences, a Stanford–Free University Berlin Graduate Exchange Fellowship, a Graduate Research Grant from the Europe Center at

Stanford, a Weter Fellowship from the Stanford History Department, a Mabelle McLeod Lewis Memorial Fund Dissertation Fellowship, grants from the George Mason Department of History and Art History Nelson Research Fund, and generous support, including research leave, from the George Mason College of Humanities and Social Sciences.

My path into the historical profession has been a long one that began as a middle school student. This book is also a product of the encouragement I received from mentors along the way, especially from Mike Ortmann at Lawrence High School and from Ute Brandes, Catherine Epstein, Heidi Gilpin, Christian Rogowski, and Ronald Rosbottom at Amherst College.

Working on this topic reminds me constantly of how fortunate I am to come from a loving family. A special thanks to my aunt and uncle Nancy Huneke and David Hamilton, who were my California home away from home; my cousins Alec Clowes, Sarah Clowes, and Edie Bowles; my aunts and uncles Mardi and Frank Bowles, Jon and Ev Clowes, Markie Clowes, and Susan Detweiler; and my German "parents" in Baden-Baden, Gisi Erbslöh and Burkhard Schlichting.

I am also lucky to have a large chosen family of friends. For their support over the years, I thank Max Alderman and Ben Cole, Chelsea Amegatcher, Nina Bernard, Casey Brennan, Olivier Bodson, Russell Burge, Rachel Chin, Nolan Danley, Nathaniel Edwards, James Frank, Isaac Gendelman and Jason Plesha, Franz Heitzer and Adrian Toschev, Richie Hofmann, Peter Johnston, Anjulie Kalsia, Akane Kanai, Jing Li, James Longbotham, Jared Miller, Julie Moorman, Sebastian Naumann, Tom Newton and Alex Chan, Roger Pellegrini and Harry Shamansky, Philip Schwada and Chris Farris, Matthew Sellers, Damien Soghoian, Alex Speir, Rebecca Wall, and David Westwood and Carolyn Brotherton.

Most important, to my partner, Hugh Ross, thank you for the years of adventure, love, and encouragement as I wrote, revised, and fretted about this book.

Finally, I feel lucky every day to have my immediate family. My brother and sister-in-law Ned and Erin Huneke are humorous, loving presences in my life, always happy to recommend a good novel or a new pie recipe. My parents, Edith Clowes and Craig Huneke, have encouraged my interest in history since I was a twelve-year-old kid reading biographies of Henry VIII. They have never ceased to support me, even when I did not always believe I would see this project through to completion. This book is dedicated to them.

A Note on Place Names

For all cities and countries, I use the English translation – Cologne, for instance, instead of Köln (see figure 0.1). For Chemnitz, which the East German government renamed Karl-Marx-Stadt in 1953 and which regained its former name after Germany's reunification, I use Karl-Marx-City. Municipal addresses, on the other hand, I leave untranslated (see figure 0.2). Street names such as Schönhauser Allee, which in English would be "Schönhaus Boulevard," or Alexanderplatz, which would be "Alexander Plaza," I render in the original German.

Terms and Abbreviations

BASIC LAW	The *Grundgesetz* was West Germany's constitution.
BUNDESTAG	The lower and more powerful house of the West German parliament.
CDU	The Christian Democratic Union (*Christlich Demokratische Union Deutschlands*) is postwar Germany's principal centre-right political party. It occupied the West German Chancellorship during 1949–69 and 1982–90.
CSU	The Christian Social Union (*Christlich-Soziale Union in Bayern*) is the CDU's sister party in Bavaria, the southern federal state where the CDU does not contest elections.
FDJ	The Free German Youth (*Freie Deutsche Jugend*) was East Germany's official youth organization.
FDP	The Free Democratic Party (*Freie Demokratische Partei*) is Germany's classically liberal party, advocating personal liberty and free markets. For most of West Germany's existence, it governed as the junior coalition partner with either the CDU/CSU or the SPD.
FRG	The Federal Republic of Germany (*Bundesrepublik Deutschland*), also known as WEST GERMANY.
GDR	The German Democratic Republic (*Deutsche Demokratische Republik*), also known as EAST GERMANY.
IM	An unofficial collaborator (*inoffizieller Mitarbeiter*) was an informant, often an ordinary citizen, recruited by the Stasi to pass information to the secret police.
KPD	The Communist Party of Germany (*Kommunistische Partei Deutschlands*). The party was a major political force in the Weimar Republic. It ceased to exist in what became the GDR in 1946 after it merged with the SPD to form the SED. The West German government banned it in 1956.

MÄNNERBUND	Homosocial associations of men, which can be translated as male association, society, or covenant. It is a cornerstone of the masculinist conceptualization of male-male desire.
MFS	The Ministry for State Security (*Ministerium für Staatssicherheit*), better known as the STASI. The MfS was East Germany's secret police and intelligence service.
NATO	The North Atlantic Treaty Organization, founded in 1949 to cement the alliance among the United States and Western European countries. West Germany was admitted to the alliance in 1955.
NVA	The National People's Army (*Nationale Volksarmee*) was East Germany's military.
REICHSTAG	The lower house of the German parliament between 1871 and 1945.
REPUBLIKFLUCHT	Literally "flight from the republic," *Republikflucht* denoted the crime of illegally leaving the GDR.
SED	The Socialist Unity Party (*Sozialistische Einheitspartei*) was East Germany's ruling party from 1949 until 1990. It was the product of a forced merger of the East German KPD and SPD in 1946. Although it technically ruled the GDR in coalition with other parties, including the CDU, it was guaranteed the leadership of the state in the 1968 East German constitution.
SEW	The Socialist Unity Party of West Berlin (*Sozialistische Einheitspartei Westberlins*) was the SED's sister party in West Berlin.
SPD	The Social Democratic Party of Germany (*Sozialdemokratische Partei Deutschlands*) is Germany's principal centre-left party and the oldest extant party in Germany. It governed West Germany from 1969 to 1982 in coalition with the FDP.
VERFASSUNGSSCHUTZ	West Germany's domestic counter-intelligence agency. It translates literally as "constitution protection."
VOLKSKAMMER	The East German parliament.

Figure 0.1. East and West Germany, c. 1975

Figure 0.2. Gay spaces in divided Berlin, c. 1975

Introduction

The click of a camera's shutter and a blinding flash: the moment is captured. He is twirling away from you, eyes skimming the sundry faces and a grin underneath his moustache. A wide-brimmed hat perches over his thick hair, encircled by a polka-dot scarf. He wears a frilly summer dress held by an enamel clasp. Behind him is another man, dressed in an open vest and fedora, with a long strand of beads cascading down. His chest glistens, his lips are pursed. All around these two dancers are men – seated, contemplative, jovial men, chattering away as their eyes linger over the dancers. It is a happy picture. It is a queer picture (figure 0.3).

Taken in 1977, the photograph depicts a gay carnival. The party takes place in the basement of a suburban villa and is humorously called Hibaré, a portmanteau of cabaret and the group's name HIB, short for Homosexual Interest-group Berlin. The hostess is Charlotte von Mahlsdorf, one of Germany's most famous trans women. She runs the villa as a museum for furniture and curios from imperial Germany and lets these rambunctious gay men – and women – use it for their festivals.

But they do not gather just for fun; they are also a political group. They believe that the state has an obligation to help them overcome the prejudices that still make many of their lives unlivable. They gather at the Mahlsdorf villa not only to don silly costumes, perform skits, and recite poetry but also to plan their next petition to the government, to discuss the stigma they all face, and to find more gay men and lesbians. They are, in fact, their country's first gay liberation movement.

It just so happens that that country is East Germany, a communist dictatorship.

Homosexuality and the State

Fast-forward almost exactly forty years and Berlin, now reunified Germany's capital, is awash in rainbow flags. It is 30 June 2017, and

Figure 0.3. Dancing figures, 1977. Courtesy of Peter Rausch

crowds celebrate in the shadow of the Brandenburg Gate. After a week of political squabbling, the German parliament has voted to legalize marriage equality, seeming to set a coda on the country's decades-long gay struggle.

The only genuinely surprising thing about that vote was that it took so long to happen. By the time marriage equality was fact in Germany, over 80 per cent of the population supported it.[1] After all, the country, and in particular its larger cities, had rapidly become a hub of global gay life. Every year, throngs of gay tourists descend on Berlin, where more than half a million people crowd the streets every summer for the city's pride festival. When The New Yorker covered the capital's nightlife in 2014, it exclaimed: "Berlin's queer culture is the city's most essential and distinguishing element."[2]

What that flourishing culture belies is that less than sixty years ago Germany still criminalized homosexual acts and imprisoned tens of thousands of gay men under its anti-homosexuality laws. Less than a century ago Nazi Germany sent gay people to concentration camps, where around six thousand of them died. Although it may seem intuitively obvious that Germany – along with much of the Western world – should accept homosexuality today, it is breathtaking that a country that so brutally persecuted sexual minorities would, only decades later, celebrate their existence.

Which brings us back to the Hibaré performance in an East Berlin basement in 1977. The picture offers startling commentary on both the idea of gay liberation and our conception of what life under state socialism looked like. Gay liberation – in the traditional telling – is something easily definable with concrete milestones. It is often supposed to come out of Western, consumer-capitalist democracies and to have been largely absent from authoritarian states. The arc of gay liberation has been closely tied, in scholarship and popular imagination alike, to the fate of liberal democracy.[3] Whatever the East German state was, it was not supposed to have been a hospitable place for gay liberation activists. And whatever gay liberation was, it certainly was not supposed to have come out of the cellar of a furniture museum in a communist dictatorship.

The HIB was only one of numerous gay activist organizations that sprang up in the two Germanies in the decades between the end of the Second World War and the fall of the Berlin Wall in 1989. Confronted as they were with the Nazi legacy of imprisonment and murder, these activists strove in ever-changing ways to win rights from and assert privileges against the East and West German governments. At the same time, those states, which had inherited anti-homosexuality laws from the National Socialists, sought to stamp out, to police, and, eventually, to understand homosexuality in their societies. Over the last few decades, a burgeoning number of scholars have turned their attention to these twin pasts, that is, to how East and West Germany each regulated male homosexuality and how, in turn, gay activists mobilized in each country.[4] Yet, these two histories have never been recounted together, as one. To tell that story – to weave together and to compare the trajectories of male homosexuality in the two German states across the span of forty years – is the aim of this book.

Although I set out to write a book that would integrate histories of male and female homosexuality, the more interviews I collected and the more time I spent in archives, the more I realized how difficult a task that would be. Part of the difficulty lies in sources. Paragraph (§) 175 of the German penal code, the law that banned homosexual acts, never criminalized female homosexuality. Thus, while historians have recourse to thousands of police and court files about gay men prosecuted under the law, there is no similar corpus of files dealing with female homosexuality. Because §175 is the focus of the book's initial chapters, women appear only fleetingly. To the East and West German governments, female homosexuality was not as pressing a concern as male homosexuality. When I write about persecution, it is primarily the persecution of gay men.

Women do appear in the book's second half, as lesbians and gay men began to theorize forms of activism that would unite rather than divide them. Nonetheless, the history that this book charts is ultimately one dominated by men and cannot claim to be representative of the experiences of lesbians, who grew increasingly – and justifiably – frustrated with the sexism they experienced from male activists. The story of lesbians' persecution and liberation in Cold War Germany is deserving of its own treatment and is too important to efface with the assumption that gay and lesbian experiences were simply the same. While lesbians do figure into *States of Liberation*, the experiences of gay men remain its focus.

States of Liberation thus traces the evolving relationships between gay men and the two postwar German states, comparing and contrasting how each country persecuted gay populations, and how, in turn, those populations expounded political, social, and economic agendas and sought to enact them. Relying on oral histories and on documents from ten archives, many of which have never before been brought to light, I advance three overarching arguments about gay citizenship and the history of Cold War Germany. First, I contend that comparing each state's persecution of gay men in the 1950s and 1960s reveals homophobia to be a much more malleable phenomenon than most historians have heretofore recognized. Second, I argue that a similar comparison of gay activism in the two Germanies illustrates both how the idea of gay liberation is historically contingent and the need to reconceptualize it independent of the Western, democratic, and consumer-capitalist contexts in which it is so often located. Finally, I assert that centring gay men as subjects in postwar German history helps us unsettle Cold War-era assumptions about the supposed success of liberal capitalism in West Germany and the alleged failures of state socialism in East Germany. In so doing, I seek to trace a more complex picture of dictatorship and democracy, both during the Cold War and in our world today.

Rethinking Homophobia

Only recently have historians begun to think about homophobia as something that changes over time. In fact, many works in the history of sexuality rely on an often-unstated assumption that anti-gay prejudices, practices, and policies in different times and places have the same origins and have served the same purposes. Since the history of sexuality arose in the 1970s, its practitioners have, surprisingly perhaps, showed little interest in the sources of, or reasons for, anti-gay views, which were first named homophobia in the 1960s.[5] These scholars were intent on the urgent work of unearthing long-submerged queer pasts, cataloguing forms of persecution, and explaining how sexual identities changed over time.

In fact, for many decades the question of homophobia seemed largely settled. There were two explanations on hand to describe its origins and function in modern society. One, which we might think of as the othering hypothesis, has a long pedigree in the history of Western thought. It posits, as the historian of medieval Europe R.I. Moore put it,

campaigns of moral repression with which newly instituted regimes so often establish their legitimacy, proclaim their adherence to traditional values, discredit their enemies and consolidate their hold on the instruments of power. Such drives tend to be directed [...] against stereotypical public enemies who may serve as the locus of rhetoric and the object of attack.[6]

It is the same hypothesis Sigmund Freud elucidated in *Civilization and Its Discontents* when he wrote, "There is an advantage, not to be under-valued, in the existence of smaller communities, through which the aggressive instinct can find an outlet in enmity towards those outside the group."[7] It is a persuasive hypothesis, which suggests that persecution and prejudice are forms of scapegoating that exist as a means for the powerful to stay in power.

The second explanation, which scholars often express with the term "biopolitics," originated in the work of Michel Foucault and has since become a standard clarification for why homosexuality arose as an identity when it did. Foucault posited that the ascent of sexual identities was the result of society's and the state's growing willingness to regulate individuals' private lives.[8] This new exercise of power – by which Foucault meant normative relations among individuals instead of hierarchical domination – served the interest of moulding a healthy population of workers and subjects. The state thus began to take an interest in suppressing sexual habits that it perceived as unhealthy or inimical to reproduction. The biopolitical hypothesis appears in many contemporary works on the history of sexuality as a sort of background assumption to explain the existence of anti-gay laws and taboos.

In recent years, though, historians have begun to think about homophobia in more careful ways, unearthing how different regimes nurtured it for different reasons and to different ends. Dan Healey's *Russian Homophobia from Stalin to Sochi*, in particular, marks one of the first attempts to think through how state animus towards queer people emerged and changed over the course of decades in a specific national context. In so doing, he reveals just how contingent the phenomenon we call homophobia is, questioning whether Western conceptions of anti-gay prejudice can be applied to Russia.[9] In *Sexual Hegemony*, Christopher Chitty similarly critiques the notion that religion sits at the root of "sexual intolerance," although his focus on imbrications of capitalism and sexuality (a conjunction to which I turn below) makes it seem at times that he is supplanting capital for religion as homophobia's source.[10]

In Germany, the high-water mark of anti-gay sentiment arrived with fascism. The National Socialists investigated approximately 100,000 men under a new, harsher version of §175 and sent between 5,000 and 15,000 to concentration camps.[11] For several decades, historians have sought to explain the fascists' extreme persecution of gay men. While they have offered various theories, many argue that the persecution stemmed from a fear that gay men were naturally conspiratorial and that gay cliques would develop in all-male organs of power, such as the Nazi party, the military, and the police.[12] The nature of these fears, alongside widespread misogyny, also meant that the fascist state persecuted primarily men who had sex with men. Nazis remained largely confident that women, whom they believed were passive and sexually pliable, did not pose a similar threat.

After the war, each German state had to decide what to do with §175. In West Germany, the new democratic government retained the Nazi version of the law. Prosecutors there used it to convict more than 50,000 men between 1949 and 1969. Why West Germany continued to employ a Nazi law is no easy question to answer. Using propaganda, court cases, and documents from the German federal archive, I argue that West German officials, weighed down by both the fear of communism and the memory of fascism, continued to cast gay men as members of a threatening conspiracy.[13] Significantly, they did not do so to rally voters. Rather, the animus was a symptom of anxieties surrounding the state's stability and legitimacy. This strange paranoia not only provided justification for the law but even led the West German intelligence services to recruit gay spies to ferret out domestic threats and to extract information from East Germany. West German animus was the result of neither scapegoating nor biopolitical preoccupations alone but rather an expression of insecurity in a state struggling to emerge from fascism.

Although the two Germanies shared a history and a legal culture, East Germany charted a very different path, adopting a fundamentally reactive posture vis-à-vis homosexuality. As a self-proclaimed anti-fascist state, it cleaned house of Nazism's remnants, including laws passed under that dictatorship. Its courts invalidated the Nazi version of §175 soon after the country came into being and replaced it with a far milder law. But the communists also feared that the population they governed was fundamentally hostile to gay people and that any association with homosexuality might delegitimize their rule. Even as the regime established criminal leniency towards gay men, it made clear, through purges and propaganda, that it would not tolerate homosexuality in the party, military, or security services. Thus, the imperative to establish a stable, legitimate government in the shadow of Nazism also shaped East Germany's schizophrenic approach to homosexuality.[14]

Comparing the two Germanies' divergent treatment of gay men – and the anxieties upon which each animus was predicated – thus reveals homophobia to be a profoundly contingent historical phenomenon. As some Jewish historians argue of antisemitism, homophobia is not a transhistorical constant but rather a constructed belief or feeling, sometimes even imposed with specific political goals in mind.[15] The history of anti-gay sentiment in Germany suggests that "homophobia" may not even be a useful term for historians, that it encompasses too many different phenomena that served different purposes in different times and places. While I do not suggest a universal replacement for the term – indeed, I argue that the contingency inherent in anti-gay prejudices and practices makes it impossible for a single term to encompass them all – I primarily employ the phrase "anti-gay animus." I do so because this book's focus remains on how states conceived of homosexuality and what effects those conceptions had on juridical and police practices. In declining to use the term "homophobia," I hope to unsettle anti-gay sentiment – to make it strange – and thereby to create space to think about its construction and purpose as a tool of the state.

Gay Liberation, East and West

Unlike the history of anti-gay animus, gay political movements have been thoroughly studied by queer theorists and historians of sexuality. Their work has led to raucous debate, among scholars and activists alike, about how to view the twentieth century's gay liberation movements – especially those in the United States.[16] Thanks to the insights of this scholarship, historians now better understand the conflicting and often counter-intuitive dynamics that shaped these movements.

While many popular accounts offer tales of liberation's triumph over the past fifty years, queer theorists have increasingly cautioned that such narratives cast both progress and its shortcomings as inevitable. "A queered history," Jennifer Evans writes, "questions claims to a singular, linear march of time and universal experience and points out the unconscious ways in which progressive narrative arcs often seep into our analyses."[17] Such work is needed because those progressive arcs can encourage us to ignore that, for example, the American gay movement's ambitions shrank drastically between 1969 and 2000, from, as Martin Duberman puts it, a "full-scale assault on sexual and gender norms, on imperialistic wars and capitalistic greed, and on the shameful mistreatment of racial and ethnic minorities" to a quest for marriage and conformity.[18] In questioning such narratives, queer scholars seek not only to get out from under the weight of Whiggish assumptions about progress but also to critique and enrich what Elizabeth Freeman has termed "our own sexually impoverished present."[19]

These queer approaches often look at the tensions and trade-offs among activists in order to draw out their contradictions and even hypocrisies. They examine who within activist movements made what claims and for what reasons, revealing how the priorities of cisgender white men typically gained precedence over the needs, desires, and programs of other groups. Most important, these studies have made it possible for scholars to examine gay and lesbian activism with an eye for its queer potential, its unpremeditated dynamics, and its unexpected consequences, no longer tethered by "liberationist pieties about the future."[20]

States of Liberation extends these approaches by comparing the trajectories of gay liberation movements in two countries, one a consumer-capitalist democracy, the other a socialist dictatorship. Examining the two countries in tandem reveals not only that what we think of as gay liberation can, in fact, occur in authoritarian and non-capitalist settings but also that it evolves on numerous planes and takes varied forms that do not always move in unison. By making these comparisons, I contend that, just as "homophobia" is a poor conceptual term, so too is "gay liberation" (along with its synonyms) an over-generalized concept that draws together too many efforts, values, and desires to be of use to historians.

Thus, my interest is not in finding the best, the correct, or the most radical project to hold up as an exemplar. Nor is it in uncovering where these movements fell short of a preconceived standard. I have written neither a triumphal history nor a pure critique of one, and this book does not ask what model of activism, statehood, or market relations delivered the best form of gay liberation. Rather, I look to describe activists' efforts as social, economic, and political movements in order to understand how they changed the societies and the governments with which they interacted. In so doing, *States of Liberation* forms a piece with other recent historical work, such as Emily Hobson's *Lavender and*

Red, Timothy Stewart-Winter's *Queer Clout*, Laurie Marhoefer's *Sex and the Weimar Republic*, and Jens Rydström's *Odd Couples*, all of which chart gay and lesbian activism in the United States and Europe. These historians unearth ways in which activists engaged social and political structures beyond their movements and how those interactions in turn changed the bounds of what gay liberation meant at a particular time, in a particular place.[21]

A comparison of these efforts in East and West Germany first allows us to divorce the idea of liberation from the democratic, consumer-capitalist context in which historians and theorists often locate it. There is a wealth of scholarship, dating back to John D'Emilio's landmark 1983 essay "Capitalism and Gay Identity" and Foucault's own sometimes-vague assertions, that situates homosexual identities, subcultures, and politics in capitalist republics. These works identify the market economy, in particular, as a necessary precondition of such phenomena.[22]

Some see the conjunction as fortunate. As Deirdre Nansen McCloskey, for instance, contends, "The market is not the enemy of queers. The restaurants and bars from which the drag queens exploded in political action in the 1960s in San Francisco and then in New York were after all profit-making entities."[23] On the other side are queer critics who, following in Foucault's footsteps, attack the ways in which capital and neoliberal values co-opt what they consider gay liberation ought to be. But *States of Liberation* illustrates that gay liberation is not, in fact, tied to a specific economic or state form. Tracing the parallel paths of gay activism in East and West Germany illuminates how liberation efforts flourished in varied ways under different economic and political conditions.

Untethering the idea of gay liberation from its liberal, consumer-capitalist, and democratic moorings allows us to view it as a changing project that arose on multiple planes, in different ways, and under diverse conditions. The kinds of demands and actions that together constituted gay liberation led to change on those different planes in profoundly different and often counter-intuitive ways. To put it another way, this book seeks to understand how the mobilization of homosexuality as a political identity – as a form of sexual citizenship – functioned under particular political and economic regimes. Following on the work of scholars such as Diane Richardson and Katie Sutton, I understand sexual citizenship as an expression of social, cultural, and political claims to belonging that sexual minorities make on the basis of their sexuality.[24] To borrow Kathleen Canning's words, gay men in postwar Germany, like women in the Weimar Republic, articulated "a 'plurality of specific allegiances' […] in a recognizable language of claims we might call 'citizenship.'"[25] *States of Liberation* compares and contrasts how East and West German activists elucidated and acted upon shifting conceptions of sexual citizenship.

After West Germany legalized adult homosexuality in 1969, gay men and lesbians enjoyed an ever-expanding subculture that encompassed a vast array of saunas, clubs, bars, and magazines. At the same time, young activists coalesced around the idea that, as a persecuted minority, gay men and lesbians should band together to exercise political power in opposition to existing social and political institutions. These efforts led to an ever richer social and cultural scene catering to queer people, with the appearance of coffee shops, bookstores, archives, and museums for gay and lesbian communities. Nonetheless, it did not lead to the changes in federal law or policy that activists had sought since the early 1970s.[26]

Across the Iron Curtain, an inverse situation obtained. In the 1970s, activists in East Germany began to elucidate a very different conception of sexual citizenship, one that sought to carve out a place for gay men and lesbians within East German socialism. This concept of sexual citizenship did not emphasize opposition or separateness, and only in the last years of the Cold War did East German cities begin allowing openly gay clubs and bars to exist. Using heretofore unanalysed files from the Stasi Archive, however, *States of Liberation* reveals how East German activists successfully pressured the dictatorship to make sweeping, pro-gay policy reforms in the 1980s. In this respect, the country far outpaced not only West Germany but also most other socialist and capitalist countries in Europe.

Ironically, by the late 1980s, activists in each country looked across the Iron Curtain with a certain jealousy at the gay scene and gay movement the other had created. Different conceptions of sexual citizenship and different relationships between activists and governments had evolved in each Germany, leading to divergent forms of gay liberation in the two countries. Looked at in this way, liberation becomes a suddenly slippery concept – a product of neither capitalism nor democracy but rather an unstable set of claims inconsistently made and counterintuitively realized. At best, we can speak of states of liberation.

Dictatorship and Democracy in the Two Germanies

While I seek to use the methods of political, legal, and social history to question the epistemological value of homophobia and gay liberation, I also look to employ queer perspectives to trouble our understanding of state and society in East and West Germany. Acknowledging gay people not only as objects of state interest but also as subjects of political and social change, I argue, gives us new insights into both German states and the relationships between them. In making these arguments, *States of Liberation* adds to recent scholarship that seeks to move past simple Cold War narratives of success or failure and instead to tell a richer story of the two Germanies' entangled history.

The earliest histories of the two states often dealt with either one or the other. Rarely were the two countries intertwined in a single narrative. Yet, as historians have moved past Cold War assumptions about the success of the Federal Republic and the failures of East Germany, so too have they increasingly sought to tell conjoined histories of the two states. Taking up Christoph Kleßmann's conception of postwar German history as one of "asymmetrical entanglement," historians now look to comprehend how the two German states were "divided, but not disconnected."[27]

Weaving together histories of male homosexuality in the two Germanies, *States of Liberation* unearths a deeply interconnected past. Cold War anxieties about the other Germany bulked large in how each state conceived of and treated gay men. Likewise, by the 1970s and 1980s, activists in each country drew inspiration from the other. The trajectories of gay liberation and persecution in the two countries would not have been the same without the motivations and anxieties each inspired in the other.

Recounting the divided German past in such a manner has gone hand in hand with historians' efforts to re-evaluate long-held assumptions about the two countries. In the case of the Federal Republic, scholars have increasingly challenged the West German success story that emerged during the Cold War. Earlier histories, Frank Biess and Astrid Eckert note, had "oddly decoupled the history of the Federal Republic from a historiography that has critically interrogated the failed promises, contradictions, multiple exclusions, and sheer violence of the so-called Western liberal tradition."[28] Looking to examine West Germany from precisely such a perspective, a substantial body of scholarship in the last twenty years has interrogated the role of race and racism in West German society, the place of gender, and how Nazi-era structures and ways of thinking outlived the "zero hour" that supposedly divided fascist Germany from the postwar order. These works reveal not only how anxieties from the Nazi past shaped the Federal Republic but also how outsider groups – including Turks, Jews, Black Germans, women, and refugees – were socially and politically marginalized.[29]

States of Liberation extends this revisionist scholarship by examining the fate of gay men in the new German democracy. It not only illustrates the long shadow Nazism cast over the Federal Republic's treatment of sexual minorities but also reveals the difficult paths gay men took toward acceptance as citizens. While this story is not a simple success narrative, it is equally not a story of failure. Rather, *States of Liberation* looks to understand the specific ways in which change came about in the Federal Republic, highlighting not only how a liberal democracy exercised violent oppression against its own citizens but also how it exhibited social and political flexibility in the *longue durée* and, quite remarkably, changed itself.

Just as West German scholarship has increasingly challenged received narratives of success, so too recent histories of East Germany have added complexity to our view of the socialist dictatorship. Although the German Democratic Republic is still compared to Nazism, labelled totalitarian, or denounced as a "Russian satrapy," over the last two decades historians have delved into East German social history to disturb such preconceptions and to recapture the GDR's "normality."[30] Their work demonstrates not only that the socialist state was far more responsive to the needs of its citizens than previously assumed but also that East Germans experienced rich private lives. Some scholars refer to this modicum of private autonomy as *Eigensinn*. The term, which German historian Alf Lüdtke coined, is difficult to translate, but refers to a spectrum of self-reliance or private independence from external structures of domination.[31]

In spite of this scholarship, however, some historians have expressed scepticism about the sincerity with which the GDR enacted pro-gay reforms in the 1980s, pointing to animus, taboo, and even persecution that lingered in East Germany's last decades.[32] And, in fact, an overview of queer activism in other Eastern bloc countries further justifies such doubt. In recent years, scholars of homosexuality in the Soviet Union, Poland, Romania, and Czechoslovakia have revealed that antigay animus remained entrenched until at least the 1990s and that gay liberation efforts gained little traction in these countries.[33]

States of Liberation intervenes in these debates by not only highlighting a rambunctious gay and lesbian subculture in East Germany but also revealing how activists' efforts extended well beyond the private sphere and into public and political realms. In addition to *Eigensinn*, gay East Germans enjoyed a sense of political citizenship, I contend, which they deployed to pressure the regime. Moreover, I show that these efforts enjoyed great success in the 1980s, convincing the East German dictatorship to enact a slew of progressive reforms. I do so by looking not only at what policies the state promulgated – from allowing gay men to serve in the military to equalizing the age of consent – but also at why it did so and how those policies were carried out. This perspective adds a new dimension to our understanding of how the East German state functioned, demonstrating that change was, in fact, possible, and that the country's leaders could be receptive to specific types of grassroots political engagement. This history of East German gay activism suggests that the GDR was not, as some scholars continue to assert, entirely unreformable.[34]

The stakes of this argument extend far beyond the realm of German history, though, and into an ongoing conversation about the shape of democracy and dictatorship in the past and in our own time, a conversation with roots in Cold War liberalism.[35] Comparing gay persecution and activism in the two Germanies highlights in new ways the deficiencies of that mindset, which could only ever make out the problems of communist rule and the beneficence of liberal democracy. That is to say, the complexities of gay persecution and activism in both Germanies illustrate that, just as the relationships between sexual minorities and states took different forms across Western Europe, so too did they east of the Iron Curtain. This history thus underscores the degree to which social and political changes, especially changes we might call progress, are localized, subjective phenomena that can occur in democracies and dictatorships alike.

Sources

States of Liberation relies on five broad groups of unpublished sources: criminal police and court records from German regional archives, the archives of the East German secret police, other East and West German government documents, the files of gay activist organizations, and oral histories. The balance of sources, which also include published documents such as articles from gay magazines, has allowed me to write a history from multiple perspectives, not just from the standpoint of either activists or state actors. Oral histories, in particular, enabled me to fill in gaps in the archival record, to place state decisions in a social and cultural context, and to better comprehend activists' thinking. While this diverse collection of sources has permitted me to write an integrated history from both below and above, problematic aspects of two source bases in particular require some reflection.

The records of the Stasi, East Germany's secret police, have been a particular boon to historians of postwar Germany. Where the Nazi dictatorship left "mountains of corpses," some Germans quipped after the fall of the Berlin Wall, the GDR left "mountains of files."[36] When the regime began to implode in 1989, it was not clear what would become of the Stasi. In January 1990, after the dictatorship had collapsed, ordinary

East Germans stormed Stasi headquarters in East Berlin. The protesters demanded that its files be preserved and made available to those on whom the secret police had spied. The federal government eventually agreed. Starting in 1990, historians and German citizens alike could access records of the secret police, albeit within strict limits to protect the privacy of those named in the files.[37] I too am constrained by these rules and, in accordance with them, have anonymized references to individuals from these files.

Access to the files of a secret police force as gargantuan as the Stasi – it was the largest such force, per capita, in modern history – provides historians with a remarkable window into both the workings of the East German government and the everyday lives of its citizens.[38] Yet the files must be read carefully, for they contain numerous embellishments and outright falsehoods.[39] Much of the information in the files came from so-called unofficial collaborators, or IMs, whom Stasi officials recruited to spy for them. These informants, and their handlers, were incentivized to find evidence of plots against the socialist state and to connect those plots to known or suspected adversaries. One informant, for instance, told the Stasi that members of the East Berlin HIB carried silver swastikas, a plainly absurd assertion that sought to paint the activists as fascist sympathizers.[40]

I employ these files in two ways. On the one hand, I use them as evidence of what Stasi officials, as members of a powerful organ of the East German state, thought about gay people and gay activism. Here the records provide surer ground, for there was less incentive for Stasi officials to falsify their own views in internal memos and reports. On the other hand, I use the files as direct evidence of gay life and gay activism in the GDR. Because such use of these sources requires corroboration, I have endeavoured to check evidence against other sources, including police and court documents, published records, and oral histories.

The oral interviews on which much of this work is based also require explanation. To find many of my interview partners, I used a snowball method, in which partners put me in contact with new interviewees.[41] I also found a large number of narrators through the queer Berlin retirement community *Lebensort Vielfalt*. Because my aim in these interviews was to understand how the narrators had comprehended their sexuality and their place in German society, I strove to direct the conversation as little as possible, allowing them to talk for as long as they wanted about whatever they wished.[42] At the end of the interview, which usually lasted between one and three hours, I sometimes asked follow-up or clarification questions. Nonetheless, the information gleaned from these interviews is primarily the spontaneous result of memory, rather

than of specific querying on my part. Aside from a handful of interviewees who are already known in the scholarship and have consented
to be cited by name, I have anonymized the names of my oral sources.

As with the Stasi files, the recollections of my interview partners are
representative of multiple, sometimes conflicting, interests and perspectives.[43] When I interviewed these men and women between 2016
and 2018, they were describing events decades old, and they sometimes
seemed to impose today's assumptions onto their memories. I occasionally had the impression, for instance, that the East Germans I interviewed were telling me what they may have subconsciously thought
that I, as an American, wanted to hear about socialist society. Similarly,
I sometimes wondered to what extend West Germans stressed their
own persecution as gay men in the 1950s and 1960s in ways they might
not have at that time. In 2016 and 2017, the German federal government
was considering a bill that would offer reparations to men convicted
under §175. Reporting on the issue might have encouraged my interlocutors to remember their own experiences in a dimmer light. As with
the Stasi files, I employ these sources in the context of other evidence as
a way of checking their factual veracity.

Ultimately, drawing on so many different kinds of sources allows me
to play them off each other, cross-referencing claims and analyses. To
take one example, Lothar de Maizière, the only freely elected prime
minister in East German history, told me, when I interviewed him in his
law offices in autumn 2016, "On the question of homosexuals, the GDR
was substantially more open than the Federal Republic. I think that
this somewhat greater tolerance has since migrated into the West."[44]
I was struck, because it seemed like a profoundly counter-intuitive
thing for a conservative, Christian-Democratic opponent of the East
German regime to say. Yet it became clear during our interview that
de Maizière – although he himself is not gay – was justifiably proud
of the legal assistance he had offered to gay and lesbian activists in the
1980s and of his efforts to include protections for minorities in East German legislation during his short tenure as the country's democratically
elected leader. His assertion, to my mind, was thus less a factual statement and more an invitation to examine the laws passed after German
reunification, to look for evidence of East Germany's spectral presence
in the development of the reunified nation.

Organization

States of Liberation is divided chronologically into nine chapters that
alternate between events in East and West Germany. Chapter 1 begins

before the Second World War, tracing the emergence of queer subcultures in Germany and activists' unsuccessful efforts to repeal §175. When the Nazi Party came to power in 1933, it stamped out the Weimar Republic's gay subculture. The fascist government promulgated a harsher version of §175 along with a new law, §175(a), using them to convict almost 50,000 gay men. The chapter concludes in the ruins of occupied Germany. When East and West Germany were founded in 1949, West Germany decided to maintain the law in its harsh, Nazi-era formulation, while East German courts reverted to the earlier, Weimar-era version.

Chapter 2 examines West Germany's persecution of gay men. Between 1949 and 1969, its courts convicted more than 50,000 men under the Nazi-era version of §175 and its sister statute, §175(a). This chapter describes the gay subculture that evolved under the threat of these laws, seeking to recapture the voices and experiences of the men who, hounded by the police, looked for sex in public baths, toilets, and parks. Furthermore, the chapter examines conservative propaganda and government documents to argue that West Germany's anti-gay animus stemmed in large part from fears of gay conspiracies, which West Germany's leaders worried would develop in the military and government bureaucracies.

Chapter 3 turns to East Germany in the same period. When it came to homosexuality, East German leaders found themselves stuck. The Communist and Social Democratic Parties had traditionally been opponents of §175. By replacing the Nazi-era version of the law with the milder Weimar-era one in 1950, communist rulers regained some stature as reformers, while casting their country as an anti-fascist bulwark. Moreover, this change meant that far fewer men were convicted between 1949 and 1968 than in West Germany. But communists had long had an ambivalent view of homosexuality, and East German leaders worried that most ordinary Germans remained inimical to it. Because those leaders were concerned about popular support for their rule, the East German government remained intolerant of homosexuality that it perceived to have tarnished its reputation, even as it rarely prosecuted adult men for consensual homosexual acts.

Unlike East Germany, which liberalized its laws in 1950, 1957, and 1968 with little fanfare, West Germany's legalization of adult homosexuality in 1969 was a public turning point. Chapter 4 traces the story of that decriminalization, arguing that legal reform did not mark a repudiation of the anti-gay animus that had sustained the laws for two decades. Rather, scientists and lawyers opposed to the laws succeeded in convincing a coalition of liberal and social-democratic politicians that they served no purpose and that gay men should be treated as patients rather than criminals. The perceived gap between decriminalization and liberation encapsulated in the reform set the stage for West Germany's gay movements of the 1970s.

Fear of gay conspiracies did not initially figure prominently in discourses about homosexuality in East Germany. Yet, the East German secret police, the Stasi, began noticing in the late 1950s that Western spy agencies were recruiting gay men to infiltrate the East German gay subculture and to gather intelligence about its military and government. Chapter 5 pieces together archival clues to tell the remarkable story of how the Stasi became convinced that gay people posed a threat to state security. By the 1970s, this view was cemented, making the Stasi deeply suspicious of gay men and their subculture. While these fears never sparked a wide-ranging persecution of gay men in East Germany, they did lead the Stasi to crack down on gay liberation efforts that sprang up around the country in the 1970s and 1980s.

Chapter 6 turns to West Germany after its 1969 reform of §175, which enabled the gay subculture there to flourish. Gay and lesbian bars, clubs, and periodicals began springing up around the country. But many gay people remained unsatisfied, convinced that legal reform had simply traded one form of oppression for another. In 1971 so-called gay action groups appeared around the country, calling for more combative political activism rooted in gay men's and lesbians' self-awareness as a persecuted minority. These activists claimed that if gay people organized, their strength in numbers could effect real political and social change. This strategy, which was predicated on a minoritizing claim of political citizenship, explicitly repudiated the rights-based rhetoric of earlier generations. The action groups' efforts eventually culminated in a much-hyped campaign during the 1980 federal election to win votes for the centrist, gay-friendly Free Democratic Party.

Many West German activists were dedicated socialists and, as such, were interested in life behind the Iron Curtain. They took frequent day trips to East Berlin and began telling gay men there about liberation efforts in the West. These conversations inspired some East Germans to found their own liberation group, the HIB, which is the subject of chapter 7. Unlike Western activists, those in the authoritarian East could not simply take to the streets or begin disseminating information. Instead, they organized in private and tried to convince government bureaucrats to sanction their meetings. In contrast to West German activism, these efforts relied on a universalizing concept of gay citizenship, one that hoped to carve out space for homosexuality within East German socialism. But the Stasi explicitly ruled these efforts out, in part on the grounds that such an organization might provide a conduit for Western espionage. Officials tolerated the group for several years before shutting it down in 1978.

The 1980s in West Germany represent something of a paradox. While the decade saw the consolidation of many of the social, cultural, and political gains of the 1980s, West German gay activists often recall the period as one of stagnation. Chapter 8 argues that activists ignored many of their own successes and described the movement as a failure because of a set of narrow political losses early in the decade. I contend that the 1980s witnessed an inspiring growth in other forms of activism, from the founding of new gay magazines and the rise of the progressive Green Party to a national campaign against AIDS that drastically reduced West German infection rates. While the decade did not bring the legislative gains activists had hoped for in 1980, it charted a strikingly different course for gay activism in medical efforts and cultural and social institutions.

Disappointed by the regime's unresponsiveness to gay concerns, activists in East Germany began searching for new ways to organize in the early 1980s. They ultimately decided to associate under the umbrella of the country's only independent organization: the Protestant church. Gay circles soon sprang up in parishes around the country. The Stasi, concerned about the groups' rapid spread and worried that they might be part of a Western plot to destabilize the regime, sprang into overdrive. Chapter 9 describes the origins of these church-based circles, Stasi officials' responses to them, and the change they spurred in the GDR. As the Stasi became ever more desperate to stop the church groups' spread, it hit upon a novel strategy: if the government simply enacted their political platform, the groups would have no reason to exist. Beginning in 1985, the dictatorship embarked on a wide-ranging program of gay-friendly measures. From a policy perspective, the late 1980s were a golden age for gay people in East Germany and a striking example of the success of gay activism in an authoritarian country.

The epilogue considers the fate of Germany's gay liberation movements after reunification. The years after the wall fell saw an increase in anti-gay violence, likely occasioned by the economic and social strains of knitting the two countries back together. But East Germany's gay emancipation efforts did not evaporate. Because the GDR had equalized its age-of-consent laws, Germany finally abolished §175 once and for all in 1994. Because gay rights were widely accepted in East Germany's political establishment, the new parliament had large numbers of new deputies who favoured expanding rights for lesbians and gay men. But in reunified Germany, too, the shape of what we call liberation remained idiosyncratic, contested, and incomplete. The epilogue dwells on that incompleteness, on the ways in which neither a triumphal narrative nor its denial can capture in their totality Germany's states of liberation

1 Dance on a Volcano

Homosexuality from the German Empire to Zero Hour

Klaus Mann, the intemperate, gay son of Nobel laureate Thomas Mann, arrived in Berlin in 1925. The city was a haven for gay men and lesbians, and Mann was a prolific author determined to chronicle its vast hedonism. That same year, only nineteen years old, he published *The Pious Dance*, a coming-out novel that sparked a small scandal with its vivid depictions of gay life.[1] When Mann fled Germany in 1933, he had penned two novels, a memoir, several plays, and numerous short stories, in the process becoming one of Weimar Germany's most famous young authors.

Symbol though Mann was for queer culture, gay Berlin had grown up decades before his arrival. Germany was home to the first homosexual rights movement, the foremost sexologists practised there, and its cities had the most raucous queer nightlife in Europe. But for all that writers have mythologized Weimar's libertinism, more recent histories have revealed how troubled a time the 1920s were. Sex between men remained illegal, gay men were still arrested and blackmailed, and radical right-wing forces raged against perceived sexual excesses. Indeed, it all abruptly ended in 1933, when Adolf Hitler took power and the Nazi government instituted a far-reaching persecution of Germany's gay men. For decades, historians have sought to understand homosexuality in these years, producing a remarkable body of scholarship that this chapter weaves together. For an appreciation of those years – years that, to paraphrase Mann, were a dance on the edge of a volcano – is necessary in order to discern homosexuality's vexed place in Cold War Germany.[2]

Early Activism

On 9 November 1918, seven years before Mann arrived in the German capital, Kaiser Wilhelm II abdicated his throne and fled to the

Netherlands. That same day, Social Democrat Philipp Scheidemann declared Germany's first democratic republic from a balcony of the *Reichstag*, Germany's parliament building. On 6 February 1919, delegates to a new National Assembly journeyed to the town of Weimar fifty miles southwest of Berlin. The representatives gathered there to escape the violence that rampaged on the streets of Germany's metropolises. In the provinces they cobbled together a democratic constitution.[3]

The new law was a radical document, not only because it introduced democracy to Germany for the first time in its history but also because it was remarkably progressive for its time. It mandated universal suffrage for both men and women. It wiped away aristocratic privileges and guaranteed a broad set of rights to citizens. The Weimar constitution abolished censorship, a tool of the old imperial government. For Germany's gay men and lesbians, this change, along with the optimism that accompanied the new democratic era, marked a profound turn.[4]

Imperial Germany – at least its large cities – had already been a remarkably open place for gay men and lesbians. Hungarian-German writer Karl-Maria Kertbeny had coined the very word "homosexuality" (*Homosexualität*), using it in an 1869 open letter excoriating the Prussian law criminalizing sex between men.[5] Karl Heinrich Ulrichs, a Hanoverian lawyer, had lobbied the Prussian government against the law in the 1860s.[6] In 1896 Adolf Brand began publishing *Der Eigene*, the world's first gay magazine.[7]

The German-speaking world was also home to famous sexologists such as Richard von Krafft-Ebing, whose *Psychopathia Sexualis* (1886) was the pre-eminent sexual reference work for a generation, and the famous Berlin activist Dr Magnus Hirschfeld.[8] More than any other figure, Hirschfeld was responsible for forging a homosexual rights movement in imperial Germany, wedding scientific research to advocacy against the law that criminalized homosexual intercourse.[9] In 1897 he founded the Scientific-Humanitarian Committee, the world's first gay lobby.[10]

These activists' and sexologists' primary goal was the abolition of Paragraph (§) 175 of the German criminal code (*Strafgesetzbuch* or StGB), which criminalized homosexual intercourse (see Appendix A for the full text of the law). The statute had its origins in §143 of the Prussian criminal code, which banned "unnatural fornication (*widernatürliche Unzucht*)" between men.[11] In 1871, over the objections of lawyers and doctors, the German Empire adopted the provision wholesale as §175.[12] Significantly, courts held that the statute's wording criminalized only "intercourse-like (*beischlafsähnliche*)" acts.[13] That is, the law proscribed only penetrative sex between men, which meant prosecutors had to prove that anal or oral intercourse had taken place to win convictions. The law's narrowness made sex between men relatively difficult to prosecute. The average number of convictions under §175 remained well below 1,000 per year between the late nineteenth century and 1935 (see figure 1.1).[14] Significantly – as was typical for such measures across Europe – the law did not criminalize sex between women.[15]

While courts only ever convicted a small fraction of Germany's male homosexual population under the law, its presence hung over gay men's lives. Unscrupulous lovers, rent boys, and conmen routinely blackmailed them, threatening to turn them over to the police. Activists began to publicize how blackmail and the law drove gay men to suicide.[16] In fact, Hirschfeld's activist career began in 1896 after he received a suicide note from one Lieutenant von X.[17] In 1914 Hirschfeld claimed that 3 per cent of gay men in Germany had committed suicide, 25 per cent had attempted it, and 75 per cent had strongly considered it.[18]

Nonetheless, in the years between Germany's 1871 unification and the outbreak of the First World War in 1914, Germany's metropolises became centres of a burgeoning homosexual subculture.[19] Recent scholarship has revealed that, in spite of §175, German police authorized gay men to congregate in certain bars and dance halls in this period.[20] Works of homoerotic literature appeared in ever-greater numbers, from authors and poets including Thomas Mann, Hermann Hesse, Frank Wedekind, and Stefan George. Something like a gay identity, with its own literature, public spaces, and cultural idioms began to emerge.

The introduction of democratic government in 1918 and the concomitant fall of censorship gave these trends a shot of adrenaline. In 1919 Hirschfeld founded the Institute for Sexology in a villa near Berlin's Tiergarten. The institute became a hub for sexological research and a centre of queer life.[21] In *Christopher and His Kind* (1976), Christopher Isherwood described wandering through the institute's museum, where he saw everything from "fantasy pictures, drawn and painted by Hirschfeld's patients" to "lacy female undies which had been worn by ferociously masculine Prussian officers." In Berlin, Isherwood wrote, he "was being brought face to face with his tribe."[22]

The Berlin subculture was a fantastical place. The mammoth Tiergarten park boasted a "gay path," where men cruised for sex.[23] Clubs and bars dotted the city, especially the Nollendorfplatz neighbourhood in Schöneberg. Transvestite balls became the city's queer calling card, and the Eldorado nightclub boasted its own kind of gay glitterati.[24] The number of gay and lesbian publications rose dramatically. New magazines such as *Eros*, *Der Freund*, *Die Freundin*, and *Die Insel* emerged, reaching substantial new audiences in the tens of thousands.[25] Novels,

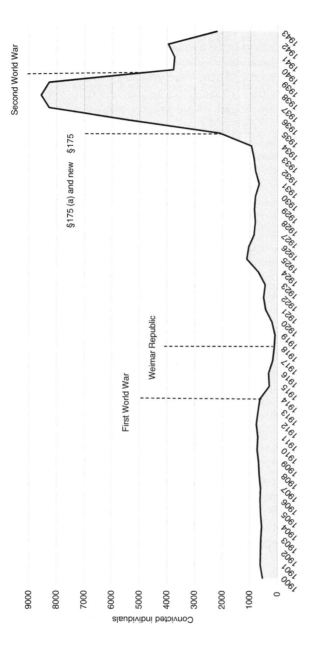

Figure 1.1. Individuals convicted under §175 and §175(a), per annum, 1900–43. NB: The figures for years 1933–43 represent convicted adults only. Sources: Stümke, *Homosexuelle in Deutschland*, 26, 90, 119; Stümke and Finkler, *Rosa Winkel, rosa Listen*, 262

plays, poetry, and films also appeared. Klaus Mann was only one of a long string of authors who began to thematize homosexuality in their works.[26] Marlene Dietrich became an icon of Weimar's sexual exuberance in films such as *The Blue Angel* (dir. Josef von Sternberg, 1930). One of the era's most famous queer films, *Girls in Uniform* (dir. Leontine Sagan, 1931), depicted a young girl's love for her teacher at a severe Prussian boarding school.

At the same time, Weimar's gay and lesbian intellectuals contested the parameters of sexual identity. The modern study of sexuality had begun in the late nineteenth century, in particular in the work of Richard von Krafft-Ebing and Albert Moll. Subsequent decades saw rapid growth in the field and counterveiling explanations for what Moll termed "contrary sexual feeling (*contrāre Sexualempfindung*)."[27] These debates, which drew in other researchers, including Hirschfeld, Sigmund Freud, Iwan Bloch, and Johanna Elberskirchen, to name just a few, encompassed the question of whether sexual desire was a congenital condition or the result of psychological development.[28] Individual sexologists rarely answered this question as a simple dichotomy, making room for both biological and psychological explanations.[29]

These scientists were among the first to suggest that homosexuals belonged to a distinct class of person possessed of a unique sexual identity. Queer theorist Eve Kosofsky Sedgwick would later call such formulations "minoritizing" because they posited homosexuals as a distinct minority.[30] Ironically, as Claudia Bruns points out, not only did these thinkers create a vocabulary of liberation, but their work also led to the pathologization of homosexuality, even as many of them advocated for more tolerant treatment of queer people.[31]

Magnus Hirschfeld and his arguments are among the best remembered today because they offered an intellectual footing for homosexual rights. Borrowing from older sexologists, Hirschfeld contended that §175 was "incompatible with advanced scientific insights."[32] Other campaigners of the era followed a similar logic. The communist intellectual Kurt Hiller, also one of Hirschfeld's collaborators, formulated the battle against §175 in legal terms as the "right to one's own body."[33] From the founding of the Scientific-Humanitarian Committee in 1897 until the Nazis' 1933 seizure of power, Hirschfeld and his allies emphasized how the law caused gay people to suffer blackmail, mental illness, and suicide. In so doing, they aimed to demonstrate that the prohibition created more problems for society than it solved. These arguments largely rested on what I call scientific liberalism, the idea that a ban on sodomy was incompatible with both liberal jurisprudence and modern scientific thought.

Hirschfeld hoped that his research would force the government to comprehend the social and medical problems caused by §175 and to repeal it. To this end, the Scientific-Humanitarian Committee circulated a petition among Germany's educated elite. In 1914 Hirschfeld boasted that more than 3,000 doctors, 750 directors and university professors, and many "outstanding jurists" had signed it.[34] The petition succeeded in its goal of fabricating a veneer of respectability for the movement, one that fitted hand-in-glove with its scientific liberalism.

As Laurie Marhoefer points out, many of these pioneers eschewed more radical forms of activism. They worried that any perception they were advocating for homosexuality (as opposed to struggling against an illiberal and ignorant law) might harm their cause with the wider public.[35] The struggle to balance activism and respectability would continue to influence homosexual politics throughout the twentieth century.[36]

While Hirschfeld and his many collaborators had fought against §175 since the late 1890s, the Weimar period saw increasingly robust efforts among political parties to repeal the statute. Allied with feminist groups that hoped to do away with Germany's abortion ban (§218 of the criminal code), and with the Communist Party (KPD), Hirschfeld was instrumental in forging the so-called Cartel for the Reform of the Sexual Penal Code. This organization brought together different groups, from the Scientific-Humanitarian Committee to Adolf Brand's Society of the *Eigenen* to activist Friedrich Radszuweit's League for Human Rights.[37]

It is important to note that while the Social Democratic Party (SPD) and the KPD were important political allies in the effort to abolish §175, German socialists had an intensely ambiguous view of homosexuality. Karl Marx and Friedrich Engels wrote very little about sex between men, and what they did write tended to be dismissive. Engels, for instance, described how Athenian men "sank into the perversion of boy-love, degrading both themselves and their gods."[38] Although August Bebel, the famous Social Democratic leader, signed Hirschfeld's petitions against §175, he also argued that "sodomy" was a symptom of the luxuriant decadence of the privileged classes.[39]

Such views were not uncommon among socialists. Many not only argued for a narrow masculine morality but also viewed homosexuality as a symptom of capitalism.[40] Moreover, German socialists had no scruples about using their enemies' homosexuality against them. In 1902 the SPD newspaper *Vorwärts* discovered that Friedrich Krupp, heir to the great manufacturing fortune and the wealthiest man in Germany, allegedly held gay orgies on the Italian island of Capri. The newspaper wasted no time publishing the information in an effort to embarrass Krupp and his friend Kaiser Wilhelm II. A week after publication, Krupp died, likely as the result of suicide.[41]

In the 1930s, socialists across Europe exhibited a rising animus against gay people. The Soviet Union led the way, recriminalizing homosexuality in 1934 after Lenin's government had decriminalized it in 1922.[42] Klaus Mann went so far as to excoriate socialists in a 1935 article, writing that homosexuals had become "the Jews of the antifascists."[43] While German socialists were convinced for most of the nineteenth and twentieth centuries that homosexual intercourse should not be criminalized, they remained conflicted about what place gay men ought to enjoy in politics, the labour movement, and society in general.

In 1929 a *Reichstag* committee advanced a bill to legalize adult homosexuality on a narrow vote, with support from socialist and centrist politicians. While the bill would have repealed §175, it would also have created a new §297, which proposed to criminalize homosexuality in three cases: prostitution, abuse of a position of influence, and sex with men under twenty-one years of age.[44] This last condition, which would have set an unusually high age of consent for male homosexuality (the age was fourteen for heterosexual acts), arose from the notion, advanced by some psychoanalysts, that homosexuality was caused by the seduction of young men and boys by older gay men.[45] The proposed law, which provided a roadmap for the Nazis' later persecution of homosexuals, fundamentally repudiated congenital theories of sexuality. Moreover, it made clear that neither society nor the government approved of homosexuality. While the bill never passed into law, it created a schism between moderates like Hirschfeld and radicals such as Hiller, who believed the bill gave too much away in the interest of repealing §175.[46]

But the notion that homosexuals (and gay men in particular) were a biologically or psychologically definable minority never had universal appeal. In the imperial and Weimar periods, a second group of German intellectuals conceived of male same-sex desire in stark opposition to the doctors, scientists, and psychologists who debated the causes of homosexuality. Historians often refer to these thinkers, many of whom published their work in *Der Eigene*, as "masculinists," because they believed erotic bonds between men to be the foundation of society, culture, and the state. They were particularly drawn to the Greek tradition of pederasty, which they understood as evidence that homosexuality was not the attribute of a diseased minority but rather a crucial element of social vitality.[47]

The masculinists thus rejected any conception of male homoeroticism as a sexual pathology. Benedict Friedlaender, the influential author of *The Renaissance of the Uranian Eros* (1904), which called for the return of Greek love, broke with Hirschfeld's Scientific-Humanitarian Committee in 1906 over its pathologizing approach to homosexuality.[48] Thinkers including Friedlaender, Brand, and Hans Blüher not only eschewed medical notions of sexuality but also believed men were innately bisexual.[49]

They contended that same-sex eroticism led men to develop powerfully romantic friendships with other men, which in turn led to the formation of healthy societies. Blüher, who wrote about the role of homoeroticism in Germany's early-twentieth-century youth movements, argued that, "Apart from the associational principle of the family, which is fed by the spring of male-female Eros, a second principle knits human society together, the 'male society' (*männliche Gesellschaft*), which exists thanks to male-male Eros and is at work in male covenant (*Männerbund*)." These two principles working at cross purposes, Blüher thought, "lead humans to the state."[50] Male-loving men, in masculinists' estimation, were not weak or effeminate. Rather, they were hypermasculine individuals who belonged to a *Männerbund* – an elite society of men. This view of homosexuality was, again using Sedgwick's language, "universalizing," insofar as it saw homoeroticism as something that potentially inhered to every man and undergirded all of society.[51]

Theirs was also a deeply misogynistic worldview, which saw no place for women in a future Germany ruled by a select class of men bound to each other through erotic ties. Women's suffrage, granted in the Weimar constitution, was, in their view, one of "the most objectionable consequences of democratization," as Harry Oosterhuis contends.[52] Masculinist writings also contained racist undertones, which became ever more pronounced as the twentieth century wore on. Blüher would eventually espouse an explicitly racist idea of an all-German *Männerbund*, while attacks on Hirschfeld in *Der Eigene* often played on antisemitic stereotypes.[53]

Unsurprisingly, many gay men belonged to far-right parties. When Radszuweit polled 50,000 gay men in 1926, 24 per cent belonged to right-wing or *völkisch* parties.[54] The allure of a racial *Männerbund* undoubtedly appealed to former soldiers and members of the paramilitary *Freikorps* that terrorized Weimar Germany's streets. Ernst Röhm, a hero of the Great War, infamous street brawler, and close friend of Adolf Hitler, was one such man. A gay Nazi who became embroiled in a politically motivated outing in 1932, Röhm was drawn to both the misogynistic, racist ideology and the homoerotic camaraderie that he believed fascism offered.[55]

One of the most famous writers associated with masculinist homo-eroticism was the renowned poet Stefan George. His life is also one of the most vivid illustrations of a *Männerbund*. Born in 1868, George began to write poetry inspired by French symbolism in the 1890s. He gathered about himself a clique of homoerotically inclined men, known as the "George Circle" (*George Kreis*). Although most of these men would eventually marry and raise families, they remained dedicated to the poet many of them referred to as their "master."[56]

George's poetry, which was published in extravagantly ornate, limited-series volumes, was heavily tinged with homoeroticism. The most famous, the "Maximin" poems, were inspired by Maximilian Kronberger, a sixteen-year-old Munich student whom George had befriended and drawn into his circle in 1903.[57] Maximilian died the following year of meningitis, and George canonized his memory with a cycle of poems adorned with photographs of Kronberger wearing Grecian dress. Other works, too, envisioned the role of the *Männerbund* in German society. "Secret Germany," one of George's best-known poems, called "you brothers" to the "greatness" of the "coming day."[58]

Many of the circle's members enjoyed glittering careers. Friedrich Gundolf became one of the most prominent literary scholars in Germany, while Ernst Bertram penned the first major book on Nietzsche's philosophy. Claus von Stauffenberg, who belonged to the circle as a boy, would lead the 20 July 1944 attempt on Hitler's life. Right before his execution by firing squad, Stauffenberg was alleged to have yelled, "Long live Secret Germany!"[59]

The *Männerbund* had more sinister faces too. The notion of an elite belonging to secret male societies struck fear into ordinary Germans, who worried that conspiracies of gay men had compromised their government. In 1906 these fears seemed to materialize when Maximilian Harden, publisher of the progressive magazine *Die Zukunft* (*The Future*), accused members of Kaiser Wilhelm II's inner circle, including Prince Philipp zu Eulenburg-Hertefeld and Count Kuno von Moltke, of being homosexual. He implied that the queer camarilla influenced the Kaiser's decision making.[60] The affair left an imprint on the German imagination: it was no longer unthinkable that cliques of influential gay men existed, possibly controlling government, society, and the fate of the nation.[61]

The imperial and Weimar eras were periods of experimentation, tolerance, and exuberance for Germany's queer populations. They were also a time when anti-gay animus became entrenched among conservatives and more than a few progressives. Even as the world's first homosexual rights movement almost won the repeal of §175, enforcement of the statute actually increased.[62] While doctors and psychologists begged for more tolerant treatment of homosexuals, believing sexuality to be a condition that the law could not change, their work also provided ammunition for conservatives, who argued that homosexuals were diseased beings. Leaders of the nascent homosexual rights movement disagreed vehemently about the best way to reform the sexual-criminal law and win greater tolerance for homosexuality. The 1920s were thus an ambiguous era for gay Germans. That ambiguity not only morphed into outright hostility under the Nazi regime but also continued to shape their lives in postwar Germany.

Nazi Persecution

It all changed on 30 January 1933, when Adolf Hitler was sworn in as chancellor of Germany. On 6 May, brownshirted Nazi storm troopers (*Sturmabteilung* or SA) descended on Magnus Hirschfeld's Institute for Sexology. They ransacked the villa, burning its library and the medical files stored there.[63] The government closed most of Germany's gay bars and periodicals, leaving the queer subculture in tatters.[64]

In 1934 Hitler, acting on the advice of his SS (*Schutzstaffel*) chief Heinrich Himmler, ordered the murder of Ernst Röhm, whom he had appointed chief of the SA in 1930, and of Röhm's close associates. While the army's disdain for the SA provided the purge's primary impetus, the so-called Night of Long Knives augured a re-entrenchment of anti-gay policy.[65] With the party's only prominent advocate for abolishing §175 gone and Himmler's star on the rise, the regime promulgated a new version of §175 on 28 June 1935. The new law made two important changes that vastly increased its scope and allowed for far harsher punishments.

First, the new law mandated prison for a man who "fornicates (*Unzucht treibt*)" with another man. This new language encompassed a far broader range of activities than did the older formulation "unnatural fornication." Under the new §175, any act that could be interpreted as homosexual in nature was punishable, whether a kiss, a flirtatious glance, or mutual masturbation.[66] Thus, prosecutors no longer had to prove that penetrative intercourse had taken place, making it significantly easier to win convictions. While this language was fundamentally different from many other laws banning sodomy or buggery, it resembled the law in the United Kingdom, which had banned "gross indecency" – an equally capacious term – since 1885.[67] Despite this similarity, the Nazi government used the statute to convict approximately the same number of men in twelve years as did British courts in eighty-two.[68]

Second, the Nazis created a new sub-paragraph, §175(a), which established several new crimes that could be punished with terms of prison with hard labour (*Zuchthaus*). The provision criminalized sexual assault between men, the abuse of a relationship of dependency, the so-called seduction (*Verführung*) of male minors (defined as younger than twenty-one), and male prostitution.[69] This measure drew on many of the same ideas that had informed the Weimar parliament's proposed §297. Although §175(a) was technically a sub-paragraph of §175, it was really a distinct law, and I will refer to the two as separate laws throughout. When I write about the Nazi version of §175, I do so in contradistinction to the Weimar version of §175. These two new laws enabled convictions for a wider range of homosexual activity as well as far crueller sentences (see Appendix A). They marked a stark turning point in how Germany treated gay men.

One key facet of the change was the seduction of youth, criminalized under §175(a)-3. In the Nazis' view, most homosexuals had not been born but rather made. Older gay men, in their understanding, recruited male youth into homosexuality. This view came out of the work of psychologists and psychiatrists such as Hans Bürger-Prinz, a researcher at the University of Hamburg.[70] In the estimation of Nazi doctors and jurists, §175(a)-3 was necessary to protect Germany's youth from corruption by adult homosexuals.[71] While criminal and psychological experts around the world at the time accepted that gay men posed a danger to youth, I know of no other country to enact such a statute.

Empowered by the new laws, police dragnets cut through Germany's gay subculture. Police demanded that arrested men turn over their former lovers. Their confessions proceeded from torture, as officers forced victims to recount their entire sexual histories.[72] Convictions surged tenfold from around 800 in 1933 to more than 8,000 by 1937 (see figure 1.1).[73] In all, Nazi courts convicted almost 50,000 men, and the regime interned between 5,000 and 15,000 in concentration camps.[74]

In recent decades, scholars have endeavoured to explain the Nazis' extreme anti-gay animus. Some contend that the persecution grew out of eugenic preoccupations. Soon after assuming power, the fascist government imposed so-called traditional gender roles and promoted what it considered to be the "positive breeding" of the Germanic-Aryan race.[75] Laws relegated married women to the domestic sphere and severely curtailed their ability to work. They offered monetary incentives to raise broods of children and encouraged so-called Aryan couples to wed.[76] At the same time, the regime murdered hundreds of thousands of handicapped Germans, including small children – so-called "life unworthy of life (*Lebensunwertes Leben*)."[77] The government legalized the sterilization of Germans whose progeny it deemed undesirable.[78] Stamping out a group of men who were supposedly unwilling to have children and whose sexual predilection itself marked them, in the state's view, as mentally damaged perverts seems to have been nothing more than a logical extension of these efforts.[79]

Yet, as numerous scholars argue, pronatalism alone did not lead to the terror.[80] The regime neither criminalized female homosexuality nor persecuted lesbians in the same way as it did gay men.[81] That discrepancy would make little sense if eugenics sat at the root of the party's animus. Moreover, National Socialists tended to evince a more pathological fear of gay men in the SS, the SA, the Nazi party, and the military. In a 1937 speech to SS leaders, Himmler infamously raved about cases of homosexuality within the SS. Lamenting that they did "not have it as easy as our forefathers," who simply "drowned [homosexuals] in a swamp," Himmler instructed that gay SS members were to "be publicly degraded, expelled, and handed over to the courts," adding that, "Following completion of the punishment imposed by the courts, they will be sent, by my order, to a concentration camp, and they will be shot in the concentration camp."[82] Significant numbers of those convicted under §175 belonged to party organizations.[83]

Gay party members and military officers were persecuted because National Socialist ideologues believed homosociality posed a threat to their authority. All-male organizations brimming with young men, the Nazis feared, were ideal recruitment fields for homosexuals. If gay men were permitted to seduce these youths, they might become numerous enough to band together as a clique, which might in turn launch a conspiracy against the regime. Nazi leaders from Hitler on down had cited this paranoia to justify the Night of Long Knives purge. On 13 July 1934, Hitler gave an hour-long address to the *Reichstag* about the coup, telling fascist deputies that Ernst Röhm and the clique of homosexual men around him had planned to topple the government. The dictator ranted that widespread homosexuality in the SA "generated the nucleus of a conspiracy against not only the morality of a healthy *Volk* but also against the security of the state."[84]

The view that gay men naturally fell into conspiratorial cliques gradually became a staple of National Socialist thought, what Geoffrey Giles describes as a "fictitious yet nonetheless powerful dread."[85] As Nazi thinker Rudolf Klare wrote in his 1937 doctoral dissertation on homosexuality and criminal law, "We do not wish to forget, that against the

overwhelmingly intensive propaganda of the homosexual organizations [...] there has still been no positive counterstroke." He warned
of an "inverted army" and "inverted youth," arguing that until only
recently "homosexuals occupied influential positions, homosexuals
dominated areas of public life."[86]

This fear of gay conspiracies drew on masculinist views. National
Socialists took the *Männerbund* and turned it on its head, fearing that
homoerotic bonds among men naturally led to conspiratorial behaviour
that posed a danger to the state. While this fear was not unique to Nazi
Germany – writers and politicians in other countries including France,
the Soviet Union, and the United States expressed similar concerns –
none of these other countries, with the possible exception of the USSR,
indulged in such brutal persecution of gay men.[87] At the same time,
the nature of these fears justified the continued non-criminalization of
female homosexuality. As one official in the Ministry of Justice put it
in 1942, lesbians did not pose a threat because of their "less influential
position in state and public offices."[88] That is, Nazi anti-gay animus had
at least as much to do with gender roles as it did with partner choice.
This distinction would have consequences for how the East and West
German states treated both gay men and lesbians.

By the end of the 1930s, police efforts had eviscerated Weimar's gay
subculture. Those who would not or could not restrain their sexual
appetites were mostly left to look for partners in public toilets, train
stations, parks, and, later in the war, the bombed-out shells of buildings. When the outbreak of the Second World War in 1939 diverted
massive numbers of adult men into the army, it also reallocated police
resources to the war effort. Consequently, convictions under §175 fell
from more than 8,000 in 1939 to fewer than 4,000 in 1940.[89] At the same
time, police tactics adapted to the mundane reality of an underground
scene increasingly populated by men too young, old, or infirm to participate in the war. While policing of civilian populations seems to have
ratcheted down by 1940, persecution within the military and the SS
continued to radicalize, albeit in an uneven manner. On 15 November
1941, Himmler decreed the death sentence for any SS or police officials
convicted of homosexuality, and Giles has shown that executions were
carried out until the very end of the war.[90]

As the terror aimed at Weimar's gay networks and subcultures
ebbed, it left behind a drearier but no less effective regime of observation aimed at discouraging homosexual acts. On the morning of 19
January 1945, mere months before the war's end, a plainclothes detective observed Georg G. cruising a Berlin public toilet.[91] The detective
arrested him on the spot. In subsequent interrogations, Georg admitted

to numerous other sexual contacts but rebuffed efforts to wrest their names out of him. In March a court sentenced him to only two months of prison.[92] In a similar case in early 1945, officers apprehended fifty-five-year-old Otto R. for soliciting a man for sex at Berlin's Friedrich-strasse train station, one of the capital's best-known cruising spots.[93] By the end of the Nazi era, these tactics had become routine, as detectives shifted from large-scale dragnet operations to the everyday surveillance of gay cruising sites.

Homosexuality in Occupied Germany

The Germany that surrendered to the Allied Powers on 8 May 1945 was a devastated land. An American visiting Berlin that October wrote, "The whole center of the city is practically flattened. The stench of corpses rising from the sewers, the flooded subways, the Spree and the canals is unbearable. But there are crowds of people in the ruins. [...] The misery of the inhabitants is pathetic."[94] Allied bombing had reduced some 50 per cent of buildings in German cities to rubble, and ordinary people struggled to access basic provisions.[95] Diseases such as typhus and diphtheria galloped through the population.[96]

The administration of law was in a similar state of uproar. That winter and spring Allied armies came upon Nazi concentration camps, horrified and confused by the starving prisoners they found and the piles of corpses they uncovered.[97] But they also took custody of German prisons, which were filled not only with political prisoners but also with those whom Nikolaus Wachsmann has termed Hitler's "awkward victims," that is, those convicted of ordinary offences.[98] Where the occupiers thought gay men fitted between Nazism's obvious and "awkward" victims was not immediately clear.

Helmuth Körner was one such man. A thirty-four-year-old blind brush maker, he had picked up an anti-aircraft soldier at a public toilet in Frankfurt am Main on 30 October 1944. The next day, Frankfurt police questioned Körner.[99] He admitted to everything but did not give the police any further names from their "homo-album." When asked if he would agree to be castrated, the record indicates, "he answered, almost in tears: 'I'd rather die!'"[100] Several months later, a court sentenced Körner to two years in prison.

Somehow, though, he managed to escape, fleeing to Würzburg some seventy miles away. In October 1945, by which point the Allied occupation was five months old, local authorities caught him and sent him to prison in Bayreuth to complete his two-year sentence.[101] It struck no one, it seems, as strange that Allied authorities should enforce Körner's

Nazi-era sentence. A letter from his father the following year begged that he be let out, insisting that the §175 charge had been a pretext. "I would guess," his father wrote, "that the Nazis marked him with this act because he was known as an anti-fascist." In January 1947, after more than a year in prison, Körner was released.[102]

Körner could still be imprisoned under a Nazi-era verdict because legally nothing had changed, insofar as homosexuality was concerned.[103] After Nazi Germany's surrender, the Allied Powers issued the so-called Berlin Declaration on 5 June 1945, which specified that the United States, the United Kingdom, France, and the Soviet Union would assume all functions of the German government.[104] The declaration laid the legal groundwork for the Allied Control Council, which in theory ruled the country between 1945 and 1949. In practice, of course, occupied Germany quickly split between the Soviet Zone in the East and the American, French, and British Zones in the West. The Allied governments faced the monumental task of not only rebuilding Germany but also ensuring it would not again pose a threat to world peace.

Denazification was thus one of the occupiers' first objectives.[105] On 20 September 1945, the Control Council promulgated Law No. 1, which repealed twenty-five particularly egregious laws that the Allied governments deemed to have been essential to Nazi rule. The law instructed that no German statute "shall be applied judicially or administratively in any instance where such application would cause injustice [...] by discriminating against any person by reason of his race, nationality, [or] religious beliefs."[106] The Council supplemented the statute with further laws and judicial instructions later in the 1940s.[107] As late as 1947, the Allied Control Authority's Legal Directorate was absorbed with denazifying the German criminal code.[108] Its efforts built the foundations of a new jurisprudence free of Nazi influence. Henceforth, laws deemed essentially National Socialist were illegitimate in Germany.

Yet none of the Control Council's laws, instructions, or directives mentioned §175 or §175(a).[109] The council's reticence concerning homosexuality created problems for courts and prosecutors, who were unsure whether §175 or §175(a) still obtained. Moreover, it was unclear which version of §175 might be enforced – the harsher version, which the Nazi regime had imposed in 1935, or the more lenient Weimar-era one.

Nonetheless, denazification fostered a sense of optimism among gay communities in occupied Germany's larger cities.[110] In 1949 *Der Kreis*, a homoerotic magazine published in Switzerland, rhapsodized, "Berlin is dancing!"[111] Jennifer Evans's study of sexuality in postwar Berlin highlights the new kinds of sexual freedom that flourished in the capital's ruins.[112] Gay men founded advocacy and social groups in the immediate postwar era alongside homophile magazines.[113] At the same time, it was a tentative optimism, what *Der Kreis*, alluding to Klaus Mann, called a "dance on a volcano."[114]

That confidence buoyed efforts to do away with §175 once and for all. Consequently, the judiciary took up numerous challenges to the law. At least eight different appellate courts in the four occupation zones ruled on the question of whether or not §175 and §175(a) were compatible with denazified jurisprudence. On this question, East and West German courts soon diverged.

The Soviet Zone, which became East Germany in 1949, quickly repudiated parts of the Nazi-era law. Already in 1945, Thuringia's regional administration attempted to abolish §175 and §175(a).[115] In 1948 the higher regional court in the city of Halle vacated both statutes, finding, "The new version of §§175 [and] 175(a) of the criminal code [are] characteristically nazistic (*nazistisch*) and therefore void."[116] Two years later, in February 1950, the Berlin high court (*Kammergericht*) partially agreed with the Halle court. Judges there found that while courts could only enforce §175 in its Weimar-era form, prosecutors could continue to employ §175(a). The court justified the decision by asserting that §175(a) offered "a necessary protection of society against socially damaging homosexual acts of a qualified nature."[117] One month later, this became national jurisprudence when the East German Supreme Court (*Oberstes Gericht*) ruled on the case. The court held that, "The new version [of §175] is nazistic (*nazistisch*)" and therefore not to be employed.[118] At the same time, the court's decision remained silent on §175(a), implicitly endorsing the Berlin *Kammergericht*'s approval of the sub-paragraph that criminalized male prostitution and the seduction of youth. This reversion to the Weimar version of §175, along with the retention of §175(a), charted a new course for East Germany's regulation of homosexuality.

Numerous courts in what became the Federal Republic of Germany, on the other hand, held that because Allied Control Council directives never mentioned them, the validity of §175 and §175(a) was unquestionable. In August 1946 the higher regional court of Braunschweig held the 1935 laws to be legitimate, as they "took up an old, not-National-Socialist body of thought, when [they] changed and extended §175."[119] The statutes, the court believed, were inspired by the Weimar parliament's own reform bill and were therefore not inherently fascist. Higher courts in Kiel, Hamburg, Celle, and Oldenburg also held in 1946 and 1947 that the laws neither represented "national socialist thought (*Gedankengut*)" nor violated any Control Council dicta.[120]

In 1951 the newly constituted Federal Court of Justice reaffirmed those rulings in a decision that maintained the 1935 version of §175.[121] Nonetheless, men continued to challenge the statute's constitutionality through the mid-1950s. The issue remained unsettled until 1957, when the Federal Constitutional Court (*Bundesverfassungsgericht*) – West Germany's highest court – ruled that the Nazi-era version of §175 and §175(a) neither represented National Socialist jurisprudence nor violated the West German constitution. They were thus admissible as law in the democratic state.[122] As the country set out on a new, divided future, its two governments held radically different views of homosexuality. East Germany, though an authoritarian state, opted for a more *laissez-faire* attitude toward gay men. West Germany, on the other hand, clung to policies and practices from the fascist past.

On 21 May 1949, two days before West Germany formally came into being, Klaus Mann overdosed on sleeping pills in a hotel room in Cannes. When news of his suicide reached Germany, gay readers mourned the loss of an author who had captured "the turmoil of [their] own hearts."[123] Early in the twentieth century, queer Germans had had good reason to believe in progress. The country saw the foundation of the first homosexual rights movement in history and the publication of periodicals dedicated to gay and lesbian readers. Blossoming queer subcultures in Germany's cities appeared as signs of growing liberalization, and the decriminalization of male homosexuality seemed to be on the horizon. Yet the Weimar era was never as open or uncontested as it might seem in hindsight. And the rise of National Socialism dashed any hopes of progress, ushering in twelve years of sustained persecution. While Germany's defeat in the Second World War offered a brief glimmer of hope, the Allied occupiers and Germany's new political leaders continued to sanction the persecution of gay men. As those men confronted two different regimes after 1949, the twin anxieties of the fascist past and the divided present would weigh heavily on them.

2 Paranoid Republic

§175 and West Germany's Persecution of Gay Men

The arrests began in summer. On 9 September 1950 alone, Fritz Thiede, the weasel-faced state's attorney in Frankfurt am Main, opened cases against more than 160 allegedly gay men. In the following months, his office investigated at least 80 more under §175 and §175(a).[1] By November the press had caught wind of the roundups, which, according to *Der Spiegel*, West Germany's periodical of record, ensnared more than 700 men.[2] They faced a special tribunal presided over by Kurt Romini. Only a few years earlier, the bespectacled judge had industriously prosecuted gay men for the Nazis.[3] Rather than submit to trial, at least two men committed suicide, one jumping to his death from a tower in the city forest.[4] The onslaught sparked curiosity around the country and even outrage.[5] Roger Baldwin, president of the American Civil Liberties Union, criticized it on a trip to the city. "It is incomprehensible," Baldwin exclaimed, "that such proceedings against irreproachable adults are still possible in the twentieth century."[6] The affair finally subsided in December when Judge Romini was assigned to a new court and most of the cases awaiting trial were closed.[7]

Between 1949 and 1969 West Germany convicted more than 50,000 men under both the Nazi-era version of §175 and §175(a) (see figure 2.1).[8] In the decades since, scholars have asked why it did so. Their work points to different facets of West German society, culture, and politics, from the country's newly resurgent Christian mores to fears about the seduction of youth.[9] Building on these interpretations, this chapter locates West German anti-gay animus, particularly that employed by different arms of the state, as a product of anxieties generated by both the Nazi past and the Cold War present. While conservative pressure groups and politicians deployed numerous justifications for §175 and §175(a), the government ultimately maintained the laws for many of the same reasons that the fascists had created them. Contemporary

Figure 2.1. Individuals convicted under §175 and §175(a), per annum, in the Federal Republic of Germany, 1950–94.
Source: *Statistisches Jahrbuch für die Bundesrepublik Deutschland*[10]

anti-gay propaganda and government documents underscore that West Germans took homosexuality seriously not only as a danger to youth and the family but also as a threat to the state itself. Nazi-era fears of gay conspiracies, that is, continued to shape West Germany's persecution of gay men long after the end of the Second World War.[11]

In fact, the question of whether West Germany's treatment of gay men can even be termed persecution has become a point of contention in recent years. Older scholarship, often the work of German historians tied to activist groups, took for granted that West German policy represented a perpetuation of the Nazi era.[12] In recent years, however, some scholars have questioned such assertions, pointing to the regeneration of a gay subculture in West Germany and its somewhat more moderate penal practices.[13] Using police and court records alongside oral interviews, I argue that the laws' continued use did constitute a clear persecution of gay men, whose voices and experiences this chapter seeks to recover.

As West Germany employed Nazi-era statutes to imprison tens of thousands of gay men in the 1950s and 1960s, moreover, other Western states also persecuted queer populations in new and more aggressive ways. The United States terminated gay federal employees in a decades-long purge remembered today as the "Lavender Scare," while British courts convicted a growing number of gay men in the postwar years.[14] While the Nazi past provided context for West Germany's policies, then, those policies did not set the Federal Republic apart from its Western peers. This chapter therefore draws out the distinctive elements of West Germany's persecution of gay men and its effects on their lives, while also locating it in a more global history of anti-gay animus.

The Shape of Animus

On 14 August 1949, the Federal Republic of Germany held its first parliamentary elections. The Christian Democratic Union (CDU), a centre-right grouping that brought political Catholicism into the same tent as Protestantism, won 31 per cent of the vote to the SPD's 29 per cent.[15] The CDU could thus name Konrad Adenauer, the Weimar-era mayor of Cologne, chancellor of the new republic. An elderly figure whom many initially considered only a caretaker, Adenauer advanced a deeply religious, conservative, and anti-communist agenda that prioritized reconciliation with the United States and Western Europe. His policies also fostered a collective forgetting of the fascist past. The eighty-one-year-old chancellor won re-election in 1953. In 1957 he achieved an absolute majority with 50 per cent of the vote, running under the slogan "No experiments!"[16]

On questions of sex and gender, Adenauer's government pursued a patriarchal family politics. The Basic Law (*Grundgesetz*, West Germany's constitution) placed the family under the state's special protection, which enabled the government to keep in place a range of sexist laws and practices.[17] Adultery, pornography, abortion, and contraception were all censured or outright banned in the Republic's early years.[18] Although Article 3 of the Basic Law guaranteed equality between men and women, Adenauer's CDU fought tooth and nail to keep women out of the workplace and to encourage large families.[19] Franz-Josef Würmeling, the minister for family affairs from 1953 to 1962, became a household name when he successfully pushed for children of families with three or more children to be allowed to ride public transportation at substantially reduced rates. The government issued these children so-called "Würmeling passes" granting them the discount.[20]

Adenauer also pursued amnesties for Nazi criminals. The Basic Law forbade the *ex post facto* application of law, meaning German prosecutors could no longer rely on Allied Control Council Law No. 10, under which many National Socialists had been convicted.[21] Adenauer's regime promulgated expansive amnesty laws in 1949 and 1954.[22] In 1951, around 150,000 Nazi bureaucrats and army officers reclaimed their pensions and, in many cases, government jobs.[23] Many judges and prosecutors regained their posts in what some called a "renazification" of the civil service.[24]

Although family politics and the Nazi past might, at first blush, seem unconnected, historians have persuasively argued that they were, in fact, deeply intertwined. Adenauer's chief concerns were to cement democratic rule and to align the new state with the United States and Western Europe. As communism appeared an ever-greater threat, Adenauer and the Western allies forgave and forgot the crimes of the Nazi years. At the same time, as Dagmar Herzog contends, the government's conservative views on sex and gender arose, in part, as a reaction against the Nazi period's perceived sexual liberties.[25] These two trends, however, left homosexuality in a rather perplexing place. If the state's aim was to forgive, forget, and move past Nazism, why did it enforce a Nazi-era law for twenty years?

The answer lies in a combination of anti-gay animus, personnel, and police practices. At the forefront, of course, stood those prosecutors and judges whom Adenauer's government had reinstated in their positions. The author of a 1949 article in *Der Kreis* reported hearing "sitting judges" lament that the still-enforced Nazi laws "'unfortunately' could no longer be employed so harshly": they could not incarcerate gay men in concentration camps.[26] The effect personnel could have on the laws' enforcement became clear in cases such as the 1950 Frankfurt trials, over which a former Nazi prosecutor presided. The failures of denazification in both the law and its enforcement thus led to astronomical numbers of arrests and prosecutions. Police registered more than 100,000 men under §175 and §175a between 1949 and 1969, of whom courts convicted more than 50,000 (figure 2.1).[27]

The anti-gay animus that motivated the law's use was a hodge-podge of ideas culled from different traditions, from Christian dogma to fascist ideology. Pamphlets published by the powerful Catholic lobby known as the *Volkswartbund* (roughly translated as Guardians of the People) stressed that West Germany's Christian culture was inimical to homosexuality. Invocations of West Germany's "moral law" and "moral energies" appeared not only in propaganda justifying animus against homosexuality but also in government publications and the Constitutional Court's 1957 ruling upholding §175 and §175(a).[28] These appeals rarely offered careful or detailed explanations of West Germany's "moral law" but were, rather, gestures to the population's assumed Christian views. Herzog argues that such rhetoric "provided a convenient strategy for erasing from view and from popular memory both Christian churches' own very strong complicity with Nazism" and distracted from the "continuities between Nazis and postwar Christians."[29]

Nazi ideas about homosexuality also enjoyed great staying power in the Federal Republic.[30] Much like the National Socialists, West Germans alleged that there was no such thing as a true homosexual: all homosexuals were products of society rather than nature. As Richard Gatzweiler, a Cologne jurist affiliated with the *Volkswartbund*, insisted in 1951, "It is today not even established that there exists congenital homosexuality."[31] This point, to which he returned in his many publications, parroted a key contention of contemporary science. Even Hans Giese, a sexologist and perennial critic of §175 in the 1950s and 1960s, accepted that homosexuality was not always a congenital condition.[32] In a different pamphlet, Gatzweiler wrote, "The oft-heard contention, the homosexual is born that way (*sei von Natur aus so*) and his predilections thus reflect his nature, is not scientifically defensible." In so doing, he relied upon widely accepted scientific views, including Giese's.[33] Indeed, one of the experts on whom the Constitutional Court relied in its 1957 ruling contended that, "Every person is homosexualizable (*homosexualitisierbar*)."[34] The widespread acceptance of these views also echoed the scientific liberalism of Weimar-era homosexual rights campaigners, who had been willing to accept that gay men posed a threat to youth in order to win limited new rights.[35]

Unsurprisingly, then, fears about the influence of older men on youth, what Clayton Whisnant refers to as fear of the "corrupting homosexual," remained a potent force in West Germany.[36] When adult gay men had sexual contact with young men and boys, conservatives insisted, the experience eventually led them also to become homosexual. As one author associated with the *Volkswartbund* put it, "Homosexuals are only the way they are because they were once seduced by older homosexual persons."[37] The state therefore had a duty to protect young men from seduction.

This paranoia was ubiquitous. It informed, for instance, a 1957 hit film by Veit Harlan, the notorious director of the viciously antisemitic Nazi movie *Jud Süß*. In *Different from You and Me* (*Anders als du und ich*), Harlan depicted a teenager's seduction by a circle of gay men attached to a wealthy antiques dealer.[38] The seduction of youth, Frank Biess argues, also coloured West Germans' moral panic over the recruitment of young men into the French Foreign Legion.[39] Significantly, courts adopted the view that homosexuality was learned behaviour. Judges frequently considered whether youth appearing before them had been seduced. The Constitutional Court's 1957 ruling mentioned "seduction" (*Verführung*) thirty-eight times.[40] The protection of youth (*Jugendschutz*) thus remained a primary rationale for the continued employment of §175 and §175(a) in West Germany.[41]

It is therefore necessary to point out that contemporary perceptions of paedophilia, child sexuality, and consent played a significant role in how the country policed homosexuality. The German criminal code, through §176, punished individuals who had sex with children under the age of fourteen. At the same time, §175(a)-3 protected men and boys under the age of twenty-one from "seduction."[42] These laws left a grey area between ages fourteen and twenty-one. German statute did not consider sex with boys and young men of those ages to be paedophilia. That is, its primary concern was not with the youth's inability to give consent, but rather with whether or not the accused's actions had turned (or could have turned) him into a homosexual.

When West Berlin police interrogated eighteen-year-old Jochen S. in 1961, for example, they discovered that an unnamed schoolteacher had molested him as a teenager. Because they determined that Jochen had at that point "already [been] active as a rent boy (*Strichjunge*)," the police decided the teacher could not possibly have seduced him. That is, the teacher was not responsible for Jochen's homosexual tendencies. The officers therefore pursued no further investigations to uncover the teacher's identity. But they did interrogate Jochen, compelling him to name other sexual partners.[43]

Thus, the rubric of seduction was vague at best. Because scientific and legal opinion held that homosexuality was a behaviour learned in puberty, the law was designed to shield male teenagers from homosexual activity. Hence, those accused of seducing male youth faced harsher penalties not because their acts were considered paedophilic but because the state worried about the effect that the seduction of youth had on society.[44] At the same time, however, police officers often assumed that youth such as Jochen were so-called rent boys and not simply teenagers looking for sex. As *Der Kreis* wryly noted, "everyone, who does not have a particularly good salary, is considered a 'rent boy.'"[45] Prosecutors could, and did, charge these young men under §175(a)-4, which outlawed male prostitution.[46] The law could thus generate harsher punishments for youthful offenders, even as its defenders argued that it was designed to protect youth.[47] Only beginning in the 1970s, after the West German government had decriminalized adult homosexuality, would national dialogue turn to issues revolving around consent.[48]

Ironically, the very policies designed to protect youth from seduction fostered opportunities for sexual relations between younger and older men that might otherwise have not existed. By limiting public discourse about homosexuality and stamping out most public venues for gay men to gather, the state restricted them to a narrow world of public swimming pools, toilets (known as the *Klappe*), parks, and train stations where they could cruise for sex.[49] Young men and boys curious to explore their sexuality ventured to these locations. Older men also frequented these cruising sites and often picked up inexperienced young men. In most cases, these encounters ended without incident. My oral history partners often spoke fondly of their first sexual experiences, which in almost every case occurred with a significantly older man at a public cruising spot. In some cases, though, men abused, raped, or even tried to kill young victims. Samuel R. recalled how, as a boy in Hamburg, he was almost murdered in a public toilet by a man looking for sex.[50] West Germans' desire to protect youth from homosexuals thus fostered an environment in which they were forced to satisfy their sexual curiosity in dangerous locations. To put it more simply: the West German preoccuption with homosexuals' alleged seduction of youth had nothing to do with actually protecting young men and boys.

While the protection of youth explains the parameters of the law's enforcement, it does not, I contend, illuminate why elements of the state actually feared homosexuality. That anxiety grew, in part, out of another paranoia inherited from the Nazi dictatorship. Just as National Socialists believed gay cliques would propagate in all-male institutions, so too their postwar successors worried about what gay circles might do to government authority and to society.[51] Numerous court judgments and police reports from the era hint at suspects' involvement in "homosexual circles" or "circles of homosexuals."[52] The Constitutional Court's 1957 ruling noted that one of its criminological experts had advised that homosexuals exhibit a "tendency to join homosexual groups alongside a rejection of non-homosexual society."[53] These groups seemed to threaten the state and the social fabric.

Volkswartbund pamphlets described in vivid detail the danger that such associations posed. One from June 1950 carried the title "Homosexuality as an Acute Public Danger" with the subtitle "1.8 Million Inverts Are Banding Together in Germany," raising the spectre that homosexuals might topple the fledgling democracy. The text declared, "In many metropolises in West Germany homosexual clubs are being founded."[54] These secretive clubs, the pamphlet hinted, had "incorporated into a central association."[55] They were a "freemasonry of the sexually perverse" that endangered the German state "exactly as Bolshevism and fascism" had done.[56]

The homosexuals' efforts, the pamphlet concluded, should leave one in "no doubt: the perverts are in the midst of establishing a state within the state (*Staat im Staate*)."[57] Commentators compared this threat to the events of 1934, when Ernst Röhm had supposedly established a "camarilla of homosexuals."[58] Another pamphlet, which Gatzweiler penned the following year, made the case in fierier language:

> The formation of clubs must be regarded as particularly dangerous. Germany learned the significance of homosexual clubs from the so-called *Röhm-Putsch*. [...] A similar formation of clubs and sects is also underway in Germany. When it succeeds, the inverts will constitute a state within the state (*Staat im Staat*). Everyone knows they hold together like lice. Therefore, they would constitute a fearsome danger for the young German democracy.[59]

As further evidence of the threat homosexuals posed to the republic, Gatzweiler encouraged his reader to "consider that, at the moment, the Eastern Zone [GDR] largely tolerates homosexuality."[60] This alleged danger to the "young German democracy" certainly justified the mass arrests of gay men. It gave grounds for the *Volkswartbund*'s call that "all homosexual clubs, events, and magazines should be immediately banned."[61] In fact, the group endorsed everything short of "the tools of dictatorship," which it coyly renounced in the fight against the "cancerous growth" of homosexuality.[62]

The notion that Ernst Röhm had tried to lead a gay coup against Hitler's government – and that homosexual cliques thus posed a serious threat to the state – was commonly accepted at the time. The Constitutional Court asserted in 1957 that, "A change in the attitude of the National Socialist authorities came about, however, after Röhm and the predominantly homosexual group of his political allies in the NSDAP were exterminated in June 1934."[63] Periodicals employed such tropes to cast homosexuality as a constitutive element of fascism and to justify the continued persecution of gay men. In 1949 *Der Spiegel* published a five-page essay by former Gestapo chief Rudolf Diels about the Night of Long Knives, in which he reiterated claims of a "homosexual clique" around Röhm. Diels alleged Hitler to have said, "This whole camarilla around Röhm is depraved through and through."[64]

If these paranoias seem absurd, recall that West Germany was not particularly secure in its existence in the early Cold War era.[65] Not only did a neighbouring German state exist that denounced the Federal Republic as heir to German fascism, but West Germany's ambivalent relationship with the Nazi past also haunted its efforts to establish democracy.[66] Former National Socialists continued to occupy prominent positions in the regional and federal governments, the bureaucracy, and the judiciary. At the same time, German citizens remained ambivalent about multiparty democracy. A 1956 poll found 16 per cent of young people receptive to re-established National Socialist rule.[67] To a state already in crisis over its own legitimacy, the potential for conspiratorial bands of gay men to further destabilize the social and political order was a serious threat indeed. These fears of gay conspiracies thus intimate that uncertainty about West Germany's social and political stability spurred the country's persecution of gay men.

The Federal Republic's relative indifference toward female homosexuality also makes more sense when viewed from this perspective. Not only did scientists, intellectuals, and politicians believe lesbians less likely to seduce women into homosexuality, they also realized that, with most women still confined to the home and traditionally female lines of work, there was little danger of lesbian conspiracies. In his 1957 report to the Constitutional Court, the famous sociologist Helmut Schelsky considered precisely this problem. "Because of the publicly oriented lifestyle and the familial responsibility of men," he insisted, "one expects the endangerment of public order, youth, and family from male homosexuality in particular." Female homosexuality was less concerning, he argued, because "the familial private life of women does not seem to offer the same social endangerments through lesbian relationships." Of course, Schelsky hedged, women were starting to encroach on the public sphere. He had heard rumours of "lesbian section leaders [who use] their positions to seduce subordinates into lesbian relationships." Nonetheless, he considered the social danger of lesbianism to be far less than that posed by male homosexuality. Lesbianism, he ventured, "leads less frequently to the formation of cliques."[68]

Fear of gay espionage – evoking the US Lavender Scare – also featured in these conservative fantasies. The connection was made plainest in a *Volkswartbund* pamphlet from 1953. The group argued that gay people "drew themselves together" in groups with "conspiracy-like bonds," and that "these groups are deployed by different sides for the purposes, for example, of espionage."[69] In another pamphlet, Gatzweiler raved, "It is anything but true that homosexuality is benign. The USA recognized the danger of secret homosexual clubs and spy groups. – Let us also be wary!"[70] He worried that because gay people already belonged to secretive cliques that cut across boundaries of class, ideology, and nationality, they were logical recruits for foreign intelligence agencies. In a 1963 op-ed about West German intelligence, the deputy editor of *Die Zeit*, Marion Dönhoff, even expressed that, "It seems to me as though someone were suggesting to work primarily with homosexuals in the intelligence agency because it is so easy for them to make contacts on the other side."[71]

Of course, the fear of gay spies was not isolated to any particular country in the twentieth century. Originating with the celebrated case of Austrian intelligence officer Alfred Redl in 1913, the stereotype had gained force over the decades.[72] Between British mathematician Alan Turing's 1952 arrest and the American case of Whittaker Chambers and Alger Hiss that began in 1948, the conviction was widespread that gay men were more likely to be turncoats.[73] The reasons were numerous, from the belief in gay men's inherently conspiratorial natures to the concern that their illicit sexual activities made them more susceptible to blackmail. Curiously, West German fears did not seem to stem from the notion that gay men were more likely to be blackmailed, as did those motivating the Lavender Scare.[74] While the panic around gay spies was not unique to the Federal Republic – and West German anti-gay rhetoric clearly took cues from the country's most important Cold War ally – it was undeniably shaped by the Nazi past.

Even more striking, this mirage had an impact on espionage practices in Germany. As we shall see in chapter 5, Western intelligence agencies recruited gay spy networks in the 1950s and 1960s, hoping to use them to gather information about the East German regime and security services. In one case that turned into a small scandal for the West German government, the Hessian counter-intelligence bureau decided to recruit a network of gay informants in order to unmask alleged East German agents in the regional government.[75]

Trouble began in 1953 when a Wiesbaden public prosecutor requested that a trial – a trial the judge believed to be "an ordinary 175 matter" – be held *in camera*, as evidence might divulge information about "the counter-intelligence bureau (*Verfassungsschutzamt*)."[76] The judge countered, "Do you seriously expect that a German court would help you shield the interests of the executive branch? What accusations were made against Nazi judges because they allowed themselves to be put under pressure? We will not be subject to pressure!"[77] Thus enraged, he rebuffed the prosecutor's motion and allowed the media access to this outlandish trial.

The accused, Dr Horst Krüger, was a former employee of the Hessian branch of the *Verfassungsschutz*.[78] The agency had first hired Krüger in January 1952. A year and a half later, local prosecutors charged him with "foster[ing] homosexual relations with a 16-year-old lad."[79] In a twist, Krüger, whom a Nazi court had convicted under §175 in 1938, claimed immunity from the statute. Krüger swore that, "The *Verfassungsschutz* promised me immunity for activity in the homosexual sphere."[80] The agency had hired him, Krüger insisted, in order to "move in homosexual circles, in order to foster a network of agents."[81] The counter-intelligence agency had wanted gay agents, according to him, because it "had become aware that, among homosexuals, who are consolidated into organizations, there are situated [intelligence] agents."[82]

This justification could easily have come straight from a *Volkswartbund* pamphlet. Unease about the gay subculture's shadowy "organizations" had led the *Verfassungsschutz* to conclude that it needed to infiltrate the gay subculture. It was in pursuit of this goal that Krüger befriended a sixteen-year-old schoolboy, "M.," whom he eventually registered as a secret agent.[83] The astonished court decided to call Krüger's boss, the former director of the Hessian *Verfassungsschutz*, Paul Schmidt, to corroborate his assertions. Schmidt affirmed that he had indeed tasked Krüger with building a network of gay agents and had promised him immunity for his acts in pursuit thereof.[84]

Krüger's gay spy network helps illustrate how and why West Germans feared homosexuality in the early decades of the Cold War. Krüger convinced the head of a counter-espionage service to hire him for the purpose of building a gay spy network, seemingly on the strength of the idea alone. He justified the project by arguing that gay people were "consolidated into organizations" teeming with foreign agents, just as

Volkswartbund propagandists considered gay people to be members of secret, international, and hostile organizations, a "freemasonry of the sexually perverse."[85] The notion that the gay subculture was honeycombed with foreign spies thus built on an already existing paranoia, underscoring just how potent the fear of gay cliques remained in the Federal Republic.[86]

These views also had an influence on the bureaucrats and politicians who decided if and how to enforce §175 and §175(a). In 1959, for instance, a federal ministerial adviser wrote, "Within public institutions homosexuals create groups, which gradually win a certain influence over certain areas of public life through constant recruitment of similarly minded individuals."[87] Likewise, an undated government report noted that, "In West Berlin there is a headquarters" that pairs gay men with young tricks, drawing on fears that the seduction of youth and gay clique formation nourished each other.[88] The government's own commentary on its failed 1962 criminal code (which would have continued to criminalize homosexuality) emphasized the "danger of the formation of homosexual groups" and of their "propaganda." When the commentary discussed the potential ramifications of decriminalizing homosexuality, it focused heavily on the perils posed by "homosexual groups" to society.[89]

In 1966 a reporter asked CDU Minister of Justice Richard Jaeger why he would not support a reform of §175. He too invoked the threat of gay associations. "My fear is this," he told the newspaper *Hamburger Abendblatt*, "that if the criminalization were repealed homosexuality would disseminate even more, that the dams would be torn asunder and clubs opened."[90] As late as 1978, a decade after adult homosexuality was decriminalized, the liberal Free Democratic Party confronted such qualms in an *Argument for the Repeal of §175*: "There was no so-called 'breaking of the dam' [...] and no homosexual political clique endangered the state."[91] The CDU politicians who ruled West Germany until 1969 – and more than a few members of other parties – accepted and advanced the view that cliques of gay people were endeavouring to corrupt young men and recruit them into a social-political conspiracy that might even be allied with Soviet intelligence. That belief sustained §175, §175(a), and the array of taboos and police practices that relegated gay men to a world of toilets, train stations, and parks for more than two decades after the end of the Second World War.

These fears not only reveal that the Federal Republic was a deeply insecure state. They also suggest that a key source of modern anxiety about gay people is not their sexual predilection *per se* but rather their ability to pass as straight and to thereby avoid detection by the heterosexual majority. Like their Nazi forebears, West Germans worried that large groups of mal-intentioned gay people were hiding in plain sight, ready to sacrifice the fledgling democracy to the Bolsheviks. It is no accident that Jews have been accused of similarly conspiratorial activities in the long history of antisemitism, for as historians have long noted, anti-gay animus and antisemitism share much of the same intellectual bedrock.[92]

The terms of this animus, which emphasized the seduction of youth and the danger that cliques posed to government and society, are furthermore remarkable in that they do not fit easily with widely held assumptions of why governments and societies persecute sexual minorities. Neither the biopolitical hypothesis nor scapegoating can explain why the West German state criminalized male homosexuality so expansively or for so long. Eugenic concerns played at best a bit part in public defence of the law, and politicians did not cynically wield animus as a way of garnering votes or support. Unlike the US Lavender Scare, which turned into a media circus, homosexuality became a broad topic of public discussion only in the late 1960s, as we shall see in chapter 4.[93] Anti-gay animus thus never became what Eric Weitz, in his discussion of anti-communism in the Federal Republic, terms an "integrating influence."[94] Rather, deep-seated concerns about stability seem to have spurred the fear of homosexuality's spread and its potentially damaging effects on society and the state.

But West Germany was not alone in persecuting gay men in this period. As Wannes Dupont notes, "a spasm of hostility toward homosexuality was rippling through Western Europe" at the time.[95] Countries where male homosexuality was not criminalized, such as Switzerland, Italy, and France, proposed recriminalization or found other ways to subject gay men to official discrimination. Annual convictions rose rapidly in the United Kingdom and in the Scandinavian countries.[96] Like recent postcolonial histories of Europe and the United States, this transnational swell of persecution throws into relief how Cold War democracies enacted fundamentally illiberal policies.[97] While Dupont suggests that social instability and anxiety after the Second World War contributed to the rise of such policies, David Johnson argues that the United States "exported" the Lavender Scare to its Cold War allies.[98] This was certainly not the case in the Federal Republic. Though undoubtedly inspired by McCarthyite practices, West German prosecutors, courts, and politicians acted on the basis of home-grown fears and prejudices. What set West Germany apart, then, was not §175 or its persecution of gay men *per se* but rather the Nazi past and the spectre of East Germany, which both shaped that persecution and gave it purpose.

Enforcing §175

When focusing on the rhetoric around §175 and §175(a), it is sometimes easy to forget the men convicted under the statute. On 9 September 1959, the Frankfurt am Main district court sentenced fifty-eight-year-old Otto S. to four years of prison with hard labour – a brutal punishment. The judges found Otto, who had already spent two years in an Ulm prison for a §175 conviction in 1949, guilty of sexual acts with several teenagers.[99] Two months later on 4 November 1959, the same court convicted twenty-two-year-old Horst S. of mutually masturbating with his fifteen-year-old co-worker Ulf F. But to Horst the court handed down the relatively modest sentence of two months' imprisonment.[100] Among the more than 50,000 men convicted under §175 and §175(a), it was common for their sentences to vary in this way, from the mild to the draconian.

The reasons for such variation often had to do with contemporary understandings of homosexuality, especially homosexuals' alleged seduction of youth. If a court concluded that a perpetrator was unlikely to continue pursuing homosexual acts and posed no threat to youth, it could respond mildly. Twenty-one-year-old Herbert L., for example, was found guilty in February 1950 of molesting more than a dozen boys, some of whom were younger than fourteen years old.[101] Despite the number and young age of Herbert's victims, the health bureau in Gelnhausen, a small town in Hessen, insisted he was simply stuck in the "homosexual phase of a young man's physical development." This period, the bureau contended, "is for L. somewhat elongated [...], but it is still likely that it will gradually abate."[102] The court agreed and sentenced Herbert to only eighteen months in prison.[103] The sentence seems shockingly mild for someone who had admitted to molesting so many young, even pre-pubescent, boys. But the court's rationale illustrates that jurists did not necessarily view the danger posed by gay men in terms of paedophilia but rather in terms of the need to prevent homosexuality's spread. Because the court believed Herbert to be living out a stage of puberty – and crucially that he was not seducing boys into homosexuality – it let him off with a relatively lenient sentence.

Some courts converted prison sentences into fines. This practice took up the precedent of a famous Hamburg case. In 1951 a court there found two men guilty under §175, but fined them only three Deutschmarks (DM) in what became known as the "Three-Mark-Decision (*Drei-Mark-Urteil*)."[104] A municipal court in Cologne in 1952 similarly sentenced salesman Karl-Ludwig W. to a monetary fine of 150 DM.[105] In a different case, a court in Hanau converted a twenty-five-day prison sentence against Hans W. into a 1,000 DM fine.[106] The man's professed heterosexuality – he claimed that he had "a certain inclination towards men exclusively in a drunken state" – along with his seventeen-year-old partner's indifference justified leniency.[107] The practice was not isolated: every year a sizeable percentage of those convicted under §175 were let off with a fine. Between 1955 and 1964, when convictions reached their height, courts fined 39 per cent of those convicted under §175 (leaving aside §175(a) convictions). In those years, 22 men were given terms of prison with hard labour for §175 convictions, and 575 men, or 4 per cent, received prison terms longer than nine months.[108]

Judges could be merciless when men in their docks were found to be repeat offenders or seducers of youth, and thus punishable under §175(a)-3. In 1957 a court in Rottweil, a small town in Baden-Württemberg, sentenced one "habitual offender" to five years of prison with hard labour for "severe same-sex fornication."[109] Georg R., who was born in German-occupied Strasbourg in 1942, told a similar story. He began having sex with older men in public baths at the age of thirteen and met a man at a carnival a year later. When the police found out, a court sentenced the man to seven and a half years of prison with hard labour for having allegedly seduced Georg. In our interview, Georg, now seventy-five, protested, "The initiative came from me."[110]

Furthermore, the range of crimes that could land a gay man in prison hints at the breadth of West German persecution. Terribly banal acts could lead to prosecution. In 1959 a court upheld a complaint against a technical university instructor for appearing in public with a known homosexual man.[111] A Stuttgart court convicted two men in 1963 for kissing in their apartment.[112] While these cases belie any argument that the FRG's enforcement of §175 was tempered, they also illustrate how varied enforcement was. Although practices and policies did carry over from the Nazi era, it is equally inaccurate to say, as would later become a rallying cry for gay activists, "for homosexuals, the Third Reich has not yet passed."[113]

Courts also pursued medical and psychological remedies to male homosexuality. As in much of the Western world, castration and other therapies intrigued even those sceptical that gay men could be cured of their predilections.[114] Some men experimented with quack solutions that purported to change their sexuality. Fifty-one-year-old convict Wilhelm A., for example, fiddled with different homeopathic cures in 1967 and 1968.[115] A report on his condition indicated that he had hoped to be chemically castrated but that doctors were not sure his health would allow it.[116] A later report to the Karlsruhe prosecutor noted that because a doctor believed "voluntary castration" would not help him to control his urges, Wilhelm was "currently undergoing medical treatment" of an unnamed sort.[117]

In fact, concrete evidence of castration in the Federal Republic has surfaced in recent years.[118] In an annotation on a petition to the federal government in 1964, for instance, a Ministry of Justice official commented that the "convict Wilhelm B." was "castrated with his consent on 26 May 1964."[119] The note's author betrayed no consternation at Wilhelm's fate. We do not yet know how common such castrations were, but it is not in doubt that they occurred. While other Western countries continued to chemically castrate gay men – one thinks in particular of Alan Turing in the United Kingdom – in West Germany, the practice was intimately linked with Nazi persecution. The fascist government had forcibly sterilized some 400,000 Germans during its twelve years in power.[120]

West German courts sometimes called on physicians or psychologists to examine men charged under §175 in order to determine if hospitalization would better serve society's interests.[121] Though they might forestall prison terms, these examinations were not necessarily better for the accused. Viewing homosexuality as a mental or even physical abnormality, doctors latched onto other evidence in the accused's medical history in order to arrive at a pathological diagnosis. Such a finding could result in long periods of institutionalization. One case that also reveals continuities between Nazi Germany and the Federal Republic involved a thirty-seven-year-old pianist named Hermann S. In 1944 he was attacked and robbed while cruising a Frankfurt toilet. Instead of looking for his assailant, the police arrested Hermann and sent him to a specialist for examination. The doctor, noting a §175 conviction in 1935, wrote, "The intellectual inferiority, weakness of character, and habituation to abnormal sexual satisfaction endangers S." He recommended that Hermann be packed off to a mental hospital.[122]

In February 1945, while the country was still under Nazi rule, a court agreed. In addition to a six-month prison sentence, it remanded Hermann to the sanatorium in Herborn, one hundred kilometres north of Frankfurt. For the next twenty-four years, the hospital sent regular reports on Hermann's condition to the court. Each time, the assessment insisted, "The purpose of his commitment has not yet been achieved." That is, Hermann was not yet cured of his homosexuality. The reports all recommended an extension of the confinement.[123] Only in 1969, after the federal government had reformed §175 to make sexual acts between adult men legal, would the court agree to free Hermann.[124] We do not know how many men suffered similar fates, but these remedies were an important part of postwar attempts to suppress homosexual behaviour.[125]

West Germany thus employed the laws in broad and varied ways to keep homosexuality underground and out of sight. The Federal Republic was one of the few European countries that criminalized homosexuality until the late 1960s, convicting a vast number of men – more in total than even the Nazi government. In those years, my oral source Holger G. said, "everyone lived in fear, everyone concealed themselves. [...] You could not lead any sort of life, you could not have any friendships."[126] Another man, Hubert U., born the fifth child of a baker in 1947, remembered the secrecy of the gay subculture and bemoaned that there were no other options for gay men. "It was a mendacious society," he insisted. "It was truly terrible. And dark."[127]

Policing and Everyday Life

Prison sentences and court rulings represent only a fraction of gay life in the first postwar decades, though. The everyday surveillance that the law sanctioned shaped the gay subculture, as it evolved through a game of cat-and-mouse between the police and men looking for sex with men. Of course, not everyone who frequented the gay subculture was gay. Hetero- and bisexual men, some of them sex workers, also haunted the places where gay men sought sexual partners. And plenty of men who might today be considered gay thought of themselves as heterosexual, or in their words "normal," only searching for sex with other men when drunk, lonely, or depressed. In that sense, the term "gay subculture" is something of a misnomer, an imposition of our own expectations onto the warp and woof of the past.

For most gay men, the horizon of sexual possibility extended only so far as the public toilet, train station, park, and swimming pool.[128] Public pools or baths were a favourite place to cruise, perhaps because they were among the least vulnerable to police surveillance. Many of the men I interviewed indicated that their first sexual exploits took place in such pools. Volker K., who was born in 1956 in Dortmund, a city in the Rhineland, recalled his first experiences in a public bath. As he put it, "I often went to swimming pools and allowed myself to be seduced by older men." At some point in his teenage years, though he did not remember when exactly, he "realized somehow that when one showered for a while there were other men who also showered for too long." These men disappeared in twos or threes into private changing rooms. One day Volker "followed one into one of these cabins and we jerked off together."[129]

Authorities knew that pools provided ample opportunities for gay men. Police records and court rulings observed that men brought to trial had almost always first been "seduced" by an older man at a swimming pool. In 1963 the Karlsruhe youth bureau noted that nineteen-year-old Rolf K. "was molested by a 45-year-old man in the Durlach pool (*Freibad*) […]. This seduction awoke sexual desire in Rolf and it must be assumed, that this first seduction was the cornerstone of [his] later failings."[130] Likewise, when prosecutors charged a different Rolf K. as a prostitute in 1950, the indictment asserted that he had first learned to masturbate at the age of fifteen in a swimming pool.[131]

Beyond the pools, a greater underground beckoned. A variety of public locations became marketplaces of sexual opportunity. Georg R., who first had sex at the age of thirteen in a pool, recollected moving to West Berlin as a young man and being introduced to the city's "cruising turf (*Cruisingsgebiete*)." These included Tiergarten and Grunewald, both public parks. He recalled that because "it is not so great to creep through the bushes in winter, we went to the public toilets."[132] Georg recognized the dangers of this kind of cruising, though. As he put it, "The door could have opened at any moment and – raid!"[133]

Plainclothes officers frequented cruising spots such as toilets and train stations. In West Berlin, the train station at the Zoo was a notorious congregation spot for male prostitutes.[134] Likewise, other cities across the country had their own sites for public cruising and sex, all fertile ground for vice squads. Even acting suspiciously in such places could end in arrest. Nineteen-year-old Heinz P. fell victim to a police raid in October 1949, when West Berlin officers picked him up at the Zoo station. Though detectives watching the station saw him commit no crime, the report justified his arrest with the observation that he "comported himself like a rent boy (*nach Strichjungenart*)."[135] The Hamburg police notoriously used two-way mirrors to catch men in the act, which often led to a ban on their use of the public toilets. In the 1960s officers issued bans to around 300 men every year.[136]

Relationships were a rarity in these years, for even if one could find someone interested in more than a quick handjob, the two would likely be found out or denounced in relatively short order. In 1949 seventeen-year-old Werner Heinz G. had lived for almost six months with thirty-year-old Hänschen W., who owned a bar in West Berlin. His landlady eventually denounced the couple to the police.[137] A similar scenario played out almost two decades later, when Holger G., a German who spent his earliest years in Columbia and New York City, lived for two weeks with his first boyfriend in Munich at age nineteen. "The state's attorney charged him" under §175, he recalled, "because a neighbour had denounced us."[138] In another case from 1960, Falko D. in West Berlin was jailed because he was eighteen and his boyfriend seventeen.

The boyfriend, Falko wrote in a petition to the federal government in 1980, "preferred the suicide of corrective therapy."[139]

Some gay bars endured in this period. The most famous of them, Elli's Beer Bar in Kreuzberg (West Berlin), stayed open from 1942 until after the fall of the Berlin Wall and was the city's best-known congregation point for gay men.[140] Charlotte von Mahlsdorf, an East Berliner and undoubtedly Germany's most famous trans person, recalled going to the bar in the 1950s: a room that smacked of the 1900s filled with "half-naked youth, often in drag or in an almost transparent nothing, [who] sat on the laps of their escorts."[141] Clutches of such establishments appeared in large cities such as Hamburg, West Berlin, Frankfurt am Main, and Munich, and their numbers slowly rose over the course of the 1950s and 1960s.[142]

In police interrogations, some men mentioned meeting each other in these bars, which the police, in their reports, typically modified with the phrase "known as a meeting spot for homosexuals (*als Treffpunkt für Homosexuelle bekannt*)."[143] As one man accused of prostitution in 1955 remembered, "I was once in a pub where 'gays' meet up. I met 'gays' in Kaiserstrasse in Frankfurt. They took me to the bar. […] In the bar I only drank, but others also danced with each other."[144] These bars resembled neither the subculture of today's metropolises nor Weimar's queer clubs. Most German men did not even know of their existence. Although homophile publications in the early 1950s advertised some locales, police interrogations suggest knowledge of them was spread primarily by word of mouth.[145]

Though some put on the kinds of racy performances that characterized the Weimar scene, they were mostly just pubs known to cater to gay men.[146] In one 1963 case from Frankfurt, the police charged the proprietor of the bar Oasis with hosting orgies in his bar after it closed each night. The police report described these "so-called 'men-parties'" in which "all participants sat around a table. On the table lay a bottle that would be spun and whoever the neck of the bottle pointed towards had to take off a piece of clothing until everyone was naked. Then there was naked dancing and obscene acts."[147] That gatherings of five or six men for the purpose of playing spin the bottle and dancing naked reckoned as a particular scandal to the Frankfurt police indicates just how inhibited the gay scene had become.

While operating a gay bar was not in itself a criminal offence, these venues were not safe from the police and were targets of large and frequent raids.[148] On 29 October 1957, for instance, more than one hundred policemen in West Berlin "undertook a great raid of a bar […] in Schöneberg, which stood under suspicion of being a meeting point of homosexually inclined men and prostitutes."[149] By 1959 the West Berlin criminal police estimated that such locales were subject to between two and three raids per month.[150]

The case of Georg R. is illustrative. In his late teenage years, he met an actor in the spa town Baden-Baden who told him, "Berlin is the city. You have to go there!" He wasted no time and left southwest Germany for the metropolis eight days after his twenty-first birthday. He recalled becoming friendly with a man on the Berlin vice squad who was married to a lesbian police officer. The man occasionally told him, "Please don't go out tonight," so Georg knew "that raids would be happening in the bars." He said his friend's advice protected him from ever being caught in a raid. It opened his eyes to the fact that "the police secretly visited these bars and picked people up."[151] In some cases, the police even allowed these institutions to exist because they presented easy targets. West Berlin police, for example, advocated the "authorizing of meeting places (pubs etc.)" because "the criminal police preserve therewith better surveillance opportunities over the homosexuals."[152]

In the late 1950s the West Berlin Senate, led by the Social Democratic ruling mayor Willy Brandt, decided to crack down on hooliganism (*Rowdytum*), which encompassed a number of perceived social ills including homosexuality. Politicians worried about the influence of deviants on Berlin youth and were determined to stamp out any contact that young people might have with homosexuals and prostitutes. These efforts came at a time when West Germans were preoccupied with hooligans, known as *Halbstarke* (literally "half-strong"), and juvenile delinquency. Though tensions had percolated through the first half of the 1950s, they boiled over after large-scale riots of young hooligans broke out in 1956. The rebels hated the cloying, conservative culture of Adenauer's Germany, and their unrest foreshadowed the revolutionary student movements of the 1960s. Older generations feared they were the product of American culture's degeneracy, Eastern influences, and "proletarianization."[153]

The West Berlin Senate's efforts centred on identifying and cracking down on bars that served homosexuals and other socially undesirable elements. Between 1959 and 1962, the interior senator's "Commission on Combatting Hooliganism" coordinated dozens of raids on gay bars and hundreds of arrests. In the thirty days between 15 September and 15 October 1959, the commission orchestrated a jaw-dropping 739 raids and detained 4,200 individuals.[154] Among those caught were almost 200 alleged rent boys, many of whom were likely just young, gay men cruising for sex.[155] The commission's records also note that a large percentage of those youth lived in East Berlin.[156] By the end of the year, the commission had succeeded in closing down a number of bars known to cater to gay men.[157]

Though the commission's zeal faded by the early 1960s, perhaps because hardline Interior Senator Joachim Lipschitz died in 1961, its efforts showcase the lengths to which municipal governments would go to control the gay subculture. The existence of gay bars and cruising areas in West Germany's cities should not be taken as evidence of tolerance, let alone acceptance. They provided some space for gay men (lesbians had fewer places to meet) but were also subject to continual surveillance and raids, which kept their clients in a perpetual state of anxiety. These venues were not symbols of a more tolerant culture, nor did their existence lead to eventual decriminalization.

West German prosecutors continued the Nazi practice of asking arrested men to name others with whom they had had sex. A 1962 petition to the federal government complained that, although the police never resorted to violent interrogation tactics, they made "promises" to arrested men, enticing them to "name this or that person."[158] These cases included that of eighteen-year-old Rolf K. from 1963. At around the age of sixteen, while at a swimming pool in his hometown of Karlsruhe in southwest Germany, he was "approached by an ostensible homosexual, who wanted to entice him to touch his penis and rub on it."[159] In the two years since, the police noted, Rolf had had sex with around twenty men between the ages of twenty-eight and sixty. Under interrogation, Rolf named eight different sexual partners.[160]

Detectives also kept photo albums of alleged homosexuals, a practice that dated to the imperial era.[161] When officers arrested a gay man, especially a male prostitute, they showed him these albums and asked him to identify those with whom he had had sex. The most infamous use of such albums occurred in the 1950 Frankfurt trials. There the police had picked up a prostitute named Otto Blankenstein in July 1950. Blankenstein, who testified in forty of the subsequent trials as the prosecution's principal or sole witness, admitted to having had sex with at least seventy men.[162] His identifications in turn set off the cascade of arrests, many from the police's albums of homosexuals.[163] Der Spiegel explained to its readers how the process worked:

> The police employ so-called rent boys in order to initiate new proceedings. They are driven, for example, through the city in private cars. They then indicate which passers-by on the sidewalk they know. The car stops, the person concerned is arrested and interrogated. He is also fingerprinted and photographed. His picture is then shown to all imprisoned prostitutes and informers, until someone recognizes him.[164]

The Munich police became notorious for charging those appearing on these "homo-lists" with unrelated crimes.[165] In 1949 *Der Kreis* compared police tactics in the postwar era to those "in the times of the Gestapo."[166] Though an exaggeration – things were certainly better for gay men than they had been under Hitler – the magazine was not entirely wrong. Such practices did mimic those of the Nazis.

This does not mean, of course, that they were particular to West Germany. In addition to campaigns of persecution directed against queer populations in Western Europe, the 1950s also saw an intensification of policing practices to control other marginalized populations. Clifford Rosenberg has described how imperial practices shaped the policing of immigrant populations in Paris, which included systems of surveillance not dissimilar to those the West German police used against gay men.[167] Likewise, the early Cold War saw the rapid growth of the American Federal Bureau of Investigation, in part due to efforts to police communists, anarchists, civil rights activists, and even homophile campaigners.[168] As a liberal democracy exercising sometimes extreme violence against its own citizens, West Germany was not unique. But the Federal Republic's uneasy relationship with its fascist past made the continuation of Nazi-era tactics and policies – from castration to the maintenance of "homo-albums" – all the more striking, as did the sheer volume of arrests and convictions.

Beyond the law's reach, gay men faced other perils. Prostitutes posed dangers to their johns past simply snitching to the police. Blackmail was a quick source of revenue: young men, even those who were not rent boys, took to lingering around train stations and threatening anyone they suspected might be gay.[169] In 1955 a gang of three fifteen-year-olds stopped a man at the Zoo train station in West Berlin and demanded money. Unfortunately for them, he was not gay and promptly turned them over to the police.[170]

In one extraordinary incident from 1958, a gang of young men led by twenty-three-year-old Fritz H. tried to extort a ministerial director K. in the Hessian government. The four men had come to Wiesbaden from Hamburg "in order to collect money from this acquaintance."[171] Fritz alleged that he had had a three-month affair with the official.[172] After K.'s relationship with Fritz came to light in an unrelated trial, prosecutors charged him under §175. In April 1959 a court sentenced K. to two months in prison and a fine of 1,500 DM.[173] Unlike the Weimar and imperial eras, when prosecutors might overlook such infractions in order to crack down on blackmail, West German courts were only too happy to send blackmail victims to prison.[174]

Rent boys also attacked men, either before or after sex, robbing them of cash or other valuables. Between 1962 and 1967 male prostitutes in Hamburg allegedly murdered at least nine gay men.[175] In 1959 a group of seventeen boys began terrorizing park-goers in West Berlin's Preußenpark. The East German *Neue Zeit* reported that they had originally banded together "in order to protect themselves from homosexuals […] this 'self-help' soon evolved into a terror brigade."[176] Even in the late 1960s, so-called "rocker bands" (likely just gangs of young men) lured gay men to arranged meeting points, then mugged them in what *Der Spiegel* called "lynching justice."[177]

Yet sex workers were victims of brutality too, a fact that has gone comparatively unremarked. In 1955 Fridolin J. in Gelnhausen was discovered severely beaten in a field. The initial police report noted that Fridolin was known as someone who "mainly hangs around 'Café Pali' around the time that the [American] soldiers are paid. He often went with the soldiers to toilets or into the open country."[178] When Fridolin had recovered from his injuries, he admitted to having had sex with three or four American men and told the detectives that he wanted to charge the soldier who attacked him "with severe assault because he smashed me up so badly."[179] There is no indication that the assailant was ever found or punished.

Where they could, gay men actually pleaded for greater police protection. One 1955 petition to the West German government enumerated "harrowing numbers" that included "5 unsolved murders, three solved murders and one attempted murder" of gay men in West Berlin alone. Its author excoriated "this democracy" for clinging "to the sinister longing to persecute innocent people, to abandon them to murderers and to chase them into death."[180] Another 1963 petition demanded that the regime immediately repeal §175 so that homosexuals "will no longer be blackmailed by criminals and hounded to suicide."[181]

West German animus thus sanctioned the far-reaching persecution of gay men in the 1950s and 1960s. It grew from multiple sources, shaped by the weight of the Nazi past as well as Cold War anxieties. Among the many paranoias informing the persecution of West German gay men stood the lingering fear of homosexual conspiracies. From Catholic pamphlet writers to constitutional court judges, West Germans worried that gay men were inherently cliquish and that they thereby posed a profound threat to social cohesion and political stability. Such rhetoric, alongside that which emphasized the danger that gay men posed to German youth, was used to justify the continued use of fascist laws to terrorize gay men for two decades.

Taking this persecution of gay men and youths seriously – and salvaging their voices – forces us to reconceptualize West Germany's first decades, which were once unironically termed the country's "miracle years."[182] While many West Germans enjoyed the benefits of a booming economy and newfound democracy, the country's stability was more fragile and its liberties far narrower than it perhaps at one time appeared. These were years marked by intense anxiety about a past that dared not speak its name and the looming presence of another German state.[183] Such fears expressed themselves, in part, in the continued persecution of gay men long after the Second World War had ended.

Across the border, gay men faced very different legal, political, and social circumstances. While the East German government, making good on the promise of socialism, liberalized §175, it refused to tolerate homosexuality among its ruling cadres. Its concern about anti-gay animus among the population it governed created a strange situation: toleration for much of the population coupled with persecution of homosexuality among, in particular, party members, police officers, and members of the military. As in the West, the 1950s and 1960s were an unhappy time for gay men living under German communism.

3 Equivocal Animus

Homosexuality and Socialism in East Germany

In 1969, in a collection of essays published in Hamburg, the East German sexologist and reform advocate Rudolf Klimmer wrote:

> In spite of [its] progressive lawmaking, homosexual life in the GDR has not changed. The difference in conduct between East and West Germany is curious. In the West, freer life in public, homosexual newspapers and bars as well as widespread homosexual prostitution, all alongside a harsher penal code. Here in the East, fewer public manifestations, no newspapers and clubs. Homosexual prostitution barely exists here.[1]

Klimmer's complaint against the GDR continues to resonate today. Historians of postwar Germany often contend that, even if East Germany's laws appeared more liberal than the Federal Republic's, gay East Germans enjoyed fewer social opportunities than did gay West Germans in the 1950s and 1960s.[2] East Germany's early liberalization of §175 is frequently dismissed, and gay people are assumed to have led cloistered lives in the Democratic Republic.

While East Germany was certainly no queer utopia, such views risk over-simplifying both gay experiences and the complex web of competing state priorities enveloping homosexuality. East Germany's early liberalization of §175 allowed most gay men to engage in sexual acts with adult men with far less fear of prosecution than gay West Germans. While the communist regime remained intolerant of public displays of homosexuality and the socialist economy made less room for queer locales, a subculture nonetheless evolved in East Germany that cannot be deemed any worse (or better) than that which existed in West Germany. Alongside cruising areas in public baths, toilets, forests, and train stations, a number of bars existed that catered to gay men. A private universe of house parties also developed in large cities by the 1960s. The gay subcultures of East and West Germany were distinct, and one cannot be judged by the standards of the other.

Because gay everyday life in East Germany was not measurably better than in West Germany, however, Klimmer's article does point to a real paradox. Why, with more progressive laws in place, did East Germany not boast a more robust subculture? In spite of early legal liberalization, East Germany did not develop a public or commercial gay scene, as one might expect in a sexually liberated country. One might reasonably anticipate that a change in the law would lead to changes in everyday life: in East Germany this was not the case. This chapter untangles the web of policy, practice, and animus that led to this confounding situation.

Drawing from police and court documents, Stasi archives, oral histories, and East German newspapers, I propose that this ostensible contradiction arose from competing impulses within the socialist tradition. East German courts invalidated the Nazi version of §175 in 1950, in large part because the communist state had cast itself as an anti-fascist bulwark. At the same time, the GDR's leaders hoped to win acceptance of their rule from East Germans, whom they believed remained hostile to homosexuality. Newspaper articles attacking the Federal Republic regularly painted it as a land infested with crime, prostitution, and homosexuality – a trifecta of perceived ills that socialists had long associated with capitalism. Courts maintained §175(a), which judges argued would protect East Germans from the twin spectres of male prostitution and the seduction of youth.

Moreover, recent scholarship underscores that the East German regime adopted conservative, patriarchal rhetoric around gender and sexuality in its early years, in part to appeal to its citizens.[3] Party members were typically held to the highest moral standards, worried as the regime was about how East Germans viewed the socialist state. Gay officials could thus find themselves charged under §175, even years after courts had ceased prosecuting most cases of consensual, adult homosexuality. The East German state's attitude – which Kyle Frackman similarly characterizes as a "persistent ambivalence" toward its queer citizens – thus arose from competing strategies to legitimize its rule and led to the seeming paradox of legal liberalization coupled with continuing discrimination and lack of social opportunity.[4]

Gay Everyday Life under Socialism

As in the West, the Democratic Republic's gay subculture was constituted as a network of public toilets, swimming pools, train stations, and forests where men cruised for sex, alongside a few bars known to cater to gay clientele. To take one example, Carsten I., a gay man born in 1954 in a small village near Potsdam, explored his sexuality in ways that would have been familiar to West German men. His first sexual experiences came in public baths, when he noticed glory holes drilled into the walls of changing cabins. Peering through one time he saw "a big male penis." That day while swimming he observed men staring at him. One even reached into his swimming trunks. After showering, Carsten went home with the man.[5]

Later in his teenage years, Carsten recalls queuing at a sausage stand near the Potsdam central station when, "I had the feeling that someone had grabbed my ass." He turned around and saw "a Russian officer" who then left the line for a nearby forest. Among the snow-covered trees, "He laid out his jacket and we fooled around." They met several more times in public places, Carsten recalled over cookies and coffee in his spacious Berlin apartment, "where we thought we would not be found out."[6]

Public sex was not uncommon. In Dresden in 1963 the police arrested two judicial clerks at the monument to victims of the Nazis in the Heidefriedhof graveyard. The officer who caught them reported, "The one person had the genitals of the other in his mouth."[7] As with the Zoo train station in West Berlin, so-called rent boys and gay men flocked to the Friedrichstrasse train station and to Alexanderplatz in the city's eastern half. Peter Rausch, who would later become a leader of East Germany's gay movement, recalls going to the toilets on both Alexanderplatz and Schönhauser Allee, one of East Berlin's main boulevards, to look for sex as a teenager in the mid-1960s.[8] Similarly, Rainer E., an East German born in the 1950s, remembers an older man picking him up on Alexanderplatz at the age of fifteen.[9]

There were fewer bars for gay men in the Democratic Republic than in West Germany. This fact had to do with socialist society, East Germany's relative poverty, and the regime's ambivalence toward homosexuality. While the provinces of Brandenburg had always been less developed than the prosperous states of southern Germany and the Rhineland, the Soviet Union exacerbated the problem by appropriating significant industrial wealth from East Germany until 1953.[10] In 1951, the government promulgated a Stalinist five-year program, which focused on developing the country's heavy industry to the detriment of consumer staples.[11] The government shuttered bars and restaurants to make way for urban housing development.[12]

At the same time, socializing was largely organized around, by, and for the party, while constrained by an oppressively family-oriented social ethic. Both economic necessity and the dictatorship's inherent suspicion of civil society hemmed in social life in East Germany. In short, gay life was not immune to the necessities of building social- ism. Even fewer opportunities were available to lesbian women. As in West Germany, women in the East were encouraged to marry and become mothers.[13] While sexual acts between consenting, adult women were never criminalized, taboo and prejudice remanded les- bians to isolated lives.[14]

In the divided capital, men regularly crossed the border in both direc- tions. Some Easterners went to West Berlin for its bars. An East German cross-dresser told the police in 1953 that they frequented a handful of Western pubs including Elli's Beer Bar and Kleist Casino in the gay neighbourhood around Nollendorfplatz.[15] They had been caught smuggling glasses and silverware out of East Berlin to use in their own West Berlin bar, which was known as a hangout for queer people.[16] At the same time, police files suggest a not inconsiderable number of West Berliners came to the East. What attracted them – whether the liberal- ized penal code, the perception that East Berlin had more male pros- titutes, or some other reason – remains a matter of speculation. Only the Berlin Wall's construction on 13 August 1961 stanched the flow of visitors in both directions.

There were some bars in East Berlin that catered to gay clientele. Their numbers expanded in the 1960s, much as they did in West Ger- many. Carsten I. remembers that during his teenage years in Potsdam there was one bar in the city known as a gathering place for intellectu- als and homosexuals. By around 1960, Möwe, Presse-Café, City-Klause, and Esterhazy Keller in East Berlin had all become popular places for gay people to socialize.[17] A Stasi informant indicated in 1961 that an acquaintance of his "is often in the tavern City-Klause with around 20 homosexuals, all young men."[18] In later decades, a number of gay- friendly locales sprang up in the Prenzlauer Berg neighbourhood.[19]

Gay men, especially those in cities, also regularly gathered in private dwellings. Reports from Stasi informant "Franz Moor," whom we will encounter again in chapter 5, offer a rich portrait of this private world in the early 1960s. On 14 November 1960, for instance, he described going to the home of one man, on Invalidenstrasse in east-central Ber- lin, at which at least eight gay men were present.[20] He reported another case of a young gay aristocrat who "is known to the whole Presse-Café- Club, knows everyone there and can say something about everyone. He goes to every single party that takes place with this group."[21] Of "Moor" himself, a different informant offered the opinion, "He declines sexual activities with more than one person, even at parties where the opportunity may present itself."[22] In her autobiography, Charlotte von Mahlsdorf described going to house parties where "many GDR-transvestites could for the first time live out their otherness."[23] In 1975 yet another informant passed information to the Stasi about a teacher in Leipzig who allegedly had "'homo-parties' in his apartment."[24] In her analysis of East German photography, Josie McLellan likewise finds evidence of queer life in 1960s East Germany that flourished in "private flats and sticky, crowded bars."[25]

Nonetheless, evidence of such parties is rare. Because they took place in private and involved no illicit activities, they were unlikely to draw the attention of the criminal police – unlike their Western counterparts. Moreover, the files I reviewed at the Stasi Archive suggest that secret police agents only began monitoring the gay subculture in the 1960s. Even then, the Stasi's interest in homosexuality was not systematic. Thus, the archival record only hints at what may have been a quite lively private gay scene in East German cities in the 1950s and 1960s.

As in West Germany, the subculture was a dangerous place. In 1957, for instance, Bernhard C. and Erich K. invited seventeen-year-old Christian K. to their apartment, plied him with schnapps and beer, and raped him.[26] In another case from 1962 two men apparently assaulted Johannes H., a gay policeman, in a toilet. One of the men "ripped his watch from his wrist," a police report described, while the other "snatched his briefcase."[27] Soon thereafter, Johannes hanged himself. The ensuing investigation into his sexual affairs and the possibility of dismissal were too much for him to live with.[28]

Of the brutalities gay men faced in their everyday lives, suicide was perhaps one of the most horrific. In Imperial and Weimar Germany, activists had begun to talk about suicide in order to illustrate the violence that §175 visited on gay men.[29] In both postwar German states, gay suicide remained an all-too-frequent phenomenon. In another case, thirty-year-old East German army officer Lukas G. shot himself after being discharged for "homosexual acts." In a final letter, recorded in his Stasi file, the young man wrote that he "parted from life in order to avoid a scandal."[30]

Gay life in East Germany thus inhabited the unlit way stations of the subculture, where men cruised for sex, picked up rent boys, and did their best to avoid public notice. Men gathered in private apartments and the few locales known to welcome queer clientele. Crime was a regular feature of gay life, though, and unknown numbers of gay men continued to take their own lives. In stark contrast to West Germany, however, East German police and the courts adopted a far more *laissez-faire* approach to homosexuality.

Homosexuality and the Law

On 6 May 1950, twenty-eight-year-old Werner L. went to a bar in central Berlin. Werner lived in Neukölln, a district in West Berlin, but travelled through the East to reach his destination. Once there, he drank seven glasses of beer and "just as many schnapps" before finally leaving after midnight. He then made his way to Alexanderplatz, in East Berlin, to look for a urinal. In the toilet, another man approached him, asking if he would like to accompany him to a bombed-out building for anal sex. Werner agreed, but when he arrived at the ruin, the other man pulled out a police badge and arrested him.[31] In West Berlin, Werner would likely have been sentenced under §175. But in East Berlin, the appeals court (*Kammergericht*) had already struck down the Nazi-era version of §175, making it significantly harder to win convictions. The police seemed open to letting Werner off with "a warning" and noted that a court would determine if he had contravened §175.[32] Unfortunately, the file is incomplete, and so we do not know for certain if Werner was let off. That it was even a question whether or not Werner had broken the law nonetheless illustrates how different the two countries' legal regimes had already become.

When it came to §175, the German Democratic Republic started off on a progressive note. The Soviet Union and the Socialist Unity Party (SED), which ruled the GDR, positioned the new country as an "anti-fascist" alternative to the supposedly fascist and imperialist Federal Republic.[33] In its early years, the regime prosecuted former Nazis and removed them from positions of power, in stark contrast to West Germany's amnesty policies.[34] Moreover, the communist regime contended that its legitimacy stemmed from its successful repudiation of (and the Federal Republic's continued complicity with) the Nazi past. In the legal realm, this meant Nazi-era laws, including §175, had to go. That Germany's socialist and communist parties had pressed for §175's repeal since the 1920s further legitimated reform of the law.[35]

The regime's anti-fascism and the party's traditional antipathy toward §175 led East Germany to change the law in 1950. Regional courts in Halle and Berlin, as well as the new Supreme Court, found the Nazi-era version of §175 to be "characteristically nazistic and therefore void."[36] The Weimar-era version that thereafter obtained made it substantially harder to win convictions, for it criminalized only "intercourse-like" acts. At the same time, both the East Berlin *Kammergericht* and the East German Supreme Court upheld the validity of §175(a) on the grounds that "the seduction of young people poses an especial danger for society." The *Kammergericht* argued that the subparagraph was thus part of a "progressive line of legal thinking."[37] Thus, the young socialist regime halfway denazified the laws criminalizing homosexuality: while the principal statute was reformed, the subparagraph criminalizing prostitution and seduction of youth remained in force until 1968 (see Appendix A).

In 1957 the government promulgated a new Supplementary Criminal Code. It mandated that no crime existed, whatever the criminal code might say, if there were no "injurious consequences for the GDR."[38] This meant that, in theory, prosecutors would no longer apply §175 in most cases of consensual sex between adult men.[39] To what extent the new law legalized consensual, adult homosexuality is still an open question. On the one hand, Klaus Berndl and Vera Kruber discovered evidence that the GDR continued to employ §175 until at least 1959. On the other hand, various publications from the late 1950s and early 1960s indicated that, in general, consensual adult homosexuality was no longer prosecuted.[40] "Homosexual activity is punished in the GDR," the 1964 *Dictionary of Sexology* averred, "only when a considerable social danger exists."[41] A Stasi report from 1966 noted that "according to court practice," offences against §175 "are no longer prosecuted."[42] Surviving criminal accounts suggest that, after 1957, prosecutors employed §175 in cases in which the accused had in some way endangered the regime.

At the very least, East German courts convicted far fewer men under §175 than West German courts.[43] In the period 1957 to 1959, the only years for which we have precise East German figures, West Germany annually convicted more than five times as many men, per capita, than did East Germany under §175.[44] Significantly, East German courts in those three years also convicted over 20 per cent fewer men under §175, per capita, per year, than the Weimar Republic had done between 1919 and 1933. This discrepancy suggests that even if the Supplementary Criminal Code did not eradicate §175 completely, the East German state was less interested in pursuing convictions of gay men than even the Weimar Republic had been (see figure 3.1). Though East Germany only formally abolished §175 and §175(a) in a new criminal code promulgated in 1968, gay men enjoyed a *de facto* liberalization after 1957, years ahead of West Germany. And while criminal reform was rarely a subject of public discussion, East Germans seemed to recognize that their country did not penalize homosexuality as harshly as other states. A 1952 newspaper article in the East German *Berliner Zeitung*, for instance, criticized a West Berlin newspaper for suggesting that homosexuals should face corporal punishment or castration.[45]

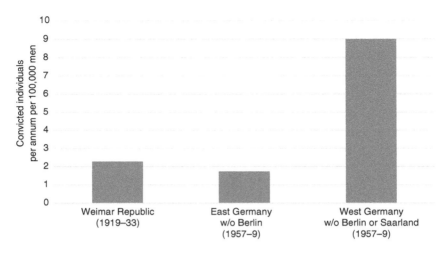

Figure 3.1. Individuals convicted under §175, per annum, per capita, in the Weimar Republic, East Germany, and West Germany. NB: this chart does not include §175(a) convictions. Sources: *Statistisches Jahrbuch für das Deutsche Reich; Statistisches Jahrbuch für die Bundesrepublik Deutschland; Statistisches Jahrbuch der Deutschen Demokratischen Republik;* Stümke, *Homosexuelle in Deutschland,* 90; BArch-Koblenz, B 141/85386, 24; Berndl, "Zeiten der Bedrohung," 21

As in the case of Werner L., these legal changes had an impact on who was charged or convicted under §175. On the evening of 30 January 1954, for example, a gay West Berliner wandered into the eastern half of the city. At a bar in central Berlin he met two young military officers, whom he invited home with him.[46] Though the men did not return with him that night, they agreed to meet again the following week.[47] On 6 February, after drinks, they made their way to his apartment in Schöneberg, one of Berlin's traditionally gay neighbourhoods. En route, the two officers arrested the man because "they arrived at the view that he was an intelligence agent who wanted to abduct them."[48] More than two months later, East German prosecutors charged him under §175 and crimes under Allied Control Council Directive Nr. 38, which governed the prosecution of Nazi sympathizers and partisans.[49]

We must imagine that the poor man would have been scared. Had he been convicted, he could have faced years of prison or hard labour. But the prosecutor abruptly reversed course after the trial and recommended that the charges under Directive Nr. 38 be dropped. To justify this decision, he pointed out that there was no proof the man had wanted to turn the officers over to an espionage agency.[50] On the charge of §175, the court declared him not guilty.[51] Had the man been caught attempting to pick up two young men in West Berlin in 1954, he almost certainly would have been convicted under the law.

Although courts had curtailed §175's application against consenting adults, §175(a) remained in force. As in West Germany, the seduction of minors remained a central preoccupation of the East German judiciary. In the case of a twenty-two-year-old paramedic convicted under the statute, for example, the district court in Potsdam found that while the accused "had been seduced (verführt) in his earliest childhood," that experience had not stopped him from seducing younger border police officers himself. The judges berated him because "he knew […] that indecent acts could lead to severe bodily and emotional damage."[52] The court thus sentenced him to two years and three months of prison with hard labour.[53]

Berndl and Kruber's statistical findings also provide evidence that prosecuting both the seduction of youth and male prostitution remained a priority for the socialist regime.[54] Whereas convictions under §175 remained six times higher per capita in West Germany than in East Germany for the period 1957–9, convictions per capita under §175(a) were roughly equal.[55] These figures include prosecutions for both seduction and prostitution, charges that sometimes overlapped in the same case. In one case from 1950, the police picked up a fourteen-year-old student named Fred V. along with one Werner W. The two had engaged in mutual masturbation and fellatio in a ruin near the Friedrichstrasse train station.[56] The police determined that because Fred had engaged in "rent boy activity for a longer time," Werner was not guilty of "seduction" under §175(a)-3. Later that year, the Berlin-Mitte district court sentenced Fred, a fourteen-year-old, to youth prison for a period of between nine and thirty-three months for male prostitution, while Werner was released.[57] Socialist thinkers had long associated both phenomena with capitalist decadence, and the regime likely considered prosecuting such offences to be a natural extension of the moral probity it sought to project.

Although some might find it surprising, given the GDR's overwhelming distrust of independent groups, the regime evinced little fear of gay cliques. While references to cliques cropped up every so often in East German sexology and political speech, they were rarely imbued with the same significance as in West Germany.[58] Nor was concern about gay cliques a common trope in East German discourse. Sexologist Kurt Freund's 1963 book Homosexuality among Men, the first East

German monograph dedicated to homosexuality, mentions cliques not once.[59] Even while reporting on gay espionage cases, major East German newspapers did not parrot the idea that gay men were likely to form conspiracies that threatened the state or society.

The East German Supreme Court even referred to the lack of gay cliques in socialist society as one reason to expunge the Nazi-era version of §175. Its judges stated that Nazism had required a draconian sodomy statute, "because the male societies (*Männerbunde*) which it fostered provided more social opportunities between men. Homosexuality thus endangered society and the army according to National Socialist thought."[60] The communist court thus believed that the masculinity which had dominated fascist society had led to the fear of gay cliques. In anti-fascist East Germany, though, which officially promoted gender equality, such protections were no longer necessary.[61]

In spite of the courts' retention of §175(a), it seemed as if a full repeal of both §175 and §175(a) was possible, even likely, in the early 1950s. In 1952 the government appointed a commission to draft revisions to the penal code. As Erik Huneke describes, the proposed law envisioned dropping both §175 and §175(a).[62] Yet, the early 1950s was an unstable time for the dictatorship. The Soviet occupiers had forced the SPD to merge with the smaller KPD in April 1946 to create the Socialist Unity Party that ruled the GDR until 1990. Though Social Democrats outnumbered Communists in the new party, the USSR ensured the latter's dominance. Between 1948 and 1950 around 200,000 Social Democrats were forced out, of whom at least 5,000 were imprisoned.[63] At the same time, the new socialist regime, led by Walter Ulbricht, a veteran of the Weimar Republic who had spent most of the Nazi years in the Soviet Union, projected a guise of democratic rule. As Ulbricht memorably told a subordinate, "It must look democratic, but everything must be in our hands."[64] To that end, the socialists authorized four other parties, including an East German CDU, whose members would hold office (but no real power) throughout East Germany's existence.[65]

These consolidations hit a speed bump when workers took to the streets in mammoth numbers on 17 June 1953, angered by low standards of living and high work quotas. The revolt, which Soviet troops quickly crushed, led to further suppression. In its wake, courts sentenced at least eighteen individuals to death and more than a thousand to terms in prison.[66] The uprisings needled the regime's insecurities in a peculiar way. Much as in the early Federal Republic, a struggle for legitimacy defined the GDR's first decades. Just as West Germany strove to secure its existence in the face of the Nazi past, so too the East scrambled to win sufferance, if not enthusiasm, for its rule. In the words of Jeffery Herf, "Vivid memories of past mass support for the Nazis [...] deepened the Communists' willingness to establish a second German dictatorship."[67] Most East German leaders, unlike their counterparts in the West, had spent the war in exile or in prison. They had returned home with a conquering army.[68] The regime's paranoia vis-à-vis its citizenry, what Andrew Port has called its "siege mentality," led to the imposition of a fantastical surveillance state.[69] This state of affairs made the regime both afraid of the population it ruled and highly sensitive to discontent.

The 1953 uprising, Evans contends, also led the state to retreat on matters that seemed to touch traditional morality. The government began advocating a more conservative, patriarchal order that flew in the face of its earlier rhetoric on gender, sexuality, and the family.[70] This morally upright, masculine ideal, often referred to as East Germany's "socialist personality," was summarized in Ulbricht's "Ten Commandments for the New Socialist Person."[71] Published in 1958, the commandments directed that East Germans should, among other things, "live cleanly and decently and respect your family."[72]

One victim of the 1953 purges was Max Fechner, East Germany's minister of justice. A former SPD member and a victim of Nazism, Fechner was accused of homosexuality and sedition in 1954.[73] After the uprisings, the secret police had delved into Fechner's sexual past, searching for compromising material. Agents discovered that he had had an affair with his chauffeur between 1952 and May 1953. They found at least one other man with whom Fechner allegedly had attempted to have sex.[74] When the police submitted a summary of their findings on 29 October 1954, it included the claim that Fechner had "repeatedly engaged in unnatural fornication (homosexual) with men who stood in a professional relationship of dependency" (also a crime under §175(a)).[75] A year later, on 24 May 1955, the East German Supreme Court sentenced Fechner to eight years of prison with hard labour. Its ruling described him as "not only politically, but also morally depraved."[76] These words mark a striking shift from a court that had struck down the Nazi version of §175 only five years earlier.

Not only did Fechner's conviction mark a shift in language around homosexuality, it also slowed government progress on the new penal code that would have repealed §175 and §175(a).[77] The government's response to the uprisings thus signalled a retreat from the progressive lawmaking of its first couple of years. The regime did not backtrack on its initial reform of §175, but it did make clear that homosexuality would have no public place under socialism. This equivocal approach – neither a commitment to socialism's more radical legacy of sexual reform nor the kinds of persecution of gay men that Stalin had introduced in the Soviet Union – defined gay life in East Germany.[78]

East Germany's Equivocal Animus

The shift after 1953 was also visible in a rising number of anti-gay newspaper articles (see figure 3.2). Just as West Germans saw in homosexuality a danger encroaching from the East, socialist newspapers – which were subject to government censorship – described homosexuality as a symptom of Western decadence. As the regime consolidated its rule, newspaper articles paid greater attention to West German politicians' gay sex scandals and held up homosexuality as a symbol of Western degeneracy.[79] Sensationalist headlines such as "Tiergarten Is a Criminal's Paradise" or "Male Prostitutes, Murderers, and Thieves" adorned stories about West German homosexuality.[80] One article reported on the alleged rapes of young Berliners by Western occupation troops. A survey of some 236 homosexual youth, the author wrote, had discovered that "more than half of them were seduced and abused by Western occupation soldiers."[81] Other articles described murders alleged to have taken place near bars known to cater to gay men.[82] One piece related how "68-year-old publican Emil Grundmann was found murdered in his pub at Friesentraße 13 (USA-Sector). […] The pub, which faces the main entrance of the West Berlin police presidium, is known as a meeting-point of homosexual circles."[83] The regime clearly believed that these stories played on the public's anti-gay sympathies and could help discredit capitalist democracy. It "marshalled homophobia," as Evans puts it, "to project a sense of normalcy."[84] Here, the "othering" hypothesis applies, as the regime sought to consolidate support by scapegoating gay men.

These articles drew on a tradition of leftist animus against homosexuality that associated sexual deviance, crime, and capitalism. As we saw in chapter 1, German socialist thinkers had long entertained ambivalent views of homosexuality. Many considered it both a symptom of capitalism and unworthy of criminalization. These ideas continued to influence thought in East Germany in the 1950s. The East German historian Günter Grau, for instance, reports that, according to a proposed East German penal reform in 1958, "The bad economic relations prevailing under capitalism […] were important contributing factors to the spread of homosexuality."[85] Herzog notes that GDR doctors, such as Rudolf Neubert, asserted that homosexuality was far more common in capitalist societies.[86] Such language even shows up in court documents, such as a 1962 ruling that condemned homosexuality as "detritus of

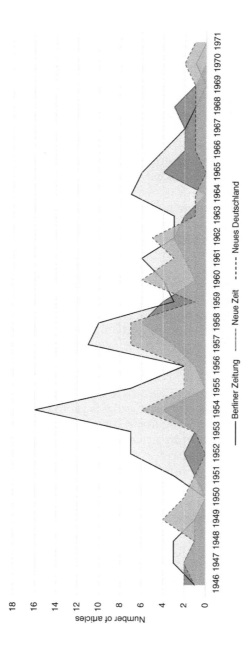

Figure 3.2. East German newspaper articles including the word "homosexual," per annum, 1946–71

the capitalist social order."[87] Curiously, while these views connected homosexuality to criminality and the excesses of capitalism, East German newspapers also often portrayed individual gay men as victims of crime, including murder and blackmail.[88] Thus, just as the East German government treated homosexuality equivocally, reforming the penal code halfway, so too did East German newspapers employ ambiguous rhetoric.

This equivocation is also visible in court cases, in particular those tried after the Supplementary Criminal Code came into force in 1957. In these cases, the desire to tarnish capitalism by association did not seem to be all that was at work in East German anti-gay animus. Rather, the regime's schizophrenic treatment of gay men also stemmed from a fear that the East German population itself remained highly inimical to homosexuality and that the regime would damage its legitimacy if it were seen to embrace it.

Consider the case of Friedrich J., a former Stasi officer living in Karl-Marx-City (now Chemnitz). In February 1961, Friedrich brought his drunken friend P. home from a bar. "Because of the consumed alcohol," Friedrich later explained to interrogators, P. "lay quite inert on the bed. How long I pleasured myself with his body, I can't say because I fell asleep during the act."[89] Although P. went to the police to report the rape, Friedrich was not charged. According to the police, he "promised to change."[90] But the problem did not go away. P. started telling anyone who would listen that "in the GDR there is no law." Nothing had happened to Friedrich, he alleged, "because he is protected by the MfS [Stasi]."[91] After P. denounced the regime in front of a crowd of around one hundred people, police officers arrested him. They charged him under §20 of the Supplementary Criminal Code, which punished "defamation of the state" with up to two years in prison.[92]

Only at that point was Friedrich prosecuted under §175. At his sentencing, the court indicated that Friedrich "was known as a former member of the Ministry for State Security and through his criminal behaviour he had endangered the trust of the populace in this government body."[93] While investigating him, his former colleagues had also discovered that Friedrich had slept with numerous other men, including one T., who was serving a twenty-five-year sentence for espionage.[94] Friedrich's behaviour, a Stasi report from June 1961 indicated, warranted prosecution under §175 because he was a public menace who "is reckless and hot-headed and has no regard for the morality or health of his fellow beings."[95] Stasi officials decided that because Friedrich's behaviour posed such a danger to the regime's reputation and to East German society in general, he had to be prosecuted. Nevertheless, he was only sentenced to eight months in prison. A convicted rapist, Friedrich received such a light sentence because the court believed he would once again be able to "create a respected place [for himself] in our society."[96]

Friedrich's case captures the equivocal animus that shaped gay life in East Germany in the 1950s and 1960s. Though the officials seemed largely uninterested in prosecuting cases of homosexuality, even those involving violent rape, it was concerned that any association between the state and homosexuality might taint its public profile. Friedrich's fate suggests that when homosexual acts became a clear danger to the state, in particular when they exposed perceived moral failings, the government would prosecute gay men.

Among the relatively few §175 prosecutions after 1957, Friedrich's case was not uncommon. Most likely, because the Supplemental Criminal Code only criminalized acts with "injurious consequences for the GDR," the judiciary fixated on gay men whose sexual exploits had tarnished the regime's moral profile. Judges harangued men convicted under §175, accusing them of denigrating the morality of the working class. In 1959 a court excoriated two men whose conduct, according to the judge, was "especially reprehensible because they both come from working families and have broken the laws of our workers' and farmers' state in such vulgar fashion." Their acts were dangerous because they "intensely injured the shame and moral feeling of the workers."[97] Evans uncovered similar language in her study of homosexuality in the Wismut uranium mining complexes. In one case, a defendant received a two-year sentence for "trampling on the moral values of the working people." In analysing these cases, she identifies a parallel dynamic, namely that such language was evidence of the regime's efforts to increase productivity and strengthen socialism through the embrace of traditional morality.[98]

From these examples, it is clear that homosexuality posed a problem for the regime's relationship to its own citizens. Its fear of popular animus against homosexuality (though no evidence exists that East Germans were more ill-inclined towards gay people than any other nationality) seems to have spurred the regime's occasional prosecutions of gay men. When prosecutors employed §175, especially by the late 1950s, they often did so to punish men whom they believed had marred the regime's reputation.

As a result, the army and Stasi were forbidding places for gay men.[99] In December 1955 Stasi minister Ernst Wollweber signed an order explicitly mentioning the case of a Stasi officer, "G.," who was found to be homosexual. "For this reason," Wollweber ordered, "his immediate dismissal had to be enacted."[100] Wollweber directed that "colleagues who are not unwavering in a moral sense" could not be appointed to "executive roles."[101] Gay soldiers and officers, such as Johannes H. or Lukas G., sometimes chose to commit suicide after being outed, rather than face the humiliation of dismissal.

Because the regime feared that homosexuality might taint its moral legitimacy, cases arising under §175 could have a political component, such as that of Max Fechner. The party sometimes relied on homosexuality as an excuse to dispose of troublesome members.[102] In 1947, for instance, party member Dr Stefan J. found himself on the wrong end of a purge. A local woman had accused him of molesting her son and his friend, who averred that when they visited Stefan, "he tried to hug us and at the same time took his penis out and played with it."[103] While such purges likely spiked after the 1953 uprisings, as late as April 1966 an SED member was faced with a party trial for having had sex with an eighteen-year-old man, thereby violating §175(a). The party eventually sentenced him to one and a half years of prison with hard labour.[104]

Although the GDR rarely prosecuted sex between adult men, homosexuality could thus become a significant liability for party members. To borrow a phrase from Marhoefer, being gay or engaging in homosexual activity reduced one's "social capital" in East Germany.[105] On their own, such proclivities would not necessarily land one in prison, but they certainly put one at greater risk for prosecution. Of course, homosexuality was not the only behaviour that the party policed among its officials. The SED went to great lengths to ensure that those in positions of authority lived up to the censorious standards of the new socialist personality.[106]

Thus, the GDR's treatment of gay men differed considerably from both Nazi and West German practices. In the Federal Republic, the Nazi version of §175 allowed for the convictions of tens of thousands of men. As we have seen, West Germany continued to employ the law out of fear of both homosexuality's spread and the threat that it might pose to West German society and the government's stability.

In East Germany, however, anti-gay animus was much more equivocally constituted and deployed. When the regime indulged in anti-gay rhetoric or prosecuted gay men, it often did so to generate support from the populace by casting the West as a place of sexual perversion. At other times, it did so to head off any perception that the East German government was friendly toward homosexuals. At the same time, traditional opposition to §175 and the state's anti-fascist rhetoric led East Germany to liberalize the law and even express sympathy at times with gay victims of crime. While some historians have drawn on medical tracts to argue that homosexuality's supposed threat to the nuclear family motivated East Germany's persecution of gay men, such language does not always show up in police records or court decisions, again pointing to the multifaceted nature of anti-gay animus.[107] Similarly, while an enduring fear of male prostitution and the seduction of youth explains why East Germany retained §175(a), it does not clarify either the regime's continued stigmatization of gay men or why its courts inconsistently prosecuted adult homosexuality.

As in West Germany, then, East Germany's treatment of gay men was wrapped up in concerns over the regime's legitimacy and stability. Unlike in West Germany, however, that impulse led the socialist dictatorship in competing directions. Whereas West German law sanctioned far-reaching campaigns against homosexuality for two decades, the communist regime's efforts were sporadic and reactive because leaders were equivocal about homosexuality's place in socialist society. Considering the role homosexuality played in the regime's efforts to fabricate legitimacy, however, allows us to place its seemingly haphazard treatment of gay men into a single explanatory framework: lenience and harshness alike aimed to shore up support for the regime.

Acknowledging that liberalization and persecution sprang from the same source allows us to make out a more complex picture of the relationship between homosexuality and elements of the East German state.[108] At the same time, it chimes with recent scholarship that has sought to temper views of the East German dictatorship that are still informed by Cold War stereotypes. These works have been especially effective at showing how East Germans were able to carve out private space for themselves, a phenomenon sometimes referred to as the country's niche society. They also reveal that, on matters of gender, East Germany remained, in important ways, more progressive than its Western twin.[109] What Elizabeth Heineman writes of women's equality in Soviet-occupied Germany – namely, that "if the stick in the Soviet zone was harder, the carrot was also sweeter" – applies to East Germany's treatment of gay men as well.[110] The regime implemented some genuinely progressive reforms and, as a result, the laws regulating homosexuality were less restrictive than in West Germany. At the same time, anti-gay animus remained a potent force in the Democratic Republic, particularly within its security services.

The outlines of East German gay life in these decades also illuminates the disconnect between legal and social change, at which Klimmer hinted in 1969. While different modes of anti-gay animus inspired divergent treatment of homosexuality in East and West German law, everyday life for gay men was not markedly better in East Germany than in West Germany, by any metric. That is, just as legal reform does not always engender a commercial subculture, so too the lack of such a subculture does not always imply the juridical persecution of queer people. Put plainly, consumer capitalism should not be our yardstick for progress. In both countries, gay men remained outsiders, albeit for different reasons and enforced in different ways.

Furthermore, the fact that East and West Germany quickly diverged on the policing and prosecution of homosexuality offers us an opportunity to probe why it is that societies in general police heterodox sexual acts and identities. What is curious about East and West Germany is that neither the "othering" hypothesis nor the "biopolitical" hypothesis described in the introduction can wholly explain their divergent treatment of gay men (to say nothing of their apathy vis-à-vis lesbianism). In both countries, the vagaries of denazification and the anxieties of the Cold War shaped the state's regulation of homosexuality. Yet, these two governments did so in divergent ways that set their countries on radically different paths. The multivalence of anti-gay animus in East and West Germany thus suggests that the policing of sexuality can fulfil a diverse set of social and political needs. It intimates that we should be cautious about using the term "homophobia," which is too broad and too divorced from historical context to be of analytical use.

While East Germany finally expunged §175 and §175(a) in 1968 with little fanfare, West German scientists and jurists engaged in ever-more-public campaigns throughout the 1960s to reform the statutes. These efforts, which only came to fruition in 1969, further illustrate the shifting nature of anti-gay animus. Liberalization of the criminal code at the end of the decade was paired with a recommitment to anti-gay prejudice as intellectuals, doctors, and politicians alike made clear that homosexuality had no place in West German society. Although gay life and politics in East and West Germany continued along divergent paths, they both expose that animus takes many guises – political, medical, legal, social, and cultural – that do not always wax and wane in unison.

4 Ever Disdained, Ever Despised

The Crooked Path of Emancipation in West Germany

The *Spiegel* cover on 12 May 1969 was meant to shock. On a bright magenta page, two naked men stood back to back (see figure 4.1). Over their heads hovered "§175." In the left corner was the question that would have bulked large that fateful year: "the law is falling – will the ostracism remain?"[1] The federal government had at last reformed the penal code, decriminalizing sexual acts between adult men.

The reform was one of the most momentous turning points in the lives of gay men in modern German history, vindicating a struggle that had started with the efforts of Karl Heinrich Ulrichs in the mid-nineteenth century. He had begun a long battle between elite, educated opinion that advocated legal reform and a succession of states hostile to it. The West German government was no different, using §175 and §175(a) to convict more than 50,000 men between 1949 and 1969. They sanctioned widespread surveillance of the gay subculture, denunciations, censorship of publications, and confinement of men to sanatoria. Yet in 1969 the law suddenly changed: sexual acts between adult men became legal. How this reform came about in a state whose functionaries were deeply sceptical, scared even, of homosexuality is no easy question to answer. Using newspapers, court decisions, parliamentary debates, and petitions to the federal government, this chapter looks to reconstruct not only how reform came about but also the strategic choices advocates of reform made and how their interactions with the state shaped decriminalization in 1969.

In recent years, a handful of scholars have described how the statutes came to be amended.[2] Following on their work, this chapter makes several arguments about how the 1969 reform occurred. Unlike other countries, including France and the United States, in which homophile organizations fought against discrimination in increasingly public ways, West Germany experienced no such enduring or public activism.[3]

Figure 4.1. The 12 May 1969 cover of *Der Spiegel*. © DER SPIEGEL 20/1969

While a number of homophile groups and publications appeared in the early 1950s, they had almost all closed down by the end of the decade. Advocacy for §175's reform was left in the hands of a small group of sexologists and lawyers.

Their arguments against §175, I show, were characterized by scientific-liberal rhetoric similar to that employed by certain Weimar-era activists. Most prominent among these postwar intellectuals was Hans Giese, a wiry Frankfurt doctor who attempted to re-found Hirschfeld's Humanitarian-Scientific Committee. In the late 1940s Giese began arguing for reform, and he continued in largely the same vein until the late 1960s. While his and his allies' arguments had little effect on policy in the 1950s, tectonic social changes in the 1960s offered more fertile ground for their reception. As the first postwar generation came of age, a new, more liberal atmosphere took hold, in which politicians were increasingly receptive to narrow arguments that the law should no longer criminalize consensual, adult homosexuality. Though scientific liberalism won the day in 1969, the terms of the reform made clear that West Germans still considered homosexuality a social ill. The debate that led to §175's reform in 1969 revealed that decriminalization never had been the same as social or political liberation.

The Scientific-Liberal Argument

In the Allied Occupation's wake, many gay West Germans hoped that their lives might return to what they had been in the 1920s. They expected the new government to repeal the Nazi-era version of §175 and §175(a), abolish censorship, and allow a return of the kinds of organizations that had formed the bedrock of gay life in Weimar Germany. Homophile groups did, in fact, reappear in West Germany's large cities starting in the late 1940s. Although the term "homophile" had originated in the 1920s as an alternative to homosexual, by the postwar era it carried specific political valences. Those identified as homophile not only pushed for the rights of same-sex desiring men but also steered clear of feminism, socialism, and especially prostitution.[4] They were often defined by their attachment to a politics of respectability.[5]

These new groups were intentionally modelled on Weimar-era organizations. Their defining figure was Hans Giese, then working as a sexologist in Frankfurt am Main. In 1949 he founded an Institute for Sexual Research, recalling Magnus Hirschfeld's Institute for Sexology. He also helped create a new German Society for Sexual Research, which his mentor, Hans Bürger-Prinz, one of the Nazi era's foremost sexologists, chaired. Furthermore, Giese worked with activists to create a new Scientific-Humanitarian Committee (*Wissenschaftlich-humanitäres Komitee* or WhK), taking the name of Hirschfeld's gay lobby founded in 1897.[6] While Giese's institute aimed to produce high-quality research, the WhK pursued a more explicitly political agenda, advocating for the repeal of §175 on the grounds of its "legal illegitimacy."[7] Although Giese was a key figure in postwar efforts to reform §175, his National Socialist training, which taught that homosexuality was a characteristic acquired in childhood rather than a congenital trait, has led some scholars to view him with distrust.[8] Their scepticism is justified, for Giese's ideas not only contributed to §175's long endurance but also had a significant impact on the terms of its eventual reform.

In other West German cities, new homophile groups also cropped up. A branch of the WhK opened its doors in Berlin in 1948. Hamburg played host to a string of short-lived organizations, including multiple iterations of the so-called Club of Friends. In Bremen both the International Friendship Lodge (IFLO) and the World League for Human Rights (WLHR) opened in 1951.[9] These groups were inspired by the work of activists in neighbouring countries, especially the Netherlands.[10] A number of homophile and homoerotic magazines also sprang up in and around West Germany. These included *Amicus-Briefbund*, *Freond*, *Der Weg*, and *Humanitas*.[11] The Swiss homophile magazine *Der Kreis*, which was published from 1942 to 1967, reported on goings-on in Germany. Some explicitly recalled their Weimar roots, such as *Die Insel*, which took the name of one of Weimar's most successful gay magazines.[12]

While these organizations entertained a diversity of aims, they all shared a basic belief that §175 had to be repealed. Much of their agitation against the law tended to advance scientific-liberal arguments similar to those prevalent before 1933. Though they evolved over time, these arguments almost always emphasized the incompatibility of modern sexological research and liberal jurisprudence with the continued criminalization of adult homosexuality.[13] Significantly, these activists' claims rarely contested mainstream characterizations of homosexuality. Campaigners accepted that gay men posed a threat to youth, that homosexuality might be a learned behaviour, and that the greater public would always disdain homosexuals. The scope of the scientific-liberal argument is important because it would set the terms for gay men's legal emancipation and continue to shape gay politics in the 1970s.

The scientific-liberal argument, which showed up in homophile publications and in petitions sent to the federal government during the 1950s, had a few hallmarks. First, these pleas typically invoked contemporary sexology in order to demonstrate both the naturalness of same-sex desire and the absurdity of laws restricting it. As one man living in Mannheim wrote to the federal government on 10 January 1955, "Homosexuality is, as has been proved, an incurable disease, that is, either a hereditary or inborn disposition."[14] Similarly, one Hermann S. writing from prison to the justice minister on 12 December 1955, compared his condition to a "sickness" just like "the flu, measles, pneumonia" and "cripples and idiots." Only "when a man is sexually ill," wrote Hermann, is he "punished for his suffering, for his constitution."[15] In 1952 the homophile magazine *Die Insel* invoked "new scientific results, which justify homosexuality as a natural human phenomenon" to argue against §175.[16] A telegram sent to Konrad Adenauer on 2 February 1956 entreated the chancellor to cease "the preservation and employ of laws that are bad [and] contradict all scientific knowledge."[17] These petitioners argued it was wrong for the law to penalize them for a natural condition they could do nothing to alter.

When Giese's institute submitted a petition to the federal Justice Ministry on 1 November 1950, it too leaned on contemporary science. The submission consisted of numerous essays by lawyers and doctors who contended that, even if homosexuality only developed in adolescence, it was still a condition rather than a choice.[18] Therapy, not punishment, presented the best course of action. Writing that modern psychology advocated against the repression of natural sexual urges, Giese complained, "The doctor must lead the individual to the acceptance of his own nature [...] But he thereby leads the patient on the sure path to prison, to social ruin." The state had placed doctors in the impossible position of pursuing a "therapy, which the lawmaker forbids."[19]

Thus, while advocates invoked medical knowledge to persuade lawmakers to repeal §175, they did so in a way that pathologized homosexuals and emphasized their difference. They also frequently endorsed §175(a), emphasizing in particular that youth needed to be protected from seduction.[20] Giese was at pains to stress that his institute and its efforts to reform §175 were not informed by "the intentions associated with Hirschfeld," by which he meant they were not a lobby for gay people. Giese even admitted that, "Undoubtedly many of these forms [of homosexuality] are treatable."[21] Gay men, he believed, could be cured of their homosexuality. The question, therefore, was not whether or not homosexuality was an equal form of human sexuality: campaigners accepted it was not. They argued instead that one had to "limit oneself to the question of punishability."[22] These narrow arguments affirmed that gay people were pathological beings in need of treatment.

In a parallel register, advocates emphasized §175's inconsistency with liberal jurisprudence founded on the rule of law. Like the medical side of their argument, this reasoning restricted itself to the question of whether homosexuality should be criminalized, leaving aside questions of whether West Germans ought to tolerate or despise it. For example, the institute's 1950 petition included an essay by Horst Pommerening, a noted jurist who later became a high bureaucrat in the West German foreign office.[23] His contribution contended that §175 was incompatible with the fundamental liberties guaranteed in West Germany's Basic Law. In his view, the paragraph contravened Articles 2 and 3, which safeguarded the right of personal development and the equality of women and men, respectively.[24] He believed that the law violated Article 2 because medical research had shown homosexuality to be a natural variation of human sexuality. It contravened Article 3 because §175 only punished acts between men. It therefore harmed men but not women, violating the equality of the sexes. The Federal Constitutional Court would consider these arguments in 1957 and reject both.

Pommerening also questioned what possible object §175 could aim to protect. He argued that consensual homosexual acts harmed no individual or state interest. Hence, the law could not rightfully criminalize sexual acts between consenting adults. "Where no legally protected interest is harmed," he asserted, "the state's penal authority fails." Except in cases of coerced homosexuality, the state had no right to intervene.[25]

These arguments were strategically narrow, making a case on legal and medical grounds that the state had better (and more legitimate) tools than prison at its disposal to address the problem of homosexuality. Scientific liberalism thus made no argument about the worth of homosexuals or homosexual acts. Instead it looked to prove that a state founded on democratic principles could find no basis on which to penalize homosexuality. Such arguments limited themselves to highlighting the futility of criminal proscriptions, the scientific consensus that considered homosexuality a natural variant of human sexuality, and the fact that homosexual acts did not pose a danger to society.

Though we have no way of knowing what effect these petitions had on the bureaucracies that processed them, notes on a 1962 petition hint at the disdain with which those in power viewed gay men. In response to the petition of one Josef T. on 5 August 1962, a bureaucrat jotted down, "It would not be advisable to grant an answer to a homosexual petitioner currently in prison."[26] To be sure, this was an extreme view. Civil servants answered most petitions regarding §175 with a polite but cold assurance that the government was in the process of reviewing the statute and would consider the petition as part of its deliberations. The note on Josef's petition, however, suggests that those reading such submissions did not take them seriously.

These petitions also reveal that, just as individual police officers, prosecutors, and judges had wide leeway in determining how they would deal with individual offenders, so too bureaucrats, politicians, and the experts on whom they relied enjoyed a great deal of agency. In this sense, the story of §175's reform becomes intelligible only if we conceive of the state, to quote Paisley Currah, as "a virtually uncountable number of state institutions, processes, offices, and political jurisdictions."[27] That is, just as we have considered a multiplicity of actors who fabricated anti-gay animus for a variety of reasons, so too the modern state's complexity led to innumerable impulses towards and away from reforming the law. In fact, when we drill down to the concrete expressions and causes of gay persecution and liberation, it becomes clear just how much of a legal fiction the state really is – a necessary fiction, certainly, but one that effaces the complex realities of human decision making beneath theories of domination and sovereignty.

Scientific-liberal arguments were also characterized by everything they did not do. While they stressed that §175 was a holdover from the Nazi regime, their authors did not usually mention gay men's fates in Nazi camps. Nor did most homophile writers define gay people as a minority in either a social or a political sense.[28] They did not envision a role for gay people in their own emancipation. Most important, their rhetoric did not foresee a future in which homosexuality would be accepted. Even Giese, whom later activists lionized, wrote in 1949, "I am no 'defender' of homosexuality."[29] Giese's contention that gay men did, in fact, seduce youth showed up not only in the Constitutional Court's 1957 ruling but also in *Volkswartbund* pamphlets.[30] Such language tracked with West German homophiles' broader socio-cultural self-representations, which emphasized bourgeois mores and respectability.[31]

These strategies inoculated their advocates against the accusation that they were apologists for homosexuality. Those arguing against §175 often did so with strikingly intolerant language. "Decriminalization should not be confused with legalization," Pommerening contended in the institute's 1950 petition. Even after the law's reform, he argued, "homosexuality will remain an incomprehensible, unsympathetic, and immoral matter." He continued: "The homosexual will always have to contend with contempt from society and with social disadvantages."[32] These narrow arguments reiterated much that we would today consider prejudicial against homosexuality. But they represented a strategic choice that campaigners likely believed they had to make in order to convince a largely sceptical population that §175 was an unjust and unnecessary law.

Interestingly, few of these texts dealt with the fear of gay cliques. One contribution to Giese and Bürger-Prinz's edited series on sexuality, for example, did try to disprove the hypothesis.[33] When liberal jurist Jürgen Baumann wrote a monograph on "the opportunity to legalize simple, non-youth-endangering and private homosexuality among adults" (again, note the long list of qualifiers), he mentioned the contention that "the emancipation of simple H[omosexuality] would promote the feasibility of the creation of homosexual cliques." Of that argument, he only pointed out that it consisted of "unprovable assertions."[34] To him, such fears were nothing more than delusion and paranoia. But these two texts were outliers: most simply ignored the theory.

In the early 1950s the federal government viewed this agitation against §175 sceptically. Convictions under §175 and §175(a) rose steadily, peaking at almost 4,000 in 1959. At the same time, police and local governments took steps to shut down nascent homophile groups. When the Hamburg Club of Friends opened its doors in 1949, Hamburg chief of police Rieck told *Der Spiegel*, "They want §175 out of the criminal code. But that won't be possible, so far as I know the conditions of the law."[35] Rieck's officers prevented the club's initial meeting from even taking place.[36] The Berlin Magistrate was similarly hostile to the Scientific-Humanitarian Committee founded in 1948. When the group applied for recognition as a non-political organization in February 1950, the municipal health bureau recommended the application's rejection.[37] The administration determined that because the city had no desire for such a group to exist, the bureaucracy should process the application in a "dilatory" fashion. If the group went ahead and functioned without a licence, the memo noted, "surveillance of the organization's activities would be appropriate, in order to [...] effect a dissolution of the organization."[38] The committee, perhaps because of the city government's hostility, faced chronic budget shortfalls and ceased to operate in the late 1950s.[39]

Homophile publications also encountered an increasingly inhospitable environment. Already in the 1940s, they were subject to suits under §184 of the criminal code, which regulated the distribution of pornographic materials. Some suits were effective, such as one against *Freond*, whose editor had to pay a 1,000 DM fine.[40] In others, however, the publications successfully repelled prosecution, convincing federal legislators of the need for more tight-fisted censorship.[41] In 1953 the *Bundestag* passed the "Law Regarding the Distribution of Youth-Endangering Texts," which created a centralized clearinghouse for all potentially "youth-endangering" texts. This board would have the power to review and index any publication in Germany. Any publication so indexed was prohibited from public sale.[42]

In addition to its profound effect upon the German pornography industry, the federal inspection authority (*Bundesprüfstelle*) began actively censoring homophile publications. In 1954 alone, the commission indexed eight "magazines for homosexuals." By 1956 twelve periodicals stood on the index, and by 1962 there were twenty-two indexed gay publications, effectively throttling their revenue.[43] The loss of income forced most of them to close down by the mid-1950s and, in Whisnant's estimation, shattered hopes for a renaissance of the Weimar-era gay public sphere.[44] Because of these measures, there was no West German equivalent to the large homophile publications in other countries, such as *Der Kreis* in Switzerland, *ONE* in the United States, or *Arcadie* in France.[45] *Der Weg* still appeared in West Berlin, but by the end of the 1960s published only 500 copies per edition.[46] Yet, the greatest loss for gay German culture was not in the novels and magazines censored but in those never written or left unpublished. The queer cultural efflorescence that had characterized Weimar Germany, above all its gay and lesbian literature, never reappeared in the postwar era. Since 1933, the country – West, East, or reunified Germany – has not witnessed a return of the same vibrant queer literary culture that left such an indelible mark on the 1920s.[47]

In the late 1940s it was not yet clear whether West Germany would keep §175 or §175(a), and homophile activists believed their political advocacy might win the day. By the mid-1950s legal and political opposition to homophile activism had extinguished it. The groups founded in Hamburg had dissolved by 1955.[48] Two years later an article in *Der Kreis* lamented, "Germany lacks an organization of the affected that is powerful and fights in word and writing with clear goals against the preservation of medieval and outdated regulations and laws."[49] Three years after that, in 1960, an assessment of the landscape in Germany concluded that a Bremen activist "is as good as the only homosexual interested party even active in West Germany."[50] Though it is difficult to know precisely when which groups failed, most had closed their doors by the end of the decade.

It is worth pausing to wonder why West Germany's homophile movement did not endure through the end of the 1960s and why its members were never as radical or public in their protests as were, for instance, American or French homophiles. No doubt part of the explanation rests, as Robert Moeller has argued, in the aggressive policing and censorship that such groups experienced, along with traumatic memories of Nazi persecution.[51] An extraordinary number of men were convicted under §175 and §175(a) in the 1950s and 1960s, and the continuation of Nazi-era policies hung heavily on homophile campaigners. Aside from the immediate effects of such persecution, we can only imagine how psychologically devastating it would have been for these men to have emerged from the Nazi years in hope of a second Weimar era only to see the new German republic recommit to fascist-era practices.

Yet homophile groups and publications in other countries were also harassed and somehow managed to survive. Generational differences may also have played a role. Homophile activism in other countries was a novelty in the 1950s, fledgling enterprises founded by young men and women full of energy. André Baudry was in his early thirties when he started *Arcadie* in Paris; Del Martin and Phyllis Lyon were in their thirties when they founded the Daughters of Bilitis in San Francisco; and Harry Hay was in his late thirties when he founded the Mattachine Society in Los Angeles. In West Germany, on the other hand, homophile activism was rather a staid tradition, a holdover from the Weimar Republic. While Giese was only in his late twenties when the new republic was founded, many of the other advocates were in their sixties, such as Erich Ritter and Kurt Hiller, who were both active in West Berlin. At the same time, many gay West Germans likely believed that the new republic would eventually get around to reforming the penal code – indeed, Adenauer himself gathered a commission of experts for precisely such a task in 1954. Generational exhaustion coupled with faith in democracy and scientific expertise may have encouraged a certain quiescence among advocates.

The passing of the homophile groups coincided roughly with another mammoth setback – the Constitutional Court's 1957 affirmation of the laws' constitutionality. Two men convicted under §175 and §175(a) had brought suit in the early 1950s, making three bold arguments against the statutes. The plaintiffs argued that the two laws were inherently National Socialist, and thus void in the Federal Republic; that they treated men and women differently and thus contravened Article 3 of the Basic Law, which guaranteed equality of the sexes; and that they contravened the Basic Law's guarantee of free development of personality, enshrined in Article 2. In a sweeping judgment, the court rejected all three arguments. The judges first found that because the Allied Control Council had not repealed them, there was no reason to see §175 and §175(a) as fascist laws worthy of repeal.[52]

In a lengthy discussion of the gendered difference inherent in the law, the court held that because male and female homosexuality were such different phenomena, the law was warranted in treating them differently. "Male homosexuals frequently aspire to join a homosexual group," the court wrote, whereas "lesbian relationships in contrast tend in general to longevity."[53] The judges further held that, while "the typical homosexual man loves the young man and is inclined to seduce him, [...] cases of the seduction of young women by lesbians [...] are unknown."[54] Finally, finding recourse in West Germany's "moral law," the court held that because homosexuality was disdained by most West Germans, the government had a legitimate interest in banning it.[55] The laws, which did impinge on gay men's personalities, therefore did so constitutionally.

Ironically, the Constitutional Court relied on contemporary sexology to justify its decision. The judges solicited testimony from seven medical and criminological experts, including Hans Giese, to inform it on the differences between male and female homosexuality. Curiously, Giese did not use the opportunity, as Moeller notes, to argue against the laws.[56] Instead, he stuck to the court's narrow question: "In what direction does male homosexuality on the one hand and lesbian love on the other represent a social danger."[57] The court wanted to know, that is, if there was good scientific reason to treat male and female homosexuality differently. Although Giese indicated that so long as homosexuality remained confined to "single relationships or long-term relationships [...] he could see no social danger," he also confirmed that "the reality, that male sexuality more easily falls into the path of perversion, is made clear by the frequency of self-indulgence among homosexual men."[58] He further noted that "promiscuity, prostitution, and the seduction of minors" were "symptomatic" of this "perversion."[59] These assertions helped convince the court to maintain the laws in the criminal code. In the 1950s, the scientific liberalism advocated by intellectuals like Giese seemed incapable of bringing about reform, in part because it reaffirmed prejudicial contentions about homosexuality.

The scientific-liberal rhetoric of Giese and other campaigners, which persisted into the late 1960s, is thus quite significant. Homophile movements in other countries, historians have recently discovered, made far more radical arguments about the innate worth of gay men or lesbians.[60] They took up Donald Webster Cory's formulation in *The Homosexual in America*, which argued that homosexuals were a minority deserving of certain legal protections.[61] When the leader of the Washington, DC, Mattachine Society, Frank Kameny, petitioned the US Supreme Court in 1961, for example, he asserted, "Homosexuality, whether by mere inclination or by overt act, is not only not immoral, but [...] for those choosing voluntarily to engage in homosexual acts, such acts are moral in a real and positive sense, and are good, right and desirable, socially and personally."[62] In stark contrast, petitions to the West German government, whether from ordinary men or from high-profile campaigners such as Giese, showed little evidence of such expansive rhetoric.

Although the language from certain homophile groups, magazines, or activists in the early 1950s might veer into the slightly more radical – Kurt Hiller, for instance, broke with Giese over the sexologist's support for maintaining §175(a) – most advocacy hewed to the scientific-liberal line.[63] Giese and his fellow advocates would continue in this vein until the laws' reform twelve years later.

An Emerging Consensus

Though continuities with the Nazi era loomed large in the first post-war decades, it bears mentioning that many of the Federal Republic's first leaders had been politicians in the Weimar Republic.[64] Theodor Heuss, the Republic's first president, had been a member of the Weimar *Reichstag*. Adenauer served as mayor of Cologne throughout the Weimar era and as president of the Prussian State Council from 1921 until 1933. Fritz Bauer, the general public prosecutor for the federal state of Hesse from 1956 until 1968, was a judge and an activist in the Social Democratic Party in the late 1920s and early 1930s.

It is no surprise then, with Weimar-era ghosts haunting the new republic, that the old, elite consensus in favour of reforming §175 would reassert itself. Already in 1951, at the 39th Association of German Jurists, Hamburg lawyer Heinrich Ackermann argued for a reform of the law. That same conference subsequently voted to recommend legalizing "simple, same-sex intercourse between adult men," but also agreed that "certain qualified cases must remain punishable."[65] Four years later, the criminal code committee of the federal bar association (*Bundesan-waltskammer*) also voted to recommend legalizing adult homosexuality. There was a sense, at least among the elite crowds that hobnobbed at these conferences, that the ban on consensual, adult homosexuality had to go. There was far less consensus, though, about §175(a). Both of these early 1950s resolutions supported the measure. The bar association even recommended an "expansion of the relevant criminal law for the protection of youth," that is, broadening §175(a)'s scope.[66]

Turning that consensus into political action took time. Pressure to reform §175 mounted only gradually, in part because the new federal government had numerous tasks ahead of it. Not only did it have to rebuild a country in ruins, negotiate West Germany's 1955 entry into the North Atlantic Treaty Organization (NATO), and justify rearma-ment to a traumatized population, it also had to carry out complete overhauls of most legal codes. Robert Moeller's study of gender in the Federal Republic's first decades reveals how tensions over women's social and economic status led to long wrangling over the civil code

(*Bürgerliches Gesetzbuch*).[67] Similarly, the Adenauer regime set up a commission in 1954 to produce a modern version of the criminal code, a reform that German parliaments under three different constitutions had attempted starting in the early twentieth century.[68]

The first sign of concrete change came from this criminal code commission. The group was composed of twenty-four prominent lawyers, judges, and civil servants.[69] Though it took five years to complete its work drafting a new code, the commission narrowly voted to recommend axing §175.[70] Taking a cue from scientific-liberal arguments, however, the commission recommended continued criminalization of homosexuality's supposed means of transmission. The proposed law prohibited men over twenty-one years of age having sex with or even "deliberately in front of" men younger than twenty-one. It further criminalized sex between a man over eighteen years of age and a man "who cohabitates with an association or a group" (such as the army).[71] This provision was intended to discourage the formation of cliques in all-male organizations. The proposed reform thus contained measures intended to continue the suppression of homosexuality. Still, by 1960, reformers had good reason to hope that the *Bundestag* would decriminalize adult homosexuality.

Two years later, Adenauer's government – the chancellor had been in power for thirteen years by this point – dashed those hopes when it released a different draft of the new criminal code, known as E 1962 (*Entwurf 1962* or *Bill 1962*). It was a horror house of reactionary morality. It punished adultery that resulted in divorce with up to one year of prison.[72] An artificially inseminated woman would face up to a year in prison, while those who had inseminated her could be imprisoned for up to three years.[73] Disseminating obscene texts could lead to prison terms of up to two years.[74] The draft was a last gasp of the Adenauer government's socio-sexual conservatism.

The law proposed to continue punishing homosexual acts. While its language returned to the Weimar-era punishment of only "intercourse-like acts," that is, only penetrative sex, the new law continued to penalize so-called "severe fornication" between men.[75] That is, it preserved §175(a) in new form. The bill foresaw punishments of up to three years in prison for those who "fornicated" – the same language as in the Nazi-era statute – with men less than twenty-one years of age.[76]

The government's official explanation for continuing to criminalize homosexuality mirrored *Volkswartbund* arguments. Clinging to what legal theorists referred to as the "morality-defining power of criminal law," the government argued that if it repealed the statute, the "degeneration of the people and the decay of its moral powers" would soon follow.[77] Gay people would then have a free hand to seduce "younger people into the spell of this movement," in turn allowing for the ever-greater "formation of homosexual groups."[78]

In fact, when it came to explaining the consequences of repeal, the regime focused heavily on the negative effects of gay cliques and groups, agonizing that if homosexuality were legalized, homosexual societies would be able to propagate "through word, text and image."[79] The possible consequences of such propagation for the state and society worried the government. It argued that gay men employed in "public service" might favour the employment and advancement of other gay men. Worse, decriminalization might enable homosexuality to spread among "the barracked units of the police and the army."[80] These were the same tired suspicions of gay conspiracy. Even by 1962, conservative fears of what homosexuality might do to West Germany, its people, its morals, and its government remained remarkably unchanged from the early 1950s and even the Nazi period.

As dark a moment as the Adenauer regime's proposed criminal law might have seemed, it became a decisive turning point against sexual conservatism. Newspapers, which had expected the reform effort to produce "one of the most modern criminal codes in the world" turned on the government's proposal.[81] A long opinion piece in *Die Zeit*, a major periodical, castigated the proposed law, accusing its authors of "mixing up sickness and vice."[82]

The clearest sign of backlash against E 1962 came in the form of an edited volume titled *Sexuality and Crime* (*Sexualität und Verbrechen*). Published in 1963 as a response to the proposed code, the volume helped to shape public debate about the relationship between law and sexuality in the 1960s.[83] The book's editors were an august bunch. Both Hans Giese and Hans Bürger-Prinz were listed on the cover along with public prosecutor Fritz Bauer and legal scholar Herbert Jäger. The four editors were sure to catch the educated public's attention, as was the star-studded list of contributors, which included none other than Frankfurt School philosopher Theodor Adorno.[84]

The book appeared with the prestigious S. Fischer publishing house and, costing only 4.80 DM, reached *Der Spiegel*'s bestseller list in the spring of 1963.[85] Positioning itself as part of the sexual revolution that had begun to sweep across the Federal Republic, the text emphasized that the "contradictions between dynamically progressing sexual-moral behaviours and the statically tenacious traditional legal order" made reform of the criminal code imperative.[86] The authors urged the *Bundestag* to review the proposed law critically and to take the advice of experts.[87] Although ostensibly about the entire sexual-criminal law, the editors made clear that "abortion and homosexuality have always stood at the centre of this discussion."[88]

Bringing arguments against the proposed code to a broader public, the book undoubtedly helped to throttle it in parliament. By the 1960s, the centre-left Social Democrats and the liberal Free Democrats had no appetite for a re-entrenchment of the conservative, almost century-old law. Most representatives in those two parties, which together composed a majority (although the Free Democrats remained in coalition with the CDU/CSU), preferred to see the criminal code liberalized.[89] The *Bundestag* never passed *E 1962*. The long-delayed criminal reform would wait until the end of the decade, after the student movement, the sexual revolution, and a shifting political landscape made the decriminalization of homosexuality thinkable to both the government and a wider swath of the West German public.

The '68 Generation

To understand how the West German government could shift from proposing an archconservative criminal code in 1962 to passing a progressive reform seven years later requires a wider consideration of the social forces that shaped the country in those years.[90] In 1961 birth control pills (*Antibabypille* in German) became available in West Germany. Images of nudity became ever more common in the media, as a new generation of younger Germans expressed increasing comfort with overt sexuality.[91] The West German pornography industry grew over the course of the 1960s, and porn became widely available in the early 1970s.[92] In short, West Germans' sexual mores were changing rapidly in what became known as the sex wave (*Sex Welle*).[93] In spite of these shifts in public conceptions of sexuality, though, attitudes toward homosexuality did not immediately change. The sex wave was a liberation of heterosexuality from the confines of the Adenauer era not a liberation of homosexuality from state-sponsored persecution.

These shifts also intersected with more explicitly political changes. They overlapped, for instance, with West Germany's increasingly robust denazification efforts in the 1960s.[94] These initiatives, many the work of public prosecutor Fritz Bauer, would not only have a profound impact on the student movements of the late 1960s and the broader impetus of leftist groups but would also open up a new discursive space for gay people to define themselves as victims of National Socialism.

The Adenauer government had pursued a politics of amnesia in its first years in power. Former Nazis regained posts in government and amnesty laws made it difficult to prosecute those affiliated with the dictatorship.[95] Politicians encouraged Germans to forget the recent past or even to think of themselves as co-victims of the Hitler state. This bargain meant that the new democratic regime stood under the simmering suspicion of protecting Nazis and fellow travellers. These misgivings, which had remained largely unspoken throughout the 1950s, emerged publicly after a set of high-profile trials of Nazi officials.

Although Germany continued to prosecute Holocaust perpetrators throughout the 1950s, these prosecutions were rarely successful (of 12,846 indicted, only 155 were convicted of murder) and never led to a public reckoning with Germans' crimes during the Nazi era.[96] But by the 1960s, this silence surrounding National Socialism began to crack. It had much to do with one man: Fritz Bauer. He was a German Jew and a Social Democrat. In 1935 he had fled Germany after a spell in the Heuberg concentration camp in southwest Germany. He was also gay and one of a coterie of elites who voiced dissent against the stultifying conservatism of the Adenauer era.[97]

The most significant single event to blast open the German past was Adolf Eichmann's 1961 trial in Jerusalem, on which the philosopher Hannah Arendt famously reported for *The New Yorker*.[98] Although Bauer, as a German prosecutor, was not officially involved in the trial, his office had covertly provided the intelligence to Mossad that enabled it to capture Eichmann in Argentina in 1960.[99] Three years later, Bauer opened the famous Auschwitz Trials in Frankfurt, charging former concentration camp officials under West Germany's murder statute. In 1965 the court sentenced seventeen of the accused to prison terms ranging from three years to life.[100] These two trials had a powerful impact, exposing the extent to which the war generation had opted to forget its culpability, trading it in for stability. Taken together, these trials formed a cornerstone of the cultural sea changes of the 1960s.[101]

These shifts made similar changes possible in how gay people recalled the Nazi era. Though West Germans were well aware that §175 had Nazi roots, they rarely acknowledged that gay men had been interned in concentration camps. Never had politicians or the media admitted queer people as co-victims of the Holocaust. Restitution laws passed in the 1950s mostly prevented gay men from claiming compensation for their imprisonment, an issue that would become significant to the West German gay liberation movement in the 1970s and 1980s.[102]

The silence surrounding the Nazi persecution of gay men began to change in 1963 when the proceedings of an academic symposium on homosexuality appeared. In it, Hans-Joachim Schoeps, a well-known Jewish religious studies professor at the University of Erlangen, tackled the history of homosexuality in the Holocaust.[103] Schoeps included homosexuals as one of "three categories of prisoner" under the Nazis, acknowledging that they were "deprived of their rights, infamously tortured and murdered."[104] He excoriated the government for maintaining §175, calling it "the last great perfidy of German justice."[105] "For homosexuals," he declared somewhat hyperbolically, "the Third Reich has not yet passed."[106]

The publication spurred further inquiry into gay men's fate during the Third Reich. In 1967 Wolfgang Harthauser published an essay, quoting extensively from Schoeps, in which he lamented that there was "no book" on the persecution of gay men under the Nazis.[107] "Now is the time to clarify the National Socialist mass murder perpetrated on homosexuals," Harthauser opined.[108] The first book on the subject appeared two years later. Harry Wilde's *The Fate of the Ostracized* provided the first in-depth treatment of homosexuality in Nazi and postwar Germany, tying the two together through gay experiences of persecution. Wilde even contended that the "torments of the prisoners with the 'pink triangle' [was] a kind of dress rehearsal for the 'final solution of the Jewish question.'"[109]

From the halls of the academy, knowledge of the National Socialist terror against gay men began to seep into the media, which had been reluctant to depict them in a sympathetic light. *Der Spiegel*, for instance, had published precious little about homosexuality in the first decade and a half of the Federal Republic's existence and nothing about the persecution of gay men in the Third Reich. Only in the 1960s did the magazine first thematize their incarceration in concentration camps.[110] By 1969, however, the magazine was calling the Nazi treatment of gay people a "pogrom," picking up Wilde's research and quoting Schoeps's pioneering article.[111]

Likewise, petitions to the federal government at the time connected gay men's plight to the National Socialist terror. One Franz M. wrote on 15 February 1966 in regard to an article in *Quick Zeitung* about the Nazis' treatment of gay men. He demanded to know why the current government did not condemn that past.[112] The next year, one H.S. wrote about efforts to reform §175: "It is finally time," he appealed, "to free this area of the law from National Socialist thought."[113] As research on this gay history grew in subsequent years, it invariably took on political valences. The pink triangle turned into a potent symbol of gay liberation, and honouring Nazism's gay victims became a political lever.[114] As Chitty argues, these early attempts to write gay history grew out of liberal political imperatives that took the form of a rights discourse.[115] In an example of what Michael Rothberg terms "the multidirectionality of memory," early research into the fate of gay men in

Nazi Germany thus constituted both a piece of West Germans' growing interest in Nazi crimes and an important element of gay men's increasingly robust claims to rights-based citizenship in the late 1960s and early 1970s.[116]

Renewed interest in Nazi crimes also helped spark the student movements that rocked the country in the late 1960s. These protests, which resembled similar movements around the world, took aim at both the politics and the culture of the Federal Republic. In conjunction with protests against Western imperialism, in particular the Vietnam War and support for the Iranian Shah's vicious dictatorship, students coalesced into new groups. This extra-parliamentary opposition, or APO, included the famous Socialist German Student Union. The movement reached its height in 1968, when activists marched on Bonn and the governing coalition passed an emergency law some feared might lead to authoritarian rule. By the 1970s, however, with Social Democrat Willy Brandt newly elected as chancellor, most activism had died down, leaving behind radical terrorist cells such as the infamous Red Army Faction.[117]

As with other 1968 movements around the world, one of the students' central demands was for liberated sexuality. It is no wonder, for the uprisings came hot on the heels of the sex wave.[118] Informed by the work of psychoanalyst Wilhelm Reich, the young rebels argued that repressed sexuality was one of the central causes of German fascism and a defining malady of the conservative Federal Republic. They therefore demanded a new, radically open sexual ethic.[119] As historian Tony Judt recalled in his memoirs, "Everyone [in West Germany] appeared unutterably serious – and alarmingly preoccupied with sex."[120]

For all the students' sexual preoccupations, however, they rarely thought about the place of queer people in Western societies. Radical publications from the 1960s often neglected homosexuality, even when explicitly addressing sexuality.[121] Much of the groups' theorizing about subculture and minorities, inspired by the American Civil Rights movement, never mentioned homosexuality.[122] The movement's obliviousness toward gay persecution lends some credence to Judt's sardonic condemnation of the revolutionaries – "how fortunate that anti-Nazism required, indeed was defined by – serial orgasm."[123] While claiming to rebel against stifling sexual mores and the lingering shadow of National Socialism, student activists neglected the one group still suffering under Nazi-era laws. Indeed, there is a certain parallel between their lack of interest in West Germany's persecution of gay men and their disregard for both female activists and the perseverance of racism and antisemitism in West German society.[124]

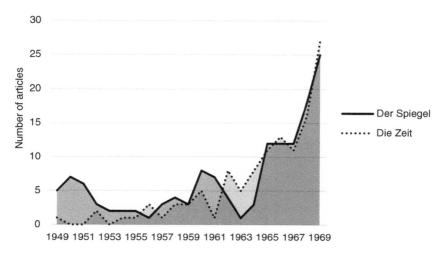

Figure 4.2. West German newspaper articles mentioning "homosexuality," per annum, 1949–69. Sources: Spiegel.de and Zeit Online

Though the student movement did nothing for gay people, surveys showed that, as young West Germans grew less religious and more accepting of extramarital sex and birth control, so too were they becoming more tolerant of homosexuality.[125] These cultural shifts created an environment in which Germans could "dare more democracy," as Brandt famously campaigned in 1969.[126] As with the prosecution of Nazi perpetrators, the sex wave, and the increasingly rosy electoral prospects of the centre-left Social Democrats, the student rebels contributed to the rapid opening up of West German society.

While these social changes were hardly noticeable in the daily lives of gay people, they began to register in newspaper and magazine articles. In two of the Federal Republic's primary periodicals, *Der Spiegel* and *Die Zeit*, articles related to homosexuality remained a relative rarity throughout the 1950s and the early 1960s, reflecting social taboos (see figure 4.2). But by the mid-1960s, mentions of homosexuality began to rise. The articles themselves also contained more sympathetic coverage of homosexuality.

Representative of this visibility surge was a 1963 article in the youth magazine *Twen*. Titled "We Discuss Paragraph 175," it consisted of five mini-essays on homosexuality in West Germany written by heavyweight intellectuals including Bauer.[127] As in the collected volume

Sexuality and Crime, each essay criticized §175 with familiar scientific-liberal arguments. As a sign of the passion the topic now aroused, the magazine received hundreds of readers' letters, of which it published a few dozen in the following issue.[128]

Not only did this one article garner a stunning public response, but it also got the federal government's attention. Some individuals mailed petitions to the Justice Ministry with the article attached, pleading for §175's repeal.[129] One high bureaucrat in the Ministry of Justice wrote his own letter to *Twen*'s editorial board, in which he defended the law. When the editors opted not to publish his letter (the thirty-two printed letters opposed §175), the ministerial aide wrote again. He petulantly complained that the magazine had only highlighted opposition to the law and insisted, "You will understand if I draw certain conclusions" from the refusal to publish his letter.[130] The article had clearly gotten under his skin, suggesting that politicians and bureaucrats had begun paying attention to West Germans' shifting views.

The Reform of §175

These cultural turns began to manifest politically in 1966 when the Free Democrats withdrew their support for Chancellor Ludwig Erhard, who had been the architect of West Germany's postwar economic recovery. The Christian Democrats were thus forced to lean on Social Democratic support in parliament. A grand coalition between the two largest parties brought Social Democrats into government for the first time since 1930 and put them in control of key federal ministries. Gustav Heinemann, a former CDU politician turned Social Democrat, was made the new minister of justice. Long-dormant efforts to reform Germany's criminal code fell to the progressive Heinemann, an opponent of §175.

By the late 1960s, reform efforts had regained steam. The arguments that Giese, Bauer, and their colleagues had advanced for the past fifteen years had finally become accepted opinion among educated West Germans and had begun to trickle into the popular press. In a sign of just how decisively views had swung against §175, the 47th Association of German Jurists, meeting in Nuremberg in 1968, chose to make sexual-criminal law the conference's focus.

Opinion there was so profoundly in the reform camp that organizers fretted that "absolutely no conservative would speak" at the conference.[131] Though one did summon the courage to address the body – an ironic reversal of fortune from Karl Heinrich Ulrichs's lonely 1867 address to the same conference – the participants voted "with a staggering majority (only three nay votes and two abstentions) for the first resolution of the day: §175 of the criminal code should be abolished."[132] The conference's official records damned the statute, excoriating "the criminalization of so-called simple homosexuality" as a provision that "cannot earnestly intend the protection of youth or dependents."[133] That is, German lawyers reaffirmed in the starkest language possible what sexologists, homophile activists, and legal theorists had been writing for decades: there was no good reason to prohibit adult homosexuality.

A publication in 1969 underscored the extent to which opinion had changed. The previous summer, author Rolf Italiaander had sent a letter to dozens of prominent politicians and intellectuals, asking them for their views on "the homophile problem."[134] In it, Italiaander entreated, "Please, allow us as scientists, authors and artists jointly to contribute so that Justice Minister Dr. G. Heinemann and others who are engaged in this matter [of repealing §175] will find public support."[135] He received more than eighty responses, almost all in favour of reforming §175. Theodor Adorno, the philosopher Max Horkheimer, conservative politician Baron Karl Theodor von und zu Guttenberg, future president Richard von Weizsäcker, celebrity sociologist Ralf Dahrendorf, Gustav Heinemann himself, and hosts of other stars in West Germany's intellectual firmament replied. Italiaander gathered their responses and published them under the title *Neither a Sickness Nor a Crime: Plea for a Minority*. Like *Sexuality and Crime* in 1963, Italiaander's volume was a cannonball aimed at the bulwarks of conservative morality. The sheer number and prestige of the volume's authors showed that §175 was untenable.

These cultural watersheds, though they undoubtedly exerted considerable pressure on the government to reform §175, were symptomatic of how decisively educated views had turned against the continued criminalization of adult homosexuality. No one cause explains this shift. Rather, as I have sought to illustrate, these changes came about gradually, through the confluence of persistent agitation by a small group of sexologists, lawyers, and scholars and the tectonic shifts Germany experienced in renewed de-nazification efforts, the sex wave, the student movement, and the Social Democratic Party's ascendance. The work of homophile thinkers such as Hans Giese and Fritz Bauer had found fertile cultural soil by the mid-1960s. Crucially, this was the handiwork not of a homophile movement or a product of the gay subculture but of a small band of scientific and legal experts. Reform of the law, significant though it was, was not a Stonewall moment in the history of German homosexuality.

Nonetheless, the tide finally reached shore on 25 June 1969, when the *Bundestag* voted to liberalize §175 and abolish §175(a). The country had criminalized adult male homosexuality for two years shy of a century, convicting well over 100,000 men.

The reform measure itself was curious. Like the scientific-liberal arguments levelled against the Nazi version of §175, the new §175 fundamentally accepted that homosexuality was an undesirable trait and that the state had an interest in preventing youth from becoming homosexual. The statute still criminalized male prostitution. More bizarrely, it punished "a man over eighteen years who fornicates with another man under twenty-one."[136] That is, the new measure legalized homosexual acts between boys younger than eighteen and between men older than twenty-one, but criminalized all homosexual acts of men aged between eighteen and twenty-one. This provision occasioned a great deal of speculation.[137]

Once again, we are brought back to gay cliques. Ministerial records from 29 January 1969 indicate that senior civil servants agonized about the possibility that homosexuality, once legalized, would spread in the military. West Germany had reintroduced universal conscription in 1956 after joining NATO the year before. Politicians and bureaucrats fretted that gay groups might form among young recruits.[138] When the *Bundestag* discussed the provision on 7 May 1969, members debated what some termed a special law for the military or *Lex Bundeswehr*.[139] Yet even the ostensibly gay-friendly Social Democrats had no better suggestion. Martin Hirsch, a Social Democratic member of parliament, proposed removing the provision because, "What would happen, when two men flirt in the barracks – they'll be killed. Really, the problem will solve itself."[140]

The provision's inclusion, which took contemporaries by surprise, reveals the terms under which emancipation had been granted. While the state had bestowed the privilege – never acknowledged as a right – of men to have sex with men, the law remained clearly set against homosexuality. The scientific-liberal argument, while contending that there was no good reason to prohibit homosexual acts between consenting adults, had for two decades accepted that homosexuality was a communicable condition and that there was every reason to try to prevent it from spreading. That the reform which followed in its wake condemned homosexuality as undesirable and dangerous to youth should not surprise us.

The bill also reflected the reality that while elite opinion had turned against §175, the broader German public remained hostile to homosexuality. A February 1969 survey indicated that 46 per cent of West Germans believed homosexuality should continue to be criminalized, while only 36 per cent were in favour of the reforms.[141] Over 80 per cent of all West Germans surveyed ranked homosexuals as a lower type of person than female prostitutes.[142] Leaving aside the question of what kind of society ranks its members in this way, these surveys indicated, as Moeller also contends, that emancipation did very little in the short term to change society's views of homosexuality.[143] The reform brought gay men a step closer to full citizenship in the Federal Republic. But it did not represent the state as "embracing minorities," as Whisnant suggests.[144] Rather, the new law demarcated all too clearly the limits of the state's tolerance.

The 1969 decriminalization and the advocacy that shaped it were the first instances of something like gay liberation in the history of the Federal Republic. The new law represented a real change in how the government treated gay men and opened new opportunities to them in subsequent years. In the decades-long effort to reform the criminal code, we see how gay activism, in particular in the strategic choices it makes vis-à-vis state authority, takes varied forms and makes counter-intuitive arguments. In the United States, an ever-more-assertive homophile movement laid the foundations for the Stonewall uprising in 1969, which in turn sparked significant national movements protesting persecution and discrimination against queer people.[145] West Germany's reform, in contrast, was a narrow legal shift made possible by broader social changes and informed by the sustained efforts of a handful of scientists and jurists.

As it was across the border, where the GDR's liberalized law never held out hope of acceptance, West Germany's reform made clear that gay men could expect very little to change in their daily lives. They would still suffer employment discrimination, violence, and social isolation. Ironically, though, even as the Federal Republic's fear of gay conspiracies slowly waned, Western intelligence practices had started to change how the East German security services viewed the gay subculture. The Stasi, discovering gay espionage rings in the 1960s, began to believe that gay men were naturally suited to be spies and that the subculture might pose an unguarded threat to the socialist state.

5 Gay Spies in Cold War Germany

anic at Radio in the American Sector," wrote the East Berlin newspaper *Berliner Zeitung* on 11 November 1961. "An atmosphere of
nervousness and mutual distrust" reigned at the West Berlin radio
station after a public announcement, on East German radio, of its secret
plan to move from West Berlin to Luxembourg. Even more scandalous,
the newspaper reported, the US Central Intelligence Agency (CIA) "is
now concentrating its investigation on the male circle of acquaintances
of the deviant [Hans] Rosenthal." The American intelligence service
allegedly had surmised that "during one of his nocturnal sex orgies,"
which "young GDR citizens" regularly attended, Rosenthal had given
away information regarding the American radio's plans.[1]

Rosenthal's case was not an isolated one. When I conducted research
in the Stasi Archive in 2016 and 2017, I came across ever more cases
of gay espionage. These perplexing, fascinating files pointed to a sub-
merged world of gay spy networks that shaped everyday life in divided
Germany. While historians today cannot always be sure of the veracity
of such records, for Stasi reports famously contain numerous exaggera-
tions and falsehoods, these reports clearly pointed to an evolution in
how the Stasi itself thought about the relationship between homosexuality and espionage. As the secret police was confronted with ever
more cases of alleged gay spies, its functionaries became increasingly
alarmed that foreign intelligence services were recruiting gay men as
agents, hoping to exploit the subculture's extensive networks that criss-
crossed society. By the 1970s Stasi officials evinced a marked interest in
and fear of gay people, worried about what they termed "the political
misuse of homosexuals."[2]

When gay East Germans founded liberation groups in the 1970s and
1980s, then, the secret police viewed them with pronounced suspicion.
To counteract this perceived threat, the Stasi would eventually recruit

a large network of gay informants within activist groups. Its infiltration of these organizations was thus predicated on its fear of gay espionage.[3] Writing about East Germany's gay movement years later, activist Eduard Stapel bewailed that the Stasi "conceived of a phantom image" of gay people, seeing them as "conspirators, [...] underminers of state authority, [...] clique-creat[ors]."[4] This chapter uncovers the origins of this paranoia, revealing, counter-intuitively, that it was not simply a "phantom image" or an expression of anti-gay animus. Rather, it was the result of a long evolution in Stasi officials' views of gay men, a consequence of the secret police's intelligence practices and the information that they generated over the course of several decades.

The Stasi's perceptions of gay people were particularly important because the secret police was the regime's eyes and ears, the branch of government that inspired the most dread and that collaborated with massive swathes of the East German citizenry. The SED had founded the Ministry for State Security in 1950, and after the failed 1953 uprising the ministry transformed into a fearsome intelligence agency. In addition to domestic counter-intelligence, one of the Stasi's chief portfolios lay in neutralizing the threats, both perceived and real, of Western intelligence.[5] The Stasi recruited a sprawling network of unofficial collaborators (*Inoffizielle Mitarbeiter* or IMs), ordinary individuals whom the Stasi persuaded or coerced to pass on information about their friends, colleagues, and even family.[6]

By 1989, the Stasi had engaged more than 170,000 IMs. Historians estimate that because of high turnover rates, somewhere between 5 and 30 per cent of the GDR's 17 million citizens worked for the Stasi in some capacity at some point.[7] Almost every East German knew someone who worked for the secret police. In turn, its penetration of society created a myth of omnipresence that was a chief source of the Stasi's power. Ordinary citizens believed its operatives were everywhere and knew everything.[8] The Stasi thus fostered a ubiquitous fear of surveillance, while co-opting vast numbers of citizens into the dictatorship's system of rule.

As one might expect in a state that had, on paper at least, repudiated the persecution of gay men, however, the Stasi did not initially perceive homosexuality as an active threat. Generally, only when a Stasi employee was found to be gay would officials investigate. Relative to inquiries in West Germany or during the Nazi era, such probes were limited in scope. Unlike the American federal government, which mounted a widespread campaign to purge gay men and lesbians from federal bureaucracies in the 1950s, the Stasi simply did not care all that much about homosexuality.[9] An emerging concern with Western gay spy networks would change that.

Early Cases of Espionage

It was a slow process. In the 1950s the regime did not perceive any causal connections between espionage and homosexuality, even when it captured gay spies and *agents provocateurs*. In March 1950, for instance, prosecutors charged the leaders of an illegal youth troop called the Falcons with distributing flyers and with homosexual acts. During a trip to West Berlin, troop leader Reinhold R. had met with Western leaders of the Falcons, who promised him work in the West in exchange for agitating against the East German state. As the leader of a Dresden chapter, prosecutors told the court, Reinhold had seduced younger members of the group.[10]

During the trial, the prosecutor denounced Reinhold, who received a sentence of thirteen years of prison with hard labour, as "a completely morally depraved person, who uses politics and youth in order to incite them with the same lies and slander against the GDR and the occupation force and to earn easy money from the western occupation force."[11] But he never suggested a causal relationship between Reinhold's sexuality and his work for Western interests. In keeping with East German propaganda, which asserted that homosexuality was a symptom of capitalist decadence, the prosecutor simply saw two unconnected forms of depravity.

In a similar case from 1953, Johann L., an officer in the Barracked People's Police, allegedly became the target of a Western agent. Since 1933, Johann had slept with dozens of men and frequented "public houses, where predominantly homosexual persons socialize, [and] was known by the name 'Princess.'"[12] In 1951, he began "a homosexual affair (*Verhältnis*) with a certain R. from West Berlin." This R., according to Johann, "made me an offer in early 1953, to gather information."[13] Johann confessed that between 1953 and 1955 he had sent ninety-three reports about the Stasi to Western intelligence and received more than 25,000 marks for his efforts.[14] In 1957 an East German court sentenced Johann to a lifetime of prison with hard labour.[15]

The Stasi's report on Johann's activities commented that, "The American intelligence service employs unscrupulous subjects, criminal elements, or incorrigible enemies of the German Democratic Republic."[16] As in the Falcons case, the Stasi's assertions elided any essential connection between homosexuality and espionage. The report neither found a causal relationship between the two nor suggested that the gay subculture posed an intelligence threat to the regime.

The connection between sex and spying is itself nothing new. It is one of the most common tropes of the Cold War, most famously captured in James Bond's exploits. There is also an ample scholarship on the Stasi's so-called Romeo agents. The regime recruited these spies to seduce intelligence targets, often foreign women employed in sensitive posts. The Stasi's head of foreign intelligence allegedly described these women as "lonely secretaries, glad of male attention, and happy to help East German intelligence for the sake of their relationships."[17] Gay Romeos, on the other hand, have received little attention from historians. John Koehler is one of the few even to mention their existence in the Stasi.[18] Agents like R. seemingly penetrated the East German subculture in order to access its networks, which connected men from all strata of society, from call boys to government ministers. The Stasi simply did not seem to realize it at the time.

As a side note, it is important to mention that these files contain no evidence that specifically American bureaus employed the agents in question. Given that the East German regime thought of the West German government as a puppet of the United States, it is entirely possible that "American" became a synonym for "Western" in these reports. Indeed, in one memo, Stasi officials described an address operated by the West German intelligence service as a "US intelligence post."[19] Moreover, Berlin was host to a small legion of espionage organizations at the time, and these often sought to recruit each other's agents.[20] One thus ought not to take allusions to "American agencies" at face value. Indeed, given the well-known possibility of exaggeration and fabrication in Stasi files, we can take very little at face value in these documents. Whereas other Stasi files, in particular those documenting East Germany's gay liberation movements in the 1970s and 1980s, can be corroborated with other evidence, these files have few parallel sources.

Nonetheless, historians know that Berlin in the 1950s and 1960s was a hotbed of espionage, a focal point of the ongoing "intelligence revolution" that turned espionage into a key element of national defence.[21] That espionage was an everyday occurrence in the divided metropolis makes these accounts plausible, if not necessarily trustworthy in all their details. Access to files from West German intelligence agencies and the CIA would, of course, shed further light on these cases and, potentially, reveal further instances of gay espionage. But this chapter's ultimate argument, that a change occurred in how Stasi officials thought about homosexuality and espionage, does not depend on the veracity of the details of each individual case.

In a late 1950s affair, officers began to suspect that something more than depravity connected intelligence work and homosexuality. The ministry imprisoned a twenty-year-old male prostitute whom officials believed an American agent M. had recruited to collect "information about the rapid response police."[22] An East Berlin court sentenced the young man on 23 August 1958 to six years of prison with hard labour under §175, for prostitution, and for "spying for the American intelligence service."[23] The court's decision lamented that the foreign agent M. "was homosexual and understood how to join his dirty profession of espionage with his homosexual urges."[24] Unlike earlier cases, in which the regime simply saw a spy's homosexuality as proof that Western intelligence services would sink to any level in order to destabilize the socialist regime, the court here recognized that M.'s sexuality had assisted him in his work. It believed the agent had intentionally manipulated acquaintances from the gay subculture to collect information. In the 1960s Stasi officials would begin to act on this suspicion and recruit agents to combat what it viewed as the spread of Western intelligence efforts in the gay subculture.

The Stasi's Emerging Awareness

On the afternoon of 21 October 1960, Joachim L., an East Berlin actor in his twenties, met with his friend Jakob H. They had been having sex regularly, and Joachim likely thought there was nothing out of the ordinary until Jakob suggested that he ought to consider dabbling in espionage. According to a Stasi IM – code-name "Deege" – who was friends with them both, Jakob and Joachim "were speaking about opportunities to earn money and H. mentioned that one can easily earn some quick money, up to 3,000 DM per month. When L. asked how that was possible, H. indicated that one could spy (*Spionage machen*)."[25] Joachim related this conversation to "Deege" soon thereafter. The informant encouraged Joachim to take the matter to the Stasi, which he soon did. "Deege" also passed the story on to his Stasi handler the next day.[26]

Two days later, on 23 October, gears began to grind at the Stasi's Berlin offices. An "operative plan" appeared suggesting that the ministry should consider recruiting Joachim. The report stressed that he was in contact with both Jakob and a certain Karl O., "who are allegedly involved in espionage against the GDR and to this end are supposedly recruiting among homosexual circles in order to prepare for and carry out their enemy activities."[27] The secret police believed Joachim, who would take the code-name "Franz Moor," could provide them with invaluable, even incriminating, evidence against Jakob and Karl. They hoped Joachim would lend "valuable support in unmasking this circle [of spies]."[28]

At the same time, Stasi officers expected that Joachim would help them infiltrate the gay subculture on both sides of the Iron Curtain. In a report two days before Joachim's official enrolment as a collaborator, officers noted that, "Because of his large circle of acquaintances, in particular among homosexuals and other negative persons, he is in a position to give us further leads, which could lead to further recruitments."[29] They anticipated that Joachim could act as their beachhead into Berlin's gay subculture and would enable them to enlist their own network of gay spies.

Over the course of almost five years, "Franz Moor" provided the Stasi with information in exchange for regular "monetary contributions" of anywhere from ten to two hundred marks.[30] In an assessment of his services, the Stasi found that he showed "individual initiative in the detection of enemy elements," and that through his efforts "one enemy person was imprisoned by the MfS."[31] Most of Joachim's tasks over those five years, however, involved not flashy scandal but rather the tedium of everyday espionage.[32]

What "Franz Moor" reported on – and what his Stasi handlers were interested in learning about – provides a glimpse into how gay spy networks shaped the East German regime's view of homosexuality in socialist society. Spanning four files and more than 700 pages, these reports paint a picture of a bureaucracy worried about its inability to surveil Berlin's gay subculture and reveal its desire to rectify the problem by enlisting gay spies.

The Stasi decided to recruit Joachim both to provide specific information about the agents who had supposedly attempted to enlist him and to give the agency access to the gay subculture. Much like Horst Krüger of the Hessian *Verfassungsschutz*, who fretted that among "homosexuals, who are consolidated into organizations, there are situated agents," the East German regime came to worry that the subculture was a target of Western intelligence agencies.[33] This paranoia reveals a distinct shift from prosecutors' fears in cases from the 1950s. In the case of Johann L., for example, the regime had only concluded that Western intelligence services were willing to employ "unscrupulous subjects [and] criminal elements," but not that there existed any necessary connection between the two.[34] Joachim's exploits, on the other hand, point to the Stasi's new fear that Western agents were "recruiting among homosexual circles," as officials noted in a report of 23 October.[35]

That concern was reflected in the tasks the ministry set for "Franz Moor." Their collaborator "Deege," one of Joachim's friends, suggested that the ministry could use him for "reconnaissance missions, for instance homosexual locales in West Berlin, which, insofar as I can judge, are of great interest for intelligence."[36] "Deege" supplied the Stasi with a list of West German organizations, such as the homophile Association for a Humanistic Way of Life and the Bremen League for Human Rights, the homophile magazine *Der Weg*, and a number of bars, on which he suggested Joachim might spy.[37] He also hinted that West Berlin politicians, such as a school administrator and a *Bundestag* member, frequented some of these locales, implying that they would be useful places to collect intelligence on the West German government.[38]

Deege's suggestions are important because they illustrate a specific process by which the Stasi came to believe gay men, and the subterranean networks to which they belonged, posed an intelligence threat. The informant, who proved far more knowledgeable about the gay underground than his Stasi handlers, applied his powers of persuasion to convince the secret police that it could employ "Franz Moor" to forge its own network of gay agents. Officials evidently took his advice, for information regarding Joachim's gay contacts dominates the reports he submitted. More than four hundred pages of accounts between 1960 and 1965 detailed his many friends and acquaintances in the East and West Berlin gay subcultures. These notes almost always indicated the person's sexuality alongside key information about their upbringing, social status, employment, and political views.

In 1960, for instance, Joachim informed officers about a party at the home of one Rudolf A. Among the seven homosexual guests was Hans G., who made a living pimping boys on both sides of the border (the Berlin Wall was built the following year). That night Hans told Joachim, according to the latter's account, that he had "around 80 boys 'to run.'"[39] In another statement, Joachim informed the Stasi of the homosexuality of a famous East German ambassador.[40] Joachim's other contacts included numerous artists, many of them from the theatres and operas in East Berlin, the State Opera (*Staatsoper*) in particular.[41]

They also included Ingolf M., a gay man the Stasi had attempted to blackmail into working for them in the 1950s; an eighteen-year-old gay ballet dancer; a twenty-two year-old prostitute; an aristocrat in his early twenties; a thirty year-old member of the SED; and the editor of a Berlin weekly.[42] In all, Joachim passed detailed information about more than eighty of his acquaintances, almost all of them gay. This material, which provided the Stasi with a fuller picture of Berlin's gay subculture, was the "good and honest collaboration" for which the secret police paid Joachim thousands of marks over the course of five years.[43]

The information was occasionally sensational. In 1961 Joachim reported evidence of a social group that called itself the *Nibelungenring* (the Nibelungen Ring) – a play on Richard Wagner's *Der Ring des Nibelungen* (The Ring of the Nibelungen). According to Stasi reports,

In Esterhazy-Keller and in City-Klause, two women supposedly socialize and maintain a circle of young men. They turn these men into spies. The men are set up with homosexual persons. There they have to pump those individuals for information and learn their political views.[44]

Although "the young men never know to whom exactly they deliver the information," the revelation provided further proof of the extent to which intelligence agencies had colonized Berlin's gay subculture.[45]

Curiously, the topic of blackmail, a concern at the heart of the US Lavender Scare and many accounts of Cold War espionage, rarely appears in these records.[46] Only once in the files I examined did the Stasi attempt to blackmail a man using his homosexuality, namely Ingolf M. mentioned above. Likewise, Western agents did not seem particularly interested in blackmail. These bureaus seemed rather more captivated by the possibility of using the subculture's dense networks to extract information about the regime, the military, and the Stasi itself. In turn, it appears the Stasi, once it began recruiting gay agents in the 1960s, focused on using the gay subculture's class-cutting nature to gather intelligence about West Germany rather than trying to blackmail gay Westerners.

The Stasi was most interested in using Joachim to get at Jakob H. and Karl O. The secret police already knew from "Deege" that Karl "shows a strong interest in people (for instance) actors at the German theatre among others, girls, youths (so-called rowdies), homosexuals" – people who existed on society's margins.[47] Karl had recently helped a female prostitute flee to West Berlin. After she successfully crossed the border, he "used the woman's apartment for frequent overnight visitors, where he hosted sexual orgies with various boys."[48] He was also friendly with the rent boys who haunted the Friedrichstrasse train station. As one Stasi report mused, "It is possible that he is only using them as a means to some end."[49] Joachim confirmed the Stasi's suspicion that Karl's lovers were "entangled in a spy affair."[50]

Joachim's collaboration with the Stasi dropped off in 1962 after an East Berlin court sentenced him to nine months in prison for having sex with a sixteen-year-old call boy.[51] His informal collaboration with the Stasi did not shield him from the law. Joachim's last reports arrived in January 1965.[52] His service underlines the Stasi's growing fear of and willingness to take action against gay agents. Unlike gay espionage cases from the 1950s, which prosecutors interpreted as evidence of Western decadence and aggression, in Joachim's case the Stasi came to believe that foreign agents were targeting the gay subculture as an avenue of infiltration. In order both to combat this danger and to take advantage of the intelligence opportunities that the gay subculture presented, the Stasi needed its own gay agents. In fact, in the early 1960s, a Stasi officer prepared a report, drawing in part on intelligence Joachim had gathered, describing how homosexual men had more of a "natural talent for conspiratorial behaviour" than heterosexuals and were therefore of interest to East German intelligence.[53] In the late 1960s and

early 1970s, that view became more ingrained. The secret police began
to consider the gay subculture as both a threat and an opportunity, a
field in which Western espionage services had gained an advantage but
also through which the Stasi, with the help of the right agents, might
better extract intelligence.

The Height of Paranoia

In 1972 the Stasi prepared a report about a gay IM named Helmut H. in
Karl-Marx-City. In it, the officers noted that he was in regular contact
with gay men from West Germany and that "leading personalities in the
FRG also belong to these [gay] circles. It should not go unnoticed, that
western agent- and spy-headquarters can find fertile soil among these
people."[54] This conclusion led Stasi officials to argue that Helmut, who
worked at a pub, "has numerous operatively interesting connections
in the entire republic as well as in socialist foreign countries because of
his homosexuality."[55] That is, the Stasi officials viewed his homosexuality as an intelligence asset. Because of their numerous contacts in the
expansive and opaque subculture, gay men were not only dangerous
to the state but also ideally situated as agents. A set of cases from the
1970s highlights just how ingrained these views had become among the
bureaucrats of the secret police.

In a particularly dramatic case, Karl-Viktor M. successfully escaped
from East Berlin in 1970. The feat perplexed the secret police. Officers
noted, "RF (*Republikflucht*) means and methods unknown" and became
obsessed with uncovering how Karl-Viktor had managed to leave.[56]
Tracing his numerous gay contacts, the secret police eventually connected him to a West Berlin anti-communist "terror group."[57] Though
officials never uncovered Karl-Viktor's way out, they remained convinced that his network of gay friends had provided the means of his
escape. The Stasi interviewed all of his friends, and their friends, and
their friends, building out a schematic of his gay network. So sure were
investigators that his flight and his homosexuality were connected that,
when they diagrammed his acquaintances, Stasi investigators shaded
pink the names of those who were homosexual (see figure 5.1).[58] Had
Karl-Viktor's case occurred in the 1950s, the Stasi likely would not
have thought to chase down his gay contacts. Now, after two decades'
experience with gay intelligence networks, secret police officials were
primed to see the subculture as a malevolent web of intrigue.

Late in the 1970s, Lothar K. of the East German border guard
absconded across the frontier he had pledged to defend. He did so with
the help of his lover, Christian N., a West Berlin resident from elsewhere

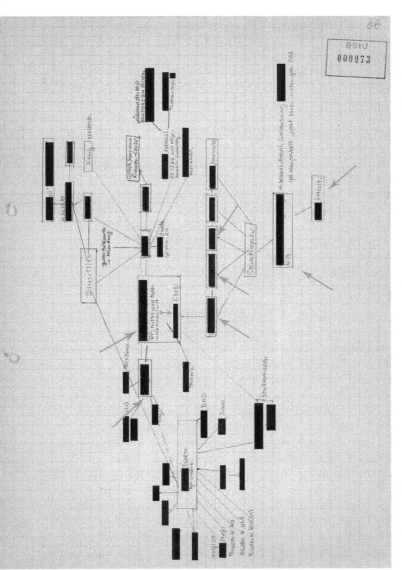

Figure 5.1. Stasi gay espionage diagram. Karl-Viktor M.'s escape so perplexed the Stasi that officers created this chart to trace his contacts. Because the Stasi suspected he was involved in a gay espionage ring, Karl-Viktor's gay contacts were shaded pink. Although most of the pink shading has been blacked out by redaction, arrows point to where it is still visible. Many of his gay acquaintances were connected to the State Opera (Staatsoper). Courtesy of the Behörde des Bundesbeauftragten für die Stasi-Unterlagen (BStU, MfS, HA XXII, Nr. 1643, page 73)

in Eastern Europe.[59] When Lothar crossed into the West, police handed him over to American intelligence agents, who interrogated him for eight days.[60] Lothar had not realized when he planned his flight that his boyfriend Christian was a CIA agent who had "informed the American intelligence" of Lothar's defection "and was waiting with armed Americans at their agreed-upon breakthrough location."[61]

Lothar, the son of a party member, had been hoping to flee from East Germany since the end of 1978. He was motivated, according to one of the numerous Stasi reports compiled about his flight, by "his homosexuality and his impression that he would be better able to fashion his life under conditions in West Berlin."[62] His sexuality had turned him, in the Stasi's view, into a dissident.

In fact, though, Lothar had lived an openly gay life in the capital, where he had a wide circle of acquaintances. At the home of one of these, he had met Christian N. and told him after a mere twenty minutes in conversation that he intended to flee the country.[63] At that point, Christian apparently told Lothar he would help him defect. Christian later brought Lothar's personal items across the border. Unbeknownst to Lothar, he also informed Western intelligence that an East German officer would be illegally crossing the border on 31 May 1979.[64]

After his eight-day interrogation at Sven-Hedin-Strasse 11 (a villa indeed owned by the West German foreign intelligence service), Lothar was allowed to leave and move into Christian's West Berlin apartment.[65] At first, Lothar's new life in the West seemed dandy. According to Lothar, Christian "was a person of trust for me. I maintained a homosexual relationship with him over several months and felt a great deal for him." At the same time, however, Lothar had numerous other friends in the city, a circumstance that, as he later relayed to his interrogators, led "repeatedly to spats" with Christian. According to him, Christian "frequently reproached me for this reason and said that I did not love him anymore."[66] Christian continued to pass into East Berlin on a regular basis, presumably in order to maintain his "connections to homosexual circles in the capital of the GDR and in the district of Halle."[67]

Around three months after his flight from the East, Lothar evidently decided he had had enough of Christian's jealousy and wanted to return to his family. A few months after his defection, the East Berlin police received an anonymous phone call informing them that Christian "was travelling to the capital of the GDR on the same day."[68] He was eventually caught.[69] Later files reveal that the tip-off came from Lothar, who, according to the Stasi's notes, betrayed Christian "after he learned of N.'s recruitment by US intelligence and because he wanted categorically to distance himself therefrom."[70] Of course, this assertion might not be true, for Lothar's own complaints about the state of his relationship suggest that he may simply have wanted to get rid of Christian and return home.

Around the time of Christian's capture, Lothar's well-connected relatives facilitated his return.[71] Over the ensuing months, the Stasi interrogated Lothar, Christian, and their gay acquaintances. The secret police wanted to know how wide Christian's network of gay contacts spread and how many others intended to flee the Republic. Lothar gave them the names of three friends, all in their mid-twenties and all gay, who intended to leave, as well as a report about another bisexual lieutenant in the border guard.[72] The names and connections here matter less than the fact that both Lothar and Christian had a wide circle of gay acquaintances, many of them in the army, and many of whom at least contemplated leaving East Germany. By the late 1970s, the Stasi had had enough experience with gay spy networks to ferret out these connections.

Also of interest to interrogators was the manner in which Christian had assembled his informal network. They learned of a lieutenant F., nicknamed "Felix," who "is homosexual and brought M. with him to the officers' bachelors quarters (*Offiziersledigenheim*)." As a Romeo agent, Christian seduced his marks in order to recruit them or extract information from them. The Stasi worried that Christian had passed "information about ["Felix's"] official position, rank and location" to Western intelligence. Their notes ominously indicated that, "Immediate measures are required."[73] After the police completed their interrogation of Christian, an East German court sentenced him to seven years in prison.[74]

Lothar's case also highlights that *Republikflucht*, the crime of fleeing East Germany, had become intimately connected in Stasi officials' imagination with both espionage and homosexuality.[75] *Republikflucht* was a serious problem for the Democratic Republic. The existence of a rival German state that refused to acknowledge the GDR's legitimacy and offered automatic citizenship to any East German who crossed the border had always posed an existential threat to the dictatorship. Though the Berlin Wall stemmed the tide of East Germans flooding into the West – flights dropped from more than 200,000 in 1961 to fewer than 10,000 per annum thereafter – and stabilized the regime, fleeing the republic or attempting to remained a grave crime.[76]

Taken together, these cases reveal that over the course of decades the Stasi grew worried about the gay subculture and its potential employment by foreign intelligence agencies. Though the ministry, like most elements of the East German regime, paid little heed to homosexuality in the regime's early years, by the 1960s its officers believed that Western governments were recruiting gay spies in order to infiltrate the subculture and gather information about the communist state. And in a sign of how the Stasi learned from previous encounters, it explicitly compared Lothar K. to a former high Stasi official "who was fired from the MfS because of homosexuality in 1977 and incarcerated in August 1978 for betrayal of military secrets."[77] The secret police began to think of homosexuality as a well-defined espionage vector.

Decades earlier, in January 1954, an author had written in *Die Zeit*, "Hardly a week passes in which we in the Federal Republic do not have to read about trials and political scandals that have to do with agents, national defence, and *Verfassungsschutz*."[78] The ubiquity of espionage in Cold War Germany illustrates how geopolitical and ideological struggles could intrude on everyday life. The individuals described here were not famous, wealthy, or well connected. Most were entirely ordinary individuals. Yet, they found themselves wrapped up in international espionage that likely seemed extremely consequential. These altercations suggest how common such everyday espionage was, particularly in Berlin, where the two regimes shared an intimate border in the heart of a metropolis.

By the 1970s, after two decades of run-ins with gay agents, secret police officials believed gay men could use their sexuality as a means to meet contacts, get in and out of the country, and gather intelligence. West Germans had accepted this far sooner. In the early 1950s, politicians and propagandists there had fretted about the threats posed to the young republic by the "freemasonry of the sexually perverse" and their collusion with communist intelligence agencies.[79] Horst Krüger, the Western counter-intelligence agent, had attempted to stitch together a band of gay agents in Hesse in order to unmask politicians whom he and his superiors believed to be East German spies. A decade later, Stasi officers thought to do the same. Even then, the secret police recruited Joachim L. only after he came to them with evidence of a gay spy ring operating in East Berlin.

As with the fear of gay cliques, East German authorities did not seem to worry that lesbians might become a conduit for Western intelligence activities. None of the files I reviewed involved lesbians, and Stasi documents did not seem to contemplate that female homosexuality posed any similar risk. Part of the reason, no doubt, lay in the fact that the subculture catered primarily to gay men in the 1950s and 1960s. Similarly, the fears of gay conspiracies, on which gay espionage efforts were predicated, rarely considered lesbian cliques to be a danger to either society or the state. Because women were less likely to occupy positions of trust and were more likely to marry and become mothers, ideologues and politicians in both countries assumed, there were far fewer opportunities for them to build groups or exert undue influence.

Though they did not change the course of the Cold War, these developments are significant because the East German regime had initially opted for a *laissez-faire* approach to homosexuality. The SED had balanced its historical opposition to criminalizing homosexuality against the anti-gay views it believed East Germans held (and that it also at times stoked). The government's policy accorded neither power nor significance to gay men or lesbians. Unlike in West Germany, where the debate over §175 became an important political struggle, the East German government rarely thematized homosexuality in public after the early 1950s.

Nonetheless, encounters with gay Western agents shaped how Stasi officials viewed the subculture. Their growing concern with gay espionage illustrates in stark terms both why the shape of anti-gay animus matters and how that animus can evolve over time. Viewed as an avenue of Western infiltration, the gay subculture acquired new significance for East Germany's rulers. The Stasi's use of gay agents in turn set off a feedback loop by which the secret police gathered ever more information about the subculture, uncovering more alleged threats, which in turn reaffirmed the danger that it believed the subculture posed.

Thus, while historians accurately characterize gay espionage as a paranoid fantasy, in Cold War Berlin it became something more, a self-reinforcing cycle of practice and prejudice.[80] This cycle informed how East Germany's sprawling surveillance apparatus thought of homosexuality and how, as we shall see, the state as a whole treated gay citizens. Both German states' exploitation of the gay subculture as a tool in intra-German geopolitics became a defining feature of gay life in the Democratic Republic. Moreover, the use of gay agents indicates perhaps that modern security states rely not merely on liminal spaces in which rules and law may be suspended – what Susan Buck-Morss terms the "wild zone of power" – but also on marginalized populations.[81] Gay men, that is, were at once both privileged and persecuted objects of state power.

Thus, when the idea of gay liberation made its way across the Iron Curtain in the mid-1970s, Stasi officials, and through them the regime, were primed to consider activists' efforts not as a legitimate quest for belonging but rather as a sinister attempt by Western intelligence outfits to disrupt socialist rule. Eventually, activists would leverage these fears to convince Stasi officials and party leaders to promulgate an ambitious pro-gay agenda that far exceeded anything activists ever extracted from the West German federal government. These liberation efforts, however, first began in West Germany, in the wake of the Federal Republic's reform of §175.

6 Three Million Votes

Gay Citizenship and Power in West Germany

On 11 February 2017, a friend and I went to see a film premiering at the Berlin International Film Festival. *My Wonderful West Berlin* (*Mein wunderbares West-Berlin*) was playing, a much-hyped documentary about queer life in West Berlin by director Jochen Hick. While the movie spanned the 1960s through the 1980s, the bulk of it dealt with West Berlin's gay movement in the 1970s. With interviews from numerous West Berliners, the film offered a snapshot of the rambunctious and joyful decade that had followed the reform of §175. Yet, when we left the theatre, my friend commented that the documentary had primarily convinced him that gay West Berlin in the 1970s was not really that different from New York or San Francisco at the time – if anything, it was a weak facsimile.

For all that it celebrated queer life and activism, the film did indeed suggest such an interpretation. In so doing, it pointed to a puzzling conflict in both the scholarship on and memories of the decade. On the one hand, the 1970s are feted as years of riotous change and new possibility. The activists who stormed onto the scene are lionized to this day. On the other hand, those same activists as well as scholars of the period often paint these years as ones of strife, as a decade in which the movement actually accomplished very little. The groups that sprang up around the country are sometimes painted as the stepchildren of supposedly more successful movements in other countries, especially the United States.[1]

The 1970s were plainly a revolutionary decade for gay West Germans. The older generation of homophile campaigners had died or were quickly sidelined – Fritz Bauer died in 1968, Hans Giese in 1970 – and a new generation of activists appeared in cities around the country. A decade that began without a substantial gay movement ended with a national push on the part of numerous activist organizations to influence federal parliamentary elections. Those years also saw the rise of an extraordinarily rich gay culture that included not only bars and cruising spots but also cafés, bookstores, and magazines dedicated to queer people.

In trying to explain the curious divergence in memories of the period, this chapter looks closely at the ideas of political citizenship on which gay activism rested, the goals of West German activists, and the strategies they pursued in service to those goals. I argue that carefully examining the shape of activism and its connection to everyday life can help us understand the scope of social and political change in the 1970s as well as how it compares to other liberation movements in other places and times. Using oral histories, articles from magazines and newspapers, and documents produced by activist organizations, this chapter contends that West German activism is a remarkable illustration of the idiosyncratic forms liberation efforts can take, of the unexpected paths they follow, and of the myriad ways in which gay people define themselves as citizens.

The New Subculture

In 1969, months after the grand coalition reformed §175, federal elections returned a majority for a new coalition of Social Democrats and Free Democrats. This new social-liberal government, led by Chancellor Willy Brandt, embarked upon a remarkable, decade-long reform of West German society under the banner of Brandt's promise to "dare more democracy."[2] His first coalition (1969–72) opened a new era of investment in the welfare state. Significantly, his government took steps to stop Turkish migration into West Germany as so-called "guest workers," while also making it easier for those Turks already in the Federal Republic to obtain residence permits.[3] Brandt also launched an era of détente in the Cold War, signing treaties with the Soviet Union, Poland, and East Germany that normalized relations with the Eastern bloc. For the first time since the Berlin Wall went up, West Germans were able to make regular trips across the border.[4]

Brandt resigned in 1974, embarrassed by the revelation that his closest aide was a Stasi agent.[5] The chancellorship passed to Helmut Schmidt, a more conservative Social Democrat, who led the coalition for another eight years.[6] While the governing coalition did not actively advance gay interests, a measure of tolerance for gay people permeated the social climate. The 1969 reform, for all its flaws, marked a sea change in how the West German state treated gay men. Convictions under §175 dropped precipitously from approximately 2,000 per annum to around 400. The new law also opened social space for gay organizations, bars, and publications. By October 1970 there were at least forty bars and clubs in West Berlin and Hamburg that publicly catered to gay people. In 1972, the *Spartacus International Gay Guide*, a kind of queer Zagat, wrote, "we therefore especially recommend Berlin, with more gay bars than the whole of Holland. A city of young care-free people, and all so attractive; Hamburg, sin city of the North (and who doesn't enjoy sinning), with a lively scene, including a live gay sex-show."[7] Some of the new bars also served lesbians, such as Sappho and Boccaccio in West Berlin.[8] The subculture, which in the 1950s and 1960s had revolved around men searching for sex with men, began to broaden into a social scene in which gay men and lesbians could meet for diversion and friendship. The number of gay establishments only expanded throughout the 1970s (see figure 6.1).

New homoerotic publications also sprang up. *Du & Ich* (*You and I*) first appeared in October 1969 in West Berlin. The magazines *Don* and *him* both came out in 1970. Alongside the reform of §175, a 1969 court ruling significantly narrowed the *Bundesprüfstelle*'s reach. Hence, the government never censored any of these magazines (though it did attempt to index *him* in 1972).[9] The new periodicals published a mélange of in-depth reporting on gay issues, soft pornography, travel accounts, and personal ads.[10]

Of these, the personals were perhaps the most momentous.[11] Although they initially took up only a handful of pages, by the end of the decade they had ballooned to become one of the magazines' most important elements and a significant source of income. *Du & Ich*, for instance, charged 20 DM for the first twenty words and 80 cents for each following word.[12] The personals were one of the most visible ways in which emancipation changed everyday life for gay people. Instead of being forced to cruise surreptitiously in public toilets, baths, or parks in order to find partners, gay men could, for the first time, look publicly for sexual companions, boyfriends and girlfriends, BDSM partners, and platonic friendships. The ads ran the gamut from a "27-year-old looks for a nice, approximately same-aged friend" to "two young masters, 29/30, wish for many tender hours with a younger boy."[13] Although they catered primarily to gay men, issues also included personal advertisements for lesbians.[14] Some men apparently even used the forum to look for lesbian friends, such as one twenty-four-year-old man who, in February 1973, wrote that he was "looking for a lesb. friend or sincere friend for a beautiful friendship."[15]

New activist organizations also appeared in the late 1960s and early 1970s, such as the International Homophile World Organization in

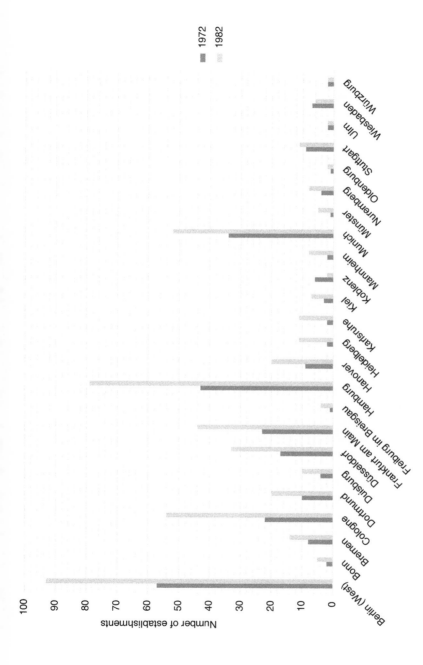

Figure 6.1. Gay and lesbian establishments in West German cities, 1972 and 1982. Sources: *Spartacus International Gay Guide*, 1972 and 1982

Hamburg, the Interest Group of Homophiles in Wiesbaden, and the German Homophile Organization in West Berlin.[16] In some ways, these groups resembled the extinct homophile organizations of the 1950s. Founded by well-educated men, they drafted charters and bylaws, registered with local authorities, and typed memoranda on official letterhead.[17] Today they are hardly discussed in scholarly literature, much less remembered in the gay community, in part because they had seemingly little impact on life or politics. Moreover, the more socially radical gay movement that arose in 1971 appeared to supersede them. Nonetheless, these homophile groups helped form West Germany's new gay public and offered a more assimilationist alternative to the better-remembered groups of the 1970s.

The homophiles, who envisioned their cause as equal parts political, social, and cultural, had their work cut out for them. Hosts of problems continued to plague gay men and lesbians. Crime remained stubbornly common in the subculture: one 1971 article estimated that gay men experienced robbery and blackmail at a rate ten to fifteen times that of the general population.[18] Anti-gay prejudices continued to colour West German social views, and police persisted in raiding bars and cruising spots.[19]

In 1973 the Constitutional Court ruled against the ban on sex between men aged eighteen to twenty-one. This ruling led the *Bundestag* again to reform §175, setting the age of consent for gay men at eighteen, still four years higher than for heterosexual and lesbian acts.[20] Nonetheless, political parties shied away from embracing homosexuality. No party in the 1969 or 1972 elections publicly advocated gay rights of any shade.[21] The federal government continued to sanction firing gay people for their sexuality. A 1978 report in the popular magazine *Stern* noted that, "The state, which according to the Basic Law must treat all citizens equally, persecutes homosexuals with employment black-lists."[22] As late as the 1980s, my oral source Georg R. learned, a conviction under §175 was still a barrier to government employment in West Germany.[23] Living in a society so deeply antipathetic to their plight, gay men became increasingly frustrated with the scientific liberalism that had brought about §175's reform. They began to realize that emancipation from social prejudice as well as state-sanctioned oppression would require new idioms, ideologies, and political stratagems.

Gay Power

At the time it might have seemed like a circle impossible to square. While scientific and liberal arguments had proved effective at describing why homosexuality should not be criminalized, they were inadequate to the task of convincing West Germans that homosexuality ought to be accepted. As an answer to this problem, however, the new gay press and homophile organizations began to shed the convictions of scientific liberalism in favour of more radical ideas. Their new rhetoric took up gay power motifs and the idea that gay people constituted a social minority.

In the 1960s the dream of gay power – that is, of the exercise of political influence by gay people – appeared in a novel by well-known author Felix Rexhausen. Titled *Lavender Sword*, the 1966 book described a fictional West Germany in which a clique of gay intellectuals and army officers overthrows the homophobic federal state after the suicide of a young gay dancer.[24] The satirical novel played on conservative fears of gay conspiracies, taking their paranoia to its logical, albeit ludicrous, end in the establishment of a lavender state governed by and for queer people. The new government, in a comi-tragic conclusion, ultimately fails because the rebels' sexual urges prove greater than their revolutionary zeal.

Credited though they were with power and influence, gay men in the 1960s were, and would have felt, powerless. Before the 1969 watershed, most would never have belonged to a homophile organization, read a gay magazine, or frequented whatever underground gay bars existed in their hometowns. Even after the seismic changes of 1969, many gay people despaired of ever living in a society that accepted their sexuality. The desperate dream of a sudden change might well have sustained any number of them in those decades. Such a radical view of gay power, which transcribed conservative fears of gay cliques in a new key, should be understood as an effect of desperation occasioned by oppression.

Rexhausen's rhetoric anticipated the discourses of gay power that, by the early 1970s, could be observed across the spectrum of homosexual activism. A letter published in *Twen* in 1963, for instance, made a similar point. Its author wrote, "The 'clever' lawmakers in the Bonn *Bundestag* apparently live on the moon, or don't realize that the shameful paragraph 175 turns the 'immoral' men – of which there are around 7,000,000 in the FRG! – into dangerous enemies of the state."[25] Using virtually identical language, *Du & Ich* wrote in March 1970 that gay people "are stronger than the F.D.P." It was a bold assertion. Although the liberals were the *Bundestag*'s smallest party, they had been in every government but two since 1949 and had enabled the Social Democrats to take power in 1969. As the article contended, "3 million homophile men! That is three million consumers, three million magazine readers, three million car drivers and last but not least, three million voters! We are stronger than the FDP!"[26]

Such language envisioned a kind of gay person who had hitherto not existed, one for whom his (and, increasingly, her) sexuality was a prime consideration in the social, economic, and political decisions they made every day. In this new estimation, the homosexual was no longer merely "a case history," to quote Michel Foucault, but also a citizen.[27] Moreover, these men and women were citizens belonging to a "minority," as activists increasingly referred to West Germany's gay population.[28] Common interests, common oppressions, and common needs bound gay citizens together culturally, socially, and, most importantly, politically.

The question of such a minority's political leanings became paramount, as is evident in *Du & Ich*'s eye-opening declaration. In January 1972 a columnist in *him* wondered if "a politics for homophiles is even thinkable." He argued: "If we can overcome our isolation as individuals and join together – yes." That is, if gay people could do the positive work of forging a minority out of the mass of gay people, then there might indeed be a chance for a gay form of politics. These new writers were no longer interested in proving to the straight majority that they were not criminals or enemies of the state. Rather, they wanted to exercise political power – much like any other constituency in a modern democracy. Doing so, however, depended on having gay people recognize themselves as members of a minority.

The most famous example of this new idea of gay political power was a 1971 film. Titled *It Is Not the Homosexual Who Is Perverse, but Rather the Situation in Which He Lives* (*Nicht der Homosexuelle ist pervers, sondern die Situation in der er lebt*), it was the work of a young director named Rosa von Praunheim (born Holger Mischwitzky) and sociologist Martin Dannecker.[29] The movie depicted the life of a gay man named Daniel in West Berlin.[30] When the film opens, Daniel is in a romantic relationship with another man. This affair soon ends, and he bounces from being the kept boy of an older, homophile man to cruising for sex at West Berlin's beaches to, finally, looking for sex in public toilets at night.

The film was a polemical attack on West Germany's gay subculture. It maintained that the 1969 reform had not brought genuine liberation. Rather, gay people still oppressed themselves by inhabiting an exploitive subculture. The film's chief complaint was that the subculture revolved solely around sex and did not encourage solidarity among gay people, precisely the kind of solidarity on which the dream of gay political power rested. In the contemporary subculture, gay individuals would never become the political minority needed to exercise power.

At the end of the film, we find Daniel demoralized, depressed, and drunk at Elli's Beer Bar. Downing his umpteenth beer, he runs into an old friend, Paul, who lives in a commune of gay student radicals. Paul invites Daniel home with him, where they engage in a theoretical discussion about homosexuals' social and political predicament with Paul's roommates. "The most important thing for all gay men," argues one of them, "is that we embrace our gay identity."[31] It fell to them, according to the film, to build a gay minority by being "proud of your homosexuality!" Only pride would lead gay people "out of the toilets [and] into the streets!"[32]

The film argued, much like Felix Rexhausen's *Lavender Sword*, that only by acting in tandem could gay people end their oppression. The film disputed the scientific liberalism of homophile activists, even accusing homophiles of perpetuating the subculture in order to more readily seduce underage boys.[33] Gay people, the film argued, were an oppressed minority who had first to develop self-conscious solidarity with each other before they could change West German society.

Although *It Is Not the Homosexual* was not, to be perfectly frank, a very good movie, it was a sensation. Conservatives, progressives, and homophiles alike attacked it – as both gay propaganda and homophobic trash. One conservative reviewer from Hanover denounced the film as "nauseating, vile and repulsive" and complained that it depicted people from the "bottom rung" of society.[34] In the university town of Heidelberg in southwest Germany, another critic lamented that society could no longer "keep our children safe from acquired homosexuality."[35]

Progressives and homophiles were also appalled. One reviewer characterized the film as a "brutal attack" because it traded in stereotypes of the sex-obsessed gay man.[36] Another raged that the film was "perversely distorted" and "full of a vicious joy in kitsch, triviality, and the extreme artificiality" of gay people.[37] An English gay publication blasted Praunheim as "perverse" and carped that the film had been "made with all the expertise of a ten-year-old psychopath."[38] Nonetheless, the movie brought the topic of homosexuality to West Germans in a novel way. For the first time, the discussion revolved not around §175, perversion, or seduction. Rather, the film depicted gay people as social and political agents. While the film's portrayal of public sex, gay cruising, and quasi-pederastic relationships aroused considerable disgust among conservatives and progressives alike, it gave West Germans an unvarnished look at the gay subculture.

Most important, the film advanced discourses of gay power that had circulated with ever-greater frequency among intellectuals and activists since the mid-1960s. It also drew clear inspiration from the 1960s student movement, in particular in its insinuation that, as the 68ers had insisted, the personal is political.[39] It conceived of a new kind of sexual citizenship, no longer predicated on homosexuals' ability to fit in with the heterosexual majority. This minoritizing vision of gay citizenship insisted instead that only by recognizing their otherness could gay people exercise social and political power.

This new rhetoric was revolutionary precisely because it reimagined homosexuality as a political identity. Comfortable as we are today with the totems of identity politics, it is hard to imagine that for much of the twentieth century most people did not see sexuality as inherently political. In the 1970s the idea that gay people should or even could behave as a social, economic, or political bloc was iconoclastic. As the Hamburg gay activist and Green Party politician Corny Littmann recalled in the 1980s, "It was unheard of, to characterize one's subjectivity as 'political.'"[40] The discourses of gay liberation that attended the new decade thus marked the birth of a new political subjectivity – the gay citizen.

The Action Groups

In the summer of 1971, *It Is Not the Homosexual* premiered at the International Forum for New Film at the 21st Berlin International Film Festival. Throngs of West Berliners came to see the movie, which sparked "angry, even brutal, discussion," according to the *Sueddeutsche Zeitung*.[41] Holger G., an activist who had moved to West Berlin in his early twenties after a two-year-long relationship with a famous director in Munich, recalled that when he first saw the film, "I was disgusted."[42] But after the "brutal discussion" that followed the film, a list circulated in the audience. Interested individuals could sign up in order to continue the debate.[43]

Several months later that group formulated a "Statement of Principles" that called for the "emancipation of homosexuals" and named itself the Homosexual Action West Berlin (*Homosexuelle Aktion Westberlin*, HAW, or here referred to as the West Berlin Action).[44] It was among the first of a new kind of gay liberation group that rejected both social animus and what it perceived as the staid tactics of its homophile predecessors. The West Berlin Action's statement formulated the problem as one of solidarity, arguing that "discrimination [...] generates a kind of communal spirit. Transforming this phony solidarity into real solidarity would be a precondition for the emancipation of homosexuals." The group hoped to get gay people "to mediate their existence as homosexuals with their economic-political existence," and to "support them in their conflict with society."[45] In this way, the Action elucidated a very different citizenship ideal than had the reformers of the 1950s and 1960s. These young activists hoped gay men and lesbians would recognize themselves as a social minority and would begin to comport themselves politically and economically in ways that furthered homosexual interests.

As *It Is Not the Homosexual* premiered in other cities around West Germany, it drew large crowds of people, who, in turn, founded local action groups. By 1976 there existed more than forty around the country.[46] These new organizations espoused political views to the left of homophile organizations, rejected much of the subculture, and were primarily composed of university students steeped in 1960s radicalism.[47] In their push to combat anti-gay animus, remake the subculture, and campaign for political power, they are today collectively remembered as Germany's "second gay movement" (the first having occurred during the Weimar Republic).[48]

In formulating their goals, the new groups drew inspiration not only from *It Is Not the Homosexual* but also from the American Civil Rights movement, feminist movements around the world, and anti-colonial movements.[49] The founding document of the group *RotZSchwul* in Frankfurt am Main, for instance, compared gay men and lesbians to "ethnic subcultures (Jews, Negros) in which one is a mandatory member from birth."[50] While comparisons with other oppressed groups allowed activists to diagnose the prejudices they continued to face, it did not prevent racism from flourishing in West Germany's gay communities, as Christopher Ewing argues. In the 1970s, and increasingly in the 1980s, Turks and Black Germans faced both racialized desire and disgust from white, gay West Germans.[51] Some of my oral sources expressed disdain for Turkish call boys in terms that echoed the respectability politics of homophile campaigners.

Recognizing social discrimination against lesbians also helped activists to formulate their goals, as exemplified in another pamphlet from the Gay Liberation Front in Cologne. It noted: "The situation of the homosexual woman has already shown that legal impunity does not equate to social acceptance: she was never prosecuted under the law but was still discriminated against."[52] These comparisons were, of course, not original to 1970s discourse. Already in 1951, Donald Webster Cory's *The Homosexual in America* had made similar contentions about American gay people, and comparisons of Germany's Jewish and homosexual populations have abounded since the early twentieth century.[53] Associating themselves with other minorities in this way helped activists elucidate a concept of citizenship grounded in their claimed minority status.

Less clear is the extent to which the American gay movement influenced events in West Germany. Although groups in the United States had radicalized and gained increasing visibility after the 1969 Stonewall riots in New York City, there is evidence that West Germans remained ignorant of events there until the mid- to late 1970s. Rosa von Praunheim insisted that when he directed *It Is Not the Homosexual,* he "still had no idea of the American gay liberation movement."[54] As Ralf Dose, a historian and West Berlin Action member, recalled, "at the beginning we didn't know [about the American movement]."[55]

Nonetheless, by the late 1970s activists insisted that the West German movement had arisen from the American one and that – in most regards – it was nothing more than a weak reflection of it.[56] In 1977 Rüdiger Lautmann, the well-known gay sociologist at the University of Bremen, noted that, "The militancy of the American Gay Liberation Front 1969–1971 [was] an impressive model for many German groups."[57] Rosa von Praunheim, who was active in the movement throughout the 1970s and 1980s, directed a subsequent film about gay liberation in the United States, *Army of Lovers or Revolt of the Perverse,* which premiered in 1979. He used the occasion to contrast it with developments in the Federal Republic, complaining that, "The movement here [in West Germany] 'has fallen into Sleeping Beauty's sleep.'"[58] The gay press too chronicled the American movement, casting it as the German movement's older, and more successful, sibling.[59]

West Germany's new gay groups saw their principal goal as twofold. First, they had to forge solidarity in order to create a minority consciousness among West Germany's gay population. The West Berlin Action, in a 1972 pamphlet, formulated it thus: "we must awaken the consciousness of these 100,000" gay Germans. Second, the movement had to radicalize that gay minority. It had to stop, as the same flyer insisted, "yammering for understanding and begging for recognition," and instead take up political arms.[60]

As with other movements of the era, outsized ambitions alongside their nebulous formulation meant that ideological differences mounted within the action groups. Many, for instance, considered the commercial subculture to be one of the primary obstacles to their efforts to build gay solidarity. Thus, activists did what they could to undermine West Germany's gay bars, magazines, and homophile organizations. One afternoon, while distributing pamphlets, around forty members of the West Berlin Action went to the bar Your Place on Grolmannstrasse near Kurfürstendamm. Though they "did not disturb the guests in any way" (or so they claimed), the bartender recognized them and refused service. "Under police escort," members grumbled, "we were thrown out of the bar." They responded by launching a new campaign, accusing bar owners of "oppressing gays."[61]

The action groups also suffered foul relations with the gay press, which they saw as commercial enterprises catering to the subculture's basest demands. In a 1972 flyer, the West Berlin Action fumed that *him* only published "masturbation templates that limit our imagination."[62] The magazines responded by ignoring the action groups. Not until the end of the decade would the press regularly report on their activities. For much of the 1970s, Germany's action groups conflated the subculture, the gay media establishment, and homophile groups in a way that radical gay movements in other countries did not. While post-Stonewall activists in the United States dismissed homophile groups such as the Mattachine Society as outdated relics, its members did not seek to undermine the subculture there in a similar way.[63] Still, the kerfuffles between the subculture and the action groups paled in comparison to the internecine struggles that gripped the movement itself in the middle of the decade. These battles were defined by four overlapping conflicts: those of radicalism, socialism, feminism, and paedophilia.

First, organizations were often divided between so-called radicals and integrationists, or pragmatists.[64] The conflict between these two camps revolved around how forcefully (and, in some cases, violently) to oppose existing social and political structures. Franz G., a founding member of both the Gay Liberation Front in Cologne and the Bonn action group, considered himself a pragmatist. He recalled that while one side "propagated radical activism including unlawful property damage like the leftist student movement," the others "sought concrete reforms for the equality of hetero- and homosexuals."[65] Pragmatists tended to advocate specific policy change, including abolition of §175, which would equalize the age of consent; reparations for Nazism's gay victims; and abolition of employment blacklists.[66] At the base of this division sat two competing views of German government and society. While the pragmatists believed existing social and political structures were adaptable to the aims of gay emancipation, radicals thought only a revolutionary overhaul could bring about genuine liberation. While these struggles, Griffiths argues, show traces of the respectability politics scholars often associate with homophile movements, it is important to remember that they were genuine answers to the novel question of how to create a politically engaged minority of gay men and lesbians.[67]

Mirroring the conflict between pragmatists and radicals was that over socialism in the movement. Many of the new action groups, such as *RotZSchwul* in Frankfurt, were explicitly socialist or communist organizations. As the Frankfurt Homosexual Working Circle – a competing group – wrote in 1973, "We strive for the realization of socialism in an enlightened society."[68] Similarly, the West Berlin Action identified closely with West Germany's leftist parties. Ralf G., one of the group's leaders, characterized its membership as "full SPD to full KPD to ... I don't know ... even anarchists."[69] "Our goal," recalled Ralf Dose playfully, "was world revolution."[70] Some members even worried that the group was too close to the Socialist Unity Party of West Berlin (the SEW, the sister party of the East German SED). As Ralf A., a technician and Action member, recalled, "The leadership-clique was infiltrated by people who worked for the SEW."[71]

Within the action groups, the principal struggle took place between those who thought the fight for gay emancipation was merely one battle within the larger socialist war against capitalism and those who believed it an independent struggle. In its "Statement of Principles," the West Berlin Action insisted that anti-gay animus was only "a special case of the general oppression of sexuality."[72] That is, liberation for gay people would only come about in the context of broader social liberation efforts. Members who questioned the group's Marxist orthodoxy would be shouted down or told, as Holger G. remembered, "shut up, you stupid cow!"[73] The conflict over socialism also echoed in activists' debates over homosexuality in East Germany, specifically over whether or not the socialist government oppressed its gay citizens.[74]

On the other side were those who argued that gender, and not class, ought to be the primary lens through which to view their oppression. Belonging to this group were the so-called *Tunten*, a term variously translated as fairies, faggots, nancies, or queens. *Tunten* were effeminate gay men who rejected stereotypical masculinity (by using eye shadow and nail polish, for instance). Many of them considered gender conformity to be a far greater foe than the capitalist class system.[75]

The conflict over gender nonconformity in the movement reached its height in the legendary *"Tuntenstreit"* (the *Tunten* controversy), which began in 1973.[76] In June of that year, a West Berlin activist, writing under the camp pseudonym Winfrieda von Rechenberg, distributed a jeremiad about a recent political demonstration in West Berlin. Winfrieda accused socialist-leaning Action members of "hiding your homosexuality behind leftist slogans." That is, the *Tunten* perceived a new kind of hetero-conforming respectability politics among socialist-leaning activists. The attack eventually led to the foundation of a feminist faction within the Action.[77] Its members saw gender as a better frame than class through which to understand the subjection of sexual minorities. The group engaged in what one of its opponents characterized as "hooligan methods [...] and perverse tricks" in order to "either conquer or destroy the HAW."[78] Franz G., who had moved to Berlin at the high point of the *Tuntenstreit*, remembered that the controversy repelled him from the group.

In addition to effeminate men, lesbians in these groups often felt alienated by the macho socialists who ran them. In the West Berlin Action's plenary meetings, according to one of its male members, "the gay men were too dominant [...] they rode roughshod [over the lesbians]."[79] Women in the West Berlin Action, and in other Actions around Germany, thus founded their own sub-groups, which in turn broke off to form independent organizations in the mid-1970s. By 1978, there existed two primary lesbian organizations, the Lesbian Action Centre in West Berlin and the Lesbian Centre in Frankfurt am Main, while women in Hamburg had plans to found their own group.[80] Though these organizations continued to coordinate with gay male groups, they often found more in common with the women's movement.[81] Dorothea R., an activist in the West Berlin Lesbian Action Centre who also experienced the lesbian scene in Münster in the late 1970s, recalled that the lesbians she knew never socialized with gay men. The first joint activity she remembered was collaboration on a museum display about gay and lesbian Berlin in the 1920s, the famed "Eldorado" exhibit of 1984.[82]

Finally, the problem of paedophilia confounded gay activists.[83] While large age gaps between same-sex sexual partners had been normal in the 1950s and 1960s, the advent of a robust public subculture made similar-age relationships more common. In fact, historians of sexuality mark the 1970s as a turning point in which gay relationships became more equal in age across the United States and Western Europe.[84] At the same time, the imposition of a higher age of consent for gay men under West Germany's rump §175 made a political issue of age.

On the one side were those who argued that there should be a unified age of consent for hetero- and homosexuals. On the other were those who wanted the age of consent abolished *tout court*. Activists thus began to distinguish between most homosexuals and those who "primarily or only feel attracted to very young partners," as *Du & Ich* opined in 1978.[85] Men attracted to boys increasingly banded together in new sub-groups, such as the Pederast Group of the West Berlin Action, the Working Group Paedophilia of the West Berlin General Homosexual Action Group, or the Pederast Group of the Homosexual Action Hamburg.[86] By the decade's end, the extent to which gay activists accepted these men began to divide the movement.

These four ideological fault-lines – radicalism, socialism, feminism, and paedophilia – led to strife within and among different groups, and even to the establishment of multiple gay organizations in the same city. Gay people in Frankfurt am Main split early in the 1970s among three different groups: *RotZSchwul*, The Homosexual Action Group (HAF), and the Gay Cell. The three groups "differ[ed] on the question of political means," explained the liberal daily *Frankfurter Rundschau*: "While, for example, Rotzschwul is more oriented towards Marxism, the HAF identifies with democratic socialism."[87] Likewise, in Cologne and Bonn in the Rhineland, action groups splintered into factions of pragmatists and radicals.[88] Göttingen, Hamburg, and West Berlin too were home to multiple action groups.

They could be vicious toward one another. When, after the 1973 *Tuntenstreit*, members of the West Berlin Action broke away to found the General Homosexual Action (AHA or here referred to as the General Action), the groups wanted nothing to do with each other. Torsten V., a General Action leader, recalled that another member "called a special member assembly of the AHA when he discovered that I was in a relationship with someone from the HAW. That's how it was then."[89]

The infighting contributed to perceptions of the movement's decline in the late 1970s. Since their exuberant birth in 1971, dozens of action groups had disbanded, and as early as 1977 gay activists insisted that the movement "is considered to have failed."[90] That same year, the West Berlin Action formally dissolved.[91] When *Stern* magazine published an eight-page spread on homosexuality in 1978, it dismissed the movement. "Their activities," the magazine averred, "often consist of nothing but unrhymed and stale agitprop [...] and nutty provocation."[92]

These divisions and the conflicts they spawned in the West German gay movement continue to colour memories of the period.[93] Those memories not only ignore how these conflicts were constitutive of the movement's zeal but also tend to obscure activists' unprecedented work. They also obscure the fact that, as members of action groups aged and left university for full-time employment, the movement for gay liberation shifted from emancipation organizations in university towns to gay and lesbian groups organized in and around professions.[94] Moreover, these memories shroud the ways in which young activists transformed West Germany's political landscape. Increasingly, both gay and straight individuals thought of homosexuals as a well-defined minority possessed of political and social agency. Through social activities, political protests, and visibility efforts, action groups reshaped how West Germany's gay men and lesbians thought of themselves.

Building Solidarity

Above all else, the action groups provided new social opportunities for gay men and lesbians in West Germany. Although the West Berlin Action denounced the subculture's bars and clubs, its members were never opposed to drinking, dancing, or sex. They hosted parties at the Action's headquarters and other spaces around the city.[95] Taking advantage of Willy Brandt's détente with East Germany, the group also organized outings to East Berlin, where members spread the gospel of liberation.[96]

Gay bookstores opened in cities around the country, such as *Prinz Eisenherz* in West Berlin, *Erlkönig* in Stuttgart, and *Männerschwarm* in Hamburg. Activists founded their own bars and cafes, such as *Schwarze Kaffee* and *Anderes Ufer* in West Berlin.[97] By the end of the decade, many groups had opened permanent centres, such as SchwuZ and the Gay and Lesbian Counselling Centre in West Berlin, the Magnus Hirschfeld Centre in Hamburg, and the Gay Communication Centre in Frankfurt am Main. The institutions the movement left behind are a testament to its impact on everyday life.

Action groups also thrust lesbians and gay men – and the problems they faced – into public discourse. As increasing numbers celebrated their sexuality, the movement capitalized on their visibility in order to show that the hundreds of thousands of gay people in West Germany belonged to a minority. In 1978 *Stern* magazine, one of West Germany's largest periodicals, published an article in which 682 gay men publicly acknowledged their homosexuality.[98] The idea was lifted straight from the feminist playbook. In 1971 *Stern* had published an article in which 374 women publicly admitted to having had abortions.[99] The 1978 article on homosexuality contained a searing indictment of West Germany, attacking government and society alike for their intolerance of one of the Federal Republic's largest minorities.

The most prominent solidarity efforts came in the form of demonstrations. In 1972 the West Berlin Action began a tradition of Pentecost meetings. These weeklong summer gatherings brought activists from around the Federal Republic as well as foreign countries to participate in discussions, parties, and protests. Its second gathering, in June 1973, is still remembered as the Action's greatest triumph: more than 600 gay men and lesbians flooded the city and marched up West Berlin's main boulevard, Kurfürstendamm.[100]

Action groups routinely organized activities such as flyer campaigns and kiss-ins, as both lesbian activist Dorothea R. and West Berlin Action member Roland R. recalled.[101] These demonstrations became ubiquitous around the Federal Republic in the 1970s and would eventually be ritualized in West Germany's summertime gay pride marches. The first march billed as a gay pride event was held in 1979 in the northern city-state of Bremen.[102] When Hamburg celebrated its first pride week a year later, the demonstration brought more than 2,000 men and women to the Hanseatic city.[103]

These demonstrations, however, were not the gay pride parades of today. Local governments frequently opposed them, and marchers often faced hostile crowds.[104] Police sometimes showed up at demonstrations to photograph participants. Many demonstrators, oftentimes teachers or other public officials, wore white masks to protect their identities (see figure 6.2).[105] West Berlin activist Holger G. described seeing older men and women who, in his view, believed the city to be "an island in a red sea." Marching along Bülowstrasse during the 1973 Pentecost demonstration, Holger recalled that an elderly woman hissed at him, "we forgot to gas you!"[106] Franz G. remembered that, at an early parade in Cologne, "there was commentary throughout filled with hate and loathing. A few of us were spit on and reviled as 'perverts.'"[107]

But the movement and its demonstrations persisted. By decade's end, activists had convinced West Germans that there existed a gay minority and had forged new institutions to serve that minority. In 1979 *Der Spiegel* noted that gay demonstrations "count in West German metropolises as a habitual street scene."[108] That tradition of protest and celebration lives on in unified Germany's Christopher Street Day Celebrations, the pride week each summer that routinely draws hundreds of thousands of people onto the streets. Without a doubt gay Germans' relatively comfortable lives today owe a great deal to activists' work in the 1970s.

But Christopher Street Day's very name, which comes from the New York City street where the Stonewall riots took place, hints at the sense of inadequacy that already tinged the activism of the 1970s. In spite of the changes they had wrought, activists felt a perpetual dissatisfaction with their efforts and a sense of inferiority when compared to their compatriots across the Atlantic. That malaise perseveres in memory today and is well summed up in Michael Holy's contention that, "The German gay movement in the FRG required almost a decade in order to identify with the militancy and the new self-consciousness of the American gays."[109]

Holy's assessment is, of course, unfair. Not only does it overestimate the success of the American movement, it also incorrectly casts the West German gay movement as a replica of the American one. West German activists remained ignorant of developments in the United States until the movement was well underway. They had to face the fascist past and contend with a social-liberal government that was neither hostile nor

Figure 6.2. Marchers in the HAW-led protest on 10 June 1973. Note the white hoods in the foreground: some activists could not risk public identification for fear of losing their jobs. Courtesy of the Landesarchiv Berlin (LAB, F Rep. 290 Nr. 0161676). Photographer: Ingeborg Lommatzsch

sympathetic to their cause. They could draw inspiration from the Weimar-era gay movement but set out upon a fundamentally new course predicated on a minoritizing understanding of sexual citizenship. Most striking about the West German movement, however, was the extent to which it never lost sight of its ultimate goal of creating a base of political power for gay people. For all that West German activists hoped to reshape the subculture and forge new ways of being for gay people, the movement always kept an eye on politics in the hope of exercising power in ways that gay people had never before dreamt.

Political Action

While American gay activists gravitated leftward in the 1970s and 1980s, propelled in part by the right-wing conservatism embodied in Anita Bryant's campaigns against homosexuality, West German activists had no obvious political home in the 1970s.[110] Many were inclined to side with the Free Democrats because of their progressive social views. In 1971, still in the early years of the social-liberal coalition, the party had adopted the so-called *Freiburg Theses* at its convention in the southwest city Freiburg im Breisgau. This document envisioned "democratization and liberalization of the state," growing from "guarantees of constitutional rights [and] protection of minorities."[111] Other gay people sided with socialist parties, from the Social Democrats to the German Communist Party. These leftists focused on socialism's traditional support for gay rights, particularly during the Weimar Republic. Yet the largest of them, Willy Brandt's Social Democratic Party, refused to endorse even the abolition of §175.

There were also parties outside the mainstream. By decade's end, a host of Alternative List (AL), Multicoloured List (*Bunte Liste* or BL), and Green Party candidates – drawn together from the feminist, green, and gay movements and vehemently opposed to sexual animus – had started contesting regional elections. The first openly gay candidate for office in Germany, twenty-five-year-old Wolfgang Krömer, campaigned for the Hamburg state parliament in June 1978 as a BL member.[112] Although his efforts failed, voters elected openly gay Reinhard Frede to the municipal legislature for West Berlin's Schöneberg neighbourhood a year later.[113]

Many gay West Germans were also conservative. A sizeable chunk, estimated in the 1965 federal election to have been as many as 27 per cent of gay voters, plumped for the Christian Democrats and their Bavarian sister party, the Christian Social Union. Homophile groups in particular encouraged their members to vote for the centre-right. In the 1972 election, the German Homophile Organization and the Association of German Homophiles (*Schutzverband deutscher Homophiler*) lobbied for the Christian parties.[114]

The lack of allegiance to one particular party seemed utterly natural at the time. And while it effectively splintered the movement, it also presented an opportunity. The magazine *him* expressed this sentiment in a 1973 article, contending that, "Readers of this magazine are not at the outset inclined to the SPD and FDP."[115] This population of politically unattached voters the magazine described as "an electoral reservoir."[116] Although gay people spread their votes across the political spectrum, most of them could still be persuaded to vote for any mainstream party that best represented their interests.

Around the same time, sociological research breathed life into the idea that gay citizens could be persuaded to vote as a block. Martin Dannecker's extensive study *The Ordinary Homosexual*, which he and his collaborator, Reimut Reiche (a former member of the 68er Socialist German Student Union), published in 1974, included a section on gay political attitudes. Their research compared how subjects had voted in the 1965 and 1969 general elections. They found that support for the Social Democrats had surged among gay men from 55 per cent in 1965 to 71 per cent in 1969 on the first ballot (*Erststimme*). Likewise, the Free Democrats had enjoyed a bump of 7 per cent in the second ballot (*Zweitstimme*).[117] Support for the Christian Democrats, on the other hand, had collapsed from 27 per cent on the first ballot in 1965 to 14 per cent in 1969 and from 21 per cent to 13 per cent on the second ballot.[118]

Dannecker and Reiche chalked the SPD and FDP gains up to "a sympathy-boom of homosexuals" for the parties' 1969 reform of §175. At the same time, they warned, "It would be false to conclude a particularly strong social democratic" tendency among gay people.[119] These results bolstered the notion that gay and lesbian people represented a large pool of uncommitted voters.

To take advantage of this fact, action groups began holding electoral debates with party representatives in the mid-1970s. These so-called podium discussions constituted the most explicit attempt to project gay political power that Germany had yet seen, and they followed on the heels of similar attempts by homophile groups to pressure the government. The German Homophile Organization had arranged a "public discussion with politicians" on 27 October 1972 in order to help gay people figure out "who best represents our interests in parliament."[120] When the *Bundestag* debated new reforms of the criminal code in 1973, the German Action Society Homosexuality (DAH) collected more than 20,000 signatures on a petition for the total repeal of §175.[121]

These early initiatives had little discernible impact. The 1973 reform kept §175 intact, though it reduced the age of consent for gay men to eighteen. Early in the decade no major party included gay rights as a plank of their national platform. But by mid-decade, action groups around the country began to hold podium discussions with the goal of changing that. At the podium discussions, party candidates standing for regional elections fielded questions on gay and lesbian issues from audiences composed primarily of queer people. The first such event occurred after the 1976 election that returned the social-liberal coalition to power under Helmut Schmidt. The Gay Liberation Front in Cologne invited representatives of the CDU, SPD, and FDP to discuss its political priorities.[122] Three years later, in March 1979, the General Action of West Berlin, the group that had broken away from the HAW, organized a similar event. Representatives from the major parties answered questions about their positions on homosexual priorities at the Charlottenburg City Hall, which was "completely overcrowded."[123] The same year, parties participated in another podium discussion in Cologne.[124] April 1980 brought yet another podium discussion in Düsseldorf attended by 400 people.[125] When Hamburg activist groups held an analogous discussion in June 1980, representatives of five parties took part, and around 1,000 attendees swamped the venue.[126] After years of talk, *Du & Ich* gushed, "Something is finally happening."[127]

At around the same time, gay people began organizing within mainstream political parties. Working circles for gay people in the youth organization of the Social Democrats, the so-called Young Socialists or *Jusos*, cropped up in West Berlin and Cologne late in the 1970s. Of course, they faced an uphill battle. Even by 1979, some SPD members did not even know §175 was still in force. Others even believed homosexuals should be barred from certain professions.[128] The Social Democrats' class-based view of politics prevented many of the old guard from taking gay concerns seriously.

Activists had more success with the Free Democrats. In October 1978 gay members of the youth group of the West Berlin FDP, so-called Young Democrats or *Judos*, met in order to establish a working circle within the party. Although the group was small, it enjoyed support from the party and began to advocate making gay rights more visible in its platform. In February 1979, the group convinced the regional party leadership to adopt a set of "Arguments on the Topic of Homosexuality."[129]

In September 1979 the group successfully lobbied the West Berlin government to alter its sexual education practices. Schools there would no longer teach homosexuality in the same breath as rape. In a particularly impressive coup, the group secured a grant of 5,000 DM from the local government for a gay and lesbian counselling centre in 1979.[130] Not only did the gay liberals achieve a new relationship between West Berlin's gay population and its government in a matter of months, they also inspired similar groups around the country. Another Young Democrats working group appeared in March 1979 in North Rhine-Westphalia, West Germany's largest state. In December of that year, party members in the southwest state of Baden-Württemberg began to come out as gay. A few months later, these groups met to discuss plans for a national organization of gay Free Democrats.

1980 seemed ripe for revolution. A general election scheduled for that year provided the impetus for the gay groups' most significant attempt to exercise political power. A number of shifts in West German politics also hastened the pace. Local and regional Green parties, the BL, the AL, and other grassroots movements united in January 1980 to form a national Green Party, which soon adopted a radically progressive stance on sexual rights.[131] At the same time, the Christian Democrats nominated Franz Josef Strauß, Bavaria's archconservative minister-president, as their lead candidate for the elections.[132] The emergence of a more conservative Christian Democratic Union and a new progressive party reshaped the political landscape.

Encouraged by positive reactions to the regional podium discussions, the West Berlin General Action decided in 1979 that the coming federal election was the moment for West Germany's gay minority to exercise its newfound power. On 12 December 1979, the group declared its intention to host a podium discussion in Bonn's Beethoven Hall, one of the largest public buildings in West Germany's capital.[133] The group described the chance to put influential politicians in front of a national audience as "a grand coup" for West Germany's gay movement.[134] A few months later *Du & Ich* exclaimed, "We are [giving] the parties a chance to remember that there are 2–3 million homosexual [voters]."[135] Those voters, it hoped, would "decide the election."[136] The Beethoven Hall discussion would be the turning point that projected gay and lesbian voters' strength.

The four big gay magazines – *Du & Ich, Don, him applaus,* and *Gay Journal* – supported the event and used it to launch an electoral initiative of their own, named "Action '80."[137] The campaign made nine demands of the parties, many of which the action groups had been demanding for years. They included demands that §175 be expunged from the criminal code; that gay victims of National Socialism be paid reparations; that an anti-discrimination law be passed to protect minorities, women, and homosexuals; that police be forbidden from keeping records of homosexuals; and that the Federal Republic advocate for the removal of homosexuality from the World Health Organization's list of illnesses.[138]

Most remarkably, the agitation had an impact on the parties. The newly formed Green Party's 1980 electoral program went furthest in declaring its support for this agenda. The party dedicated a full section of its platform to "socially marginalized groups" and called for "an end to discrimination against homosexuals."[139] The Young Democrats proposed advocating the repeal of §175 at the FDP congress in June 1980.[140] Delegates voted to adopt the measure, breaking with the Social Democrats, who voted down a similar proposal at their party congress.[141] The Free Democratic Party, the embodiment of West German establishment politics, thus became the first parliamentary party in postwar German history to endorse part of the gay movement's agenda.

As the October election drew closer, activists pulled harder for the Free Democrats, whom they believed represented the movement's best chance at political power. In September 1980, a full-page advertisement ran in the gay magazines asking readers to vote for the Free Democrats.[142] One reader wrote to *Du & Ich*, "The only party that openly and honestly fields our issues – and not merely as an electoral tactic – is the F.D.P."[143]

But the campaign's centrepiece remained the podium discussion in Bonn. It is not difficult to see why, for the organizers had managed to orchestrate a grand affair. The Social Democrats dispatched Herbert Brückner, senator for health in the city-state of Bremen, to the event. The FDP was represented by its general secretary, Günther Verheugen. Famous TV host Reinhard Münchenhagen was engaged as moderator. Gay magazines ran stories about the podium discussion and urged readers to come to Bonn. Large posters adorned with pink triangles called for gay people to "come in masses" to the capital.[144] When 12 July 1980, rolled around, more than 1,000 gay men and lesbians from across the country surged into the town. They took to its streets in public demonstration and crowded into the Beethoven Hall. They expected to hear, for the first time in history, national parties ask for their votes as gay and lesbian citizens.

What they got instead was chaos. About ten minutes into debating whether and how to grant gay people reparations for Nazi-era persecution, catcalls broke out from the audience. Two radical paedophile groups, the Indian Commune from Nuremberg and the Oranien Commune from West Berlin, had come to the event to protest their exclusion.[145] The meeting soon dissolved in pandemonium. Various members of the protesting communes yelled out and one unidentified voice cried, "how terribly sad it is, that gays discriminate against each other," while another screamed that the event organizers were a "destructive gay dictatorship." Thousands of people streamed out of the hall to avoid the madness, leaving the movement's "grand coup" in shambles.[146]

Yet if activists left the Beethoven Hall event dejected, their spirits surely rose after the election on 5 October 1980. Voters returned Helmut Schmidt's social-liberal coalition and delivered a drubbing to the Christian Democrats under Franz Josef Strauß. In sum, the Christian Democratic Union and Christian Social Union lost 4 per cent of the popular vote. Most heartening to the movement was the fact that the Free Democrats saw a bump of over 1 million votes. Those new votes might well have come from lesbians and gay men enthused by the liberal party's dedication to homosexual rights. Gay activists certainly believed so. A week after the election, the General Action took out a full-page advertisement in major West German newspapers in which it declared, "The electoral results of October 5 came about with the votes of homosexual men" (forgetting, unsurprisingly, that lesbian activists too had been involved).[147] While there is no way of knowing how gay and lesbian West Germans actually voted in the election, there is evidence that the Free Democrats accepted activists' logic that gay votes had delivered their electoral victory. A couple of years later, a parliamentary report for the party noted that, "It cannot be ruled out that the FDP was able to mobilize a significant share of homosexual voters [in 1980]."[148] Most important was the fact that the Free Democrats seemed intent on making good on their promises to gay voters. In coalition talks, they pressed the Social Democrats to repeal §175.[149]

Thus, while the 1970s are today remembered ambivalently – the internal strife often drowning out the movement's radical possibility – activists had achieved something remarkable in just nine years. The 1970s in West Germany were a period of incredible social and political ferment for gay people, and by the end of 1980 the dream of gay political power seemed well on its way to becoming reality. The decade saw the multiplication of new gay scenes and forms of gay life. Rejecting scientific liberalism, the movement forged a new vision of gay citizenship, one that aimed to turn the country's atomized population of gay people into a unified minority that could project power through protests and the ballot. While activists largely agreed on this conception of gay citizenship, they disagreed vehemently about both the movement's end goals and the means to get there. While the ideological skirmishes that many historians have taken as the West German gay movement's hallmark throw into relief divergent conceptions of gay liberation, the movement's impact on West German politics and society illustrates how those differences ultimately led to the evolution of particular kinds of social and political liberation for West German gay men.

The 1970s also reveal the winding path that change can take. The action groups not only propelled West Germany's gay men and lesbians onto the streets, they also inspired a generation of activists in East Germany. West Germans' trips across the border into the eastern capital brought them face to face with gay men and lesbians living under socialism. In the same years that West German activists sought recognition from society and political parties, these East German men and women struggled to convince the dictatorship of their plight, to organize as an independent group, and to carve out a space for themselves in the Democratic Republic.

7 Into the Labyrinth

When Gay Activists Met the Socialist State

Berlin's old city hall (*Altes Stadthaus*) is an imposing historicist structure just south of Alexanderplatz. A soaring tower dominates its façade. From 1955 until 1989, it served as the seat of East Germany's Council of Ministers, the country's chief executive organ. On 20 September 1979, four men and one woman came to meet with council representatives.[1] Over the past six years, they had laboured to create a socialist analogue to the West German gay movement. They came on that autumn day to gain official approval for their plans for a homosexual "recreation and communication centre."[2] They were "euphoric," for they believed the government was on the verge of acknowledging, for the first time in its history, its gay and lesbian citizens' particular needs.[3] For a state so reluctant to admit the existence of homosexuals, let alone the legitimacy of their social and political demands, it was a triumph. Arriving on tides of liberation, they had won their government's attention.

The meeting came about thanks to the activism of a handful of gay men and lesbian women. Early in the 1970s, Western ideas about gay liberation had migrated into the Democratic Republic. Those ideas had arrived as stowaways with members of the West Berlin Action, who travelled sporadically across the border, and in the broadcast of Rosa von Praunheim's emancipation film. East Germans began to regard their sexuality as a political issue, and they started to press the regime to implement new policies that would benefit gay men and lesbians. In so doing they ran up against a paranoid, authoritarian state that had recently begun taking the threat of espionage in the gay subculture seriously. These new activists found themselves entangled in the socialist bureaucracy's labyrinthine workings.

While these early gay liberation initiatives have received attention from scholars in recent years, little has been written about the relationship between these activists and the East German state or the ways in which the security services, in particular, responded to their efforts.[4] Unsurprisingly, they aroused considerable fear and perplexity within the regime, whose haphazard reaction helped to define the terms of East German gay activism. The state's inconsistent approach underlined not only the regime's indiscriminate nature but also the ways in which bureaucratic obfuscation was a core feature of East German authoritarianism. Moreover, a look at the regime's reactions to various gay initiatives exposes the Stasi's role behind the bureaucracy's façades. The grey men of the secret police not only represented the lurking threat of violence that kept socialism in power but were also decision makers who could either compel the bureaucratic machine to act or sanction its inefficiency.

At the same time, activists' experiences reveal some of the political strategies available to East German citizens. Though the Democratic Republic was an authoritarian dictatorship, it was also Janus-faced. While the regime stayed in power thanks to its awesome surveillance apparatus, it also strove to maintain an appearance of the rule of law. Prioritizing rights and rules, the government inadvertently opened space for activists to organize independently and press for reform.

Everyday Life under Honecker

As in the West, the 1970s were transformative years in East Germany, and the most visible change was political. In 1971 Erich Honecker, a high-ranking Politburo member, orchestrated a palace coup against Walter Ulbricht.[5] Honecker assumed the position of General Secretary, which he would hold until 1989, and set upon a course of social, economic, and cultural détente. He inaugurated a new approach aimed at the "unity of economic and social policy," retooling the economy to better serve citizens' everyday needs.[6] In practice, this policy meant greater production of consumer staples.[7] The government also promulgated a number of measures in the 1970s aimed at assisting women, from extended maternity leave to shorter work weeks for mothers to legalizing abortion, building on its "welfare dictatorship."[8]

The regime also authorized a greater breadth of leisure activities and relaxed censorship. It ceased Operation Oxhead (*Aktion Ochsenkopf*), the code name for the regime's efforts to keep Western radio and television programs from East German ears and eyes.[9] By 1971 the vast majority of East Germans owned television sets and could tune in to West German programs.[10] Honecker's government negotiated the Basic Treaty with Willy Brandt's new government in Bonn, easing travel restrictions on West Germans coming into the Democratic Republic.[11] While the

Stasi also swelled in size under Honecker, these changes marked a real opening up from the probity and rigidity of the Ulbricht years.[12]

For gay people in East Germany the thaw had mixed results. Although newspapers, for example, had largely ceased printing prejudicial coverage of homosexuality, they published nothing positive either. While this vacuum condemned lesbians and gay men to a kind of neglect, it also meant an end of the regime's overt efforts to cultivate anti-gay animus. The SED no longer painted the West as a paradise for "criminals and homosexuals."

That shift was likely the result of two forces. On the one hand, the Berlin Wall had stanched the flood of refugees fleeing the GDR, stabilizing the country in the early 1960s.[13] As socialist rule normalized, the need to populate propaganda with homosexual bogeymen dissipated. On the other hand, the government officially decriminalized homosexuality in 1968 when it promulgated a new criminal code. The measure replaced §175 with §151, which set a higher age of consent for male and female homosexual acts than for heterosexual acts. Interestingly, §151 is the only statute in modern German history to criminalize any lesbian act.[14] Equally strangely, government records give no obvious reason for why lesbians were suddenly also subject to a higher age of consent.[15]

All the while, discrimination persisted. Gay people still could not serve in the army, the police, or the Stasi. Gay partners were unable to find living space together, which the state carefully controlled.[16] It was even difficult to acquire information about homosexuality. Dr Ursula Sillge, a lesbian activist who was raised in a rural corner of Thuringia, recalled hearing about a library in the Saxon Ore Mountains that refused to lend a book because the volume discussed homosexuality.[17]

Gay people also could not place personal advertisements in newspapers, although some tried to circumvent the ban. Sillge recalled how the weekly *Wochenpost* allowed "pen pal ads" in which "one had to name two hobbies." She bought an ad to find a correspondent who enjoyed "sports and theatre." Because she could not specify the gender of the desired contact, she received forty responses from men and only three from women.[18] While gay West Germans were forging new friendships in the 1970s through personal ads, coagulating the subculture's bonds, taboo still excluded gay East Germans from most of public life.

Gay men thus continued to rely on public toilets, swimming pools, parks, and train stations to pick up tricks. The most famous of these was the Fairy Tale Fountain (*Märchenbrunnen*) in the Friedrichshain People's Park (*Volkspark Friedrichshain*), a large fountain with statues of fairy-tale characters in one of East Berlin's largest parks.[19] The police continued to monitor these cruising sites and registered men for publicly soliciting sex, though such patrolling became increasingly rare.[20]

Worse, thugs knew about these locations and loitered there in order to extort and beat gay men. "When I became a lawyer," former Prime Minister Lothar de Maizière recollected, "it was quite common to have trials of young people who made a game of smacking gays around (*Schwule aufklatschen*), that's what it was called. In particular in special toilets or elsewhere, where one knew that they met. The hooligans went there and roughed them up."[21] While the *Klappe* remained dangerous, it presented one of gay men's only opportunities to meet sexual partners and make friends.

If anything, lesbians were worse off, for they had virtually no means of finding each other.[22] As Sillge notes in her book on lesbians in the GDR, there was no lesbian equivalent of the *Klappe*. She argues that this absence arose because "most lesbians do not divide their wish for sexual release from their need for emotional comfort."[23] Moreover, lesbians who married or had children could be disadvantaged in divorce and custody trials. The law allowed children to be taken away from mothers found to have "gravely abnormal development of personality," which homosexuality might still be considered in the 1970s.[24]

Yet, the regime's newfound interest in citizens' leisure activities did mean one positive change for gay people. By the early 1970s, more bars and cafés catered to gay clientele in certain cities.[25] Although the concomitant boom in West German locales dwarfed that in the East, the change was palpable. Certain spheres of employment also became havens for queer people. "There were areas where gays were absolutely tolerated," recalled de Maizière, who began his career in the Berlin Symphony Orchestra as a violist: "it was the theatre, it was the ballet, it was especially so in gastronomy."[26] House parties also continued to be popular. Lesbians and gay men hosted gatherings in their apartments or houses, ranging from a handful of guests to dozens or even hundreds. In 1977, for example, one gay man allegedly invited at least 100 guests to his house just southwest of Berlin for an evening fete.[27] Of course, these pubs, cafés, and parties were largely confined to cities – East Berlin, Dresden, Karl-Marx-City, and Leipzig – and most gay people did not know about, let alone experience, them. The early 1970s was still an ambiguous period for East Germany's gay and lesbian populations.

In this brave new world, we encounter a young man named Peter Rausch.[28] Rausch was born in 1950 to parents who belonged to the SED. He spent his teenage years exploring the capital's gay subculture, learning about the public toilets on Alexanderplatz and how to cruise men at the large public bath on Gartenstrasse. In 1968 he joined the East

German army, which stationed him in Frankfurt an der Oder near the Polish border. In the military, Rausch recalled, there reigned "a macho cult," which forced him to lead a double life. "You can really live for a long time with this schizophrenia," he told me. "I never saw myself as gay, rather that it was a practice that you did in your youth."

After his service, Rausch returned to East Berlin in 1972. There he began frequenting bars that welcomed gay people, in particular Johannes Eck on Friedrichstrasse in the city centre, which catered to both gay and straight clientele. He returned often to the baths at Gartenstrasse, where "one could have good sex." One day, Rausch noticed a man who "rose out of the water like an Adonis." That man, Michael Eggert, sat down next to Rausch and from that day on, Rausch said, "we were good friends."

Their meeting was significant because Eggert had, earlier that year, serendipitously met West German gay activists. During the West Berlin Action's 1972 Pentecost gathering, a group of them had crossed the border and spent the day in East Berlin. In Mocca Bar, a "very gay bar filled with boisterous fairies," according to Rausch, they had met Eggert. The Westerners told him about their "emancipation work" and gave him various documents including their recently formulated Statement of Principles. Eggert relayed all this to Rausch, opening his eyes to the idea of social and political discrimination. "It had never occurred to me that the paragraph [§175] was wrong," he remembered, "rather that I was wrong."

Rausch and Eggert began meeting with a third man later that year to discuss gay liberation in East Germany. They called themselves "the group" and were spurred to further action on 17 January 1973, when they watched Rosa von Praunheim's *It Is Not the Homosexual*. West German television broadcast the film that day, alongside a follow-up discussion with gay activists. As with most West German programming, the signal reached antennae in East Germany. A week after seeing the film, the group decided, as had so many West German gay men, that "we are a political group."

They got their first taste of activism later that year. In summer 1973 East Berlin hosted the tenth World Festival of Youth and Students, an international exposition held periodically since 1947, primarily in Soviet-bloc countries. One attendee that year was London Gay Liberation Front activist Peter Tatchell. Determined to make gay emancipation a topic of conversation, he smuggled 300 gay rights brochures and 10,000 flyers into the GDR.[29] On 3 August, Tatchell spoke to a room full of members of the Free German Youth (*Freie Deutsche Jugend* or FDJ), East Germany's official youth organization, including Rausch and Eggert. Once it became clear that he would talk about homosexuality, the organizers cut Tatchell's microphone. But those assembled wanted Tatchell to finish, and the organizers eventually allowed him to speak. Two days later, as the festival wound down, Tatchell and a few other gay men, including members of Rausch's group, distributed flyers and carried a banner that proclaimed "Homosexual Emancipation! Revolutionary Homosexuals Support Socialism!"[30] Surprisingly, the demonstrators managed to escape without incident.

A decade later, Tatchell published an account of the events, titled "Ten Gay Days That Shook East Berlin."[31] The protests – and contact with Western activists in general – were certainly important for the group.[32] At the time, curiously, the security services barely seemed to care. In the mountains of documentation that the Stasi eventually gathered on gay activism in the 1970s and 1980s, I discovered only two reports that mentioned the fact that gay East Germans had met with Western gay activists during the World Festival.[33] For reasons that are unclear, it simply did not register in a significant way with the secret police.

Nonetheless, Tatchell's protest pointed to the problems activists faced in a socialist dictatorship. Agitation of the sort that West German lesbians and gay men employed was simply not an option for Rausch's group. The regime allowed neither public demonstrations nor political opposition nor independent groups of any kind. Rausch explained the difficulty thus: "You could not just create an organization. You always needed someone there in that centralized country who, from above, allowed [new] structures." The group had been meeting at the so-called House of Health in Potsdam just southwest of Berlin.[34] But the centre's medical director could not offer them official recognition of the sort needed to create a genuine social alternative. The group therefore decided to try to win approval from the state itself.

The Gay Socialist Citizen

In 1974 a remarkable document began circulating within the East German government. Titled "Plan (*Konzept*) for the Creation of a Homosexual Communication Centre," it laid out a new vision of homosexual men's and women's place in socialist society. The paper elucidated a claim of citizenship based neither on human rights nor on gay power but rather on the ideals of socialist society. Its authors argued that anti-gay taboos were not native to socialism but rather a holdover from the capitalist past. It pointed out that social progress had led to "a deep-seated change in consciousness" among gay men and lesbians, causing them to begin "to question the social justification for their situation from a Marxist perspective."[35] Its authors, who were members of Rausch's group, meant that the continued stigmatization of gay men and lesbians was incompatible with socialism's utopian promise.[36] They wanted to help the state create "opportunities for us homosexuals for the full development of our socialist personalities."[37]

The plan listed a catalogue of complaints, such as lesbians' and gay men's inability to marry, their difficulty finding partner housing, and that there were few social opportunities for gay people in East Germany beyond the dangerous *Klappe*.[38] Like their Western counterparts, East German activists wanted new ways of socializing with fellow gay people that would make cruising public toilets obsolete. They suggested that the regime authorize a "homosexual communication centre," which would serve as a place for gay people to socialize and as an institution that could spread information "about the true causes of our misery [...] in particular the fascist persecution."[39] They hoped such an institution would lead to a more welcoming subculture and would combat anti-gay prejudices.

The plan is intriguing for how it articulated West German notions of gay liberation in the language of East German Marxism. Its authors not only went out of their way to express their devotion to the regime (in stark contrast to West German activists who viewed their movement as one of opposition) but also catalogued the numerous benefits the regime might enjoy from such a centre. Playing on the regime's paranoia about Western influences, they wrote that Western countries, while "seemingly paradise on earth for us," were actually places of exploitation. "That homosexual life is so commercialized there," the group wrote, "is not seen" in East Germany.[40] A communication centre would not only make life better for gay East Germans but would also help combat their (misplaced) exasperation with East German society. While the paper adopted West German activists' fixation with forming a gay minority through an overhaul of the subculture, it turned the formulation on its head. In their rendition, the state was not an enemy that gay liberation would have to overcome but rather a prospective ally.

The paper's provenance was something of a mystery to the secret police. A "leading doctor in the 'House of Health,'" the institution that Rausch and Eggert had hoped could serve as a home for their group, had submitted a copy to the government, showing it to a judge on the East German Supreme Court some time in 1974 or early 1975. That jurist had then written to the chief of police and deputy minister of the interior on 21 January 1975.[41] By 24 January 1975, the criminal police – for which Department VII of the Stasi was responsible – had issued a memorandum regarding the plan.[42] A month later, Stasi Department

XX, responsible for the state, culture, church, and underground, was in contact with Department VII about it.[43] The Health Ministry was also drawn into the government's internal debate about what to do with the document.[44] Because these bureaucracies' reaction to this plan shaped their future interactions with gay activists in the 1970s and 1980s, it is worth pausing to consider precisely how they assessed and responded to it.

On 24 January 1975, the criminal police authored the first of several memoranda about the plan. This memo did three important things. First, it argued that the government must not allow homosexuality to become a "comprehensive problem of society and the state."[45] That is, the security services thought it unwise for the government to address the group's concerns. Second, the police offered five justifications for this view. In an echo of §175 trials in the 1950s and 1960s, it contended that most East Germans would not tolerate homosexuality. Any government act seen to be promoting homosexuality might endanger its standing with the population. The memo further contended, somewhat perversely, that gay people already enjoyed support from the state.

The three remaining reasons all dealt with the state's fear of gay conspiracies. The police argued that such a centre would lead to the "advocacy" of homosexuality and that it would gather criminal elements together under one umbrella. Most remarkably, the memo insisted, "It would necessarily foster significant connections with foreigners. Assuredly enemy intelligence services would concentrate on such an establishment." They would do so, the report went on, because "homosexuals with their labile personalities are known to have long been a target of enemy activities."[46] That is, the police's and, by extension, the Stasi's experiences with gay espionage led it to dismiss out of hand the possibility of allowing pro-regime gay activists the right to organize in a tightly regulated institution.

Third and finally, the memo suggested a solution by which to defuse the problem. The police noted that, as an agency, it could "only have an opinion from the standpoint of the fight against crime." Homosexuality, it averred, "currently plays an unimportant role" in crime. The memo therefore suggested that homosexuality was actually a medical-social problem and that the Ministry of Health ought to assess the petition from that standpoint.[47] Bouncing gay activists from one bureau to another became a favoured strategy to frustrate the group's efforts.

To that end, the East German Central Medical Service sent a letter to Stasi Department VII on 21 February 1975. In it, the bureau declined to endorse the idea of a communication centre. Referencing "medical literature," it maintained that although homosexuality was a congenital condition, "It is fully erroneous to believe that (generally speaking) our population could be led to a realistic, positive attitude about homosexuals."[48] Such a centre would, the letter argued, only inflame the public's prejudice and make things worse for gay people in East Germany.[49]

Further Stasi memoranda appeared later that also summarized these opinions. The memos reiterated that there was no need for such an organization because "homosexuals also have the same rights and responsibilities of citizenship" as heterosexuals.[50] The Stasi averred that a centre would lead to their social isolation, which "stands in opposition to the evolution of the personality of a socialist citizen as well as the principles of cohabitation in our socialist state."[51] Gay men and lesbians, that is, were already full citizens and their desire for an association would only lead to their segregation from society.

Beyond invocations of gay espionage, these documents do not exhibit much overt anti-gay animus (some even cast their authors as enlightened vis-à-vis the presumed prejudicial views of ordinary East Germans). These and later memoranda were largely free of the kinds of pathologizing and moralizing language historians of sexuality are accustomed to seeing in state responses to homosexuality. The documents themselves give few indications as to why this might be. The government, as we have seen, was certainly no advocate for gay causes. Yet, the relative absence of animus suggests that officials were genuinely concerned about the dangers they believed gay activism might pose. The dictatorship thought of homosexuality in political rather than moral terms.[52]

Becoming the HIB

Though the group never received an official response from the government, Rausch, Eggert, and their comrades pressed ahead. By 1975 their group had around fifteen members and, Rausch remembered, "met every Friday evening at eight o'clock in one of our apartments."[53] These events became ever more cramped as they grew from the original core to dozens of people.[54] Because clubs required government approval, the group could not simply show up at an event space like a dance hall or even a restaurant. Private gatherings of the sort queer people had long organized in East German cities were one of the only ways to circumvent the state's stranglehold on social life.

Finding new members for the group initially seemed difficult. Under the dictatorship, after all, citizens did not enjoy unfettered freedoms of speech, expression, or assembly. Even organizations that had government permits could find it difficult to print necessary materials.

Distributing information about the group's private parties thus proved to be a particularly nettlesome problem. Members resorted to typing out multiple copies of flyers and programs on home typewriters to spread word.[55]

They distributed these flyers in East Berlin bars, using the subculture to recruit new members.[56] In February 1976, a Stasi informant described several planned parties at bars around the city. He anticipated that these gatherings would draw anywhere from 150 to 300 people. While those numbers might have been somewhat inflated, the IM was correct that the group used such parties to expand their numbers.[57]

By 1976, the group had grown to at least twenty members.[58] As one report noted, the group included "members of the intelligentsia, artists, students, service professions, and workers."[59] The group was more socially diverse than its West German counterparts, which were dominated by university students.[60] As their gatherings grew correspondingly larger, however, there came ever greater strain on the group's ability to find suitable space. On 10 July 1976, for instance, around sixty people showed up to one apartment.[61] Organizers began finding creative solutions to the problem of how to gather that many people together. Some events had to be held in multiple apartments such as one on 24 October 1976, when an IM reported that the group hosted simultaneous parties in two separate apartments in order to accommodate everyone who wanted to attend.[62]

The group planned ever more events for its expanding membership. Rausch recalled that, "On Sundays once every month – or maybe every fourteen days – we organized public events, again in a private apartment."[63] The group planned outings such as "trips to the theatre" and "steam boat trips and excursions."[64] They even managed to organize a public lecture about homosexuality at the city library on 1 June 1976.[65] The activists were also occasionally able to secure public space under the guise of state-sanctioned activities such as birthday parties.[66] Of course, the group could only engage in such activities by outfoxing officials. At a certain point, Rausch said, the police realized they were using the venues for gay parties and stopped permitting them.[67]

Pressure to find a permanent space would likely have continued mounting if not for one of East Germany's most colourful personalities: Charlotte von Mahlsdorf (see figure 7.1). After a difficult youth in the Nazi era (her violent father was a Nazi whom she allegedly killed in 1944), she began living as a woman in East Germany.[68] In the late 1950s, Charlotte convinced officials to allow her to take ownership of a decaying villa in the East Berlin neighbourhood of Mahlsdorf. She moved in with her sizeable collection of furniture and curios from

Figure 7.1. Peter Rausch (right), Michael Eggert (left), and Charlotte von Mahlsdorf (centre) in the 1970s. Courtesy of Peter Rausch

the late nineteenth century (known in German as the *Gründerzeit* or "Founding Period," because of the economic expansion around the time of Germany's 1871 unification) and opened a museum dedicated to the era.[69]

At the June 1976 library lecture, Peter Rausch met Mahlsdorf.[70] They got to chatting, in particular about Rausch's group's need for meeting space. Mahlsdorf mentioned that she had three vacant basement rooms, where she had resurrected an old Berlin queer bar called Mulackritze.[71] In her autobiography, she recalled hearing the group at the library complain, "How are we actually living? Ban on public meetings, no advertising opportunities." She turned around and said to them, "Well, children, if you are looking for rooms for a get-together, you can visit me in Mahlsdorf."[72]

From the mid-1970s onward, the group hosted events in the villa's basement rooms.[73] They were able to organize their Sunday gatherings there as well as larger parties. According to the club's ledger, these events attracted dozens of people, such as the "Autumn Ball" on 22 October 1977, attended by sixty guests, or their Advent party on

4 December 1977, to which forty-five people came.[74] They hosted lectures, poetry readings, and performances such as Hibaré.[75] Sillge recalled a "cabaret – well how should I say it? – men dressed as women."[76] An essay about Mahlsdorf published in *Der Spiegel* in 1992 described how "gays and lesbians bopped and danced like it was 1904."[77]

It is significant, too, that lesbians were involved in the group. As in West German gay groups, men dominated both the group's leadership and the larger body of members. This is not terribly surprising given that the subculture catered almost exclusively to men. Lesbians had few ways of finding each other and certainly nothing resembling the network of cruising places where men could meet. Nonetheless, by 1976 the group's leadership included at least two women, and, according to Stasi records, around twenty women attended its events.[78] In that year fourteen of them decided to found a "branch organization of lesbian women."[79] According to a Stasi report, they did so after one of the men in the group "gave a lecture on lesbian problems," encouraging the group's women to become more involved.[80] Unlike the lesbian groups in the West, however, which often broke off from their male-dominated counterparts because of the misogyny they experienced, lesbians in East Germany founded their own committee in cooperation with the men in the group, of which they remained an integral part.

Insofar as the group's members hoped to create a gay-friendly space within East German society, they had partially succeeded. Mahlsdorf became a relatively well-known centre for gay and lesbian activity in East Berlin, implicitly tolerated by the regime. It was a place where gay men and lesbians could meet, discuss, drink, and dance without fear of persecution or violence. For some members, the group offered their first foray into the gay subculture, such as it existed in East Germany. Those years were, according to Peter Rausch, "the most beautiful time in the group's existence."[81]

Although coordinating social events consumed much of the group's energy, its leadership remained committed to the political goals laid out in the "Plan for a Homosexual Communication Centre." Rausch remembered that even after finding Mahlsdorf, "We wanted our own space, public rooms."[82] The group also aspired to combat anti-gay prejudice, encourage the police to investigate violence against gay people, and demand the right to place personal advertisements in newspapers. While West Germany's gay movement embraced strategies of gay power in the 1970s, its East German counterpart modulated scientific-liberal rhetoric to a socialist key. They hoped to cajole the government into granting them rights and privileges. The regime's complete intolerance of civil society and political opposition left them few other options.

The group's political work often took the form of petition writing, a well-studied phenomenon in East German history.[83] On 12 April 1975, the group submitted a petition to the government to protest the closure of the café Mocca Bar in Hotel Sofia on Friedrichstrasse. The letter insisted that, "It is certainly no secret that, first and foremost, Berlin's homosexual population frequents this coffee shop." It described homosexuals as a "minority" who were "in general not tolerated." In spite of its pugnacious tone, however, the letter also adopted the regime's own Marxist language. It insisted that "because [homosexuals] fulfil equal tasks in labour, they have the right to equitable satisfaction in leisure."[84] On 9 January 1976, another activist wrote to the German Promotional and Advertisement Society (*Deutsche Werbe- und Anzeigengesellschaft* or DEWAG) to protest gay people's inability to publish personal advertisements.[85]

The group also corresponded with medical researchers whom they suspected might sympathize with their cause. Dr Siegfried Schnabl, who directed the marriage and sex counselling centre in Karl-Marx-City, published a magazine article in 1973 titled "Plea for a Minority." The article was a fairly accurate representation of how the regime thought about gay men and lesbians at the time. Schnabl recommended an "easy recipe for dealing with homosexuals: treat them exactly as you would treat any other person, and tactfully ignore their love of the same sex."[86] Not only did Schnabl advocate the kind of know-nothing tolerance that, by the 1970s, the regime seemed perfectly happy to maintain, he even contended that, "Research will someday find a way to obviate homosexuality or to overcome it through therapeutic measures."[87]

While Schnabl's views seem retrograde today, gay people at the time thought them enlightened. The activists in East Berlin believed he might be a useful ally. Rausch wrote to him on 23 August 1976 explaining the group's efforts. He insisted that Schnabl's professional standing could help the group convince the government to allow them to organize officially.[88] When Schnabl replied the next month, however, he parroted the government line. "You all have the right," he wrote to Rausch, "to be treated and respected like every other citizen."[89] He did not offer to help in their fight for government recognition, instead suggesting that they instigate court cases against restaurants and other venues they alleged to have denied them service based on their sexuality. He discreetly ignored that the security services had sanctioned these denials of service.

The group also tried to make the criminal police aware of violence against gay people. In one case, group member Bodo Amelang wrote to officers on 24 June 1978 and described how two men had attacked a gay man near Dimitroffstrasse, a well-known cruising site. As Amelang insisted in his letter, "For the homosexual minority of the East German population there do not yet exist meeting spots fit for humans. These people (myself included) are thus forced to take up bad traditions," such as meeting in unsafe public toilets.[90] When the police replied a few weeks later, they assured Amelang "that the homosexual minority you describe enjoys the same legal protections as all other GDR citizens."[91] Attempts to draw attention to specific problems were met with gaslighting – bureaucrats asserted that those very problems did not exist.

The group's leadership realized that official recognition remained a necessary first step. Such endorsement would make it easier to communicate, to secure space, and to work towards deconstructing animus. Luckily for them, the Honecker regime, as part of its effort to foster a richer civil society, had recently introduced a new civil code and, with it, new regulations regarding the formation of clubs.[92] The new code, which the regime promulgated in 1975, allowed citizens to create interest communities (*Gemeinschaft*) by simply writing up a charter. Members had only to register that document with the appropriate government bureau. That is, the regime seemingly had not reserved the right to approve or disapprove of such a "community of citizens" (*Gemeinschaft von Bürgern*).[93]

Peter Rausch and his compatriots knew about the new law and thought that their group was perfectly suited to its purposes. In 1975 they drafted a charter to form the Homosexual Interest-group Berlin (*Homosexuelle Interessengemeinschaft Berlin* or HIB). The contract adopted statutory language, averring that, "The community has the goal to improve the life conditions of its members through the creation of community-oriented leisure activities."[94] Incorporating would have allowed the group to collect money and rent space for their activities. The regime's new relaxation of social control seemed to have solved their organizational problems.

In January 1976 the group sent the contract to the Berlin Magistrate's office for registration. Yet, on 12 May 1976, a missive appeared from criminal police headquarters directing the Magistrate's office in no uncertain terms that "there can be no social interest served by the foundation of such an association."[95] In a move strikingly similar to how the West Berlin government had treated the Scientific-Humanitarian Committee in the 1950s, the Magistrate's office refused to register the contract, leaving the group in a kind of legal limbo. A month later, three group members met with representatives from the office, who again declined to register their contract.

That meeting with the Magistrate's office had two immediate consequences. First, and unbeknownst to the activists themselves, the office informed the "security organs," a euphemism for the Stasi, of the application.[96] Second, the three members who attended the meeting told their interlocutors that they would not accept the decision. They decided to appeal to higher authorities within the Ministry of the Interior.[97] The following day, 10 June 1976, around the time they started meeting in Mahlsdorf, the group submitted a new petition. It bumbled around within the government and eventually landed at the bureau for Health and Public Services within the Berlin Magistrate. The Ministry of the Interior asked that the department meet with the petitioners and make clear to them that the government would not sanction their organization. Once again, functionaries emphasized that there was no discrimination against gay people in East Germany and that an association would further isolate them from society.[98]

The process of being ping-ponged from one office to another and of having bureaucrats deal with the organization in bad faith left a sour taste in the activists' mouths. A 1977 government report described how the group "was referred from one government office to another and 'fobbed off' by them all with untenable and unscientific arguments."[99] In a separate account, an informant from within the group described how "the conversation" with Magistrate officials "renewed a dim opinion of the GDR's state organs in this matter."[100] The experience eventually caused the group to give up on its quest for state approval. Members saw it as pointless.

Their engagement with the government suggests that the East German state was set up to work in precisely this manner. There exists a mass of scholarship on the Stasi, how it functioned within the East German state, and the ways in which it socially, culturally, and morally coopted large swathes of the East German citizenry. But historians have written far less about how the bureaucracy, specifically the government agencies with which ordinary individuals had to deal on a regular basis, helped to maintain a Janus-faced semblance of legal order, while doing much to ensure that the population remained docile. When scholars mention the bureaucracy, they often maintain that it helped the Democratic Republic forge a semblance of normality by serving citizens in a relatively efficient manner.[101] The HIB's experience suggests that, just as in liberal, democratic states, the bureaucracy could also act sluggishly in order to prevent citizens from exercising their alleged rights.

While the Democratic Republic was neither democratic nor a republic, it did attempt to maintain a façade of republican rule, of the rule of law (the *Rechtsstaat*), and of civil rights – more so than many of its

Eastern-bloc allies. Its 1968 constitution, though it enshrined the dictatorship in its allocation of the republic's "leadership" to "the working classes and their Marxist-Leninist Party," also "guaranteed to all citizens the exercise of their rights."[102] While such guarantees were nothing more than empty propaganda in some socialist countries, East German citizens did enjoy certain liberties.[103] They could avail themselves, for example, of a more than nominally independent Protestant church, of the right to a trial, and of the right to submit petitions to the government. This reality also set the GDR apart from the Nazi dictatorship, whose functionaries railed against the rule of law and dreamed of justice meted out according to the sentiment of the *Volk*.[104]

In order to balance the exercise of these rights against the state's desire for control, East German authoritarianism had to function in a curious way. Although the Stasi was the largest secret police force, per capita, ever created, it did not operate on terror in the same way as had the Gestapo. Ultimately, the East German government wanted to have it both ways: to convince its citizens that they enjoyed fundamental rights while ensuring that they would never use them in a way contrary to the regime's aims. It wanted to be able to cash in its counterfeit democracy for real legitimacy.

In practice this meant allowing each arm of the government to throw up roadblocks to citizen initiatives. The regime spun off mazes of ministries, functionaries, and formalities so dense that the average East German would not have the patience let alone the wherewithal to navigate them. The HIB's experiences suggest that bureaucratic muddle was an effective tool for siphoning off displeasure and regulating behaviour. Acknowledging this facet of East German governance should also make the socialist regime more legible to Western Europeans and Americans, who are accustomed to inefficient bureaucracies. After all, the Federal Republic had treated homophile groups in similar ways in the 1950s. Most of the time, the Stasi, the terror-inducing secret police, was far less an enforcer of this state of affairs than, as Fulbrook argues, the apparatus's central nervous system, shuttling information around and reaching decisions that other arms of the state would ultimately execute.[105] It could also, as it did with gay activism, ensure that the bureaucracy ceased to function for citizens who pressed too hard against the prevailing order.

The State Steps In

Of course, the security services – including both the Stasi itself and K-1, the political branch of the criminal police that also recruited informants

and worked closely under the Stasi's supervision – were already atten-
tive to the threat posed by gay espionage.[106] For that reason officials had
taken an interest in the 1974 communication centre proposal. Again in
1976, the bureaucracies to which activists submitted petitions informed
the security services of the group's existence. Because the secret police
was feared for its alleged omniscience, though, it is striking that it did
not take a systematic interest in the HIB until the group attempted to
register as an interest group in 1976. Between January and June 1976,
different departments within the Stasi and the criminal police produced at least four memoranda and reports regarding the new "centre of homosexual people" in Berlin and what the ministry ought to
do about it.[107] Though each described the problems the group posed
slightly differently, they all shared a handful of concerns and proposed
solutions to them.

Contact with the West caused officials the most worry. After all, the
HIB got its start through interactions with West German gay activists.
These reports noted that, "Among the circle of people there are also
homosexual citizens of West Berlin and capitalist countries" and that
some members even had "relationships with West Berlin homosexuals."[108] Given that contact, and because Western agents had allegedly
been trying to infiltrate the gay subculture for decades, they wondered
whether or not the HIB had aims inimical to the socialist state. Functionaries voiced concern that the group might work "against the state, and
thus [against] the GDR."[109] The anxiety about West German influence
over gay people suggests just how seriously the Stasi took the group.

Two memoranda offered specific recommendations for measures to
restrain the HIB. Of these two, one from 10 June 1976 deserves particular attention because it was sent from the leader of Department VII to
the first deputy minister, that is, to the Stasi's second-in-command. In
the stilted language of the East German bureaucracy, the letter insisted
that, "For a thorough evaluation of the influence of homosexuality
and its problems on our political-operational work, further special-
ized investigations, especially regarding IM work, are required."[110] To
ensure that neither the activists nor their West German friends had
nefarious designs upon the East German state, the department thus recommended recruiting more informants in gay and lesbian circles and
from within the HIB.

Over the course of the decade, the security services succeeded in
doing so. At least six individuals in Berlin and Leipzig helped the
secret police collect information on the HIB in the 1970s. But what did it
mean for these individuals to inform for the secret police? This question
touches on a core question about the East German state. In the years

following the Berlin Wall's fall in 1989, collaboration with the Stasi became a black mark against many German citizens.[111] Around 5 per cent of the population had collaborated with the secret police in some way, and almost everyone knew friends or family members who had passed information to the Stasi at one point or another. In recent years, however, an increasingly robust body of scholarship has looked more closely at the quality of collaboration – what information informants divulged and their reasons for doing so.[112]

While it is certainly easy, at first blush, to denounce any association with the Stasi, examination of the methods of recruitment and the manners of collaboration reveals a far more ambiguous picture. The HIB's desire for official recognition had captured the Stasi's attention. Its contacts with the West caused the Stasi concern that members might become tools of foreign provocation. Still, Stasi officials were not yet convinced that the HIB posed a threat *per se*, nor did they take direct action to prevent the group from meeting privately. The Stasi's desire for information about the group was genuine, and informants played a crucial role in shaping its view of gay activism.

The case of one particularly well-placed IM is illustrative. On 14 April 1975, the informant, code-named "Burgunder," met for the second time with his handlers from the criminal police branch K-1. The file I reviewed does not reveal the specifics of his recruitment, but this second encounter sheds light on the stakes at play for him. "Burgunder" was a member of the HIB, and the handlers were eager for him to provide information about the group's membership and intentions. That April day, however, he complained to his handlers, "that in completing certain assignments" he felt like a "snitch."[113] It was difficult, he explained, for him to justify to himself passing information about his friends.

The officers explained to "Burgunder" that, "The tasks of the security services and collaboration with the population cannot even be compared to 'snitching' in the sense of bourgeois morality." They clearly hoped this clarification would appeal to Burgunder's "political maturity," as he was sympathetic to the SED.[114] "It was pointed out to him," the report elucidated, "that the formation of such a group could also be exploited in the sense of purposes hostile to the state."[115] The officers put Burgunder in a double bind. They appealed to his political sensibilities while also menacing the group to which he belonged. Beneath the agents' reminder that treasonous forces might exploit such a group lurked the threat that they would construe non-cooperation as evidence of such. "Burgunder" was left with little choice other than to collaborate. At the same time, as we will see below, informants such as

"Burgunder" could use their relationship with officers to shape how the Stasi and the criminal police viewed the circles in which they moved.

Security officials were interested in three broad questions. First, following on their work in building gay spy networks in the 1960s, they wanted more information about the gay subculture. IM reports provided rich detail about the bars and parties gay people frequented in the socialist capital.[116] Some IMs also used their reports to underscore the subculture's more dangerous facets. They reported on unsolved crimes with gay victims and pressed the secret police to do something about them. IM "Burgunder" expressed concern to his handlers in November 1976 about two men who regularly cruised public bathrooms at the intersection of Schönhauser Allee and Dimitroffstrasse. Apparently, they would flirt with gay men then "later demand money and threaten violence."[117] In several further reports, he informed officers about violence perpetrated on gay men.[118]

Second, the officials wanted detailed information on HIB members, their friends, and their political leanings, looking for evidence of subversive influence.[119] The HIB was aware of this risk and made every effort to cast their activities in a favourable light. The group wrote petitions in Marxist-Leninist idiom. They spoke about integrating gay people into socialist society. The group's leaders also did everything possible to ensure that individuals whom the state might consider criminally or ideologically suspect not take part in their gatherings. A police report in 1975 conveyed how the group tried "immediately to recognize asocial and criminal individuals and not to admit [them] in the group."[120] Two years later, "Burgunder" reported that two group members were expelled because of their "negative political views."[121] Just as the old homophile reformers in West Germany had emphasized their respectability, so too the HIB excluded members it feared might reflect poorly on its efforts. Other alternative groups in the GDR took similar steps to reassure the regime of their loyalty.[122]

Third, and perhaps most significant, the group's contacts with Westerners took up substantial portions of both IM statements and Stasi records on the HIB. Agents directed one IM "Krüger," for example, to focus "especially on foreigners and West Germans."[123] IM "Kunze," another HIB member, reported in October 1976, that the group consisted of fifty individuals, of whom ten lived in West Berlin. This information, which echoed reports from other informants, not only suggests that there existed substantial cross-pollination of ideas between gay activist circles in East and West Germany but also spurred the Stasi's fear that harmful foreign influences could reach East German society through the gay subculture.

Interestingly, there is evidence that informants' efforts to influence the Stasi's views of homosexuality succeeded. For example, documents produced by security forces in late 1976 and 1977 often mentioned that group members were politically reliable. One police report from August 1977 noted that HIB leaders "endeavoured that no criminal or asocial people are brought" to their meetings.[124] A letter from Berlin police headquarters to the Ministry of the Interior in 1978 indicated that, "It can be estimated that the [HIB], or at least insofar as the so-called leadership is concerned, is composed of progressive citizens (*fortschrittliche Bürger*)."[125] In socialist jargon, this was high praise: a mark of confidence in a citizen's political reliability.

Similarly, the security services began to take violence committed against gay people seriously, perhaps as a result of IM reports. In 1976 a K-1 memo listed seven objectives of their surveillance of the subculture. The sixth in the list read, "Exposure of latent and unknown criminal acts directed against homosexuals (extortion, robbery, and blackmail)."[126] This objective is striking because it marks the first time – to my knowledge – that an East German government document, since the repeal of §175, advocated an explicitly gay-friendly policy. Moreover, it indicates that informants may have been able to shape officials' views of the groups on which they reported. In this case, collaborators seem to have convinced secret police organs that anti-gay crime was a significant problem in need of redress. This shift in policy suggests that collaboration was not always a nefarious act. It could also be a form of productive engagement with authority.

At the same time, certain information exacerbated officials' concerns. Although the police realized that, by 1977, "there [was] no more regular contact with the 'HAW'-Group in West Berlin," it still wanted information about "known and new contacts and connections to capitalist foreign countries."[127] Furthermore, officials fretted about contacts between gay people in different cities within East Germany. As early as 1975 the Stasi had evidence that the activists in Berlin were in communication with gay people in Leipzig, East Germany's second-largest city.[128]

Related to these concerns, Stasi officials also worried about the HIB's growing size. Most reports put the group's leadership at around fifteen and its total membership at about fifty, although officials understood even in early 1976 "that the circle of people who come to any particular event is much larger."[129] By late 1976, the Stasi estimated membership at around two hundred.[130] The activists themselves often stressed the large number of homosexuals – and thus of possible activists – in East Germany as a way of underscoring the magnitude of the problems they described and the potential population served by an institution for gay men and lesbians.

Government documents sometimes adopted their figures. The Berlin Magistrate, for instance, put "the number of people in the capital who are inclined in this way at 40–50,000."[131] To the security services, these numbers spelled danger. Over the course of the decade, fears grew that "the [HIB's] influence on homosexuals and even on other circles is increasing."[132] They even warned that with a critical mass the HIB might begin to win sympathy among heterosexuals. Officers worried that, "The group [wants] to be as strong as possible, precisely by the enlistment of non-homosexual and lesbian circles, in order to enable a certain oppositional position towards functionaries."[133] Ironically, while gay activists in West Germany trumpeted their electoral might but were dismissed by establishment politicians until the very end of the decade, East German activists protested their loyalty to the regime and were instead taken seriously as a potential opposition group.

The camel's back broke in April 1978 when Ursula Sillge decided to "organize a gathering of lesbians" from around the country. She was motivated to do so by the extreme isolation in which most East German lesbians lived. She wrote to those women with whom she had come into contact, who then wrote to their acquaintances in what she described to me as "a snowball system." Though forty women RSVPed for the gathering, more than one hundred would show up from all over East Germany.[134]

One week before the meeting, Sillge was summoned to criminal police headquarters to explain the meeting. She and the police argued for the entire day. By evening, she thought she had convinced them to allow the event to go forward. But the morning of the gathering, she arrived at Mahlsdorf two hours before the other women were due to appear. "There sat two police officers at the entrance to the villa and wouldn't let anyone in," she remembered. She and the other organizer went to the nearby train station, where more than one hundred women were waiting for them. The women split up into different apartments, and the meeting went ahead, albeit under strained circumstances.[135]

Why the criminal police showed up that April morning to cordon off the Mahlsdorf villa is unknown. I found no Stasi records that indicate who made the decision or what motivated them. When IM "Burgunder" reported the event to his handlers a couple of weeks later, there was no indication that they already knew about it. Nonetheless, it heralded the HIB's demise. According to a police report on 26 April 1978, Charlotte von Mahlsdorf, apparently concerned that the group's activities could endanger her museum, "declined to make [her] rooms available anymore."[136] This meant that the HIB had to return to gathering in apartments or attempting to get meeting permits surreptitiously. "We were dispirited," Peter Rausch recalled. "And so, we simply resumed our protest."[137]

This protest took the form of renewed petitions to the government for the right to organize officially. On 22 October 1978, the group wrote directly to the *Volkskammer*. As always, the petition's authors couched their language in socialist rhetoric, contending that the "situation is in no way characteristic of socialism; it belongs to the inheritance of capitalism."[138] As in other petitions, the HIB asked for a leisure and communication centre that would allow for the "well-rounded integration of homosexual workers into socialist society."[139]

Once again, the group's petition disappeared into the bureaucratic labyrinth. The *Volkskammer* replied to Peter Rausch a month later to inform him that it had forwarded the petition to the Ministry of the Interior. A further seven months later, in July 1979, after the HIB had exhausted all other avenues, the *Volkskammer* Secretariat wrote to Peter Rausch. "We hold your view," the letter said, "that the Ministry for Health Care cannot comprehensively process the problems you have raised. We have therefore sent your petition to the Secretariat of the Council of Ministers and asked that they include the other Ministries in the evaluation and coordinate from there."[140]

Two and a half months later, five activists, including Peter Rausch, Ursula Sillge, and Michael Eggert, took a meeting with officials working for the Council of Ministers. In minutes of the meeting, the activists described the get-together as "officious" and noted the platitudes with which the two officials responded to their complaints. They were told that "the state cannot promote homosexuals" and that "all citizens have the same opportunities." The bureaucrats even mentioned a lack of financial resources as a reason why the state could not help the petitioners.[141] Though their reasoning was specious, the message was clear. There was to be no gay liberation in the Democratic Republic. The five activists left the meeting dejected and disheartened. No further attempts were made to resurrect the HIB or to continue the meetings and parties they had hosted for so many years.

The end of the decade left gay activism in the two Germanies in radically different places. In the East, the sole organization, which had claimed no more than a couple of hundred members, closed in the face of government opposition. Although the group's relationship with the socialist state, especially its security organs, casts East Germany in a more nuanced light, in the 1970s the dictatorship proved unwilling even to acknowledge activists' demands. In the West, activist organizations were on the cusp of a major political victory. Activism had not only spread across the Federal Republic but had also fundamentally reshaped queer life there in ways that East German gay men and lesbians could only imagine. Yet the subsequent decade would see, if not a reversal in fortunes, then profoundly unexpected developments in each country. In the West, in spite of the gains of the 1970s, activists began to consider their efforts a failure and to speak of the movement's "stagnation." While the 1980s saw remarkable change, it was a fraught decade for West German gay activists as they navigated life under a new, conservative government, a string of public scandals, and the terrifying advent of AIDS.

8 "I'm Not the Chancellor of the Gays"

Homosexual Politics in 1980s West Germany

On 13 September 1987, *Der Spiegel* reported that Uwe Barschel, the Christian-Democratic leader of West Germany's northernmost state, Schleswig-Holstein, had directed underlings "to snoop on the supposedly 'rakish' sexual life of his 'homosexual' SPD-opponent Björn Engholm."[1] In addition to spying on Engholm, Barschel tried to con the tabloid *Bild* into publishing that his rival had tested positive for HIV.[2] Homosexuality, Barschel wagered, was still detested enough that his shenanigans would discredit Engholm in upcoming regional elections. The so-called Barschel Affair, which caused a national uproar and led the regional parliament to investigate, was one of a handful of gay scandals that coloured West German politics in the 1980s.

Strangely, the incident sparked no major protest from West Germany's gay and lesbian community. In fact, the affair was only one prominent example of what many activists called the "stagnation" of the 1980s.[3] Texts from the era characterize the period as one of quiescence after the raucous 1970s. Activists at the time, and memory today, had a favourite scapegoat: the Beethoven Hall podium discussion. That fiasco, activists later argued, destroyed "the basis for the overarching coordination of the gay groups" and led to the torpor of the 1980s.[4] An article from 1987 described the Beethoven Hall gathering as a "trauma."[5] Later historians have referred to it as a "scandal," a "failure," and a "disaster."[6] "At the beginning of the 80s," historian Martin Reichert wrote, "the movement was paralyzed and faltering."[7] The gathering – and paedophile activists' disruption of it – came to mark an ebb in West German gay liberation efforts. In spite of the wild success of Action '80 and the Free Democrats' electoral gains, 1980 is today remembered as a moment of defeat for West Germany's gay movement.

A closer look at the decade reveals a more complicated picture. In federal politics, it is true, the Free Democrats failed to make good on their campaign promises, sowing cynicism among activists, while a resurgent CDU seized power in 1982. But the movement also inserted itself into institutions of power to such a degree that activists ceased to see the need to organize. The Green Party, cobbled together in 1980 from various social and political efforts, including the gay and lesbian movements, won *Bundestag* seats in 1983, from which it was able to articulate gay and lesbian concerns at a national level. Socially and culturally, the movement remained as active as ever, and the decade saw the rise of new institutions, such as gay museums and new publications. When HIV hit the Federal Republic, the new Christian Democratic government proved remarkably willing to work with gay men and lesbians to halt the virus's spread. While the 1980s did not bring the kind of political liberation that some activists had hoped for, the decade saw remarkable changes that gay men and lesbians could welcome. In taking a second look at the 1980s, this chapter argues that these years reveal a different face of liberation, a social and cultural one no longer tethered to the previous decade's parliamentary political aims.

Political Tremors

The decade began propitiously as voters returned the social-liberal coalition with wide margins. The Free Democrats enjoyed one of their greatest electoral triumphs in West German history, in no small part thanks to gay voters. Moreover, the liberals attempted to make good on the promises that had won them those votes. In coalition talks with Helmut Schmidt's Social Democrats, Hans-Dietrich Genscher, the FDP leader and vice-chancellor, brought up abolition of §175.[8] Meanwhile, action groups around the country continued to exert pressure. At least three wrote to the federal government in 1980, demanding that the coalition honour the FDP's campaign pledge to strike §175 from the criminal code.[9] The General Action in West Berlin took out a half-page advertisement in the *Frankfurter Rundschau*, a major newspaper, on 13 October 1980. The ad insisted that the coalition had won its electoral victory with "votes of homosexual men," its authors evidently ignoring that lesbians also likely voted for the progressive parties. They declared that, "The repeal of §175 must be a component of the coalition agreement."[10]

There was certainly reason enough to think the government would repeal the law. Genscher and his fellow liberals had taken a firm stance on the measure, and the SPD, which had historically backed reform efforts, seemed amenable. But Helmut Schmidt, who as Hamburg senator for the interior between 1961 and 1965 had been responsible for that city's persecution of gay men, would have none of it.[11] In coalition talks between the parties, *Der Spiegel* reported, the chancellor treated the liberals' desire to repeal the statute as "a curiosity" and told the party that they ought to "find another coalition partner" if repeal was so important to them.[12] Sources later claimed that Schmidt even sniped, "I'm not the chancellor of the gays."[13]

The vice-chancellor, who, as the Federal Republic's longest-serving foreign minister, was a fixture in Bonn's political establishment, expressed consternation "with how little sympathy the chancellor could muster for the problem of minorities." A morose Genscher allegedly even reminded Schmidt that homosexuals had suffered in the concentration camps.[14] But to no avail. Repeal was not part of the coalition agreement.[15] The FDP's failure to make repeal a condition of the coalition was the first in a series of events that led lesbians and gay men to shy away from further parliamentary activism.

Over the next two years the FDP enjoined the Social Democrats to reconsider. On 5 May 1981, the liberals conducted a parliamentary inquiry on the question of homosexuality and the criminal code. They invited scholars, activists, and representatives of the churches to testify. The party published documentation from the hearing, and its representatives voted on whether or not the government ought to repeal §175. A large majority advocated repeal, though a handful of highly placed grumps plumped against it.[16] The liberals' tactics put renewed pressure on Schmidt, whose party agreed to hold its own investigations in August 1982. These hearings were the closest the West German *Bundestag* ever came to repealing §175.

At the same time, the social-liberal coalition that had ruled West Germany for thirteen years was fraying. While the utopian *Freiburg Theses* had guided the FDP after 1971, the party took a rightward turn in 1977 with the adoption of the so-called *Kiel Theses*. This new party program, which represented a compromise between the party's economically and socially liberal wings, consecrated the place of the so-called free market in West German society.[17] The liberals' heady identity politics of the late 1970s was, in a sense, a veneer that disguised the party's rightward economic lurch – a tendency that critics of homonormativity and neoliberalism will recognize all too well.[18]

Since the 1980 general election, economic problems had eaten away at the goodwill between Schmidt and the FDP. The breaking point came in mid-1982. The chancellor decided to raise taxes early that year, leading to conflict with his liberal ministers. At the same time, Helmut Kohl, the Christian Democrats' new, moderate leader began making overtures to disgruntled Free Democrats. Eventually, he convinced them to jump ship. On 1 October 1982, the FDP and CDU/CSU ousted Schmidt in a dramatic parliamentary vote and formed a new coalition with Kohl as chancellor. Genscher continued in his roles as foreign minister and vice-chancellor – positions he held until 1992.[19] The new government swung West Germany rightward after almost a decade and a half of centre-left rule. As did Ronald Reagan in the United States and Margaret Thatcher in the United Kingdom, Kohl set West Germany on a new, conservative path. He remained chancellor for sixteen years.

On the question of homosexuality, the new coalition was hostile in a thoroughly unremarkable way. There was never any serious talk of recriminalizing adult homosexuality, although gay activists had certainly feared such a possibility under the arch-reactionary CSU leader Franz Josef Strauß.[20] West Germany never experienced anything like the religious revival that had boosted both anti-gay animus and the electoral chances of the Republican party in the United States. While gay men and lesbians faced a hostile regime, things did not seem particularly worse than they had under Schmidt. Historians have long puzzled over the Kohl government's moderation, seeing 1982 as a watershed that wasn't. The Free Democrats clearly are part of the explanation, their liberalism a tempering influence on the centre-right coalition. Moreover, the cultural changes of the late 1960s and 1970s had not passed the CDU by. Many of the new members of government were of the 1968 generation and had much more socially liberal views than the Adenauer generation of Christian Democrats.[21]

Yet the change in government brought about a change in the Free Democrats themselves. The parliamentary coup cemented the schism within the party between social and market liberals. Up to 20 per cent of its members fled to left-leaning parties. A number of its *Bundestag* deputies voted against the new government, while the party's most illiberal parliamentarians were elevated.[22]

The new justice minister, for example, was Hans Engelhard, a politician who hailed from conservative Bavaria. He was one of the few FDP *Bundestag* members opposed to the repeal of §175. Soon after he assumed the role, *Der Spiegel* noted, he "rejected the legal reforms of the FDP's 1980 electoral program because the intended repeal of the homosexual paragraph 175 [did not] suit him."[23] Any change in the law was decidedly off the table. While the liberal party did not outright renege on its promise to repeal §175, never again did it make reform a priority.[24]

The only bright spot in the early 1980s came from elections that the new government held on 6 March 1983. The FDP's share of the vote sank by about one and a half million, while the Green Party surged by 4 per cent, bringing its representatives into the *Bundestag* for the first time. Some of the votes that propelled the Greens into parliament undoubtedly came from gay men and lesbians disillusioned with the liberals. As a product of the 1970s alternative movements, the Green Party institutionalized gay politics in a way that activists in the previous decade could not have anticipated.

Nonetheless, Schmidt's refusal to countenance §175's repeal, the liberals' turn away from its gay and lesbian constituents, and the new conservative regime left many activists bitterly disappointed with party politics. They had staked their hopes on winning the kinds of victories that the 1980 election seemed to have brought. Their inability to turn electoral gains into policy change led many to scorn the political process. One action group in southwest Germany, for instance, printed a pamphlet before the snap elections in 1983. The flyer considered what each party had to offer gay people. The liberals' recent action, it wrote, "justifies considerable doubt." The Social Democrats arouse "a certain apprehension," and only "gullibility" would get someone to vote for the Greens. The leaflet finally alluded to rumours that CDU Defence Minister Manfred Wörner was gay and sardonically endorsed the conservative party for this reason: "a gay defence minister is better than nothing."[25] Their rationale reveals an undercurrent of cynicism from activists who only a couple of years earlier had believed themselves on the cusp of major parliamentary victories.

Before the 1987 election, which saw gains for both the Greens and the FDP, and kept the coalition in power, *Du & Ich* similarly complained that, "Instead of representing the whole people, [the parties] play a remarkable game: they talk incessantly about 'liberality' and 'protection of minorities,' but only before the election – this is when the wolves don sheep skins and pretend to be tolerant: all, SPD, CDU and FDP." Its author remained sceptical even of the Greens. The reason for his incredulity was clear: "in 1980 there was the FDP, which was genuinely progressive; but they were that way really only for a few months. After the turn [in government] everything was forgotten."[26] The liberal party's betrayal and the country's rightward swerve – much more than the fiasco at the Beethoven Hall – had soured West Germany's gay and lesbian activists on the possibilities of parliamentary politics.

Social and Cultural Growth

It is no surprise, then, that the 1980s saw a decline in overtly political activism. When in 1985 luminaries including Martin Dannecker published a collected volume, *Gay Stirrings – Gay Movements*, it opened with the assertion that "the feeling of stagnation within gay movements is so widespread" that it was time for a book about it.[27] Dorothea R., who had moved to Berlin from southwest Germany in the 1970s and was active in the lesbian movement, remembered that by the mid-1980s, "the high point had passed." Only around twenty people ever came to the Lesbian Action Centre in Berlin anymore.

But such assertions often seem to conceive of political engagement in a particularly narrow way and therefore appear curiously at odds with gay social and cultural developments in the 1980s. Activist groups, which still existed in most West German cities, continued to organize activities like book clubs, gay bowling, lectures, meet-ups for gay fathers, movie nights, and discos.[28] They also offered counselling for gay men and lesbians and programming for those suffering from AIDS.[29] At the time, their members seemed to see many of these activities as political. For instance, a new action group in the university town of Heidelberg that described itself as "a group of politically engaged gays" rolled out a program that consisted primarily of lectures, film weeks, and parties.[30] The movement that had once denounced the gay subculture as an impediment to political change now embraced the "diversity of our subculture, [from] the gay sauna to the gay bookstore."[31]

The subculture had thrived in the 1970s and continued to grow through the 1980s. At least thirty new gay bars opened in West Berlin between 1983 and 1988.[32] By the mid-1980s, gay establishments crowded the blocks around Nollendorfplatz in West Berlin's Schöneberg district (see figure 8.1). The number of bars and saunas in other West German cities also continued to grow. Sylt, a barrier island in the North Sea off the coast of Schleswig-Holstein, was a popular gay tourist destination, akin to Provincetown in the United States. Each summer, gay men flooded the train – *Du & Ich* called it "the Fairy Express" – between Hamburg and the beach resort.[33]

The gay scene did not just include bars, saunas, and discos, though. An increasingly diverse array of cultural institutions sprang up around the country. Activists founded organizations dedicated to the preservation of queer history, including West Berlin's Gay Museum (which got its start in 1984), Lesbian Archive (1980), and Magnus Hirschfeld Society (1982), and Cologne's Centre for Gay History (1984). Black lesbian poet Audre Lorde took up a visiting professorship at the Free University Berlin in 1984. As Tiffany Florvil shows, Lorde helped launch West Germany's Black feminist movement, which also took up the struggles of Black German lesbians.[34] Gay and lesbian activists collaborated in the summer of 1984 on a major exhibit at West Berlin's Märkisches Museum. Titled *Eldorado*, it explored gay and lesbian

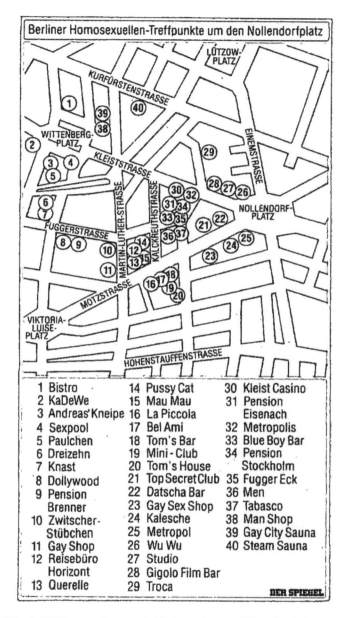

Figure 8.1. A 1985 map of gay establishments near West Berlin's
Nollendorfplatz. © DER SPIEGEL 5/1985. Source: "Plötzlich stirbst du ein
stück weit," *Der Spiegel*, 5/1985, 181

history in Germany between 1850 and 1950, one of the first such exhibits in history.[35] Pride demonstrations – now called "Christopher Street Day" or "Stonewall Demonstrations" after the 1969 Stonewall riots in New York City – continued to take place in most major cities.[36] Personal advertisements continued to play an important role in gay socialization, especially for those who, in the words of one man from Duisburg, "don't like gay discos."[37] These new institutions and expanding opportunities showed a genuine commitment to diversifying gay and lesbian social, intellectual, and cultural life as well as a fundamental rethinking of what activism meant.

Of course, violence continued to plague the subculture. Stories of street thugs attacking gay people peppered magazines and the memories of my oral sources. Georg R., who had been convicted under §175 as a teenager, remembered that once, while he was cruising Preußenpark in West Berlin, "two young men came up to me and wanted to thrash me." Chuckling to himself, he recalled, "But they made the calculation without me in mind. I walloped one after the other."[38] Around the same time, two young men attacked the owner of a gay bar in Hamburg, robbing him of 2,000 DM.[39] In 1983, a gay student at West Berlin's Free University discovered bathroom graffiti depicting a gay man, tied up and blindfolded, being shot by a firing squad. Underneath were the words "the solution to the gay question!"[40]

Gay people remained wary of the police. Homophile groups had once tried to build trust between law enforcement and West Germany's gay population. Articles from the early 1970s encouraged gay men to report crimes to the authorities, insisting that, "Homophiles should finally give up their misplaced dread of the police."[41] Activists had believed legal reform would usher in a new era of cooperation with officers. Yet 1980 shattered that illusion too. On 1 July of that year, gay men and lesbians, led by activist and Green Party politician Corny Littmann, "battered down the mirror in the public bathroom on Spielbudenplatz in St. Pauli [in Hamburg]. They discovered a room with a person." The two-way mirror had allowed officers to spy on men cruising for sex in the toilet.[42] In the ensuing scandal – labelled the "Mirror Affair" by the *Hamburger Abendblatt* – it surfaced that the Hamburg police had similar installations in seven other bathrooms and maintained a list of 2,000 gay men, known as a "pink list."[43]

In subsequent years, West Germany's gay periodicals published story after story about other cities' pink lists and police raids. Officers gave them plenty to write about: between 24 February and 3 March 1982, for example, police stormed eight gay bars thirteen times in West Berlin, alongside searches of public bathrooms at the Berlin Siegessäule

(Victory Column) and Wittenbergplatz.[44] A raid in Hanover raised hackles around the country: sixty police officers descended on five gay bars there on the night of 20 July 1984. While officers justified the sweep as necessary to protect youth from homosexuality, older patrons compared the raids unfavourably to the GDR and to the Nazi era. One grumbled it was "as with Adolf."[45] In a 1985 article titled "The Snitches Are among Us!," *Du & Ich* reported on the regularity with which police continued to raid gay bars. "Every homosexual is a potential criminal," the magazine protested: "this is the police's motto."[46]

Many gay men and lesbians still perceived the subculture as a "ghetto" from which they hoped to escape. Of the scores who moved to West Germany's metropolises from small towns and rural villages across the country, one named Frank told *Der Spiegel* in 1985 that he had come to the gay "mecca" of West Berlin full of hope for a new life of "freed sexuality." "His dreams did not come true," *Der Spiegel* reported: "Instead of grand camaraderie, continued loneliness. Mounting isolation in the midst of the diversity of opportunity, the typical pleasures, the water sports in the 'steam saunas' or the quick standing fucks at Tom's."[47] For all that was still wrong in gay everyday life, however, the subculture's possibilities expanded in the Cold War's final decade. While some activists may remember a period of stagnation, the work of liberation continued.

The Kießling Affair

On 5 January 1984, *Süddeutsche Zeitung*, one of West Germany's largest centre-left newspapers, reported that Minister of Defence Manfred Wörner had abruptly relieved four-star general Günter Kießling of his duties. The newspaper alleged that conflicts between Kießling, who served as deputy Supreme Allied Commander of NATO, and both Wörner and US Supreme Allied Commander General Bernard Rogers had led to his sacking. But the next day, the tabloid *Bild* divulged that rumours of Kießling's homosexuality had triggered his removal.[48]

The outcry was immediate. Kießling went on the offensive, giving interviews in major newspapers. He denied the allegations of homosexuality, and his lawyer sued the government for slander and attempted blackmail. He insisted on a military disciplinary hearing to clear him of the charges.[49] In the *Bundestag*, politicians demanded explanations, in particular of the government's tactics while investigating the general. A formal inquiry was launched later that month. Over its course, which the press covered in painstaking detail, it became clear that the entire affair had begun in July of the previous year. That summer, mandarins

in the Defence Ministry had discovered that Kießling was allegedly seen holding hands with a colonel. The sighting spawned the rumour that he was gay, which in turn led to Bernard Rogers's refusal to meet with him.[50]
Fretting bureaucrats had then tasked the Military Counterintelligence Service with examining the accusation. Agents asked the Cologne criminal police to investigate whether or not anyone in the city's gay subculture knew the general. Officers took a photograph of Kießling to Café Wüsten and Tom-Tom, both Cologne gay bars, and showed it to patrons and employees there. At the former, the barkeep claimed Kießling had regularly spent time there ten or twelve years ago. At Tom-Tom, the bartender recognized him as "a member of the army with the first name 'Günter.'" Through a bureaucratic game of telephone, the bartender's identification morphed into the accusation that, "General Kießling was identified as a regular visitor of the Cologne homosexual scene; he also bought rent boys there."[51]

A counterintelligence report that December described Kießling as a homosexual who cavorted in "the rent boy/criminal scene." It continued, "because homosexuals are targets of enemy intelligence services," the general posed a security risk.[52] Though the language echoed West Germans' older obsession with gay conspiracies, the military's principal concern was now blackmail. Parliamentary reports and newspapers fretted that gay officers were blackmail targets for enemy spies, even though Green politicians noted that the government itself could not provide any evidence of a link between homosexuality and blackmail.[53]

The allegations against Kießling came at a time of heightened Cold War anxiety. Soviet troops had marched into Afghanistan on Christmas Eve 1979, marking an end to the period of détente. The following year, Ronald Reagan won the American presidential election in a landslide and set the United States on a more confrontational course with the Soviet Union. In 1983, NATO deployed Pershing II nuclear missiles in West Germany – a decision that occasioned groundswells of protest in both East and West Germany.[54] Relations with NATO and the US government were more significant than ever in the early 1980s. Kohl's government certainly did not want to antagonize the American NATO commander with an allegedly queer deputy.

Although Wörner – who himself had faced accusations of homosexuality – removed Kießling in December 1983, General Kießling's counteroffensive was successful.[55] It brought parliament into chaos and even threatened Kohl's grip on power.[56] By mid-January, the chancellor decided that Kießling would have to be rehabilitated. On 1 February 1984, Wörner restored Kießling to his position, from which he retired with full honours two months later.

As far as the main political parties were concerned, this settled the matter. Although the parliamentary investigation continued for four more months, its final report, endorsed by the three traditional parties – SPD, CDU/CSU, and FDP – only noted that military counterintelligence would have to agree to more robust oversight in the future. It did not vigorously dispute that sexual behaviour might constitute a legitimate security threat.[57] In spite of the Social Democrats' and the liberals' sometimes progressive rhetoric on gay issues, when push came to shove, both parties viewed gay men as second-class citizens (also, presumably, lesbians, although the West German military still excluded women from most positions).[58]

That is precisely how West Germany's gay community interpreted the scandal. For most West Germans, the affair had revolved around the intelligence service's abuse of power. But to gay men and women, the "unhappy Kießling/Wörner Affair" had led to "a growing climate of intolerance against us homosexuals," as one Franz M. wrote in a petition to the federal government in 1984.[59] Likewise, an assembly of gay action groups from around the country published a critique of the scandal in *Du & Ich* in April 1984. They wrote, "Kießling is 'rehabilitated,' Wörner remains – but what will happen to the homosexuals?"[60]

In opposition to the larger parties, Green politicians used the scandal to cast light on the problems still facing West Germany's lesbian and gay population. For months, Green *Bundestag* members quizzed Defence Ministry officials about the place of homosexuality in the army. Thanks to their efforts, it became clear that the military actively discriminated against gay soldiers. During questioning on 19 January 1984, the defence minister's parliamentary state secretary maintained that gay GIs were only discharged when their sexuality limited their "ability to integrate." Yet he admitted that an officer's homosexuality "diminishes his official authority, and sometimes gravely endangers military discipline and can hurt the force's reputation."[61] As *Der Spiegel* put it shortly thereafter, "if a homoerotic inclination is discovered, one's career is ended."[62]

In *Bundestag* speeches, Green politicians lambasted the large parties in sardonic tones. Joschka Fischer, a future foreign minister, gave an incensed speech on 8 February 1984. In the eyes of the government, Kießling must have been "an attack on the moral foundations of our democracy," Fischer proclaimed. But the true security risk, he sarcastically noted, "lies in the endangerment of the deterrence doctrine. How could one have stood before the Warsaw Pact with a gay deputy Supreme Commander?"[63] Only such absurdly outdated ideas, in Fischer's view, could have justified Kießling's dismissal.

It came as no surprise that, when the commission investigating the Kießling Affair released its report on 13 June 1984, the Green Party published its own minority report. Its account battered both the army and the political establishment for how each had handled the events and ridiculed the fact that the army viewed consenting adult homosexuality as a security risk.[64] The Greens' objections did nothing to change the military's policy vis-à-vis homosexuality or to reorient the scandal into a national conversation about lingering anti-gay animus. But it proved that the party was far more dedicated to gay political priorities than the Free Democrats had ever been.

The decade's scandals, alongside the continued police raids and pink lists, all pointed to a resurgence of anti-gay animus in West Germany. In fact, researchers at the time found that the number of West Germans who thought homosexuality was "very bad or somewhat bad" rose from 28 per cent of the population in 1982 to 35 per cent in 1987.[65] Unlike the rhetoric of the 1950s and 1960s, however, the language of the 1980s had little to do with anxieties surrounding West Germany's legitimacy or stability. The Republic had proved itself durable. Rather, right-wing revanchism provided an opening for anti-gay stereotypes to creep back into everyday discourse. The CDU and CSU, in particular, employed animus as a dog whistle to cast their foes as outside the social and political mainstream and thereby solidify their own support.

Perhaps most astonishing is that Kohl's government did not wield anti-gay animus as aggressively as did Margaret Thatcher's or Ronald Reagan's governments to gin up support. In 1986, for instance, the UK Conservative party promulgated a new law banning local governments and schools from promoting homosexuality, while the US Republican party intentionally ignored the AIDS crisis in the United States for six years.[66] Likewise, there was no moral backlash in the Federal Republic comparable to that in the United States.[67] Under Kohl, casual prejudice in politics and society was on the rise, but the federal government never took such blatantly discriminatory action, which counter-intuitively may have deprived the movement of any external impetus for more overt political activism. This curious dynamic is illustrated most clearly in the government's response to AIDS, in which prompt and technocratic action from national and regional bureaucrats staved off the kind of mass suffering experienced in other Western countries.

The AIDS Crisis

Death came to the Federal Republic in 1982. Acquired Immunodeficiency Syndrome (AIDS) is a disease of the immune system caused by the Human Immunodeficiency Virus (HIV), which attacks white blood cells. The virus is transmitted through contact with infected bodily liquids, which puts intravenous drug users, haemophiliacs, and men who have unprotected anal sex at heightened risk of acquiring it. Once HIV has destroyed enough white blood cells, the body is left open to any number of diseases.

As it had in the United States, the disease spread fear and confusion.[68] On 6 June 1983, a year after the first cases appeared in West Germany, *Der Spiegel* printed its now-infamous AIDS cover (see figure 8.2). It depicted two naked men fondling each other behind the headline "Deadly Pestilence: AIDS: The mysterious illness." The lead article, accompanied by images of plagues past, including the Black Death, smallpox, and an artistic depiction of death playing a fiddle, amplified the terror that had already gripped the nation, a panic reflected in some politicians' responses to the crisis.[69]

The Christian Socialists, who governed the southern state of Bavaria, and their pugilistic leader Franz Josef Strauß seized on the disease as an opportunity to enact reactionary social policies. Culture Minister Hans Zehetmair and State Secretary Peter Gauweiler (called "black Peter" for his role in the epidemic) used fear to justify draconian new health policies.[70] Horst Seehofer, who eventually rose to lead the CSU, suggested bringing HIV-positive people into "special homes."[71]

By 1987 the Bavarian government had given itself the power to forcibly test those it suspected of infection (it employed this provision against people as young as fourteen and as old as eighty-four). It compelled foreigners with the disease to leave. It required prisoners and applicants for public positions to take HIV tests. Zehetmair was particularly prone to inflammatory outbursts, seething at one point that homosexuals belonged to a "periphery of decadence" that needed to be "thinned out" by the disease.[72]

Unsurprisingly, the epidemic and Bavaria's response to it terrified gay West Germans. Not only were they dying of an unknown, incurable (and, until 1985, untestable) disease, but conservative politicians seemed hell-bent on using it to stamp out the subculture built in the 1970s. So incensed were some gay West Berliners at *Der Spiegel*'s fear mongering that they founded a new gay magazine, *Siegessäule* ("Victory Column," named for the phallic monument at the centre of Berlin's Tiergarten) and banned *Spiegel* editors from gay establishments.[73] Gay magazines printed article after article about the disease, urging readers, "We must protect ourselves against AIDS and the political consequences."[74]

In a decade of anti-gay scandals, no scandal occupied more bandwidth than the epidemic. It was unexpected, then, that none of my oral

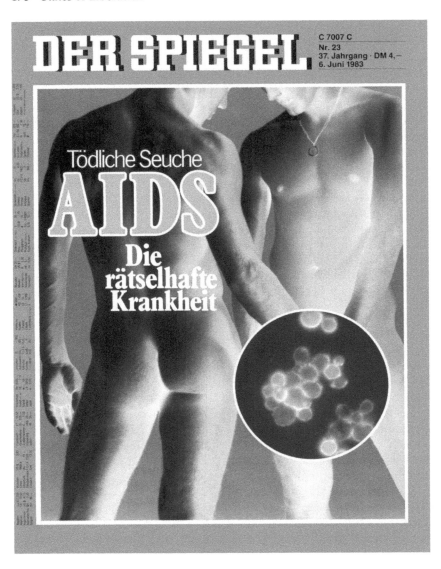

Figure 8.2. *Der Spiegel*'s infamous AIDS cover from 6 June 1983.
© DER SPIEGEL 23/1983

sources had much to say about it. Most of them did not mention AIDS of their own volition, waiting for me to bring the topic up. When, at the end of our interview, I asked Volker K. about the disease, he paused and said, "Yes, well what do I think of AIDS? I think it's not good!"[75] Of course, he knew people who had died from the disease. But it was not a prominent memory. In fact, while most people I interviewed knew victims, they either said or implied that, as Dorothea R. recalled, "it was a theme that was somewhat further away."[76] It did not always leave the same kinds of mental scars on West Germans as it did on American gay men.[77]

Even more curious, the disease did not spawn anything resembling the gay political movement that it unleashed in the United States or in other Western countries.[78] The AIDS crisis, and the Reagan government's malicious neglect of it, ignited the contemporary American gay rights movement, which would eventually command mammoth financial resources, membership, and political clout. West Germany experienced nothing remotely comparable.

What accounts for this apparent paradox? AIDS was undoubtedly a dominant topic for West Germans, homo- and heterosexual alike, in the 1980s. Gay people were terrified that the regime would use it to stoke popular hatred and take away their rights. Yet in the final accounting, it had less of an impact on how gay people there lived or how they related to their government.

The main reason was luck. If gay men were unlucky that Bavaria's government used the disease to stoke animus, they were extraordinarily lucky that representatives of the Christian Democrats' moderate wing occupied two key offices in West Berlin and Bonn. In West Berlin, Ulf Fink had filled the role of health and social senator since 1981. In that position, he directed financial resources to gay people who had organized to spread information about the disease in the early 1980s.[79]

More significant, in 1985, an unassuming pedagogy professor from Dortmund named Rita Süßmuth became federal health minister.[80] In stark opposition to her CSU colleagues, she set upon a course of education, hoping to halt the disease's spread and to ratchet down public fear. Her ministry distributed some 27 million pamphlets about AIDS to West German homes in 1985. "I hope that through our mailers, which are going to all households," Süßmuth told Der Spiegel in an October 1985 interview, "some of the fear will be massively dismantled." She refused to give in to pressure to force the infected to register with the government or to implement a quarantine.[81]

Fink and Süßmuth put gobs of government money behind AIDS education and safer sex campaigns, organized in conjunction with lesbian and gay activists. In the early 1980s, AIDS self-help groups sprang up in West Germany's major cities. By 1985, there were chapters in West Berlin, Munich, Cologne, Hamburg, and Frankfurt am Main.[82] They distributed information about safer sex and how the disease spread. Action groups also redirected their efforts toward AIDS education and outreach. As Dorothea R. recalled, "A lesbian counselling centre was founded and there were informational events, including about HIV and lesbians."[83]

Ulf Fink's efforts brought initial funding to the West Berlin *AIDS-Hilfe*. In 1985 the *Deutsche AIDS-Hilfe* (German AIDS Help, which still exists today) was founded as a partnership between the local self-help organizations and the federal government. Its funding, which came from the Federal Centre for Health Education, within Süßmuth's ministry, swelled from 300,000 DM in 1985 to 7 million DM in 1987.[84] The lucre was a boon to the groups and made it possible to spread information widely. "Money," Ralf Dose recalled, "flowed into the scene for the first time." While it made it possible to fight the disease, Dose sighed, "There was a tendency really to subordinate everything else to the AIDS question." What was left of the gay movement, he said, became an "AIDS movement."[85] While too sweeping a formulation, Dose's memory captures the fact that the new AIDS groups were focused specifically on getting information about the disease into the hands of queer people.

By any measure, those efforts were a success. Compared to those in other developed countries, West German infection rates fell precipitously after 1983. The United States, for example, had seven times as many new cases per capita as West Germany in 1985. By 1989 it was eleven times as many.[86] The even-handed approach that the *AIDS-Hilfe* pioneered and that Süßmuth's Health Ministry adopted meant gay individuals were provided with information about safer sex while the straight population (outside of Bavaria, at least) did not succumb to the mass hysteria that gripped the United States. As *Der Spiegel* reported in 1984,

"Every AIDS patient receives visitors, every one," Professor Pohle reported. The AIDS helpers, who are ready to visit the abandoned, have in this regard almost nothing to do. If this will change, as it has in the USA? There, firemen, the police, and nurses refused to do their duty for AIDS patients. "There is no hysteria here among caregivers," said Frau Professor Eilke-Brigitte Helm […] "and there will not be."[87]

Moreover, panic of the sort that took hold of gay communities in other countries did not in West Germany. Yes, there was fear, but that fear never turned gay people against each other as it did elsewhere.

In New York City, for instance, noxious debates over promiscuity and sexual liberation rent early responses to AIDS.[88] Larry Kramer, a prominent gay intellectual, saw the disease as the ultimate vindication of his condemnation of gay hedonism.[89] Randy Shilts, author of the first major English-language history of the AIDS crisis took much the same line, blaming 1970s licentiousness for HIV's advance.[90] As Richard McKay subsequently demonstrated, Shilts unfairly blamed Gaétan Dugas, often referred to as "Patient Zero," and his alleged promiscuity for the disease's spread.[91]

In West Germany there were some debates about safer sex. Martin Dannecker and Rosa von Praunheim publicly broke on the question, the filmmaker denouncing the "motto of the sex scientists" that it is "better to die than reduce the amount of sex."[92] But campaigners, including Dannecker, mostly took the line that safer sex could also be promiscuous sex.[93] Gay bathhouses, which authorities closed in other countries, remained open in West Germany.[94] The panic that gripped other European nations, even Sweden and the Netherlands, turned countries that had once boasted hedonistic subcultures into prudish deserts. Only in 2015, more than three decades after the crisis, Reichert notes, did Sweden's first gay sauna reopen.[95] In contrast, *Deutsche AIDS-Hilfe* posters proudly trumpeted the pleasures of gay sex with vivid, pornographic images (see figures 8.3.a-d).[96] While conservatives such as Peter Gauweiler tried to paint these efforts as "pathetic propaganda leaflets" and "a bad joke," AIDS workers stood by them.[97] Gay men were going to have sex, they reasoned, and it was better if it were safe.[98]

Ultimately, the level-headed response of West Germany's health officials and gay communities staved off the worst of the plague. AIDS brought death, it brought suffering, and it brought fear. But through happenstance of personnel and policy, it never became the kind of consciousness-altering watershed that it would in other countries. While the AIDS memoir is a staple of American gay literature, characterized by its heart-wrenching accounts of preventable suffering, it is telling that the most famous such work to come out of West Germany is a satire titled *Pigs Must Be Naked*.[99]

Ironically, the Federal Republic's exemplary response to the epidemic deepened activists' withdrawal from overt political agitation. The AIDS campaign's relative success turned the gay community away from political activism. Ralf Dose affirmed that it made what was left of the movement "no longer society-changing."[100] On the one hand, this was a sign of undeniably welcome change. Gay people were worth enough in society's and the government's view to save them from the plague: in this regard they were recognized as full citizens. On the other

Figure 8.3.a. *Deutsche AIDS-Hilfe* safer sex poster from 1985: "Living consciously. Sexuality has many possibilities. Safer Sex means, using his imagination. And the condom."

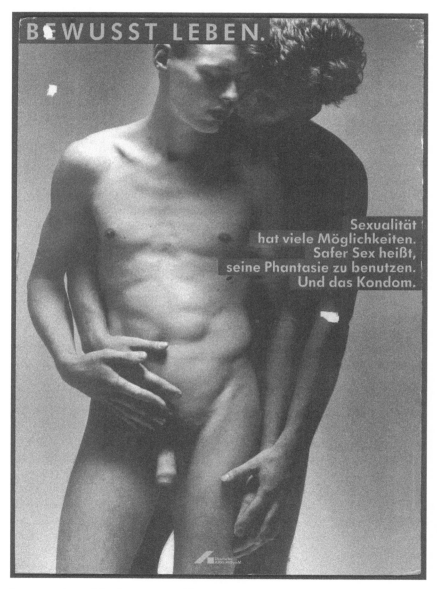

Image courtesy of the Department of Special Collections, Stanford University Libraries (SLSC). SLSC, M1463, Stop Aids Project Records, Series 4, Map Folder 16, Item 2, "Bewusst Leben," photographed by Will McBride, graphics by Detlev Pusch. © Deutsche AIDS-Hilfe

Figure 8.3.b. *Deutsche AIDS-Hilfe* safer sex poster from 1985: "Sweating Spraying Safer Sex"

Image courtesy of the Department of Special Collections, Stanford University Libraries. SLSC, M1463, Stop Aids Project Records, Series 4, Map Folder 14, Item 2, "Schwitzen Spritzen Safe Sex." © Deutsche AIDS-Hilfe

Figure 8.3.c. *Deutsche AIDS-Hilfe* safer sex poster from 1985: "Everyone has his thing. We don't know what the Health Minister recommends. We advise using dildos and whips with only *one* partner."

Image courtesy of the Department of Special Collections, Stanford University Libraries. SLSC, M1463, Stop Aids Project Records, Series 4, Map Folder 13, Item 3, "Jeder hat so sein Ding," photographed by J. Mang, graphics by trash line design. © Deutsche AIDS-Hilfe

Figure 8.3.d. *Deutsche AIDS-Hilfe* safer sex poster from 1985: "Just here? But *of course!*"

Image courtesy of the Department of Special Collections, Stanford University Libraries. SLSC, M1463, Stop Aids Project Records, Series 4, Map Folder 13, Item 8, "Gleich Hier?" photographed by Ingo Taubhorn, graphics by Wolfgang Mudra. © Deutsche AIDS-Hilfe

186 States of Liberation

hand, the government's response forestalled the kind of broad-based coalition building into which gay activists in the United States were forced in the 1980s. More than any other event of the West German 1980s, the handling of the AIDS crisis is an illustration of the messy path that which we call progress usually takes. Advance in one realm is not only not accompanied by development in another but is sometimes even detrimental to it. There is no teleology of liberation.

The Greens and the End of the Decade

Scandal defined the West German gay political experience of the 1980s. AIDS, along with the Barschel, Kießling, and Hamburg Mirror Affairs, alienated gay men and lesbians from the political process and, in some ways, re-entrenched anti-gay animus. The activist-historian Michael Holy wrote in 1985 of AIDS and Kießling that, "vis-à-vis both phenomena, organized homosexuals could not fashion anything resembling an adequate response."[101] Though the events legitimated social prejudice, they never sparked profound backlash among gay men or lesbians, in stark contrast to events in other Western countries in the same period.

Yet in another regard, the 1970s bequeathed gay and lesbian activists a far more prominent and powerful political mouthpiece in the form of the Green party. It had become the first new, major party to win seats in the *Bundestag* since the country's founding in 1949. Its representatives stood for a novel kind of progressive politics. The Greens, for instance, elected the first openly gay *Bundestag* member, thirty-four-year-old Herbert Rusche, in October 1985.[102] He got his start in the gay movement as a teenager, helping to found the group Homo Heidelbergensis in Heidelberg. Two months after the start of Rusche's parliamentary career, he gave an impassioned address to the *Bundestag*, advocating for the reform of §175 and describing himself to his colleagues as "homosexual."[103]

In the late 1980s, the Greens – in particular Rusche and two female members, Jutta Oesterle-Schwerin and Angelika Beer – peppered the regime with questions, investigations, and proposed laws related to homosexuality in the Federal Republic. Not only did the party issue its own report on the Kießling Affair, but it also pressed Kohl's regime on whether gay victims of Nazism could apply for reparations (they could not), the question of employment discrimination against gay and lesbian citizens, the existence of police pink lists, the use of gay denunciations as a political tool, and the repeal of §175.[104]

To the extent that the Green party's electoral successes were successes of the gay movement, they also illustrated its new phase. With their interests represented, gay people undoubtedly felt less inclined to organize politically. In fact, as Corny Littmann, the Green party politician and leader of the Hamburg action group HAH, lamented in 1985, "The electoral alliance with the '*Bunten*' and the 'Greens,' that whole parliamentary line. That was really the end of the HAH as a group."[105] The party itself realized this fact. At times it practically begged gay and lesbian citizens to rediscover their revolutionary zeal. In a press release on 10 July 1985, announcing its ultimately unsuccessful bill to repeal §175, the party exhorted, "We still warn against too great a fixation on parliament and advise instead more individual initiative [...] lesbians and gay men, rise up!"[106] That is, the feeling of stagnation was, perhaps, merely the result of greater representation. Gay and lesbian activists had begun, to adopt the words of the 68ers, their own long march through the institutions.[107]

Moreover, the anti-gay animus of the 1980s was not a reprise of that from the 1950s and 1960s. The Nazi past no longer defined it. Rather, it was a weak reflection of an attitude that was spreading across other Western countries. It was abetted by the rise of conservatism in West Germany and the gay movement's retreat in party politics. West Germany never again experienced the kind of storm surge of gay political activism that had defined the 1970s. That high-water mark had passed. But the decade was also marked with profound and welcome change. The subculture continued to expand, as activists founded a new array of institutions catering to gay men's and lesbians' intellectual and social needs. The political impetuses of the movement found new voice in the Green party, and even the Christian Democratic Union worked with activists to stop the wildfire spread of HIV. Far from a decade of stagnation, the 1980s pointed to new forms of liberation, to new partnerships and ways of being that continue to characterize queer life in Germany today.

At the same time, gay West Germans' gaze also wandered eastward. Across the Iron Curtain, change seemed to have finally arrived in the Democratic Republic. Precisely what that change was did not immediately become clear to those in the West. Yet by the mid-1980s, more and more articles in mainstream and gay publications alike were reporting that the dictatorship was becoming friendlier toward gay men and lesbians.[108] As these reports multiplied, gay people in the West began travelling to the East. The *Spartacus International Gay Guide*, which earlier in the decade had described the East German subculture as one defined by "oppression," wrote in 1988, "The gay scene in East Germany is beginning to develop [...] Homosexuality is gradually becoming a topic suitable for discussion within the media, and the socialist government is in favour of more tolerance from the general population."[109] An ever-increasing number of Westerners travelled to the East to experience the subculture there, some finding its insular, friendly atmosphere preferable to the commercialized scene in the West. As one twenty-four-year-old man wrote to *Du & Ich* in 1985, "I would really like to spend my vacation this year in the GDR. Who can give me the addresses of people around my age (24)?"[110]

Norton G. is a gay American man who studied in West Berlin in the autumn of 1985, the year after he graduated from college in Massachusetts. During his time in the divided city, he travelled to the eastern capital about once a week to see friends, and he got to know the scene of gay locales on Schönhauser Allee. Norton recalled that, "It was becoming common in East Berlin for there to be gay nights at discos and other kinds of opportunities for gay men." The bars were becoming "more explicitly gay places." He also had the sense that while "in the West there was certainly harassment and violence against gay men," the East German government had "a much lower tolerance for any kind of, you know, violence or harassment of gay people."[111] He was not wrong, for much had changed in the socialist republic.

9 A Golden Age in the Grey Republic

Liberation and the Stasi in East Germany

East Germany was an extraordinary place for gay people in the 1980s. The decade saw the emergence of a second liberation movement, which pursued strategies that diverged from the 1970s activists' non-confrontational stance. Then, in the middle of the decade, the state suddenly began to promulgate new policies similar to those demanded by activists. The last years of the 1980s saw an exponential growth in new opportunities, social tolerance, and gay-friendly legislation.

That East Germany adopted these policies in the late 1980s is known among German scholars and activists alike. Peter Rausch, the HIB founder, described the period to me as a gay and lesbian "turning point (*Wende*)" that occurred several years before the *Wende* that ended in Germany's 1990 reunification.[1] The late historian Hans-Georg Stümke called the changes a "radical rupture."[2] Activist Eduard Stapel relates some of the reforms in his monograph, as do Ursula Sillge in her book on lesbians in East Germany and historian Günter Grau in an article on gay activism and the Stasi.[3] But no work has yet explained how the changes came about or what precisely spurred the dictatorship to act.

This chapter offers a comprehensive history of the 1980s gay movement in East Germany, looking to understand how the regime's policy changes came about and to place these events in the broader context of the history of homosexuality in Cold War Germany. Ironically, writing this history is possible precisely because of the East German state's massive surveillance apparatus and the records it collected on activist movements. This chapter is based on thousands of pages of documents from the Stasi archive as well as oral histories and published documents, which are especially useful in verifying the information contained in the Stasi records. Piecing these sources together reveals a remarkable story of gay activism – and its success – in an oppressive surveillance state.

Organizing in the Church

In the years immediately after the HIB's 1979 demise, very little changed for gay East Germans. In the early 1980s, however, a new kind of activist group emerged. In what might seem like *déjà vu*, a theologian named Eduard Stapel met a man named Christian Pulz in autumn 1981 in a public toilet in Leipzig. Much as Peter Rausch and Michael Eggert had done almost a decade before, they eventually "came to talk about the difficult situation of gays" in their country. Soon thereafter, they started meeting at private apartments with a "gaggle of gays," in Stapel's words – nine in total, according to Stasi records – to discuss those concerns.[4]

Several months later, in January 1982, the Evangelical Academy of Berlin-Brandenburg hosted a conference about the problems of gay men in socialist society.[5] The meeting heartened Pulz and Stapel, and on 25 April 1982, their group organized as a "homosexual working circle" under the umbrella of the Leipzig Evangelical Student Congregation, a branch of East Germany's Protestant (Evangelical) church. This was the first gay organization to surface in East Germany since the HIB.[6]

To understand the significance of Pulz and Stapel's decision to mobilize under religious auspices, we must take a brief detour through the history of the East German dictatorship's relationship with the Protestant church. The church, actually a loose union of eight regional churches, was the only institution in the country that could claim any genuine independence from the regime. In the Second World War's immediate aftermath, the church, which then claimed 15 million members from East Germany's 17 million citizens, was exempted from the various land reforms instituted under Soviet occupation. The state never subjected it to the same institutional takeovers that befell other mass organizations.[7] In the GDR's "thoroughly dominated society (*durchherrschte Gesellschaft*)," the church represented a singular island of autonomy.[8]

While the regime never wiped away religious institutions, it did discriminate against practising Christians and introduced secular alternatives to religious ceremonies. It used the church as a sort of catchall vent for dissent. For those who had aroused the regime's ire, theology was often the only educational path available.[9]

Over the course of the GDR's existence, the church grew closer to the state. In 1969 it formally split from the West German Protestant church and in 1978 entered into a concordat with the dictatorship. The agreement of 6 March 1978 legitimized the church's role in East German society, acknowledged its independence, and gave it, among other things, the task of "providing social services and integrating marginal groups."[10] At the same time, the church conceded socialism's legitimacy and permanence. By the late 1970s the government had more or less succeeded in co-opting the church into its system of rule. For all its independence, the church hierarchy was riddled with Stasi informants, its leadership under the SED's influence. Yet the 1978 accord, the church's formal independence, and its loose structure gave oppositional groups, such as the GDR's peace and environmental movements, a chance to coordinate under its roof in ways the regime would never have otherwise allowed.

For Stapel and Pulz, this meant that where the HIB had relied on the state's tacit cooperation to survive, their group could meet without so much as applying for a permit. Their working circle began hosting activities that regularly drew crowds of 50 to 60 people.[11] Like the HIB, the group strove to offer diverse programming. On 26 June 1982, for instance, a pastor in Halle, a city less than an hour's drive from Leipzig, hosted a garden party on the Petersberg, a nearby hill.[12] The group also organized cultural and scientific lectures. One given by a well-known sexologist took place in Leipzig's Andreas Church in April 1983 and attracted around 150 people, including about 80 women.[13] By spring 1983, the group had a regular membership of between 30 and 100 people.[14] While these numbers, reported by Stasi informants, might be inflated, accounts from activists themselves confirm the group's popularity and rapid expansion.[15]

The circle was more aggressive than the HIB had been about bringing its ideas to other parts of the country. It sought to foster ties with congregations and groups of gay people around East Germany.[16] The network of Protestant academies played a significant role in spreading word of the new movement by hosting conferences on homosexuality. On 1 October 1983, for example, around 200 people from "all corners of the GDR" attended a conference at the Evangelical Academy of Saxony-Anhalt titled "A Plea against Deep-Seated Prejudices – Homosexuality and Homosexuals in Our Society."[17] These national meetings offered a way for disparate groups to coordinate.

Church-based working circles soon sprang up in other East German towns and cities. Word spread through the Leipzig group's contacts as well as Pulz and Stapel's proselytizing. In June 1983, a "homosexual self-help group" was founded within the Berlin-Brandenburg Protestant Church. Around 150 people, including fifteen lesbians, attended its first meeting.[18] On 12 October 1984, Stapel founded a group in Magdeburg, where he had moved to take up a vicarage.[19] By the summer of 1984 the Stasi knew of groups in Dresden, Berlin, Leipzig, Karl-Marx-City, Magdeburg, Erfurt, and Rostock.[20]

Among them were also lesbian groups in several cities, including Berlin and Leipzig.[21] Sillge explains that these groups broke away from the original working circles, much as West German lesbian activists in the 1970s had from male-dominated groups.[22] In our interview, Sillge recalled that misogyny was rife among the movement's male leaders. When a national "Gay Union" (*Schwulenverband*) was founded in 1990, for example, Sillge remembered asking, "What about lesbians? You only ever speak about gays." She recalled that one activist responded, "'Yes lesbians can become members if they want, but they have nothing to say.' That's a quote."[23] In spite of friction between gay and lesbian members, women made up a significant portion of activists and attendees. By January 1986 there were at least twelve circles claiming a total membership of more than 800 men and women.[24]

The circles' spread did not mean their existence remained unproblematic among church leaders. Many religious officials were profoundly opposed to homosexuality. Lothar de Maizière, a Protestant attorney and later prime minister, tactfully told me that opinion within the church was "differentiated" on the question.[25] In the early 1980s, for instance, a number of articles in religious periodicals appeared calling for greater tolerance toward homosexuals. In response, an anonymous official distributed a letter to church leaders arguing that gay people had no place in the Protestant ministry.[26] Three months later, in June 1983, the *Landesbruderrat*, an informal collective of ministers, adopted "32 Theses" on the question of homosexuality. The collection included the contentions that homosexuality was not part of "God's order of creation" and that homosexuals could only be employed by the church if they "do not practice or propagate homosexuality."[27] Although we have no statistics about how church members and ministers perceived gay people, tolerance was a contentious subject within the religious community.

Notwithstanding opposition from within the church, its decentralized structure made it possible for congregations, ministers, and vicars to endorse gay working circles and provide them with resources. As striking as this cooperation was, it was not unique at the time. There were efforts to reconcile religion and homosexuality in other countries, including the West German group "Homosexuality and the Church" and various local initiatives of American activists in the 1970s.[28] While it is fashionable to view religion and homosexuality as inexorably opposed, such movements remind us that this was not always the case.

The East German homosexual working circles had two distinct goals, one social and one political. Socially, they largely resembled both the HIB and the West German action groups from the 1970s. In a country that lacked social opportunities for lesbians and gay men, the working circles offered a variety of activities for their members. At a minimum, they typically met twice a month for conversation.[29] In spite of the difficulty of accessing copiers or, sometimes, even telephones, the groups managed to spread word effectively and draw large crowds to their events. As Ralf Dose, the West Berlin activist and historian, jovially recalled,

> When we used to do it, when we organized something, we had to do lots of advertising, send out lots of invitations, and then ten people would show up to the event. Or maybe fifteen, but not much more. They [in the East] were used to just hanging up one small note on a billboard in the Sophia parish (*Sophiengemeinde*) and then two hundred fifty folks showed up.[30]

One sample calendar for the "Gays in the Church" working circle in Berlin included a "coming out evening" in September; a "gay song evening," a lecture about the experiences of the Leipzig group, and an author lecture in October; a cabaret in November; and in December a Christmas party with the Berlin lesbian group as well as a debate about the public cruising scene.[31] Many of the gatherings were intellectual in nature, and the groups read widely, from James Baldwin to Klaus Mann.[32]

Groups also organized outdoor activities, such as a bike tour in April 1985 with the motto "gays on the street" (the German, "*Schwule auf die Strasse*," alliterates).[33] The working circle in Halle arranged a boat trip every year. In 1987 more than ninety people tooled down the Saale River.[34] Likewise, the Halle group organized gay sports leagues for both swimming and volleyball.[35] These events lured anywhere from dozens to hundreds of participants. A 1987 convention for lesbians in Leipzig drew, according to the perhaps inflated figures of an IM, more than 1,000 women from across the country.[36]

But their activities did not just fill members' leisure time. Activists also endeavoured to create an ersatz social safety net for lesbians and gay men. In 1986, for example, Berlin's "Gays in the Church" opened an account at a local bank. "This account," leaders informed the members, "will serve to finance speakers and homosexuals who have stumbled into social crisis."[37] In similar fashion, Lothar de Maizière offered legal advice to gay people in the 1980s. "As a lawyer, I stumbled onto it quite fortuitously," he recalled: "When homosexuals lived together and then separated, there was unbelievable dispute because there were no rules." That mayhem bothered him. When members of the "Gays in the Church" circle requested his help in fashioning a legal facsimile of marriage for gay couples, he instructed them to draw up documents that would "stipulate in writing what, for [heterosexuals], stands in the law

books." He made a "succession of suggestions," including formulating lists of common and individual property, agreeing on a household
budget, drawing up wills, and signing medical powers of attorney.[38] De
Maizière eventually suggested holding a seminar for the leaders of several circles so that they could then bring the relevant legal knowledge
back to their own communities.[39] The CDU-aligned newspaper *Neue
Zeit* even carried an advertisement for the workshop.[40]

The groups' stated goals were also determinedly political, far more
so than the HIB's had been. And by organizing beyond the state's pur-
view, they were able to pressure the regime far more aggressively. Early
in the 1980s they instituted an annual national meeting, which continued throughout the decade, where gay and lesbian leaders could coordinate messages, goals, and strategies.[41]

This synchronization allowed the working circles to develop a fairly
consistent set of sweeping demands. While the HIB had stuck primarily to its request for a communication centre, the new movement asked
the state for at least nine separate reforms. One of the most commonly
requested changes was for more published information about homosexuality. Newspapers ran precious few articles about homosexuality
in the 1960s, 1970s, and early 1980s, and forbade the publication of personal advertisements. What sexological or medical research existed on
the topic was either out of date or had an anti-gay perspective. The
appeal for more publications was thus a plea for the regime to relax its
unstated censorship.[42]

Activists further demanded that sex education include better and
more material on homosexuality. They complained that the country's
network of marriage- and sex-counselling centres were not available to
counsel lesbians and gay men on issues specific to their homosexuality. These centres had originated in 1965, and by 1974 there were more
than 241 of them.[43] When Sillge had gone to one in the 1970s in search
of more information about homosexuality, the doctors there rebuffed
her.[44] Likewise, the groups wanted public venues dedicated to serving
gay clientele, including "restaurants, discotheques, lecture halls."[45]

Memorializing Nazi persecution of homosexuals also became a key
demand.[46] Reparations for gay victims of Nazism had been a banner
issue for West German activists since the early 1970s, but the HIB had
never made much of it. Why the church circles suddenly took it up is
not entirely clear, though it flew in the face of East Germany's official
version of history. The communist regime maintained that anti-fascists
had been National Socialism's primary victims and consequently down-
played the suffering of other groups, including the disabled, Roma and
Sinti, and, most significantly, Jews.[47]

The groups also demanded the repeal of §151, the statute that set a higher age of consent for both lesbians and gay men.[48] They wanted homosexual couples to be allowed to adopt their own children and sought the right for gay and lesbian couples to acquire homes together.[49] Some Stasi reports even mentioned calls for same-sex marriage.[50] Activists sought equal treatment for gay people in employment, particularly in the police forces and in the army, which officially excluded them from service.[51] It is striking that these priorities so closely aligned with the priorities of activist groups in Western countries.

Activists expected resistance from the regime. After all, the HIB's relatively modest proposal for a communication centre had disappeared into the state's bureaucratic labyrinth. That group's strategy of accommodation had proved incapable of achieving its aim and eventually led to its forcible disbanding. What this meant for the working circles, however, was less clear. The church's autonomy protected them from outright interference. At the same time, they knew there was little chance of bringing about policy change and that their actions would make them targets of the secret police.

The question of how confrontational the groups should be therefore took centre stage in debates among activists. In one illustrative conversation among fourteen gay men and three lesbians on 22 October 1983, some members "criticized the manner of [one activist], which was too aggressive." Another participant "who had applied to leave the country and had tried, through provocations […] to speed up his departure" stood up for him. He argued that "the problem of homosexuals is a social problem, and you can't ever just 'leave the politics out.'" A group organizer insisted, on the other hand, that the leadership could not allow itself any "provocative words."[52] In a different meeting at the Philippus Chapel several weeks later, a leader suggested a "strategy of small steps" that would "carry the problems of homosexuals into the public sphere."[53] A year later, the same activist formulated this strategy more explicitly, telling a small gathering of lesbians and gay men that, "An elite of homosexuals should remain, which will still be active in the church and act as leverage vis-à-vis the state."[54] Not all gay men and lesbians could be expected to join working circles, but the movement would nonetheless exert pressure on their behalf. At the same time, he insisted, activists should look for ways to "work with the state."[55]

This vise-like "strategy of small steps," by which the working circles sought both to pressure the state and to cooperate with it, would become a guiding principle of the movement.[56] Through it, one Stasi functionary noted, the groups "wish to amplify pressure on the state. They thus invoke examples of the discrimination against homosexuals in professional and social life [...] and confront the responsible [state] organs with them in concentrated form."⁵⁷ The working circles hoped this strategy, a departure from that of the more accommodationist HIB, would force the state to take their complaints seriously. It provided a novel answer to the question of how minorities could practice politics under a paranoid dictatorship.

The movement sought to pressure the regime through a variety of quasi-public channels. The most prominent strategy was to write petitions to SED leaders. Historians of East Germany have long noted the zeal with which citizens submitted petitions (*Eingaben*) to the government. By the late 1980s, more than 1 million petitions arrived per year, complaining of everything imaginable from coal pollution to the difficulty of finding an apartment.⁵⁸

Gay activists decided that peppering the regime with *Eingaben* presented a good way to influence officials. The Leipzig group, for example, hoped in 1984 to force the repeal of §151 with petitions.⁵⁹ The minutes of a Berlin working circle meeting in 1985 noted that, "We are happily ready [...] to speak with those people who have been discriminated against and to help them formulate petitions."⁶⁰ Through these missives, activists insisted upon the rights theoretically guaranteed to them under East German law and sought to convince the state that gay men and lesbians did in fact face discrimination. One annoyed Stasi functionary complained that these petitions were "one-sided and ossified."⁶¹

One petition campaign in spring 1986 illustrates just how tenacious activists were – and just how frustrating authorities found them. On 28 April 1986, the chief editor of the *Leipziger Volkszeitung*, a daily newspaper, wrote to one Frau B. She had tried to place a personal ad seeking female companionship, and the paper had refused her.⁶² A few days later, on 1 May, one Dr R. wrote to the editors to complain. "As I am homosexual myself," he wrote, "and am thinking about placing a similar ad in your newspaper, it now interests me, whether this is a blanket regulation in the GDR [...] or if this only affects the *Leipziger Volkszeitung*."⁶³ The director of the press wrote back to Dr R. on 7 May and sanctimoniously told him, "I, like you, am of the view, that minorities such as homosexuals should experience no legal harm in our society because of their same-sex sexual desire."⁶⁴ But he refused to budge on the question of personal ads.

At least two more people wrote to the press, including a Marxist philosopher at an East German university, who chastised the press director for his "misuse of the Marxist worldview."⁶⁵ Eventually, activists took to a voter forum, where they questioned a representative about the ads. According to a Stasi report, "This representative promised to concern herself with the matter."[66] Such coordinated petitioning allowed activists to press their views within existing political frameworks. The government allowed petitions as a way of remaining halfway responsive to citizens' needs, and activists employed them to inform the regime of the problems they faced as lesbians and gay men.

The groups also tried more ambitious provocation. One of the activists' key demands was that the regime admit to the National Socialists' persecution of homosexuals. Activists believed that assumption into the canon of officially recognized victims would bestow on homosexuality a kind of legitimacy in anti-fascist East Germany. To that end, they planned trips to former concentration camps, where they would lay wreaths to honour gay victims. On 2 July 1983, the Leipzig working circle invited activists from across the country to participate in a wreath laying at Buchenwald concentration camp. The wreath bore a banner that read, "In memory of those persecuted because of their homosexuality."[67] About fifty men and women from around the country participated.[68] The following year, the Leipzig group again laid a wreath at the Buchenwald memorial, while the Berlin group "Lesbians in the Church" organized a similar commemoration at the all-female concentration camp Ravensbrück.[69] These ceremonies became an annual tradition, one that usually took place in June as a macabre variation on Western Europe's annual gay pride festivities. They were the most public demonstrations the working circles organized under the dictatorship.

The memorializations succeeded in attracting the regime's attention. Three members of the Leipzig group met with officials at the Buchenwald memorial on 14 June 1984, asking where they could lay a wreath to honour persecuted homosexuals. The officials in turn went to the secret police.[70] Two weeks later an order went out to the directors of the Sachsenhausen and Buchenwald sites, ordering them to "inhibit the planned appearance of homosexual groups [...] at these memorials."[71]

In spite of the regime's efforts, forty-nine activists laid a wreath at Buchenwald on 30 June 1984.[72] In the groups' first years, demonstrating peaceably at memorial sites was one of their most effective strategies. It won them the state's attention. Through the submission of petitions and letters, the organizing of national conferences, and the commemoration of Nazi victims, East Germany's new movement sought to force the state to acknowledge its existence and to recognize the legitimacy of its demands. The strategy of small steps eventually compelled the

Stasi to think comprehensively about homosexuality and the problems it posed for the dictatorship.

The Stasi's Early Response

Two dynamics in particular captured the Stasi's attention. First, the working circles were organized within the church. Second, the movement had spread quickly. An early report on the Leipzig group noted that already in 1982 it had "stable contact with members of a Berlin 'lesbian group.'"[73] Curiously, officials somewhat inaccurately connected the new working circles to the HIB. One report in July 1983 noted that the "Mahlsdorf circle in Berlin" had been suggested as "one possible model" for the church groups.[74] Another from December 1983 described the Berlin working circle as a reincarnation of the HIB.[75] Subsequent reports obsessively catalogued the number of groups, their participants, and their contacts with each other.[76]

In order to comprehend why the Stasi panicked the way it did, it is first necessary to understand the broader political context of the early 1980s. While the state had long used religion as a safety valve for social and political frustration, it got more than it bargained for with the advent of a grassroots peace movement in the late 1970s, also organized within the Protestant church.[77] Although East Germany had fostered an official peace movement, it worried that the church groups might pose a real threat to its military. Worse, it feared that Western powers were manipulating them in order to bring about socialism's downfall.[78]

Around the same time, environmental groups began forming under church auspices. East Germany, like most Eastern bloc states, was a notoriously bad steward of the environment. Rapid industrialization had ravaged the country's natural resources, polluted its air, and contaminated its water. Historians have gone so far as to call East Germany an ecological "failed state."[79] By the late 1980s, catalysed in particular by the Chernobyl nuclear disaster, more than 100 grassroots environmental groups had sprung up in the GDR. Unsurprisingly, the Stasi viewed these too as a threat.[80]

Thus, by the early 1980s several groups had loosely organized within the church, making it a kind of repository of dissent. The Stasi fretted that "enemy-negative powers" both internal and external – by which it meant the church and Western states, respectively – were employing these movements to destabilize the regime.[81] Worse yet, some early gay working circles were loosely affiliated with the peace movement. A peace activist, for instance, had founded one of the groups in Berlin in 1983.[82] These affiliations caused the Stasi to fear that they too would turn on the regime. In the early 1980s, Stasi officials became increasingly paranoid about this threat:

> Enemy-negative church powers and homosexual individuals are developing activities to create "homosexual working groups" in the GDR, to join these with already existing "women's groups" into an "alternative movement" and to integrate these into a "peace movement" independent of the state.[83]

Officials fretted that these groups could unite into a movement that might challenge the party's monopoly on power.[84]

The Stasi's still-festering fear of gay espionage compounded the regime's alarm. For example, a 1983 law dissertation on homosexuality in East Berlin, written by one Gerhard Fehr, a Stasi official at East Berlin's Humboldt University, described gay men as "persons, who from a young age often behave conspiratorially."[85] He claimed that many homosexuals led a "double life" and that they "recognize each other immediately."[86] Furthermore, he maintained (in now-familiar language) that homosexuals are "active in all spheres of our society and because of their sociability and their constant efforts to meet new partners for sexual manipulation are especially interesting people for the class enemy and its intelligence headquarters (*Agentenzentralen*)."[87] Likewise, in 1984 the Brandenburg branch of the Stasi investigated "a suspicion of espionage" related to a certain B., even investigating a "contact of B. [who is] the possible third party in the network [of spies]."[88]

The Stasi was slow to formulate a response to the perceived threat. The secret police was a lumbering bureaucracy that, in its final years, employed around 90,000 individuals and engaged another 173,000 as informants.[89] At the national level it was divided into thirty-three departments and fifteen separate district offices, which in turn administered more than 200 county offices.[90] Because officers from two different central departments and numerous local bureaus around the country were the first to encounter the new gay movement, the secret police's initial reactions were uncoordinated.

Most offices set informants on the groups, hoping to uncover more information about who their participants were and what danger they posed to the regime. The director of the Stasi district administration in Halle, for instance, instructed his subordinates to "select homophile informants" to spy on the new church group there. These informants were to answer questions, including, "Which people are members of a homosexual working circle? [...] Where are meeting spots, residences, and conference venues? [...] Members of other so-called homo-rings."[91]

As they had with gay IMs in the 1970s, the security services hoped informants would find out who was involved in the circles and what their goals were.

Responses to wreath layings at former concentration camps provide an example of the lack of coordination between different offices and departments. Each year at Buchenwald, in spite of the Stasi's instructions to prevent activists from honouring gay Holocaust victims at the memorial site, lesbians and gay men successfully laid a wreath commemorating these victims.[92] But when the Berlin group "Lesbians in the Church" attempted to visit the female concentration camp Ravensbrück on 20 April 1985, the police forcibly prevented them from doing so. As the group wrote of their experiences that day, "We had planned to order a bouquet of flowers, on the ribbon of which we commemorated the suffering of our lesbian sisters and signed our first names." The day before the trip, local police summoned the women who had ordered the bouquet. After an interrogation, the police told the group that because their names appeared on the ribbon, they "had announced [themselves] as a group, which was not lawfully recognized." The police therefore forbade them to visit Ravensbrück.[93]

Nonetheless, the women persisted. The author of the testimonial wrote: "When I left the house on Saturday morning with two female friends, two plainclothes men were already waiting across the street. They followed us to the S-Bahn." Once the group of eleven reached Fürstenberg, the town north of Berlin where Ravensbrück is located, they were "detained by the transportation police on the pretence of a manhunt, our IDs were collected, and we were asked to wait in the train station." They were soon hustled into a riot police van with "constant bodily molestation" and words such as "Go! Get up there. Look sharp! You're going to get fat sitting there!" The van took them to an empty school building, where the police interrogated them before allowing them to leave.[94]

Why officials allowed predominantly male groups to memorialize victims of the Holocaust unmolested while forcibly preventing a relatively small group of women from doing the same is difficult to say. As we have already seen with the HIB's planned meeting of lesbians from around the country, something about lesbians' organizational efforts struck fear into the regime in a way that those of gay men did not. It could be that such efforts troubled both gender and sexuality norms. On the other hand, one Stasi report from May 1985 noted that, "The circle of lesbians is the most politically active of all the homosexual working circles."[95] Perhaps the secret police believed lesbians presented a greater threat than gay men. Perhaps it viewed such efforts as an outgrowth of both the feminist and the homosexual movements and thus as an incipient attempt to create the larger "alternative movement" it so feared. Whatever the case, these differing reactions highlight that the Stasi operated without a coherent plan vis-à-vis gay and lesbian activism. Its responses were localized and ad hoc.

As the number of groups expanded and came into contact with different arms of the Stasi bureaucracy, there grew an institutional impetus to address gay activism in a comprehensive way. Homosexuality's portfolio, if you will, was slowly expanding within the secret police. It required coordination between two different departments and among their numerous regional offices, each with its own information bases, informant networks, and institutional agendas. Whereas municipal and regional authorities had worked on the HIB case, the national scope of the 1980s movement compelled the attention of more senior officials.

The Stasi took a step toward a coordinated response in late 1983 when Department XX circulated a memo suggesting that it "take complex, operative leadership of the uncovering and repression of attempts by enemy and politically negative powers to organize homosexually inclined people."[96] The memo proposed continuing some policies, such as using the Stasi's informant network to gain more information about homosexuals. It also indicated that some of these informants could be installed as "sympathizers" within the movement, from where they could exercise a "positive influence" on the working circles. Yet more sinister, it proposed working to strengthen "resistance from within the church" against the circles. Finally, the memo suggested that individual ringleaders of the movement "be processed operatively."[97] That is, the secret police would observe and possibly even prosecute certain activists. This first attempt at coordination came well over a year after the first working circle had appeared. Only then did the Stasi begin to come to grips with the burgeoning gay rights movement at a national level.

A Secular Alternative

The working circles, however, were not the only groups the government had to worry about. Just as disagreements about the morality of sheltering gay activists had divided the Protestant church, so too disagreements about the morality of cooperating with Christians divided gay activists. No one was quite sure if the circles were religious or if their partnership with the church was purely one of convenience. The groups themselves did little to answer this question, for their activity calendars were sprinkled with lectures on and discussions of religious topics.[98]

Some activists thus began looking for secular alternatives. In 1983, Peter Rausch recalled that, "Uschi [Sillge] called a group of people to her home and said, 'Don't we want to found another group?'"[99] This new group, which eventually came to be called the "Sunday Club," was a sort of cross-pollination of the working circles' political gumption and the HIB's largely pro-regime outlook. The group was not attached to the Protestant church in any way. Its members, according to one IM report, "stand completely behind the politics of the party and of the state."[100] Like the HIB, the group emphasized that it posed no threat to the political order. It hoped to offer community to lesbians and gay men turned off by the working circles' Christian affiliations.

Rausch confided, "For myself, I always stayed away from the church circles." He did so because he did not believe "the church was suddenly our saviour. Because until then they were, for me, the incarnation of our repression. They embodied the morality, ethics, and homophobia of the last century."[101] Similarly, Stasi information from January 1985 indicated that, "A large number of homosexuals are clamouring for the [Leipzig] working circle to leave the church, as the church does not represent their interests and because individual members of the working circle have no religious attachments."[102] Many gay people in the GDR did not want to associate with the church, leading to the creation of secular gay and lesbian organizations.

On 2 November 1983, a letter arrived for the minister of the interior asking for "a personal meeting about the question of homosexuality in the GDR." East German gay men and lesbians, the letter explained, wanted to be able to meet others "without having to go to church."[103] These individuals "go to the working circles, although they are neither devout nor religious sympathizers."[104] Because only the Protestant church allowed homosexual activities, the letter argued, the party "is giving away a huge influence over half a million residents" of the GDR.[105] "So long as a facet of our personality, namely homosexuality, is not accepted," the letter concluded, "there will be conflict."[106]

The petition employed two particular levers to convince the regime of the urgency of pursuing gay-friendly policies. On the one hand, it argued that the regime could weaken church-affiliated working circles by authorizing secular alternatives. Allowing lesbians and gay men to organize, the petition implied, would give the regime "great influence" over them. On the other hand, it contended that that population was substantial – around 500,000 people – and could pose a danger to the regime. The argument bears striking similarities to those that West German activists advanced in the 1970s. Just as gay people in the Federal Republic contended that they were too numerous a bloc of voters to

dismiss, so too activists in East Germany suggested that gay and lesbian citizens were too large a population for the dictatorship to ignore.

The minister of the interior forwarded the petition to Stasi Minister
Erich Mielke on 17 November 1983. His accompanying letter explained
that the group desired "the creation of activity centres for homosexuals
(club-, culture-, and counselling centres)." He asked the Stasi to coordinate with the criminal police to keep the group under observation.[107]
Soon thereafter, on 3 January 1984, the first secretary of the Berlin SED,
Konrad Naumann, received a letter from the director of the local Stasi
bureau. The letter mentioned, adapting language from the 2 November
petition, that most homosexuals were not interested in politics. They
primarily wanted "to meet new partners" or "discuss the problems
that arise from their sexual identity."[108] It was rather a small number
of "politically negative" homosexuals who were misusing the larger
population "to realize a political impact" from the new homosexual circles. As evidence, the letter offered "cooperation with religious 'peace
circles'" and the "successful wreath laying at the memorials at Buchenwald and Sachsenhausen."[109] The working circles' strategy of small
steps showed up as proof of the danger they posed to the regime.

During the drafting of this 3 January letter to Comrade Naumann,
Stasi Department XX/9, which was responsible for the political underground, also produced a memorandum, on 30 December 1983, that contained a radical proposal. It suggested that the letter sent to Secretary
Naumann include "the aim, that at the central level a consultation be
conducted with representatives of the Ministries for Health, Culture,
and the Interior as well as of the Magistrate of the Capital, Internal
Affairs, with the objective to create a state response centre for such circles of people."[110] That is, it recommended that the central government
convene representatives of at least four different ministries and departments for the purpose of crafting a unified response to the country's
burgeoning gay and lesbian movement.

The role of different Stasi departments in this decision is curious and
difficult to untangle. Department VII had taken the lead in dealing with
the HIB. When the working circles sprang up in the early 1980s, Department XX became involved in a much more prominent way, as it was
responsible for observing the church and underground political activities. Once new secular groups appeared, asking for state approval,
however, the offices connected to Department VII, namely the Ministry
of the Interior, again entered the conversation.

Moreover, whereas Department VII's inclination had been to block
state recognition of the HIB and similar groups, it was Department XX,
which was used to dealing with a state-recognized institution, namely

the church, that suggested a new approach. It was perhaps conceivable to officials in Department XX that allowing gay people to organize in controlled ways would be a more efficacious way of blunting their political impact. The differing perspectives of these two departments not only illustrate that the Stasi itself was not always an internally well-coordinated bureaucracy but also suggest how different strands of gay activism (unwittingly) played different elements of the state off against each other.

On 8 March 1984, the director of Department VII sent the director of Department XX a memorandum titled "Information Concerning the Efforts of Homosexual Circles to Establish Organizations." He opened with a brief history of homosexual activism in the GDR, including the HIB's efforts to win state approval between 1974 and 1976, the 1976 decision to reject the HIB's application, the constant stream of petitions from gay citizens, and the creation of religious working circles.[111]

The paper asserted that, "There are increasing signs that the Evangelical church is attempting to bind different homosexual circles closer to the church through directed political-ideological influence." This influence, the memo asserted in language sympathetic to activists, grew from the fact that "in the GDR there are no special restaurants or other meeting spots for [homosexuals]."[112] Among their motives, the paper listed, in painful bureaucratese, "the satisfaction of personal interests that derive from the particularity of this kind of interpersonal relationship." That is, lesbians and gay men wanted places where they could meet other lesbians and gay men.[113] In its own stilted way, this March memorandum reveals that the Stasi was revising its view of East Germany's gay citizens. It had begun to acknowledge the legitimacy of their social and political demands.

Moreover, the memo noted, "In present state practice all applications and petitions from these circles containing the demand for the formation of organizations or facilities have been declined."[114] But this policy, it asserted, "has not led to the confinement of the activities of these powers, but rather induced them to search for new opportunities," such as affiliation with the church. "In order to guarantee security and to hinder enemy activities," the memo concluded, "it seems necessary to rethink the position of state organs to the aforementioned problems."[115]

The director of Department VII thus effectively agreed with the suggestion of Department XX/9 and informed his colleagues that the existing policy of rebuffing gay activism was a failure, precisely because it had driven otherwise politically docile gay men and lesbians into the arms of the church. In his view, the regime needed to rethink its strategy.

The memo represents a striking admission of failure and evinces an equally remarkable empathy with lesbians' and gay men's concerns. That empathy, it should of course be noted, came not out of concern for gay and lesbian East Germans but was rather born of a fear that their political agenda imperilled the regime's stability.

Things began to move rapidly. On 29 August 1984, the director of Department XX replied that, "From our perspective it now seems particularly necessary to convince state organs, including the Ministry of the Interior, that they seriously consider eligible claims from homosexuals."[116] With the stroke of a pen, he suggested overturning an eight-year ban on gay activism, instructing the Ministry of the Interior to begin processing gay petitions in a more normal fashion. Two weeks later, he received a reply from Department VII, which argued for the formation of "a commission of accountable representatives of various ministries in order to develop a state viewpoint" regarding gay rights.[117]

Activists, these memos reveal, were beginning to have an impact at the very highest levels of government. Stasi mandarins had begun to demand change. That change, curiously, had come about because secular lesbian and gay activists were able to leverage the regime's fear of church-affiliated groups. Telling the dictatorship that gay people had no innate desire to organize within the church or to oppose the regime, they set off a chain reaction within the secret police that would have incredible ramifications in the coming years.

About the government commission proposed in these Stasi memoranda we can, for the time being, only speculate. I found no direct evidence that such a commission ever met, and the Stasi archivists with whom I worked also did not find any such documentation. In the kilometres of files that make up the Stasi archive, it is, of course, possible that such records may one day be found, just as it is possible that no such commission ever existed.

Nonetheless, circumstantial evidence suggests that a group of high officials did convene. Beginning in 1985, identical language about a new, coordinated strategy to combat gay activism began showing up in memoranda produced by different Stasi offices. One document, originating in Department XX on 6 June 1985 was titled "Central Plan of Action for the Political-Operative Processing of Negative-Enemy Inspirers and Organizers of Unions of Homosexual Individuals." Department XX/9 was to be responsible for this "Plan of Action," which officially targeted the "political misuse of homosexuals." This formulation reaffirmed the Stasi's view that most gay people's desires were apolitical and that the danger came from the possibility that enemies might use those desires to destabilize the government.[118]

In order to combat this alleged "political misuse," the memo recommended that the Stasi pursue a few specific goals. First, agents had to "uncover if and how enemy individuals, organizations, and institutions [...] misuse individuals in the GDR through exploitation of their homosexuality for negative-enemy activities." Much as with existing IM work, the Stasi wanted information about precisely how (and even if) homosexuals were being "misused" for political ends. The memo further argued that "operative work" should concentrate on developing "proof of violations of criminal law" on the part of activists.[119] Both of these aims pointed to ramped up surveillance and repression of activism.

But the memo continued with eight "categorical tasks for all departments." The first seven were all oppressive in nature, including elevated intelligence gathering, efforts to sabotage the working circles, and criminal prosecutions of leading activists. Yet, the eighth task read:

> Reinforcement of social positions for confrontation with negative-enemy powers and their views, in particular through the resolution of the humanitarian problems of homosexual people in the GDR's socialist society.[120]

This language is sensational. As a way of combatting gay activism, the East German Ministry for State Security proposed resolving the very "humanitarian problems" that gay and lesbian activists had for years been telling the regime they faced. The Stasi had come around to the activists' view that government policy needed to address anti-gay animus in law, society, and culture. The secret police seemed to believe that the only way to neutralize the political threat of gay and lesbian activism was to accede to its demands.[121]

Identical language appeared in documents from other Stasi offices over the next two years. Memos from bureaus in Magdeburg, Dresden, and Berlin all urged the government to solve the "humanitarian problems" facing East Germany's homosexual citizens.[122] By 1986 the notion that the Stasi had a role to play in ensuring that the state addressed gay men and lesbians' social and political demands seemed to have taken root. Ironically, the Stasi's paranoia about the political threat posed by such activism had transformed it into East Germany's greatest institutional proponent for the interests of gay men and lesbians.

A Policy of Liberation

As gears ground within the Stasi, Sillge and her comrades continued to pressure the regime. In her book, she recalls that a group of "despairing lesbians" wrote to the Ministry of the Interior in 1984 demanding "expert rationales for [government] decisions to decline" homosexual petitions. Soon thereafter the women were granted an audience with officials at the Berlin Magistrate, who told them that the matter first had to be "scientifically researched." As a consequence of that discussion, the prorector for social sciences at Berlin's Humboldt University convened a research group on homosexuality, which began meeting in the autumn of 1984.[123]

The committee worked for the next several months and on 25 January 1985 produced a remarkable report titled "On the Situation of Homophile Citizens in the GDR." It argued that gay people in East Germany had a right to feel at home in socialist society and that the East German constitution forbade "discrimination against homophile citizens."[124] It acknowledged both the Nazi persecution of homosexuals and prejudices that festered in East German society. The paper discussed the extraordinary suicide rate among gay people, remarking that it was four to five times higher than in the rest of the population.[125] Adopting activists' language, the academics wrote that the state's "disregard for the personal and sometimes grave social problems of homophiles" had led to "purposefully negative political reactions."[126] Among these reactions, the paper observed that lesbians and gay men had joined church-affiliated working circles and that homosexual citizens "are increasingly applying to migrate to the FRG and West Berlin."[127] In short, East German anti-gay animus came with consequences for gay people and the state alike.

The report made ten suggestions about how to address those problems. It recommended:

1. that there be more publishing on the topic of homosexuality;
2. that Humboldt University host a permanent homosexuality research group;
3. that the government create "consultation centres at the communal level," which would help homosexuals with questions of "way of life," "counselling for family members" of homosexuals, "sexual counselling," suicide counselling, and counselling related to coming out;
4. that the government change the make-up of existing marriage and sex counselling centres;
5. that the government review §151, which set a higher age of consent for gay men and lesbians;
6. that workplace discrimination against gay people be examined;
7. that the government allow coupled lesbians and gay men to live together;

8. that the government revisit regulations governing the publication of personal advertisements and approval of public events;
9. that there be research on the situation of older homosexuals;
10. and that it be examined how living conditions for gay people differ between "metropolis, medium city, town and villages" in the GDR.[128]

These recommendations – which were compiled at the behest of the East Berlin municipal government and undoubtedly with the approval of Stasi functionaries – represent another rupture with past practices. Although the report itself was couched in the stilted idiom of East German Marxism and used questionable language (such as the decision to use "homophile" instead of "homosexual"), its recommendations largely overlapped with activists' own requests.

It proved a harbinger of things to come: more remarkable than the reports that bureaucrats and professors had produced were the actual changes they engendered. In 1985 censors suddenly started to permit the publication of personal advertisements, which until then had been nearly impossible to place. Although each newspaper could still decide whether or not to publish such ads, by December 1985 at least two periodicals were accepting them.[129] East German presses also began to publish more information about homosexuality. This shift began among Christian publications. *Neue Zeit*, the East German CDU's organ, had begun to include articles about homosexuality as early as 1982. These pieces discussed sexological research, gay men's and lesbians' experiences at marriage and sex counselling centres, and AIDS.[130] *Neue Zeit* also printed notices advertising the working circles' activities.[131]

Beginning in 1985, state-aligned organs started including positive articles on homosexuality. Both the *Berliner Zeitung* and *Neues Deutschland*, for example, published coverage of a scientific conference on homosexuality in June 1985.[132] As the 1980s progressed, these newspapers published an increasing number of articles about homosexuality, in particular information about AIDS and new government policies. Some magazines, in particular youth periodicals such as *Für Dich* (*For You*) and *Neues Leben* (*New Life*), published progressive articles on homosexuality.[133] Over the next several years, ever more coverage of homosexuality appeared in the pages of East Germany's periodicals (see figure 9.1).

Around the same time, the regime commissioned Reiner Werner, a psychologist at Humboldt University, to write a book about homosexuality.[134] Titled *Homosexuality: A Call for Knowledge and Tolerance*, it

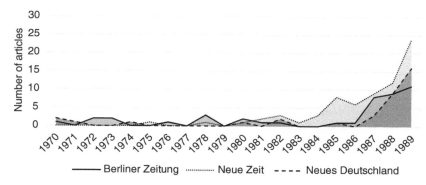

Figure 9.1. East German newspaper articles including the word
"homosexual," per annum, 1970–89

appeared in 1987 in an initial run of 50,000.[135] It was the first progressive,
state-sanctioned monograph about homosexuality in East Germany,
and within three weeks the first printing had sold out.[136] True, the book
had numerous problems and was widely criticized. One Stasi report
noted that, "among hetero- and homosexual individuals there is an
overwhelmingly deprecating view" of the book.[137] Not only had Werner
devoted the vast majority of the text to gay men, as Ursula Sillge, among
others, complained, he had also invented a nonsense term "lesbicity"
("*Lesbizität*") with which to discuss female homosexuality.[138] Yet, for all
its flaws, the book signalled a rupture with decades-old taboos. *Neue
Zeit* praised the monograph as "the first book to appear in our country
that deals with homosexuality as its sole topic."[139] Other authors pressured the regime to adopt school texts that addressed homosexuality
more tolerantly. A doctor in Jena campaigned for the publication of a
book that would help the parents of gay and lesbian children. Although
authorities initially resisted his entreaties, by 1987 his manuscript was
under consideration at a press.[140]

In 1988 the regime green-lighted the country's first feature film about
homosexuality. On 24 May, the East German film studio DEFA had
written to Kurt Hager, a member of the Politburo. Noting that Hager
"required us to inform you about film material that would be expected
to create a broad social discussion," the studio told him about *Coming
Out*. The proposed film about gay life in East Germany would be produced by renowned director Heiner Carow.[141]

DEFA had already solicited three academic evaluations of the screenplay, each of which endorsed the film. After back and forth with officials and some censorship (bureaucrats insisted that a scene in which police officers raid a cruising area be cut), Hager endorsed the project.[142] As with the rise in publishing, the authorizing of a film about homosexuality did not itself change the regime or East German attitudes overnight. Rather, it served as a sign of just how rapidly things were moving.[143] By curious coincidence, *Coming Out* premiered on 9 November 1989, the night East Germans breached the Berlin Wall.[144]

The greatest transformations came not in the realm of culture, though, but in concrete policy changes and the foundation of new institutions to serve gay people. In 1985 the Berlin government opened East Germany's first gay discotheque on Buschallee, known colloquially as "the *Busche*," in the neighbourhood Weißensee.[145] As Carsten I., a gay man living in East Berlin in the 1980s, recalled, "the *Busche* – in any event the first gay discotheque – for [my partner] Werner it was important. It was, so to say, his time, and his coming out was much easier."[146] The government allowed other bars to host discos, and the gay scene grew at a steady clip in the years after 1985.

At the same time, Ursula Sillge's secular group found a home in 1986 after years of bureaucratic obfuscation. As with the HIB, her club required state approval. Thus, Sillge and her friends embarked on campaigns of letter writing in the early 1980s. Much as in the 1970s, however, the local government once again shuffled Sillge from office to office. She recalled that, after the government had ignored multiple petitions, she was determined to meet with someone in person. She eventually went to the local government offices with a gay man. "There sat the two secretaries and also two police officers," Sillge remembered, "who asked 'Who are you then?'" She replied, "We wrote a letter and still have not received a reply and want to speak with the comrades." The secretaries wanted to know what they wished to speak to them about, and she simply responded, "Homosexuality." "They looked at us," she recalled, "as if we came from the moon." The secretaries soon began making telephone call after telephone call as she and her friend waited. Finally, someone appeared to speak with them and rebuffed their inquiries.[147]

Unsurprisingly, it took her a long time to find a venue that would host a gay and lesbian group. As Sillge remembered, "finally I found a youth club on Veteranstrasse. It was led by a lesbian and her assistant was a gay man." They agreed that her group could host events in their space. It turned out to be a felicitous relationship for both parties. The group was able to organize gatherings that drew "twenty or thirty" participants. For their part, the club directors could report to their superiors, "Oh, we're successful, we have lots of visitors." Once the municipal government discovered that those visitors were primarily lesbians and gay men, however, "the hassle started again." According to Sillge, the government decided to close the club for renovations rather than allow them to meet there.[148] Eventually, the Berlin Magistrate officially sanctioned the group. This recognition meant that it became far easier for the group, which had adopted the name "Sunday Club" because it met on Sundays, to organize and advertise its functions.[149]

Amusingly, the government began using the Sunday Club for official purposes. Bert Thinius, a scholar at Humboldt University, reported that in the late 1980s all youth clubs in the GDR were ordered to organize monthly events dealing with homosexuality. The state was moving so rapidly to accommodate activists' demands that it created, in Thinius's words, an "absurd situation."[150] Years of repression meant that there was not the necessary infrastructure to meet the state's new demand for gay-friendly programming. Peter Rausch, who was also involved with the Sunday Club, remembered rumours flying at the time that the central committee of the Free German Youth (FDJ) had promulgated this decision. "The joke was," Rausch told me, "that suddenly everyone was standing in line to get into the Sunday Club."[151]

Similarly, in 1987, a *Volkskammer* member wrote to the Berlin SED regarding a "dialogue with members of parliament at the so-called Berlin Sunday Club." The activists planned to discuss "questions of homosexuality in the GDR and the position of the people's representatives [with regard] to these problems."[152] That same year, members of the group met with SED representatives to discuss using the Sunday Club as a way to disseminate information about AIDS.[153] The state found the Sunday Club useful not only to combat the growth of the church-affiliated working circles but also as a way of coordinating services for lesbians and gay men and thereby cultivating their loyalty.

The regime began to encourage non-religious gay organizations in other cities. In Leipzig, members of the church circle broke away to form a group named "Rosa Linde" under the umbrella of the Free German Youth, which the FDJ's central committee sanctioned in 1989.[154] Around the same time, an FDJ youth club in the city of Weimar founded a group "for homosexual and lesbian youth away from religious influence." It took the name "Felix Halle" after the communist and sexual reform advocate from the Weimar era, who had been executed in the Stalinist Great Terror of 1936–8.[155] These were the first FDJ societies for gay youth in East Germany. A comparable change in the United States would be founding a Boy Scout troop for gay boys, something that has never happened in an organization that as late as 2013 still expelled openly gay members.

Other groups for lesbians and gay men also sprang up around the country. In March 1987, the Club for Youth and Athletes in Dresden began hosting a bimonthly "club evening for and with homosexuals."[156] In 1988 the Potsdam culture centre opened its doors to a local gay organization. The Potsdam centre agreed both to hold a monthly forum on issues concerning homosexuality and that gay members could conduct an additional monthly "internal roundtable."[157] By 1989 there existed at least five state-sanctioned organizations around the country dedicated to providing cultural and social opportunities to lesbians and gay men.

The regime also came to terms with the working circles' efforts to commemorate Nazism's homosexual victims. By 1987 the state had authorized these activities on the condition that the wreaths' ribbons contained "no subversive content."[158] Likewise, an increasing number of government documents acknowledged the Nazi persecution of homosexuals, breaking with the GDR's official history.[159] I have found no evidence, however, that the regime ever considered paying reparations to those victims. That tenet of West German activism never, it seems, became a central demand among East German campaigners.

The regime also took to heart the particular medical and psychological needs of lesbians and gay men. On 5 March 1985, the executive of the Marriage and Family Section of the East German Society for Social Hygiene, an agency that oversaw the country's network of marriage and sexual counselling centres, handed down a new decision. Describing homosexuals as "a minority" in need of the heterosexual majority's "goodwill" for the "assertion and recognition of their legitimate interests," the board rejected the view that homosexuality is a medical or psychological condition.[160] Instead it recognized homosexuality as a "biopsychic variant of human sexuality."[161] The board blasted the "one-sided heterosexually oriented environment" in East Germany and the "heterosexually oriented sexual education [that] offers homosexuals no assistance." It concluded by insisting that, "There is no humane alternative to the full recognition of homosexuals as emancipated and equal citizens."[162] The hundreds of marriage and sexual counselling centres around the country began to accept gay and lesbian patients for counselling on medical and psychological concerns specific to their sexuality.[163] It was a monumental victory for activists, who had been fighting both with and against the East German medical establishment since the early 1970s.

The regime was also quite aggressive in its response to HIV and AIDS.[164] Unlike in West Germany, the disease spread at a sluggish rate

Figure 9.2. New HIV infections in East and West Berlin, 1985–9

Year	West Berlin new HIV infections (1985 population: 1,853,000)	East Berlin new HIV infections (1985 population: 1,215,586)
1985	1576	0
1986	1458	3
1987	1332	19
1988	1067	12
1989	717	12

Sources: Michael Bochow, "Reactions of the Gay Community to AIDS in East and West Berlin," 38; *Statistisches Jahrbuch der Deutschen Demokratischen Republik*; *Statistisches Jahrbuch für die Bundesrepublik Deutschland*

in the East. Not until 1986 was there a single HIV infection in East Berlin, and not until 1987 was there a case of AIDS (see figure 9.2). The government also worked to educate East Germans about the virus.[165] Working circles and state-sanctioned groups organized joint programming to spread information about the disease.[166] By 20 June 1985, there were five AIDS consulting centres in various cities.[167] The low infection rate also seems to have been the result of the country's sealed borders and more conservative sexual culture: the lack of bathhouses and sex clubs likely blunted the disease's spread.[168] Ironically, the country's self-isolation did such a good job of blunting the disease that *Der Spiegel* ran a story after reunification claiming that, "The Wall Was East Germany's Condom."[169]

AIDS was not a central concern for activists. Of course, they discussed it at their meetings. But with extraordinarily low infection rates in East Germany, it was never a defining political demand or even life experience for most gay men in the country. Rainer E., a gay border guard, recalled that the disease was not a prominent topic in East Germany in the 1980s. Its slow spread meant that no sense of panic gripped the gay scene. "For me," he remembered, "it was not a theme at all."[170]

Finally, two further policy changes in the late 1980s helped open society in East Germany to lesbians and gay men. The first dealt with §151, the criminal provision that set the age of consent for both male and female homosexual encounters at eighteen. The age of consent for heterosexual acts was sixteen, which made §151's abolition one of the activists' foremost goals.

On 11 August 1987, the East German Supreme Court forbade prosecutors from employing §151 in cases with youth between ages sixteen and eighteen, effectively expunging the statute from the criminal code.[171] A little over a year later, on 14 December 1988, the *Volkskammer* formally repealed §151.[172] Its annulment meant that the penal code no longer discriminated against gay men and lesbians. West Germany, on the other hand, retained the rump §175 throughout the 1980s. Not until after reunification would the Federal Republic catch up to East Germany.

Finally, and perhaps most astonishingly, East Germany moved to allow openly gay people into the military. On 28 September 1988, the Defence Ministry distributed a set of new rules regarding homosexuality in the National People's Army (NVA). These tenets, it should be pointed out, were not published as an official part of "military policies" but were rather "an internal working basis" for the army, including its border troops. Nonetheless, the document asserted that homosexuality was natural and insisted that "from a political-moral standpoint every citizen has the right to live according to his sexual orientation."[173]

The new policy determined that "members of the NVA in military professions and termed employment who are known homosexuals are to continue in active military service so long as no complications arise."[174] Moreover, it instructed officers that, "in possible discussions in relevant military collectives, enlightened discussions" should "deconstruct traditional moral prejudices against homosexuality."[175] On paper, at least, the policy enlisted the military into the fight against anti-gay animus.

From our perspective today, the policy seems imperfect. It left the military a loophole, allowing officers to discharge gay soldiers if "complications" arose.[176] Moreover, it required that officers advise openly homosexual enlistees or recruits that a civil profession would better suit them.[177] For all its flaws, though, the new policy marked a schism, not only with the East German military's previous ban on homosexuality but indeed with what was then common practice in most democratic and communist countries alike. East Germany was one of the first to explicitly allow gay people to serve in its military.

Thus, in the span of four years, the East German dictatorship introduced a far-reaching set of pro-gay reforms. For an authoritarian regime that had refused to acknowledge the legitimacy of gay and lesbian activists' demands until 1984, the period between 1985 and 1989 represented a *volte face* the likes of which has not been seen before or since in the history of homosexuality. It is a striking example of a dictatorship acting in its citizens' social interests by constructively responding to public pressure from a committed group of activists.

The government pursued these policies in large part because the Stasi believed them to be an effective strategy to suppress gay and lesbian political organizing. We know this because not only did the Stasi take credit for the changes, but its officials also viewed the strategy as a success. As one bureaucrat noted in 1986, "State and social organs have recently introduced strengthened measures for dealing with questions from homosexuals" in order to prevent their "political misuse" by "enemy-negative powers." These measures, the official wrote, included "increased publications about the problem of homosexuality [...] in the press of the GDR, the opportunity to publish personal advertisements in the daily newspapers of the GDR [...] and the promulgation of a decision" to open the marriage and sexual counselling centres to homosexual patients.[178] Another memo from 1988 cited publications such as Reiner Werner's monograph as part of the Stasi's plan to combat activism's spread.[179] These documents, which typically described the plan as a triumph, suggest such changes would not have come about if they had not been part of the secret police's strategy to counter the perceived political threat of gay and lesbian activism. Of course, these progressive policies were only one part of that strategy.

Cracking Down

In early 1987 a member of the homosexual working circle in Karl-Marx-City became the subject of an ugly rumour. Other participants were whispering that he was a Stasi informant. He likely did not know, however, that the person spreading the rumour actually was a secret police collaborator – code-named IMB "Klaus Jäger."[180] Ironically, "Jäger" had spread the rumour to deflect suspicion that he himself might be a secret police agent. His designation as an "IMB" (*Inoffizieller Mitarbeiter der Abwehr mit Feindverbindung* or Unofficial Defence Collaborator with Enemy Liaisons) indicated that he enjoyed the Stasi's highest confidence and that his assignment involved actively sabotaging the group.

Despite all the progressive changes that the regime enacted between 1985 and 1989, the Stasi also implemented a host of new repressive measures against activists. These measures, aimed at disrupting or even destroying the working circles, reveal the Janus face of East Germany's pro-gay reforms and call into question what, precisely, we mean when we talk about gay liberation. Between 1985 and the fall of the Berlin Wall, liberation and oppression were quite literally two sides of the same coin.

How the secret police dealt with the Karl-Marx-City working circle is a particularly enlightening illustration of how agents could hobble activists. Between October 1985 and October 1988, the Stasi spied on the circle using at least eleven informants. These numbers – eleven IMs for a group of perhaps twenty or thirty activists – reflect the mammoth number of gay informants recruited around East Germany. I found archival records of at least 125 unique IMs who gathered information on homosexuality in the 1980s. That is, upwards of 10 per cent of all working circle members informed for the Stasi.[181] These collaborators provided information about the activist circles to which they belonged and the gay subcultures in their cities (see figure 9.3). At least fifteen were IMBs, meaning that the secret police tasked them with actively sabotaging the groups.

In Karl-Marx-City, the sabotage took numerous forms. When a priest and a circle member attempted to negotiate a union of the city's two gay groups, an informant intervened and successfully stopped the planned merger. Another collaborator staged a debate on the question "Lesbians in the working circle – yes or no," which resulted in talk that "the working circle is [...] misogynistic."[182] Thereafter, another collaborator, IM "Carolin," succeeded in convincing the remaining lesbian members to break away, further splintering the movement.

The Stasi's informants sowed conflict between those planning gay dances and the rest of the group, and even drove activists out of the group's leadership. Eventually the IMs succeeded in maintaining "a high rate of fluctuation among the remaining 10–15 participants." They focused discussion on topics with a "purely religious character" rather than subjects "that touch on the problems of homosexuals."[183] As early as April 1986, secret police officials could satisfactorily note that, "the number of participants has steadily decreased. [...] The reason is that a great deal of conflict and contention exists at the moment."[184] These tactics exploited existing divisions within the movement and resemble the Stasi's methods in dealing with other opposition figures.[185]

Operatives employed similar tactics in other cities. In Leipzig, Stasi officers recommended that, "The deployment of sources should [...] serve to accelerate conflicts within the working circle."[186] A list of measures taken against a different working circle in 1986 mentioned that informants "are constantly used offensively to speak out against planned or proposed enemy-negative actions." This memorandum further indicated that, "The most essential legend in use for this [is] that one must not give the state any excuse to intervene in the working circles."[187] That is, the Stasi employed the ostensible threat of its own interference to influence movement leadership.

The secret police also employed ostensibly emancipatory policies to counteract the church's influence. A report from January 1986 claimed that,

Figure 9.3. A map of the gay subculture in Berlin's Prenzlauer Berg neighbourhood produced by the Stasi, with dots indicating apartments where gay people lived, gay bars, and an "internationally known public toilet" where gay men cruised for sex. Courtesy of the Behörde des Bundesbeauftragten für die Stasi-Unterlagen (BStU, BVfS Berlin, Abt. VII, Nr. 1627, page 94)

> Through considered measures concerning the approval procedure for events of "homosexuals," such as the multi-purpose venue Buschallee […], a significant decline in the number of visits to events in the church [working circle] could be confirmed. The number of visitors declined to fifteen individuals, whereas previously between 80 and 150 had participated.[188]

That is, most gay people preferred to go out dancing rather than attend a church discussion about the place of homosexuality in East German society. Strangely enough, East German activists were beginning to discover that the logic of emancipation worked much as it did in the West: social progress often impeded political solidarity. And the secret police had figured out that this dynamic could serve its own interests.

In another case of suspected sabotage, a group of particularly pro-regime Sunday Club members broke away in February 1989 to found a new club with the name "Courage."[189] As Sillge wrote in her monograph, "Representatives of the group 'Courage' believed that the Sunday Club was not close enough to the party."[190] Rausch even went so far as to speculate that Courage "broke away from the Sunday Club through manipulation." He suggested that, "Courage was an initiative of the state security forces."[191] Those suspicions were correct: as a Stasi memorandum on 16 March 1989 relayed in no uncertain terms, "The schism of the Sunday Club has finally been executed. The positive core of the Sunday Club (party members) have […] founded their own working group 'Courage.'"[192]

As part of these efforts, the Stasi also spied on movement leaders. Eduard Stapel, for example, described in his book how the Stasi opened his mail and tapped his telephone.[193] Members of the working circles, of course, knew that the Stasi was likely spying on them and did what they could to mitigate the flow of information. They soon began to mark documents with the heading "only for use within the church" ("*nur für den innerkirchlichen Gebrauch*"), a practice that peace activists also employed.[194] Likewise, members avoided certain words such as "movement" and "gay youth group" when writing minutes of their meetings. They did not mention Westerners in attendance, again for fear of arousing the regime's suspicions.[195] My oral sources were all reluctant to discuss the Stasi, perhaps because so many activists supported the regime or perhaps because it was widely suspected just how thoroughly the secret police had infiltrated the movement.

In addition to sabotaging church groups, the Stasi hoped to prosecute activist leaders. As was specifically noted in the centralized plan circulated by Department XX in 1985, the goal of surveillance was to prove that activists had committed crimes, in particular crimes related to unlawful organizing.[196] Another memo from 1987 mentioned that one activist was being investigated for allegedly breaking §107 of the criminal code, which covered "treasonous group-organizing."[197] Likewise, the secret police considered fining another leader of a working circle for distributing printed materials without a licence.[198]

The police punished other activists by withholding certain privileges. In 1987 for example, an activist applied to travel to Frankfurt am Main in West Germany in order to take part in a conference on queer activism. The Stasi denied permission on the grounds that they might use the trip as a platform to discredit East Germany.[199] In another case, the Stasi determined that an activist's application for doctoral study would be denied as punishment for their constant petitioning of the government.[200] Such retaliation was common in the communist state. The dictatorship routinely doled out favours to those who toed the line and withheld them from those who did not.[201]

What *Is* Liberation?

In late October 1989, a certain X. in Zittau on the East German-Czechoslovak border wrote to Egon Krenz, the newly appointed secretary of the Socialist Unity Party. He complained that, "I, as a professional soldier, was discharged as a homosexual." He had already written twice to Erich Honecker, in June 1988 and April 1989, he explained. A previous reply had assured him that, "No professional soldier is encumbered because of homosexuality."[202] He also named other soldiers whom he alleged had been terminated because of their homosexuality.

I do not know what the regime might have eventually done about X., for his petition reached the government very near its demise. Nevertheless, it presents a good example of the perplexing reality that confronted gay and lesbian East Germans in the late 1980s. Although change had come rapidly to the Democratic Republic, it did not always alter the contours of everyday life. It can take time, after all, to learn new habits and paper over old prejudices. What, then, do we make of the curious admixture of emancipation and repression that characterized gay life in East Germany during the late 1980s? How do we reconcile the policy of allowing gay people in the military with X.'s discharge?

Some dismiss the changes of the 1980s as window dressing. When discussing the late 1980s with me, Peter Rausch contended that, had the regime survived, it would eventually have reverted to less progressive policies.[203] Likewise, Eduard Stapel, who recognized some of these changes as a strategy on the Stasi's part to "'dry out' our movement," dismissed them as "one part – though quite small – of our demands."[204]

Bert Thinius, in his treatment of the Humboldt University report on homosexuality in East Germany, remained sceptical of what he termed "enlightenment from the princes – or integration from above."[205]

Historians have also noted the disconnect between policy and practice. Evans describes the 1980s as bearing only the "semblance of toleration," while Dennis Sweet argues that, "Notwithstanding the decriminalization of homosexual acts [...], the interests of this regime and the interests of its lesbian and gay citizens were by no means in harmony." In a similar vein, Josie McLellan contends that, "There was no revolution in attitudes towards homosexuality. Despite a slow liberalization, gay men and lesbians faced a dual problem of homophobia and invisibility."[206]

These scholars have a point, especially insofar as the reforms were part of a strategy to deprive the gay and lesbian movement of internal impetus. Yet, the sources considered here – many of them new to the scholarship – underscore both the remarkable accomplishments of the activists themselves and the real change that had come in very short order to East Germany. Activists demonstrated incredible tenacity in the face of state opposition. In spite of constant harassment, they continued to press their case with any government body that might listen. They also, whether intentionally or not, exploited the regime's paranoias. With church and secular groups alike emphasizing that gay men and lesbians just wanted to be fuller, better socialist citizens, the regime eventually agreed with them. Apparatchiks decided that providing more robust legal protections, better social opportunities, and more information for gay and lesbian East Germans would indeed diffuse the movement's oppositional nature, precisely because they believed activists' own assertions that they had no desire to resist the regime.

Moreover, the Stasi's repressive strategies did not work. When the gay liberation groups of East Germany met for their ninth annual conference on 6 June 1989, representatives from twenty-one church-affiliated working circles and at least three state-sanctioned clubs attended.[207] The number of politically active lesbians and gay men grew between 1985 and 1989 in spite of the secret police's efforts. Of course, we cannot know what might have been, but the East German gay and lesbian movement had transformed society and government, making it a place more accepting of sexual minorities. The movement succeeded in pressing a remarkably progressive agenda in one of the century's most infamously repressive states.

If we return to the case of X., who had been expelled from the East German military because of his homosexuality, we ought to acknowledge a set of seemingly contradictory realities about him and the state he inhabited. He had been discharged, it is true, but still retained enough faith in the regime that he wrote at least three petitions to its executive, hoping the discharge would be reversed. Likewise, he wrote that he had attended meetings of the Sunday Club, which by that time enjoyed official state support. The government, for its part, had responded to his petition, but with the perplexing and mealy-mouthed excuse that gay soldiers were no longer discharged for their homosexuality. X.'s is a picture of how change takes time and is imperfect in its manifestations. It is an example of bureaucratic incompetence and unwillingness to admit error. His fate should stand as a warning against both triumphalist narratives of progress and overly bleak appraisals of the past.

In my interviews with former East Germans, I came across similar contradictions. Ulrich Z., a gay man who lived in Dresden in the 1980s, hated the East German regime and migrated to West Germany in 1988. Nonetheless, when we talked about his life in Dresden, he described it as "the most beautiful gay time."[208] Similarly, Carsten I., who fled to West Germany in the late 1980s, recalled living openly as a gay man in East Berlin in that decade and meeting his partner of almost thirty years in that time.[209] These were memories of neither the euphoria of liberation nor the despair of persecution.

The East German regime had been confronted with a savvy political movement that sought to make the cause of gay liberation politically expedient. As we have seen, activists did so in numerous ways with the hope that the regime would enact policies and with the knowledge that they would be subject to the repressive machinery of the secret police. The Stasi's decision to pressure the government to accede to that catalogue of demands was certainly part of a strategy to suppress the gay and lesbian movement. But that realization does not negate the fact that East Germany liberated its gay and lesbian populations in a way very few other states had done at that point in history. Its government and bureaucracy authorized a host of new policies that came to West Germany only in the years after the fall of the Berlin Wall.

Over the last decade or so, revisionist histories of East Germany have unearthed ways in which East German private life evolved independently of the regime. Scholars have done so to highlight that, in Fulbrook's words, "There was, in curious and multiple ways, also a 'normality' about the history of the GDR."[210] While I sympathize with this project – and argue that the history of gay everyday life supports it – I also think something more is at work in the successes of East German gay and lesbian activism. After all, there was nothing normal about their experiences in the GDR. Rather, their efforts reveal something extraordinary: a public, political idea of gay, socialist citizenship that developed in East Germany, at least by the 1980s, and that provided activists with a foundation from which to seek change within an authoritarian system. That is, they fashioned an understanding of their own political subjectivity that allowed them to pressure the regime in ways both public and private. The history of gay and lesbian activism in East Germany is, quite simply, a story of public life and political engagement under state socialism.

Comparing this activism in the GDR to similar developments in other socialist dictatorships reveals just how striking the East German case really was. To begin with, many Eastern-bloc states continued to criminalize homosexuality well past their transition into post-communist republics. Russia only decriminalized homosexuality in 1993, while Romania kept its statute on the books until 2001.[211] Both Poland and Czechoslovakia, however, saw activist efforts in the 1980s more in line with what East Germany experienced. In Poland, gay friendship circles arose in the mid-1980s. Yet, as Lukasz Szulc describes, the Polish government launched mass arrests of homosexuals in 1985, code-named "Operation Hyacinth." While historians still do not know precisely why the Polish government cracked down on the gay scene in so ruthless a fashion, some have speculated that it was intended to stymie gay political efforts.[212]

Though Czechoslovak activists saw nothing so brutal, only in 1988 did two sexologists found the country's first gay and lesbian social circle. While the group did have some success, winning the right to place personal advertisements in the fall of 1989, there were no reforms of comparable scope to those in East Germany.[213] In fact, the overwhelmingly grim condition of gay and lesbian life in the Eastern bloc has led Conor O'Dwyer to assert that, "After communism's collapse, activism had not crossed any of these thresholds: it was local, informal, and apolitical – comprised of friendship networks oriented toward self-help and services."[214] His assessment clearly does not apply to the East German case.

Moreover, a comparison of East German policies with those in countries beyond the socialist bloc reveals just how extraordinary they were. Many of the new measures were particular to East Germany – there is no real way to compare the regime's decision to allow marriage and sexual counselling centres to see homosexual patients because no similar, centrally controlled network of clinics existed in Western countries. Nonetheless, we can compare two policies with laws in other countries, namely the repeal of §151 and the decision to stop discharging soldiers because of their homosexuality. In the 1980s, most countries around the world both forbade gay people from serving in the military and set a higher age of consent for homosexual sex (or continued to criminalize homosexuality). A comparison (see figure 9.4) of when countries changed these two policies reveals that East Germany was one of the very first countries explicitly to allow homosexuals to serve in the military. It was also among the first to equalize ages of consent. Most countries only followed suit in the 1990s and early 2000s.

The case of gay liberation in East Germany is thus something of an anomaly when compared both to socialist dictatorships and to liberal democracies. Why is it that the Democratic Republic, one of the most notoriously inflexible states in the region, pursued reform? Part of the answer, as I have argued, lies in how activists couched their demands to the regime and the ways they envisioned their own political subjectivity. Their efforts were framed in ways that, by the 1980s, made sense to East Germany's rulers. Moreover, in spite of German socialism's long ambivalence about homosexuality, there was an undeniably progressive heritage that activists could draw on, from the KPD's Weimar-era push to decriminalize homosexuality to gay victims' suffering in Nazi camps. Finally, West German activism not only inspired gay men and lesbians in the GDR but also weighed in the calculations of the East German government. That is to say, as remarkable as East Germany's gay and lesbian movement was, it does not offer a road map for other social and political movements. It was an extraordinary result of its time and its place.

Nonetheless, this messy reality suggests a few tentative conclusions about democracy and dictatorship in the Cold War. It indicates that change, and specifically change motivated by the kinds of activism historians typically associate with liberal democracy, was and is possible in authoritarian systems. Histories of the Cold War still sometimes indulge in essentialist frameworks, casting Western countries as capable of transformation and Eastern dictatorships as static. If anything, the success that gay activists had in pushing through an ambitious reform agenda in an authoritarian state should underscore just how limited that model is. Communist countries too had forms of civil society, albeit different from that typical in Western states at the time. They were never fully totalitarian in practice (and scholars have cast evergreater doubt on that term's utility) or, by the 1970s at the latest, even in aspiration.[215] Even as the Stasi swelled in size under the Honecker regime, the East German government grew increasingly responsive to its citizens' desires.[216] Political activism can, did, and does shape life in authoritarian states.

Furthermore, the fact that one of the most wide-ranging pro-gay policy agendas to have been enacted in the 1980s came out of the fraught

Figure 9.4. Comparison of when different countries equalized ages of consent and formally allowed gay men to serve in the military

Acceptance of Homosexuality in Military		Equalization of Age of Consent	
Country	Year Policy Changed	Country	Year Equalized
Netherlands	1974	*Poland*	1932
Sweden	1976	Netherlands	1971
Norway	1979	Norway	1972
Spain	1984	Denmark	1976
East Germany	1988	Sweden	1978
Portugal	1989	Colombia	1981
Australia	1992	France	1982
Canada	1992	New Zealand	1986
Switzerland	1992	**East Germany**	1987
Ireland	1993	*Czechoslovakia*	1990
Israel	1993	Iceland	1992
New Zealand	1994	Ireland	1993
Italy	1995	Germany (FRG)	1994
South Africa	1998	Spain	1995
Colombia	1999	Finland	1998
United Kingdom	2000	Israel	2000
Germany (FRG)	2000	United Kingdom	2000
Czech Republic	2001	*Albania*	2001
Peru	2004	Austria	2002
Bulgaria	2004	*Bulgaria*	2002

These charts compare two of East Germany's policies with when other countries around the world made similar changes. Policies concerning homosexuality in the military are more difficult to pin a date on than statutory ages of consent because some militaries removed bans on allowing gay people to serve only to replace them with policies that *de facto* banned them. The Federal Republic of Germany, for instance, gradually eliminated some official barriers to gay military service over the course of the 1970s and 1980s but still banned gay men from military careers until 2000. As we have seen, some gay East German soldiers were expelled from the army even after the 1988 guidelines appeared. The dates in the left-hand column should thus be taken with a grain of salt. Countries in italics are former communist states. For sources, see Appendix B.

Figure 9.4. (Continued)

Acceptance of Homosexuality in Military		Equalization of Age of Consent	
Country	Year Policy Changed	Country	Year Equalized
Argentina	2009	*Hungary*	2002
Philippines	2009	*Romania*	2002
Uruguay	2009	United States	2003
Serbia	2010	*Serbia*	2006
United States	2011	South Africa	2007
Chile	2012	Australia	2016

relationship between activists and a paranoid surveillance state should remind us that gay liberation is not simply a product of liberal, consumer-capitalist democracy. Likewise, it is not always allied with other causes deemed progressive, and it often arrives in haphazard fashion. Gay liberation was not and is not always hitched to the van of progress. The experiences of East German gay liberation throw into contention whether historians can even write of progress or progressive change. In East Germany, many activists promoted the dictatorial regime and saw liberation as a way of bolstering its support among gay and lesbian citizens.

The events of the 1980s should thus give us pause when evaluating the contours and even the definition of gay liberation. Advocates and historians alike frequently assume that the existence of a flourishing subculture and political progress go hand-in-hand. Comparing the fates of activist efforts in West Germany, which enjoyed a huge commercial subculture but lacked legal reforms, and in East Germany, where the opposite was true, indicates that these two horsemen of gay liberation do not always ride together. Historically speaking, there is no reason to expect that they should.

Epilogue

Revolutions are not always brought about by a gradual decline from bad to worse. Nations that have endured patiently and almost unconsciously the most overwhelming oppression often burst into rebellion against the yoke the moment it begins to grow lighter. The regime which is destroyed by a revolution is almost always an improvement on its immediate predecessor, and experience teaches that the most critical moment for bad governments is the one which witnesses their first steps toward reform.[1]

These words, which Alexis de Tocqueville penned in 1856, have become standard fare in our understanding of revolutions. Mediated by mid-century thinkers, including the American sociologist J.C. Davies and the German historian Reinhart Koselleck, the notion that reform precedes revolution and even makes it thinkable turns up in histories of virtually every upheaval in the modern era.[2] The *annus mirabilis* 1989 is no different. Prevailing views hold that the East German regime's gradually slackening grip led to its rapid unravelling in autumn 1989, to the breaching of the Berlin Wall on the night of 9 November, and to the regime's demise shortly thereafter.[3] Reform made revolution possible.

Whether or not Tocqueville's hypothesis helps explain the course of Germany's gay liberations may be asked with two inflections. The first queries whether or not East German pro-gay reforms contributed to the regime's collapse at the end of the 1980s. After all, Peter Rausch spoke of a "gay and lesbian *Wende*" that took place before the *Wende* of 1989.[4] That language mirrors what Edith Sheffer found in her 2011 study of the Iron Curtain. Late in the decade, panicked border officials began granting travel permits with ever-greater frequency, thereby allowing an ever-swelling flood of East Germans to flee westward.[5] That shift played a part in the regime's collapse soon thereafter. Did the "gay and lesbian *Wende*" also play a role in the end of German communism?

A number of signs suggest that the answer is no. East Germany's gay and lesbian movement was heavily populated with pro-regime individuals, many of whom belonged to the SED. The HIB and its secular successors in the 1980s explicitly favoured the regime, while members of church-affiliated working circles held varied opinions. Peace activists more openly hostile to the dictatorship, it is true, led some of the working circles. Nonetheless, most leaders were, at the very least, aware of the dangers of opposing the regime and tried to work within existing social and legal frameworks. Moreover, the movement, unlike the peace and environmental movements, was largely successful in pressing the regime to institute new policies. This meant that gay and lesbian activists had concrete reasons to think well of and cooperate with the regime, for it had granted them new rights and opportunities.

The East German electoral campaign of 1990 provides further evidence that these reforms had little to do with opposition to the regime. After droves of East Germans crossed the border on 9 November 1989, the party allowed the country's first-ever democratic elections on 18 March. The elections were governed by a new law that, among other things, forbade parties that discriminated on the basis of sexual orientation from participating.[6]

Twelve parties contested the election, though the main vote-getters were the Christian Democratic Union, led by Lothar de Maizière; a newly reconstituted SPD; and the Party of Democratic Socialism (PDS), the SED's successor.[7] Although sexual policies never became a dominant topic in an election that revolved around the question of whether East Germany should reunify with West Germany, they were discussed and contested. Most left-wing parties, including the Green Party and the SPD, supported gay rights in their electoral platforms.[8] Even the centre-right Christian Democrats advocated for gay men and lesbians. When we spoke, Lothar de Maizière told me that one of his core interests, as leader of the East German CDU, had been in finding ways "in which the state can prevent the discrimination of minorities." When he became chairman of the party that fateful November, he and other reformers set about writing a new platform. "In the program," de Maizière said, "it stood that we respect all forms of cohabitation, hetero- and homosexual and so forth."[9]

I have found no evidence that the CDU, which led the charge for reunification, campaigned on its support for homosexual rights. The PDS, on the other hand, tried to make electoral hay from its pro-gay policies. Its program argued for the "equalization of homosexual

Figure 10.1. Party of Democratic Socialism 1990 campaign poster. It states:
"For the emancipation of all foreign fellow citizens, all those who think
differently, who live differently, who love differently."

Für
die Gleichberechtigung
aller ausländischen
Mitbürger,
aller Andersdenkenden,
Anderslebenden,
Andersliebenden.

PDS

Partei des Demokratischen Sozialismus

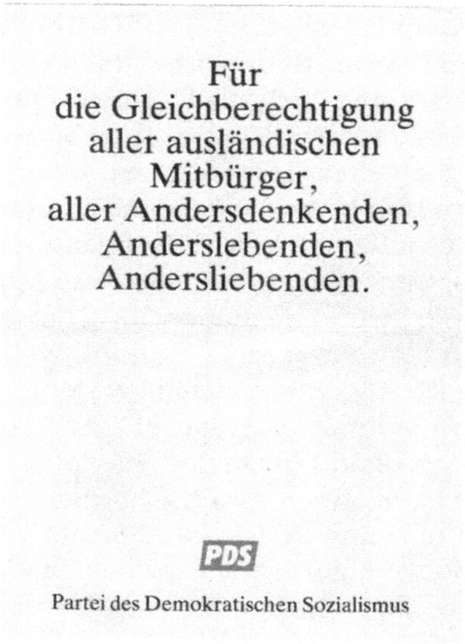

Courtesy of the Hoover Institution Library and Archives ("Elections 1990 March 18 PDS,"
German Subject Collection, Box 46, Folder "Partei des Demokratischen Sozialismus
[PDS]," HA) and the Rosa Luxemburg Stiftung (Rosa Luxemburg Stiftung e.V. Archiv,
Signatur P_Volkskammer 11.02.07.01–1249)

women and men vis-à-vis heterosexuals in all social spheres of life."[10] It
made its support public in ways the CDU did not, printing large posters that declared, "For the emancipation of all foreign fellow citizens,
all those who think differently, who live differently, who love differently" (see figure 10.1).[11] East Germany's former rulers clearly thought
their support for gay men and lesbians in the 1980s would make their
calls for a more equitable and open society believable – and generate
electoral support.

The ways in which homosexuality showed up in the campaign suggest two conclusions. First, there existed a broad political consensus in
favour of gay and lesbian interests in East Germany. Parties from the far
left to the centre-right supported equitable sexual citizenship in a way
not yet accepted in West Germany. Not only would the West German
CDU remain resistant to similar policies until well after reunification,

but as late as 1987 the West German SPD's party program also made no mention of either homosexuality or §175.[12] On the other hand, the PDS's vocalization of its policies suggests it believed gay people would support it because of its track record. Although the party won only about 16 per cent of the vote on 18 March, its willingness to campaign on gay rights illustrates the party's belief that gay and lesbian voters were not enemies of state socialism or of the GDR.

Second, there is virtually no indication that gay activism helped push East Germany into revolution. Instead, the evidence intimates that the regime's pro-gay policies bolstered its standing among gay men and lesbians. This is not to say that the Tocqueville hypothesis is incorrect but rather that different flavours of reform have differing effects. Those instituted in the late 1980s were revolutionary in comparison to sexual policies that then obtained in most of the rest of the world. But they affected a relatively small subset of the population and were reforms of a cultural-legal nature, as opposed to the kinds of socio-economic reforms to which Tocqueville, Koselleck, Davies, and others refer.

The other inflection with which we can read Tocqueville's assertion is that which asks whether or not the gradual reform of laws regulating homosexuality in both East and West Germany – starting with reforms in 1950, 1957, and 1968 in the GDR and 1969 in the FRG – led to a revolution in the treatment of homosexuality or in moral thought more generally. To answer that question requires a cursory glance at what came after the end of the Cold War in Germany – at how homosexual life and politics evolved in the reunified nation.

The reunification process was not a happy one. West Germans arrived in the new states, taking positions of authority away from East Germans and privatizing the socialist economy. Professors, politicians, and bureaucrats lost their jobs in the upheaval.[13] A state organization known as the *Treuhand* took over East German industries after the Wall fell and auctioned them off at fire-sale prices.[14] These policies quickly led to resentment from Easterners and attacks on marginalized groups. Immigrant populations in particular became targets in these waves of violence in the early 1990s.[15]

The progress of the 1980s did not immunize East Germany's queer populations from the reaction. Gay men and lesbians too faced increased violence in the post-reunification era – a fact that many studies of the period do not mention. Neo-Nazis attacked a party at Charlotte von Mahlsdorf's villa, for instance, in May 1991. In her autobiography she describes seeing "thirty skinheads [who] advanced on Mahlsdorf with crowbars" in order to attack the eighty people at her spring festival.[16] The incursion prompted gay groups to protest their still precarious position in society more aggressively. Man-O-Meter, a gay clinic in Schöneberg, reported in 1991 that at least 648 gay people had been attacked in Germany in the past year.[17] Newspapers reported that, "Violence against homosexuals in Germany has markedly increased in magnitude and intensity since reunification."[18] While gay men had been victims of crime for decades, the surge of violence directed against homosexuals, along with concomitant waves of xenophobia, suggests that East Germans were taking deep-seated social frustrations out on already vulnerable minority populations.

The renewed animus against gay men and lesbians makes clear just how fragile change can be. Although East Germany was in some ways at the forefront of gay and lesbian activism in the late 1980s, that did not prevent the subsequent decade's surge of violence. Animus became a convenient outlet for the frustrations and anxieties of a population undergoing radical social, political, and economic changes. The violence of the early 1990s illustrates how all progress on so-called social questions is provisional.

Politically speaking, the *Wende* did make the Federal Republic friendlier to lesbians and gay men. As early as 1990, as West German politicians scurried to prepare elections in reunified Germany, the Green Party tried to leverage the GDR's progressive record in parliament. The party's *Bundestag* caucus introduced a resolution which insisted that "the lesbian and gay movement is an integral piece of the citizens' movement in the GDR." It noted that laws passed by de Maizière's government had made sexual orientation a protected class under GDR antidiscrimination provisions. The party insisted that the West German *Bundestag* not allow reunification to wipe away this progress, asking Kohl's government to adopt East German measures into federal law.[19]

Although the conservative government rejected the Greens' suggestions, elections on 2 December 1990 brought scores of new politicians sympathetic to gay and lesbian concerns into an enlarged *Bundestag*. A shotgun marriage with the East German party Alliance '90 saved the West German Green Party that year, preserving in parliament one of the most significant institutional advocates for gay and lesbian interests.[20] The PDS, though it won less than 3 per cent of the popular vote, campaigned on a program that included homosexual rights.[21] As *Der Spiegel* reported, the PDS argued that East Germany's repeal of §175 meant it had "reached a higher cultural stage than the BRD."[22] Although the CDU retained the chancellorship under Helmut Kohl, the new parliament included more politicians openly sympathetic to sexual reform.

One particular sticking point for the new government was reconciling the East and West German penal codes. East Germany's laws were considerably more progressive than West Germany's. Statutes regulating abortion, divorce, and inheritance, for example, were all far more equitable in East Germany than in the Federal Republic.[23] Moreover, while the *Volkskammer* had repealed §151 in 1988, thereby equalizing the age of consent for homo- and heterosexual acts, §175 remained on the books in the Federal Republic. The statute was no dead letter: even in the early 1990s, West German courts convicted scores of men under it. East German negotiators, however, were loath to allow West Germany's more conservative criminal code to encroach on their country, and thus the reunification treaty signed on 31 August 1990 mandated that §175 would continue to obtain in the West German states, but not in those of the former GDR.[24]

In 1991 the Free Democrats, still the CDU's junior coalition partner, suggested liberalizing the criminal code in order to bring it into line with the progressive laws of the Democratic Republic. Unsurprisingly, their conservative partners balked at the thought.[25] Their intransigence was not surprising, for when the East German CDU had brought its progressive platform to the West German party after reunification, de Maizière told me, "Kohl threw it out *at once*." For three years the parliament dithered, allowing the bizarre reality of two mutually exclusive laws obtaining in different parts of the same country.[26]

Finally, in 1994, seven months before new federal elections, the government repealed §175, bringing to pass a core demand of West Germany's gay movement. For all its historical significance, though, the *Bundestag* approved the bill in more of a whimper than a bang. In an early debate, one CDU representative had complained that the fact "that we still have §175 in the penal code is used by some homosexual groups to spread the notion that homosexual acts are still punished in the Federal Republic."[27] He apparently favoured repeal to deprive gay groups of what he considered no more than a propaganda device. On 10 March 1994, §175 finally passed out of existence, extinguishing what one parliamentarian called "the most famous statute of all."[28] Its ultimate repeal, which arose from the need to reconcile the GDR's progressive criminal code with the FRG's regressive one, is one of the most concrete examples of East German gay liberation's afterlife. These developments suggest there is merit in Lothar de Maizière's striking contention that, "On the question of homosexuals, the GDR was substantially more open than the Federal Republic. I think that this somewhat greater tolerance has since migrated into the West."[29]

Four years later, on 27 September 1998, federal elections swept the SPD back into power for the first time since 1982. With support from the new federal states, it won its highest proportion of votes vis-à-vis the CDU in postwar history and entered into coalition with the Green Party. The following year Lieutenant Winfried Stecher, whom superiors described as a "supersoldier (*Supersoldat*)," was discovered to be gay.[30] Stecher's commanders subsequently demoted him to a desk job under army guidelines that allowed gay men as general infantry but not as officers. Stecher sued the Defence Ministry and his case went to the Federal Constitutional Court. Before the judges could rule on the merits of the case, however, SPD Defence Minister Rudolf Scharping decided to withdraw the discriminatory rules and allow Stecher to return to his old position, thereby equalizing homo- and heterosexuals within the military.[31] It is hard to imagine that a government led by the conservative CDU would have volunteered such a change in military practice.

These changes indicate that reform brought not revolution but the opportunity for new reform. Events of the last three decades imply, moreover, that such reform is unstable and moves in a jagged fashion. Lesbians and gay men continued to be the victims of violence, while legal advances often materialized slowly. Germany's path has not allowed it to break free of history's moorings and chart a revolutionary new sexual ethic. Rather, its history bequeathed it a kind of steady evolution in the recognition of homosexual citizenship. In fact, when one pauses to consider it, gay liberation is rarely a story of revolution. Much oftener it is one of slow – sometimes infuriatingly slow – change over time that, as queer scholars increasingly recognize, typically brings in its train hosts of new worries and repressions. One might even ask if revolution is ever an appropriate term to describe changes in sexual law, policing, or morality.

On closer inspection, the progress of Germany's gay liberations thus reveals a deeply uneven process. The symbols we today take as evidence of liberation – thundering nightclubs and rainbow-festooned streets – often dissemble, telling a different story than that of science or the law. Examining social, medical, cultural, political, and legal evidence offers at least five different stories of gay liberation, some moving faster than others, some steadily, some haphazardly, all unexpectedly. East German gay men and lesbians undeniably enjoyed greater legal protections than did their counterparts in the Federal Republic, who in turn enjoyed a richer commercial subculture of bars, saunas, magazines, museums, and clubs.

The fate of gay liberation efforts in both Germanies is a reminder that all political systems generate their own incentive structures that reward and penalize particular behaviours: there is nothing inherently good or evil – or progressive or revanchist – about them. The East and West German trajectories are evidence that what we think of as gay liberation is not easily defined, for it consists of multiple, conflicting phenomena. Moreover, it was not always coterminous with the triumph of liberal democracy or consumer capitalism. These paths suggest that the process of sexual citizenship formation is too contingent and nationally situated to be lumped together under a term such as gay liberation. That is to say, there is no one path that gay liberation takes – it has no telos. At best, we can speak of states of liberation.

I began this book by noting the utopian quality of queer life in contemporary Germany, particularly in Berlin. What I hope has become apparent is how convoluted the path to that present was, how slow and contingent the processes of reform were, and the scepticism with which we should regard claims about the alleged success of liberation movements. At best there were many small liberations that brought slow and tentative change. These processes should also prompt us to question just how utopian the present really is. Is there a greyer reality that hides behind the images of rainbow-bedecked Pride floats? The answer, of course, is that there is.

Germany does lead the pack in many respects. Berlin and Germany's other large cities are remarkably queer-friendly places. They boast overwhelming numbers of gay bars and clubs. Hundreds of thousands of people attend Pride celebrations every summer in German cities. Politicians and the public overwhelmingly support queer rights. When Donald Trump unexpectedly won the US presidential election in 2016, Chancellor Angela Merkel pointedly reminded the President-elect that, "Germany and America are bound by common values – democracy, freedom, as well as respect for the rule of law and the dignity of each and every person, regardless of their origin, skin colour, creed, gender, sexual orientation, or political views."[32] When the *Bundestag* passed marriage equality legislation in 2017, the measure enjoyed the support of a crushing majority of the population.[33] Some research even suggests that a higher percentage of Germans identify as LGBT than any other European nationality.[34]

Yet in other regards the country lags. In homosexual healthcare, curiously, Germany is nowhere close to the fore. Though Berlin, a city of roughly a quarter of a million LGBT people, is home to two STI-dedicated clinics, they are open only a few hours per day and require payment.[35] San Francisco, by contrast, is a city with roughly 50,000 LGBT individuals and boasts a free STI clinic open eight hours a day, six days a week.[36] Berlin ranks squarely in the middle of European cities in terms of access to STI-related healthcare.[37] Likewise, Germany was slow to adopt Truvada as pre-exposure prophylaxis against HIV infection, more commonly known as PrEP.[38] This neglect is symptomatic of an institutional indifference to LGBT priorities. Queer studies, for example, have lagged in German universities in comparison to other Western countries. In my own experience, the kind of superficial anti-gay prejudice that was banished from polite society in the United States at least a decade ago is alive and well, even in supposedly progressive German social circles. Rita Chin has argued that Germans struggle to conceptualize racial difference.[39] So too, I would argue, many Germans continue not to see sexual difference. At the same time, Germany's queer communities continue to exhibit racism and xenophobia, especially against Germany's Muslim populations.[40]

Germany also lacks the kind of large gay political organizations – such as the Gay and Lesbian Alliance Against Defamation (GLAAD) or the Human Rights Campaign (HRC) in the United States – that have shaped sexual politics in other countries over the past few decades. The national organization that does exist, the German Lesbian and Gay Association (LSVD), claims a membership of around 4,000.[41] The American HRC, by comparison, has a membership of 3 million.[42] The dearth of gay political groups is one legacy of the rapid decline in gay electoral activism in West Germany after 1980. It is also likely the result of the consensus support for gay rights across the political spectrum. Even Germany's neo-fascist party, the Alternative for Germany (AfD), pays lip service to equal rights for gay men and lesbians, as increasingly do conservative politicians around the democratic West.[43]

But this confused amalgamation of progress and regress should not be a surprise. Just as a comparison of animus in each Germany reveals there to be no one homophobia, so too the history of liberation efforts in postwar Germany is a story of strange bedfellows, of the uneven and unexpected advance of gay priorities. Gay life and politics in modern Germany are nothing more or less than the result of the contingent paths they took over the last seven decades. To look at queer life in Germany today is to take in a palimpsest of the past century, of the shattered utopias that defined gay liberation's paths. Moments of failure, from 1933 and 1980 to 1949 and 1989, shaped the routes of gay liberation in Cold War Germany as much as its triumphs. But moments of utopian promise have also left lasting marks on gay life, whether in the existence of a federal endowment named for Magnus Hirschfeld, the persistence of the East German Buschallee disco and the HAW successor SchwuZ, or the radicalness of Berlin's alternative Pride parades.

It is not, after all, all bad. Not by any stretch of the imagination. Gay and lesbian citizens mobilized in extraordinary ways in Cold War Germany. They forced the hand of one of the era's most infamously

Figure 10.2. The Sunday Club in Prenzlauer Berg. Courtesy of Sebastian Naumann

inflexible dictatorships. They brought politicians in the West German democracy to heel in a remarkably public way in the late 1970s. More than anything, they survived the legacy of a murderous fascist regime to carve out a place of acceptance and celebration for themselves in the heart of Europe. And if you wander over to the beautiful East Berlin neighbourhood of Prenzlauer Berg some afternoon, you will find, standing on a leafy street-corner, a café, tended by queer people young and old, offering everything from trans evenings and lesbian hangouts to soccer viewing parties and roundtables with elderly LGBT people (figure 10.2). It is the Sunday Club, the same organization that Ursula Sillge founded in 1983 and a happy reminder of the impermanent permanence of the past.

Appendix A

Versions of §175 and Associated Laws[*]

German Reich

1 January 1872 (Imperial Germany)
§175
Unnatural fornication (*widernatürliche Unzucht*), which is committed between persons of the male sex or by humans with animals, shall be punished with prison (*Gefängniß*); the loss of civil rights is also possible.

1 September 1935 (Nazi Germany)
§175
1) A man who fornicates (*Unzucht treibt*) with another man or allows himself to be misused for the purposes of fornication shall be punished with prison.
2) In the case of a participant, who at the time of the act was not yet twenty-one years old, the court can, in particularly slight cases, abstain from punishment.

§175(a)
The following will be punished by prison with hard labour (*Zuchthaus*) of up to ten years or, under mitigating circumstances, with prison of not less than three months:
1. a man who coerces another man with force or with threat of imminent danger to life or limb in order to fornicate with him or allow himself to be misused for the purposes of fornication by him;

---

* Original German in Schäfer, *"Widernatürliche Unzucht,"* 315–26; and online at https://lexetius.com/StGB/175. Translations are my own.

2. a man who influences another man by abuse of a relationship of dependence grounded in service, employment, or subordination in order to fornicate with him or allow himself to be misused for the purposes of fornication by him;
3. a man over twenty-one years who seduces (*verführt*) a male person under twenty-one years in order to fornicate with him or allow himself to be misused for the purposes of fornication by him;
4. a man who commercially fornicates with men or allows himself to be misused for the purposes of fornication by men or offers himself therefor.

Federal Republic of Germany

1 September 1969[†]

§175

(1) The following will be punished with prison:[‡]

1. a man over eighteen years who fornicates (*Unzucht treibt*) with or allows himself to be misused for the purposes of fornication by a man under twenty-one years,
2. a man who influences another man by abuse of a relationship of dependence grounded in service, employment, or subordination in order to fornicate with him or allow himself to be misused for the purposes of fornication by him,
3. a man who commercially fornicates with men or allows himself to be misused for the purposes of fornication by men or offers himself therefor.

(2) In cases under subparagraph 1, Nr. 2 the attempt is punishable.

(3) In the case of a participant, who at the time of the act was not yet twenty-one years old, the court can abstain from punishment.

---

† The 1935 versions of the two laws remained in force in the Federal Republic until 1 September 1969.

‡ On 1 April 1970, "prison" was replaced with "a prison term of up to five years."

24 November 1973[§]

§175

(1) A man over eighteen years who undertakes sexual acts with a man under eighteen years or allows a man under eighteen years to undertake sexual acts with him shall be punished with a prison sentence of up to five years or with a fine.

(2) The court can abstain from punishment under this provision if:
  1. the perpetrator was not yet twenty-one years old at the time of the act or
  2. upon consideration of the behaviour of those, against whom the act was directed, the injustice of the act was minimal.

11 June 1994

§175

(repealed)

German Democratic Republic

28 March 1950[¶]

§175

Unnatural fornication (*widernatürliche Unzucht*), which is committed between persons of the male sex or by humans with animals, shall be punished with prison (*Gefängniß*); the loss of civil rights is also possible.

§175(a)

The following will be punished by prison with hard labour (*Zuchthaus*) of up to ten years or, under mitigating circumstances, with prison of not less than three months:

1. a man who coerces another man with force or with threat of imminent danger to life or limb in order to fornicate with him or allow himself to be misused for the purposes of fornication by him;

---

§ The West German Constitutional Court ruled on 2 October 1973 that §175-(1)-1 was only constitutional when applied to men over eighteen years fornicating with or being misused for the purposes of fornication by men under eighteen years. This ruling was codified in the 24 November 1973 amendment to the law.

¶ As the result of an East German Supreme Court ruling on 28 March 1950, the old version of §175 was coupled with the Nazi-era §175(a).

2. a man who influences another man by abuse of a relationship of dependence grounded in service, employment, or subordination in order to fornicate with him or allow himself to be misused for the purposes of fornication by him;
3. a man over twenty-one years who seduces (*verführt*) a male person under twenty-one years in order to fornicate with him or allow himself to be misused for the purposes of fornication by him;
4. a man who commercially fornicates with men or allows himself to be misused for the purposes of fornication by men or offers himself therefor.

12 January 1968
§151
An adult who undertakes sexual acts with a youth of the same sex will be punished with a prison sentence of up to three years or with probation.**

14 December 1988
§151
(repealed)††

** §65 of the penal code defined a youth as one who is "over fourteen, but not yet eighteen years old."

†† The law of 14 December 1988 codified an East German Supreme Court ruling of 11 August 1987, which nullified §151.

Appendix B

Sources for Figure 9.4

Albania: Myers, *Historical Dictionary of the Lesbian and Gay Liberation Movements*, liv.

Argentina: Immigration and Refugee Board of Canada Research Directorate, *Argentina: Situation of Homosexual Men and Women*, 8 December 2009, accessed 31 July 2020: https://www.refworld.org/docid/4b7cee77c.html.

Australia: Scott and Stanley, *Gays and Lesbians in the Military*, 224; Gail Burke, "Queensland Government Lowers Age of Consent for Anal Sex to 16," *ABC News*, 15 September 2016, accessed 31 July 2020: https://www.abc.net.au /news/2016-09-15/queensland-standardises-age-of-consent-laws-anal-sex /7850112.

Austria: Myers, *Historical Dictionary of the Lesbian and Gay Liberation Movements*, lv.

Bulgaria: Immigration and Refugee Board of Canada Research Directorate, *Bulgaria: Situation of Homosexuals*, 22 August 2006, accessed 31 July 2020: https://www.refworld.org/docid/45f146fd2f.html; Myers, *Historical Dictionary of the Lesbian and Gay Liberation Movements*, lv.

Canada: Scott and Stanley, *Gays and Lesbians in the Military*, 224.

Chile: "Chilean Sailor Makes History after Announcing He Is Gay," *BBC*, 28 August 2014, accessed 31 July 2020: https://www.bbc.com/news /world-latin-america-28961883.

Colombia: "Sentencia C-507/99, Constitutional Court of Colombia (14 July 1999)," *International Commission of Jurists*, accessed 31 July 2020: https:// www.icj.org/sogicasebook/sentencia-c-50799-constitutional-court-of -colombia-14-july-1999/; Myers, *Historical Dictionary of the Lesbian and Gay Liberation Movements*, xlv.

Czech Republic/Czechoslovakia: "Czech Republic LGBTI Resources," *Rights in Exile Programme*, accessed 31 July 2020: http://www.refugeelegal aidinformation.org/czech-republic-lgbti-resources; Myers, *Historical Dictionary of the Lesbian and Gay Liberation Movements*, xlix.

Denmark: Eskridge, *Equality Practice*, 116.

Finland: Eskridge, *Equality Practice*, 116.

France: Eskridge, *Equality Practice*, 116.

Germany (Federal Republic): Deutscher Bundestag, "Antwort der Bundesregierung auf die Kleine Anfrage der Abgeordneten Alexander Müller, Dr. Jens Brandenburg (Rhein-Neckar), Konstantin Kuhle, weiterer Abgeordneter und der Franktion der FDP: Rehabilitierung homosexueller deutscher Soldatinnen und Soldaten," Drucksache 19/17305, 20 February 2020.

Hungary: Myers, *Historical Dictionary of the Lesbian and Gay Liberation Movements*, lv.

Iceland: Eskridge, *Equality Practice*, 116.

Ireland: Pond, "A Comparative Survey and Analysis of Military Policies with Regard to Service by Gay Persons," 1020; Myers, *Historical Dictionary of the Lesbian and Gay Liberation Movements*, l.

Israel: D'Amico, "Race-ing and Gendering the Military Closet," 21–2; Myers, *Historical Dictionary of the Lesbian and Gay Liberation Movements*, liv.

Italy: Pond, "A Comparative Survey and Analysis of Military Policies with Regard to Service by Gay Persons," 980; Duncan, *Reading and Writing Italian Homosexuality*, 108.

Netherlands: D'Amico, "Race-ing and Gendering the Military Closet," 11 and 22; Sandfort, "Pedophilia and the Gay Movement," 97–8.

New Zealand: New Zealand Defence Force, "NZDF Celebrates 25 Years of Open Lgbt+ Service," Scoop Regional, 7 February 2019, accessed 31 July 2020: https://www.scoop.co.nz/stories/AK1902/S00160/nzdf-celebrates -25-years-of-open-lgbt-service.htm; "Homosexual Law Reform Act 1986," New Zealand Public Act 1986 No 33 (1986).

Norway: Gade, Segal, and Johnson, "The Experience of Foreign Militaries," 124; Eskridge, *Equality Practice*, 254.

Peru: "Sentencia 0023–2003-AI/TC, Constitutional Tribunal of Peru (9 June 2004)," *International Commission of Jurists*, accessed 31 July 2020: https:// www.icj.org/sogicasebook/sentencia-0023-2003-aitc-constitutional -tribunal-of-peru-9-june-2004/.

Philippines: "Argentinien und die Philippinen beenden Homo-Verbot im Militär," *Queer.de*, 4 March 2009, accessed 31 July 2020: https://www.queer .de/detail.php?article_id=10083.

Poland: Crahan et al., *The Oxford Companion to Politics of the World*, 308.

Portugal: D'Amico, "Race-ing and Gendering the Military Closet," 11;

Romania: Myers, *Historical Dictionary of the Lesbian and Gay Liberation Movements*, lv.

Serbia: Bajoana Barlovac, "Timeline: LGBT history in Serbia," *Balkan Insight*, 25 September 2014: https://balkaninsight.com/2014/09/25 /timeline-lgbt-history-in-serbia/; Myers, *Historical Dictionary of the Lesbian and Gay Liberation Movements*, lviii.

South Africa: Belkin and Canaday, "Assessing the Integration of Gays and Lesbians into the South African National Defence Force," 1; Myers, *Historical Dictionary of the Lesbian and Gay Liberation Movements*, lviii.

Spain: Gade, Segal, and Johnson, "The Experience of Foreign Militaries," 119; "On Penal Guarantees and on the Application of the Criminal Law," Spain Organic Act 10/1995 (23 November 1995).

Sweden: D'Amico, "Race-ing and Gendering the Military Closet," 7; Eskridge, *Equality Practice*, 116.

Switzerland: Herr Bossart, "Militär und schwul – natürlich geht das zusammen," *Mannschaft Magazin*, 29 July 2019, accessed 31 July 2020: https://mannschaft.com/2019/07/29/militaer-und-schwul-geht/.

United Kingdom: Eleanor Tucker, "The Military's Rainbow Revolution – from Dishonourable Discharge to Model Employer," *The Guardian*, 10 June 2015, accessed 31 July 2020: https://www.theguardian.com/society/2015 /jun/10/rainbow-revolution-military-lgbt-personnel; Eskridge, *Equality Practice*, 116.

United States: "Don't Ask, Don't Tell Repeal Act of 2010," United States Public Law 111–321 (2010); Lawrence et al. v. Texas, 539 US 558 (2003).

Uruguay: "Gay in the Military in Uruguay," *Americas Quarterly*, 18 May 2009, accessed 31 July 2020: https://www.americasquarterly.org/blog /daily-focus-gays-in-the-military-in-uruguay/.

Notes

Introduction

1 Antidiskriminierungsstelle des Bundes, "Studie zu Einstellung gegenüber Lesben, Schwulen und Bisexuellen."

2 Nick Paumgarten, "Berlin Nights: The Thrall of Techno," *The New Yorker*, 24 March 2014: http://www.newyorker.com/magazine/2014/03/24 /berlin-nights.

3 President Barack Obama's second inaugural address is a good example of this tendency. In it, he located gay activism as one of several moments in a progressive narrative of American democracy's evolution: "the most evident of truths – that all of us are created equal – is the star that guides us still; just as it guided our forebears through Seneca Falls, and Selma, and Stonewall." Craig Griffiths critiques this tendency, warning against "the conception that Western liberal democracy and sexual and minority rights are somehow inevitable historical bedfellows." Obama, "Inaugural Address"; Griffiths, "Between Triumph and Myth," 58.

4 *States of Liberation* is deeply indebted to this historiography, for it would have been impossible to write what aspires to be a comprehensive account of male homosexuality and the two Cold War German states without the work of these scholars. Because each chapter builds on and challenges their work in different ways, specific discussions of this scholarship can be found in individual chapters. In the Anglophone world, these works include those of Kate Davison, Jennifer Evans, Christopher Ewing, Kyle Frackman, Craig Griffiths, Elizabeth Heineman, Dagmar Herzog, Erik Huneke, Josie McLellan, Robert Moeller, Jake Newsome, Andrea Rottmann, Tom Smith, and Clayton Whisnant, among others. In Germany, this scholarship includes work by Magdalena Beljan, Klaus Berndl, Michael Bochow, Maria Borowski, Jens Dobler, Benno Gammerl, Patrick Henze (Patsy l'Amour laLove), Michael Holy, Vera Kruber, Gottfried

Lorenz, Stefan Micheler, Kirsten Plötz, Andreas Pretzel, Martin Reichert, Christian Schäfer, Hans-Georg Stümke, Teresa Tammer, Sébastien Tremblay, and Volker Weiß.

5 Fone, *Homophobia*, 5.

6 Moore, *The Formation of a Persecuting Society*, 135.

7 Freud, *Civilization and Its Discontents*, 90.

8 Foucault, *"Society Must Be Defended,"* 243.

9 Likewise, the essays in *Global Homophobia*, a volume edited by Meredith Weiss and Michael Bosia, "explore the how and why of the transnational diffusion and domestic enactment of political homophobia." Healey, *Russian Homophobia*, 19; Bosia and Weiss, "Political Homophobia in Comparative Perspective," 3; see too Canaday, *The Straight State*, 12.

10 Chitty, *Sexual Hegemony*, 27.

11 Stümke, *Homosexuelle in Deutschland*, 92–131.

12 See, in particular, Oosterhuis, "Medicine, Male Bonding and Homosexuality in Nazi Germany."

13 This argument builds on the work of numerous other scholars, including Herzog, *Sex after Fascism*, 82–105; Whisnant, *Male Homosexuality in West Germany*; Whisnant, "Styles of Masculinity in the West German Gay Scene, 1950–1965"; Evans, *Life among the Ruins*, esp. 124–47; Evans, "Bahnhof Boys"; Moeller, *Protecting Motherhood*, 190–3; Moeller, "The Homosexual Man Is a 'Man,' the Homosexual Woman Is a 'Woman'"; Moeller, "Private Acts, Public Anxieties, and the Fight to Decriminalize Male Homosexuality in West Germany."

14 These arguments enrich our understanding of homosexuality in East Germany's early years. Most scholarship has largely focused on how anti-gay animus continued to shape gay life in East Germany. Borowski, *Parallelwelten*, 86–103; McLellan, *Love in the Time of Communism*, 114–43; Evans, "Decriminalization, Seduction, and 'Unnatural Desire' in East Germany"; Evans, "The Moral State."

15 Judaken, "Introduction," 1122.

16 The debate over US queer activism and how to assess it is a vast one that spans multiple academic and non-academic discourses. For a snapshot, see Duberman, *Has the Gay Movement Failed?*; Faderman, *The Gay Revolution*; Chauncey, *Why Marriage*; Cervini, *The Deviant's War*; Hirshman, *Victory*; Downs, *Stand by Me*; Warner, *The Trouble with Normal*.

17 Evans, "Introduction: Why Queer German History?," 371.

18 Duberman, *Has the Gay Movement Failed?*, xiv.

19 Elizabeth Freeman, "Introduction," 163. These queer approaches often draw on the concept of "gay shame," about which Heather Love writes, and on Lisa Duggan's concept of "homonormativity." They look to deconstruct the strategic trade-offs activists made, often in the interest of

appearing respectable to political leaders and to society at large. See, *inter alia*, Love, *Feeling Backward*, 19–20; Duggan, "The New Homonormativity," 179; Marhoefer, *Sex and the Weimar Republic*, 207; Griffiths, "Sex, Shame and West German Gay Liberation," 445–6; Griffiths, "Konkurrierende Pfade der Emanzipation," 143–59.

20 Elizabeth Freeman, "Introduction," 165.

21 Hobson, *Lavender and Red*, 3; Stewart-Winter, *Queer Clout*, 10; Marhoefer, *Sex and the Weimar Republic*, 207–18; Rydström, *Odd Couples*, 16.

22 D'Emilio, "Capitalism and Gay Identity," 100–13; Foucault, *The History of Sexuality*, 140–1. See too David Johnson, *Buying Gay*; Sender, *Business, Not Politics*; Chasin, *Selling Out*; Chitty, *Sexual Hegemony*.

23 McCloskey, *Why Liberalism Works*, 281. David Johnson makes similar arguments in *Buying Gay*, 229–30.

24 Richardson, "Citizenship and Sexuality," 222–3; Richardson, "Sexuality and Citizenship," 83–100; Sutton, "A Tale of Origins," 193.

25 Canning, "Class vs. Citizenship," 242. See too Sheehan, "The Problem of Sovereignty in European History," 3.

26 My treatment of West German gay activism in the 1970s and 1980s adds to current scholarship and memory's focus on the divisions and failures of the movement in order to understand how the kinds of citizenship claims made by these activists shaped their relationships with society and government. See Brown, *West Germany and the Global Sixties*, 323–8; Griffiths, *The Ambivalence of Gay Liberation*; Griffiths, "Sex, Shame and West German Gay Liberation"; Henze, *Schwule Emanzipation und ihre Konflikte*.

27 Kleßmann, *Zwei Staaten, eine Nation*, 13; Hochscherf, Laucht, and Plowman, "Introduction," 3. Edith Sheffer's *Burned Bridge*, for instance, illustrates how ordinary East and West Germans alike were intimately involved in constructing the border—both its physical demarcations and the famed "wall in the head" that continues to divide the former East and West. Other examples of this approach include Eckert, *West Germany and the Iron Curtain*; von der Goltz, "Attraction and Aversion in Germany's '1968'"; Fleischmann, *Communist Pigs*; Wolff, *Die Mauergesellschaft*.

28 Biess and Eckert, "Introduction: Why Do We Need New Narratives for the History of the Federal Republic?," 7.

29 These tendencies are aptly summarized in Frank Biess's new history of West Germany, in which he argues, "The history of the Federal Republic is also the history of its anxieties." Biess, *Republik der Angst*, 17. See, *inter alia*, Black, *A Demon-Haunted Land*; Chin, "Thinking Difference in Postwar Germany"; Chin, *The Guest Worker Question in Postwar Germany*; Florvil, *Mobilizing Black Germany*; Fulbrook, *Reckonings*; Glienke, Paulmann, and Perels, *Erfolgsgeschichte Bundesrepublik?*; Heineman, *Before Porn Was Legal*; Heineman, *What Difference Does a Husband Make?*; von Hodenberg,

"Writing Women's Agency into the History of the Federal Republic"; Moeller, *Protecting Motherhood*; Moeller, *War Stories*; Poiger, *Jazz, Rock, and Rebels*; Stokes, "The Permanent Refugee Crisis in the Federal Republic of Germany, 1949–"; Stokes, "The Protagonists of Democratization in the Federal Republic."

30 Wehler, "Ein deutsches Säkulum?," 18; Fulbrook, *The People's State*, 10. See Corey Ross, *The East German Dictatorship*, 149–74; Jesse, *Diktaturen in Deutschland*; Betts, *Within Walls*; Harsch, *Revenge of the Domestic*; Port, *Conflict and Stability in the German Democratic Republic*; Fulbrook, *Anatomy of a Dictatorship*; Ghodsee, *Why Women Have Better Sex under Socialism*.

31 Lüdtke, *Eigen-Sinn*, 10–14; Lüdtke, "Organizational Order or Eigensinn?" 303–34; Epstein, "East Germany and Its History since 1989," 645; Fenemore, *Sex, Thugs and Rock 'n' Roll*, 12.

32 E.g., Evans, "Decriminalization, Seduction, and 'Unnatural Desire' in East Germany," 567; McLellan, *Love in the Time of Communism*, 212; Sweet, "The Church, the Stasi, and Socialist Integration," 364.

33 Healey, *Russian Homophobia*, 95–104; O'Dwyer, *Coming Out of Communism*, 87–94; Szulc, *Transnational Homosexuals in Communist Poland*, 106–17; Clech, "Between the Labor Camp and the Clinic"; Alexander, "Soviet Legal and Criminological Debates on the Decriminalization of Homosexuality (1965–75)," 30.

34 Bruce, *The Firm*, 183.

35 This conversation is so broad and encompasses so many different fields that it would be impossible to provide even a cursory overview. Suffice it to say, scholars are increasingly critical of the Cold War dichotomy of democracy and dictatorship developed in the works of, among many others, Hannah Arendt, Carl Friedrich and Zbigniew Brzezinski, and Isaiah Berlin. This critical scholarship has drawn, in particular, from revisionist histories of state socialism and postcolonial critiques of liberal democracy.

36 Sheffer, *Burned Bridge*, 143.

37 Miller, *The Stasi Files Unveiled*, 6–7.

38 Bruce, *The Firm*, 13.

39 Miller, *The Stasi Files Unveiled*, 14.

40 BStU, AIM Nr. 10017/77 Bd. 1/II, 70–1. Josie McLellan too notes this strange assertion as evidence that informants "were not necessarily a reliable source of information." McLellan, "Glad to Be Gay behind the Wall," 123.

41 Leavy, *Oral History*, 34.

42 In like manner, Nan Alamilla Boyd relates how she would "follow rather than lead the conversation" with her narrators. Boyd, "Talking about Sex," 104.

43 Numerous other scholars have commented on the non-linearity and inherent inconsistency of oral history as a source. These include Alexander Freund, who notes the ways in which the interviewer shapes the

interview, and Alessandro Portelli, whose classic article comments on the unfinishedness and subjectivity of oral sources. Freund, "Oral History as Process-generated Data," 31; Portelli, "The Peculiarities of Oral History," 103–4. See too Gammerl, "Erinnerte Liebe," 316–21.

44 Lothar de Maizière, interview, 11 October 2016. Unless otherwise noted, all translations are my own.

1 Homosexuality from the German Empire to Zero Hour

1 Samuel Clowes Huneke, "The Reception of Homosexuality in Klaus Mann's Weimar Era Works," 90.
2 Mann, *Der Vulkan*, 130.
3 Weitz, *Weimar Germany*, 31–3
4 Canning, "Class vs. Citizenship," 243; Canning, "Claiming Citizenship," 120.
5 Kertbeny, *§143 des Preussischen Strafgesetzbuches vom 14. April 1851 und seine Aufrechterhaltung als §152 im Entwurfe eines Strafgesetzbuches für den Norddeutschen Bund*; Beachy, "The German Invention of Homosexuality," 804.
6 Beachy, *Gay Berlin*, 3ff.
7 Ibid., 101.
8 Oosterhuis, "Sexual Modernity in the Works of Richard von Krafft-Ebing and Albert Moll," 135; Dose, *Magnus Hirschfeld*.
9 A number of female sexologists also began working in Germany and Austria in the early twentieth century. For more on their work related to female homosexuality, see Leng, *Sexual Politics and Feminist Science*, 115–51.
10 Dose, *Magnus Hirschfeld*, 14, 49.
11 Lautmann, "Das Verbrechen der widernatürlichen Unzucht," 308.
12 Beachy, "The German Invention of Homosexuality," 804, 808.
13 Marhoefer, *Sex and the Weimar Republic*, 73–4; Evans, "Bahnhof Boys," 613.
14 Stümke, *Homosexuelle in Deutschland*, 26, 90.
15 Lybeck, *Desiring Emancipation*, 108–15; Leng, *Sexual Politics and Feminist Science*, 124–5; Sutton, *The Masculine Woman in Weimar Germany*, 7.
16 Samuel Clowes Huneke, "Death Wish," 132–8; Beachy, *Gay Berlin*, 69–84.
17 Samuel Clowes Huneke, "Death Wish," 135.
18 Hirschfeld, *Die Homosexualität des Mannes und des Weibes*, 902.
19 There is a massive scholarship on sexuality in imperial and Weimar Germany, without which it would have been impossible to write this chapter. See, *inter alia*, Claudia Bruns, *Politik des Eros*; Beachy, *Gay Berlin*; Beachy, "The German Invention of Homosexuality"; Dickinson, "Policing Sex in Germany, 1882–1982"; Dickinson, "Not So Scary after All?"; Dickinson, *Sex, Freedom, and Power in Imperial Germany, 1880–1914*; Dose, *Magnus Hirschfeld*; Keilson-Lauritz, *Die Geschichte der eigenen Geschichte*; Keilson-Lauritz, *Kentaurenliebe*; Keilson-Lauritz, *Von der*

Liebe die Freundschaft heisst; Lybeck, *Desiring Emancipation*; Marhoefer, "Degeneration, Sexual Freedom, and the Politics of the Weimar Republic, 1918–1933"; Marhoefer, *Sex and the Weimar Republic*; Oosterhuis, *Stepchildren of Nature*; Samper Vendrell, *The Seduction of Youth*.

20 Dobler, *Zwischen Duldungspolitik und Verbrechensbekämpfung*; Beachy, *Gay Berlin*, 42–84.

21 Beachy, *Gay Berlin*, 160–3; Marhoefer, *Sex and the Weimar Republic*, 3–5.

22 Isherwood, *Christopher and His Kind*, 16.

23 Whisnant, *Queer Identities and Politics in Germany*, 88.

24 Ibid., 94; Gordon, *Voluptuous Panic*, 92–6.

25 Beachy, *Gay Berlin*, 164; Samper Vendrell, *The Seduction of Youth*, 38–61; Whisnant, *Queer Identities and Politics in Germany*, 188.

26 Samuel Clowes Huneke, "Death Wish," 145–7.

27 Oosterhuis, "Sexual Modernity in the Works of Richard von Krafft-Ebing and Albert Moll," 135–6.

28 Sutton, *Sex between Body and Mind*, 1–30; Leng, *Sexual Politics and Feminist Science*, 115–51; Oosterhuis, *Stepchildren of Nature*; Sigusch, "The Sexologist Albert Moll"; Whisnant, *Queer Identities and Politics in Germany*, 122–61.

29 Oosterhuis, "Sexual Modernity in the Works of Richard von Krafft-Ebing and Albert Moll," 149–50.

30 Sedgwick, *Epistemology of the Closet*, 88.

31 Claudia Bruns, *Politik des Eros*, 130.

32 Hirschfeld, *Die Homosexualität des Mannes und des Weibes*, 977; Dickinson, *Sex, Freedom, and Power in Imperial Germany*, 153, 156.

33 Hiller, *Das Recht über sich selbst*.

34 Hirschfeld, *Die Homosexualität des Mannes und des Weibes*, 973, 977.

35 Marhoefer, *Sex and the Weimar Republic*, 121–2.

36 Griffiths, for instance, asserts that, "the history of homosexual emancipation can be read as the history of a quest for respectability." Griffiths, "Sex, Shame and West German Gay Liberation," 446.

37 Beachy, *Gay Berlin*, 185.

38 Qtd in Hekma, Oosterhuis, and Steakley, "Leftist Sexual Politics and Homosexuality," 12.

39 Bebel, *Woman and Socialism*, 204

40 Hekma, Oosterhuis, and Steakley, "Leftist Sexual Politics and Homosexuality," 13 and 25.

41 Samuel Clowes Huneke, "Death Wish," 136.

42 Healey, *Russian Homophobia*, xiv, 32.

43 Mann, "Homosexualität und Fascismus," 137.

44 Marhoefer, *Sex and the Weimar Republic*, 120.

45 Samper Vendrell, *The Seduction of Youth*, 150–1; Whisnant, *Queer Identities and Politics in Germany*, 179.

46 Marhoefer, *Sex and the Weimar Republic*, 129. Hirschfeld has also recently come under scrutiny for his ambivalent views on colonialism and racism. Heike Bauer, *The Hirschfeld Archives*, 13ff. See too Leng's work on the appeal of racial thinking to female sexologists. Leng, *Sexual Politics and Feminist Science*, 184–220.

47 For more on *Der Eigene* and the masculinists, see Oosterhuis, "Eros and Male Bonding in Society"; Beachy, *Gay Berlin*, 140–59; Claudia Bruns, "The Politics of Masculinity."

48 Dickinson, *Sex, Freedom, and Power in Imperial Germany*, 167.

49 Whisnant, *Queer Identities and Politics in Germany*, 35.

50 Blüher, *Die Rolle der Erotik in der männlichen Gesellschaft*, 7.

51 Sedgwick, *Epistemology of the Closet*, 88.

52 Oosterhuis, "Political Issues and the Rise of Nazism: Introduction," 186.

53 Beachy, *Gay Berlin*, 222ff; Oosterhuis, "Eros and Male Bonding in Society: Introduction," 123; Claudia Bruns, "The Politics of Masculinity," 315–18.

54 Beachy, *Gay Berlin*, 236.

55 Hancock, "'Only the Real, the True, the Masculine Held Its Value,'" 616–21; Wackerfuss, *Stormtrooper Families*, 61–3; zur Nieden, "Aufstieg und Fall des virilen Männerhelden."

56 Norton, *Secret Germany*, 223.

57 Ibid., 339ff.

58 George, *Die Gedichte*, 802.

59 Ash, *The File*, 45.

60 Claudia Bruns, *Politik des Eros*, 180; for more on Eulenburg and Moltke, see Hull, *The Entourage of Kaiser Wilhelm II*, esp. 52–3.

61 Whisnant, *Queer Identities and Politics in Germany*, 78.

62 Stümke, *Homosexuelle in Deutschland*, 90.

63 Marhoefer, *Sex and the Weimar Republic*, 174.

64 The literature on homosexuality in Nazi Germany is vast. See, *inter alia*, Giles, "The Denial of Homosexuality"; Giles, "The Institutionalization of Homosexual Panic in the Third Reich"; Giles, "'The Most Unkindest Cut of All'"; Heger, *Die Männer mit dem rosa Winkel*; Jellonnek, *Homosexuelle unter dem Hakenkreuz*; Grau and Lautmann, *Lexikon zur Homosexuellenverfolgung 1933–1945*; Hájková, *Menschen ohne Geschichte sind Staub*; Samuel Clowes Huneke, "The Duplicity of Tolerance"; Samuel Clowes Huneke, "Heterogeneous Persecution"; Samuel Clowes Huneke, "Die Grenzen der Homophobie"; Marhoefer, "Lesbianism, Transvestitism, and the Nazi State"; Oosterhuis, "Medicine, Male Bonding and Homosexuality in Nazi Germany"; Schoppmann, *Days of Masquerade*; Schoppmann, "National Socialist Policies towards Female Homosexuality"; Schoppmann, "The Position of Lesbian Women in the Nazi Period"; Schoppmann, *Nationalsozialistische Sexualpolitik und*

weibliche Homosexualität; Schoppmann, *Verbotene Verhältnisse*; Schoppmann, "Zwischen strafrechtlicher Verfolgung und gesellschaftlicher Ächtung"; Stümke, *Homosexuelle in Deutschland*, 92–131; Zinn, *"Aus dem Volkskörper entfernt"?*

65 Hancock, "The Purge of the SA Reconsidered," 670; Schoppmann, "The Position of Lesbian Women in the Nazi Period," 11–14; Whisnant, *Queer Identities and Politics in Germany*, 214.
66 Jellonnek, *Homosexuelle unter dem Hakenkreuz*, 114ff; Schäfer, *"Widernatürliche Unzucht,"* 39–42.
67 Cook, *London and the Culture of Homosexuality*, 42–3.
68 Sarah Kaplan, "Inspired by 'Imitation Game,' Petition Calls for Pardon of 49,000 British Men Prosecuted for Being Gay," *The Washington Post*, 23 February 2015, accessed 8 June 2020: https://www.washingtonpost.com/news/morning-mix/wp/2015/02/23/inspired-by-imitation-game-petition-calls-for-pardon-of-49000-british-men-prosecuted-for-being-gay/.
69 The German *verführen* and *Verführung* can be translated in numerous ways. "To seduce" and "seduction" come closest to the legal meaning, which carries the further implication that the victim had been led astray or debauched.
70 Whisnant, *Queer Identities and Politics in Germany*, 236–7; Herzog, *Sex after Fascism*, 34–5.
71 Giles, "'The Most Unkindest Cut of All,'" 50.
72 Eric Johnson, *Nazi Terror*, 292.
73 Stümke, *Homosexuelle in Deutschland*, 119.
74 Lautmann, Grikschat, and Schmidt, "Der rosa Winkel in den nationalsozialistischen Konzentrationslagern," 332; Jellonnek, *Homosexuelle unter dem Hakenkreuz*, 12–13; Eric Johnson, *Nazi Terror*, 288.
75 Schoppmann, *Nationalsozialistische Sexualpolitik und weibliche Homosexualität*, 6; Heineman, *What Difference Does a Husband Make?*, 17–43.
76 Koonz, *Mothers in the Fatherland*, 185–6.
77 Sheffer, *Asperger's Children*, 20.
78 Proctor, *Racial Hygiene*, 95ff.
79 E.g., Müller, *Ausgrenzung der Homosexuellen aus der "Volksgemeinschaft,"* 28.
80 See in particular Oosterhuis, "Medicine, Male Bonding and Homosexuality in Nazi Germany," 194–205; Jellonnek, *Homosexuelle unter dem Hakenkreuz*, 98.
81 See, *inter alia*, Schoppmann, *Nationalsozialistische Sexualpolitik und weibliche Homosexualität*, 79–97; Schoppmann, "National Socialist Policies towards Female Homosexuality," 179; Marhoefer, "Lesbianism, Transvestitism, and the Nazi State," 1167–72; Zinn, *"Aus dem Volkskörper Entfernt"?*, 30–1; Dobler, "Unzucht und Kuppelei," 61–2; Samuel Clowes Huneke, "The Duplicity of Tolerance," 34–5; Samuel Clowes Huneke, "Heterogeneous Persecution," 325.

82 Qtd in Burleigh and Wippermann, *The Racial State*, 193.

83 Giles, "The Denial of Homosexuality," 256.

84 Hitler, "Reichstagsrede."

85 Giles, "The Denial of Homosexuality," note 35.

86 Klare, "Homosexualität und Strafrecht," 119.

87 Healey, *Russian Homophobia*, 158–60; Jackson, *Living in Arcadia*, 83; David Johnson, *The Lavender Scare*, 34–6.

88 Dr Schäfer (Reich Ministry of Justice) to the Reich Commissar for occupied Norway, 18 June 1942, printed in Kokula, "Zur Situation lesbischer Frauen während des NS-Zeit," 34.

89 Stümke and Finkler, *Rosa Winkel, rosa Listen*, 262.

90 Giles, "The Denial of Homosexuality," 265, 284.

91 LAB, A Rep. 341–02, Nr. 6515, 1.

92 LAB, A Rep. 341–02, Nr. 6515, 17.

93 LAB, A Rep. 341–02, Nr. 6522, 2–3.

94 Letter from Berlin, 8 October 1945, 1, The Hoover Institution Library and Archives (HA), Günter Reimann Collection, Folder 3. Evans, too, evokes the olfactory sensations of occupied Berlin. Evans, *Life among the Ruins*, 53–60.

95 Diefendorf, *In the Wake of War*, 11.

96 Grossmann, *Jews, Germans, and Allies*, 40.

97 Stone, *The Liberation of the Camps*, 1–28.

98 Wachsmann, *Hitler's Prisons*, 6.

99 HHStAW, Abt. 461, Nr. 18808, 6.

100 Ibid., 8.

101 Ibid., 36 and 39.

102 Ibid., 50.

103 Evans, *Life among the Ruins*, 124–6; Whisnant, *Male Homosexuality in West Germany*, 29. Some gay concentration camp prisoners were even re-imprisoned under the Allied Occupation. Micheler, "'…und verbleibt weiter in Sicherungsverwahrung,'" 64–5.

104 "Declaration Regarding the Defeat of Germany and the Assumption of Supreme Authority by Allied Powers."

105 Vogt, *Denazification in Soviet-Occupied Germany*, 1–2; Herf, *Divided Memory*, 72–4.

106 Plischke, "Denazification Law and Procedure," 811.

107 Allied Control Authority of Germany, "Control Council Law No. 11: Repealing of Certain Provisions of the German Criminal Law," in *Enactments and Approved Papers*, vol. 2, 1946, 71; "Control Council Law No. 55: Repeal of Certain Provisions of Criminal Legislation," in *Enactments and Approved Papers of the Control Council and Coordinating Committee 1 April 1947–30 June 1947*, 1947, 150–1; Weber, "Zur Auswirkung der Gesetzgebung der Besatzungsmächte auf das deutsche

Strafgesetzbuch," 238–40; Werner, "Die Bedeutung der Ziffer 8 b der allgemeinen Anweisungen der Militärregierung an Richter Nr. 1 für die Anwendbarkeit strafrechtlicher Vorschriften, insbesondere des §175 a StGB," 74–7.

108 "CONL/P(47)33 Appendix D," 2, HA, Germany (Territory under Allied Occupation, 1945–1955), Box 4, Folder 12; "CONL/P(47)35," HA, Germany (Territory under Allied Occupation, 1945–1955), Box 4, Folder 12.

109 There was discussion among Allied officials about repealing the Nazi-era version of the law. Harthauser, "Der Massenmord an Homosexuellen im dritten Reich," 25; Pretzel, "Wiedergutmachung unter Vorbehalt und mit neuer Perspektive," 93–4; Schäfer, "Widernatürliche Unzucht," 50–1.

110 Whisnant, *Male Homosexuality in West Germany*, 117–37.

111 Akantha, "Berlin tanzt!," *Der Kreis: Ein Monatsschrift* 17, no. 9 (1949): 8.

112 Evans, *Life among the Ruins*, 16–45. See too Rottmann, "Queer Home Berlin?," 45–50, 121–4.

113 Whisnant, *Male Homosexuality in West Germany*, 64–111; Rosenkranz and Lorenz, *Hamburg auf anderen Wegen*, 80–93.

114 Akantha, "Berlin tanzt!," 22.

115 Harthauser, "Der Massenmord an Homosexuellen im dritten Reich," 25; Grau, "Return of the Past," 4.

116 OLG Halle, "Beschluß v. 20.9.1948–1 Ws 53/48," 144.

117 Kammergericht Berlin, "Urteil vom 21. Februar 1950–1 Ss 165/49," 100.

118 Oberstes Gericht, "Urteil vom 28. März 1950–3 Tst. 9/50," 215.

119 OLG Braunschweig, "Urteil v. 7.6.46 – Ss 5/46," 119.

120 OLG Hamburg, "Urteil vom 22. Januar 1947," 75; OLG Oldenburg, "Urteil v. 15.4.46 (JustBl Oldenburg S. 60)," 96; OLG Kiel, "Strafsenat v. 22.1.1947, Ss 208/46," 198; OLG Celle, "Urteil von 20.12.46, Ss 94/46," 134.

121 Bundesgerichtshof, "Urt. v. 13.03.1951"; Whisnant, *Male Homosexuality in West Germany*, 28–9.

122 Bundesverfassungsgericht, "Urteil des Ersten Senats vom 10. Mai 1957."

123 Rolf, "Klaus Mann," *Der Kreis: Ein Monatsschrift* 17, no. 9 (1949): 28.

2 §175 and West Germany's Persecution of Gay Men

1 HHStAW, Abt. 461, Nr. 29109; Schiefelbein, "Wiederbeginn der juristischen Verfolgung homosexueller Männer in der Bundesrepublik Deutschland," 63.

2 "Homosexuelle: Eine Million Delikte," *Der Spiegel*, 29 November 1950, 7.

3 Ibid., 7–8.

4 BArch-Koblenz, B 141/4071, 185; Schiefelbein, "Wiederbeginn der juristischen Verfolgung homosexueller Männer in der Bundesrepublik Deutschland," 63.

5 Schiefelbein, "Wiederbeginn der juristischen Verfolgung homosexueller Männer in der Bundesrepublik Deutschland," 65.

6 "Homosexuelle: Eine Million Delikte," 7.

7 Schiefelbein, "Wiederbeginn der juristischen Verfolgung homosexueller Männer in der Bundesrepublik Deutschland," 67.

8 This number is also cited in Lorenz and Bollmann, "Die Rechtsprechung nach §§175 und 175a StGB in der Freien und Hansestadt Hamburg im Spiegel der Haupt- und Vorverfahrensregister der Staatsanwaltschaft der Jahre 1948 bis 1969," 253–4. Other scholars cite numbers for slightly different date ranges, such as in Moeller, "'The Homosexual Man Is a "Man," the Homosexual Woman Is a "Woman,"'" 427. Stümke notes 100,000 cases of homosexuality registered by the police between 1953 and 1969. Stümke, *Homosexuelle in Deutschland*, 147.

9 Hans-Georg Stümke attributes the persecution to the Federal Republic's "Christian ethics." In her magisterial study of sexuality in postwar Germany, Dagmar Herzog suggests that concerns surrounding the so-called seduction of youth as well as gendered anxieties originating in the war years played a role in the persecution. Similarly, Clayton Whisnant argues that "the alleged threat that predatory homosexuals posed to children and families" alongside "associations between homosexuality, criminality, and mental illness" justified the laws' continued use in West Germany. Stümke, *Homosexuelle in Deutschland*, 142; Herzog, *Sex after Fascism*, 90–5; Whisnant, *Male Homosexuality in West Germany*, 63; Whisnant, "Styles of Masculinity in the West German Gay Scene, 1950–1965," 367–73; see too Gammerl, *anders fühlen*, 46–52. On anxieties surrounding male prostitution and its connection to the criminalization of male homosexuality in West Germany, see Evans, "Bahnhof Boys," 610–16.

10 There are slight discrepancies between my data, which come from the *Statistiches Jahrbuch für die Bundesrepublik Deutschland*, and that presented by Rainer Hoffschildt, who relies on *Statistik der Bundesrepublik Deutschland*. I believe these discrepancies stem from the fact that the *Statistisches Jahrbuch* conveys the number of convicted individuals (*Verurteilte*), while *Statistik der Bundesrepbulik Deutschland* reports the number of convictions (*Verurteilungen*). Hoffschildt, "140.000 Verurteilungen nach '§175,'" 141.

11 Arguing that the fear of gay conspiracies was a particularly potent element of West German anti-gay animus, this chapter also augments the growing scholarship on the history of this paranoia and puts it in conversation with the historiography of homosexuality in Cold War Germany. See Schwartz, *Homosexuelle, Seilschaft, Verrat*, esp. 237–48; Woods, *Homintern*, 303–39.

12 E.g., Stümke, *Homosexuelle in Deutschland*, 142; Micheler, "'… und verbleibt weiter in Sicherungsverwahrung,'" 62; See too the collected volume

Himmel und Hölle, which is billed as a contribution to our understanding of "the discrimination and persecution of homosexuals [...] in recent German history." Balser, Kramp, Müller, and Götzmann, *Himmel und Hölle*, 8.

13 Whisnant, for instance, emphasizes that the 1950s and 1960s were "not simply an era in which the Nazi persecution of homosexuality persisted," and that these years instead "brought a revival of the urban gay scenes that had been destroyed by the Nazis." Gottfriend Lorenz and Ulf Bollmann go further, suggesting that these decades were ones of "discrimination" rather than "persecution." Whisnant, *Male Homosexuality in West Germany*, 204; Lorenz and Bollmann, "Die Rechtsprechung nach §§175 und 175a StGB in der Freien und Hansestadt Hamburg im Spiegel der Haupt- und Vorverfahrensregister der Staatsanwaltschaft der Jahre 1948 bis 1969," 277–9.

14 David Johnson, *Lavender Scare*, 166; Houlbrook, *Queer London*, 32–6.

15 Moeller, *Protecting Motherhood*, 80–1.

16 Granieri, "Politics in C Minor," 12.

17 Moeller, *Protecting Motherhood*, 63ff; "Grundgesetz für die Bundesrepublik Deutschland," Art. 6.

18 Herzog, *Sex after Fascism*, 143; Heineman, *Before Porn Was Legal*, 2.

19 Heineman, *What Difference Does a Husband Make?*, 137–75; "Grundgesetz für die Bundesrepublik Deutschland," Art. 3.

20 Schewe, "Die Kontinuität der Sozialgesetzgebung in den letzten 50 Jahren in Deutschland," 5.

21 Wittmann, *Beyond Justice*, 34; "Grundgesetz für die Bundesrepublik Deutschland," Art. 103.

22 Frei, *Adenauer's Germany and the Nazi Past*, 5–26, and 67–92.

23 Herf, *Divided Memory*, 289.

24 Fulbrook, *Reckonings*, 251.

25 Herzog, *Sex after Fascism*, 2–3.

26 "Die deutsche Situation ... 1949!," *Der Kreis: Ein Monatsschrift* 17, no. 4 (1949): 34.

27 Stümke, *Homosexuelle in Deutschland*, 147.

28 Gatzweiler, *Die Homosexualität des Mannes und das Strafgesetz*, 10, 18; Bundesverfassungsgericht, "Urteil des Ersten Senats vom 10. Mai 1957," 434–6; Deutscher Bundestag, "Entwurf eines Strafgesetzbuches (StGB) E 1962," 377.

29 Herzog, *Sex after Fascism*, 105.

30 E.g., Herzog, *Sex after Fascism*, 94–5; Whisnant, *Male Homosexuality in West Germany*, 43–7.

31 Gatzweiler, *Das Dritte Geschlecht*, 16.

32 Giese, *Der Homosexuelle Mann in der Welt*, 70–6.

33 Gatzweiler, *Die Homosexualität des Mannes und die Strafrechtreform*, 9; Whisnant, *Male Homosexuality in West Germany*, 72; Whisnant, *Queer Identities and Politics in Germany*, 236–7; Herzog, *Sex after Fascism*, 94.
34 Bundesverfassungsgericht, "Urteil des Ersten Senats vom 10. Mai 1957," 408.
35 Marhoefer, *Sex and the Weimar Republic*, 112–45; Samper Vendrell, *The Seduction of Youth*, 130–53.
36 Whisnant, "Styles of Masculinity in the West German Gay Scene, 1950–1965," 367; Whisnant, *Male Homosexuality in West Germany*, 57.
37 Becker, *Homosexualität und Jugendschutz*, 15; Gatzweiler too argued that "many homosexuals" admitted that their sexuality stemmed from "seduction during their youth." Gatzweiler, *Gleichberechtigung der Homosexuellen?*, 8.
38 For detailed analysis of *Anders als du und ich* see Baer, *Dismantling the Dream Factory*, 183–208; Evans, *Life among the Ruins*, 86–7; Whisnant, *Male Homosexuality in West Germany*, 51–2.
39 Biess, "Moral Panic in Postwar Germany," 808–13; Biess, *Republik der Angst*, 98–104.
40 Bundesverfassungsgericht, "Urteil des Ersten Senats vom 10. Mai 1957."
41 Herzog, for instance, contends that, "the notion that men had a potentially bisexual disposition, and that young men in particular were vulnerable to conversion via seduction, was explicitly named as the reason for retaining Paragraph 175." Herzog, *Sex after Fascism*, 94. See too Evans, *Life among the Ruins*, 138–9; Whisnant, *Male Homosexuality in West Germany*, 48; Whisnant, "Styles of Masculinity in the West German Gay Scene," 367–72; Samper Vendrell, *The Seduction of Youth*, 161–2; Rosenkranz and Lorenz, *Hamburg auf anderen Wegen*, 84–6.
42 Schäfer, *"Widernatürliche Unzucht,"* 264, 318–19.
43 HHStAW, Abt. 461, Nr. 30774, 6.
44 This concern for youth resembles the early-twentieth-century sex panic in the United States, when sodomy laws began to be applied as a deterrent to the alleged conversion of young men into homosexuals. Estelle Freedman notes of this panic that, "While ostensibly about preventing sexual violence against boys or male youths, the moral panic that culminated in the sexual psychopath laws was as concerned with protecting boys from acquiring homosexual identity as it was about protecting them from assault." Freedman, *Redefining Rape*, 189.
45 Erwin, "Die Freiheit der Persönlichkeit: Nächtliche Razzia auf Andersartige im Berlin von heute," *Der Kreis* 29, no. 2 (1961): 5.
46 Schäfer, *"Widernatürliche Unzucht,"* 319.
47 Evans, "Bahnhof Boys," 624.
48 Hensel, Neef, and Pausch, "Von 'Knabenliebhabern' und 'Power-Pädos,'" 137ff.

49 For a brief history of the origins of public toilets as cruising sites, see Chitty, *Sexual Hegemony*, 124–7.

50 Samuel R., interview, 15 November 2016.

51 Other scholars have noted the endurance of this paranoia but, other than Schwartz, who also argues that it was an important part of West German anti-gay animus, none have analysed its pervasiveness in the anti-gay rhetoric of the first postwar decades. See Schwartz, *Homosexuelle, Seilschaft, Verrat*, 214, 244–6; Whisnant, "Styles of Masculinity in the West German Gay Scene, 1950–1965," 372–3; Whisnant, *Male Homosexuality in West Germany*, 63; Moeller, "'The Homosexual Man Is a "Man," the Homosexual Woman Is a "Woman,"'" 411; Moeller, "Private Acts, Public Anxieties, and the Fight to Decriminalize Male Homosexuality in West Germany," 533.

52 GLAK, Abt. 309 Karlsruhe, Nr. 1330, 4; GLAK, Abt. 309 Karlsruhe, Nr. 1394, 3; HHStAW, Abt. 461, Nr. 30970, 18; HHStAW, Abt. 461, Nr. 30774, 10.

53 Bundesverfassungsgericht, "Urteil des Ersten Senats vom 10. Mai 1957," 410.

54 BArch-Koblenz, B 141/4071, 121.

55 Ibid., 122.

56 Ibid., 124.

57 Ibid., 122.

58 Ibid.

59 Gatzweiler, *Das Dritte Geschlecht*, 30.

60 Ibid., 30

61 Ibid., 31.

62 BArch-Koblenz, B 141/4071, 122.

63 Bundesverfassungsgericht, "Urteil des Ersten Senats vom 10. Mai 1957," 394.

64 Rudolf Diels, "Die Nacht der langen Messer ... fand nicht statt," *Der Spiegel*, 7 July 1949, 19; see too Whisnant, *Male Homosexuality in West Germany*, 43.

65 Biess, *Republik der Angst*, 195–238.

66 Herf, *Divided Memory*, 271–6, 293–5; Frei, *Adenauer's Germany and the Nazi Past*; Art, *The Politics of the Nazi Past in Germany and Austria*, 50–6; Olick, *The Sins of the Fathers*, 113–212.

67 Ashkenasi, *Modern German Nationalism*, 66.

68 Bundesverfassungsgericht, "Urteil des Ersten Senats vom 10. Mai 1957," 408. For more on lesbian experiences in West Germany during the 1950s and 1960s, see Plötz, "Verfolgung und Diskriminierung der weiblichen Homosexualität in Rheinland-Pfalz 1947 bis 1973," esp. 217–311; Rottmann, "Queer Home Berlin?"; Heineman, *What Difference Does a Husband Make?*, 130; Leidinger, "Lesbische Existenz 1945–1969."

69 Gatzweiler, *Gleichberechtigung der Homosexuellen?*, 8.

70 Gatzweiler, *Das Dritte Geschlecht*, 30.

71 Marion Gräfin Dönhoff, "Gehlens Geheimdienst," *Die Zeit*, 26 July 1963.

72 Schwartz, *Homosexuelle, Seilschaften, Verrat*, 112–47; David Johnson, *Lavender Scare*, 108–9; Woods, *Homintern*, 10; Whisnant, *Male Homosexuality in West Germany*, 62.

73 Schwartz, *Homosexuelle, Seilschaften, Verrat*, 212–13, 217; Hodges, *Alan Turing*, 574ff; David Johnson, *Lavender Scare*, 31–3. See too Gentile, "Queering Subversives in Cold War Canada"; Kinsman and Gentile, *The Canadian War on Queers*; David Johnson, "America's Cold War Empire."

74 David Johnson, *The Lavender Scare*, 108; D'Emilio, "The Homosexual Menace," 64.

75 The *Verfassungsschutz*, West Germany's domestic counter-espionage and intelligence service, translates literally as "constitution protection."

76 "Verfassungsschutz – platonisch," *Die Zeit*, 22 October 1953, sec. II.

77 Ibid.; "Wie bei Edgar Wallace," *Der Spiegel*, 4 November 1953, 16.

78 "Der Sumpf ist noch tiefer," *Die Zeit*, 8 December 1955.

79 Cobra, "'Verfassungsschutz' mit §175: Riesenskandal um 'Verfassungsschutzamt' als Agentenzentrale," *Berliner Zeitung*, 4 December 1953, 2.

80 "Verfassungsschutz – platonisch," *Die Zeit*, 22 October 1953, sec. I.

81 Ibid.

82 "Wie bei Edgar Wallace," *Der Spiegel*, 4 November 1953, 16.

83 "Verfassungsschutz – platonisch," *Die Zeit*, 22 October 1953, sec. I.

84 Cobra, "'Verfassungsschutz' mit §175: Riesenskandal um 'Verfassungsschutzamt' als Agentenzentrale," *Berliner Zeitung*, 4 December 1953, 2.

85 Volkswartbund, *Homosexualität als akute öffentliche Gefahr*, 7.

86 Historians also know of several cases of gay men in the employ of Soviet intelligence, such as John Vassall, Guy Burgess, and Anthony Blunt in the United Kingdom, and Whittaker Chambers in the United States. At the time, the Soviet Union criminalized homosexuality and, as Healey suggests, sent numerous gay men to the Gulag. These cases illustrate the hypocrisy of Cold War states that both demonized and employed gay men. What makes the case of Krüger, and others discussed in chapter 5, distinctive is that the *Verfassungsschutz* recruited Krüger specifically to penetrate the gay subculture, which it feared was a vector for enemy intelligence. Healey, *Russian Homophobia*, 158–70. For more on Vassall, Burgess, Blunt, or Chambers, see Haynes and Kehr, *Early Cold War Spies*, 119–32; Shepherd, "Gay Sex Spy Orgy"; Woods, *Homintern*, 343; Lownie, *Stalin's Englishman*, 20–1, 54–6; Conrad, *Locked in the Family Cell*, 40; Schwartz, *Homosexuelle, Seilschaften, Verrat*, 212–36. Evans makes a similar point about the hypocrisy of the Stasi's use of gay informants. Evans, "Decriminalization, Seduction, and 'Unnatural Desire' in East Germany," 569.

87 BArch-Koblenz, B 141/85386, 7.

88 BArch-Koblenz, B 141/17453, 170.

89 Deutscher Bundestag, "Entwurf eines Strafgesetzbuches (StGB) E 1962," 376.

90 "Die 1,5-Promille-Grenze nicht herabsetzen! Jaeger drängt auf Reformen," *Hamburger Abendlblatt*, 5 February 1966, 2.

91 BArch-Koblenz, B 141/85387, 34.

92 See, for example, Fone, *Homophobia*, 5–6; Bunzl, *Symptoms of Modernity*, 216; Biess, *Republik der Angst*, 104.

93 David Johnson, *The Lavender Scare*, 18–30.

94 Weitz, "The Ever-Present Other," 229.

95 Dupont, "The Two-faced Fifties," 361.

96 "Report of the Committee on Homosexual Offences and Prostitution," 130–42; Rydström, "Introduction," 27; Herzog, "Syncopated Sex," 1299–1300.

97 See, *inter alia*, House and MacMaster, *Paris 1961*, 30; Shepard, *The Invention of Decolonization*, 45; Kristin Ross, *Fast Cars, Clean Bodies*, 126; Gilroy, *Postcolonial Melancholia*, 102; Rasberry, *Race and the Totalitarian Century*.

98 Dupont, "The Two-faced Fifties," 363; David Johnson, "America's Cold War Empire," 56; see too Gentile, "Queering Subversives in Cold War Canada," 54; Davison, "The Sexual (Geo)Politics of Loyalty," 134–5.

99 HHStAW, Abt. 461, Nr. 36418, 201–5.

100 Ibid., 31–6.

101 HHStAW, Abt. 471, Nr. 187, 2ff.

102 Ibid., 74.

103 Ibid., 87.

104 Whisnant, *Male Homosexuality in West Germany*, 28–9; Lorenz, "Hamburg als Homosexuellenhauptstadt der 1950er Jahre," 121.

105 HHStAW, Abt. 461, Nr. 36418, 66–7.

106 HHStAW, Abt. 471 Nr. 307, 35.

107 Ibid., 5, 35. Evans argues that men often pled extenuating circumstances to win milder punishments. Evans, "Bahnhof Boys," 630–3.

108 BArch-Koblenz, B 141/85386, 24.

109 GLAK, Abt. 309 Karlsruhe, Nr. 2262, 19.

110 Georg R., interview, 7 January 2017.

111 "Gesellschaft: Homosexualität: Späte Milde," *Der Spiegel*, 12 May 1969, 57.

112 OLG Stuttgart, "1 Ss 431/63," 21 June 1963; discussed in Wilde, *Das Schicksal der Verfemten*, 62; Xerxes, "Ein neues homosexuelles Vergehen," *Der Kreis* 31, no. 10 (1963): 8.

113 Schoeps, "Überlegungen zum Problem der Homosexualität," 86.

114 Gatzweiler, *Die Homosexualität des Mannes und die Strafrechtreform*, 65–6.

115 GLAK, Abt. 309 Karlsruhe, Nr. 6662, 5.

116 Ibid., 7.

117 Ibid., 23.
118 Micheler, "'… und verbleibt weiter in Sicherungsverwahrung,'" 66;
    Sascha Maier, "Homosexualität in der Nachkriegszeit: Kastriert, der Liebe
    wegen," *Stuttgarter-Zeitung*, 25 January 2017: http://www.stuttgarter
    -zeitung.de/inhalt.homosexualitaet-in-der-nachkriegszeit-kastriert-der
    -liebe-wegen.88a90ef9-f68b-4ddb-a298-76bf59916508.html.
119 BArch-Koblenz, B 141/85394, 45.
120 Proctor, *Racial Hygiene*, 108.
121 GLAK, Abt. 309 Karlsruhe, Nr. 2262, 159; GLAK, Abt. 309 Mannheim,
    Nr. 3489, 205; LAB, C Rep. 341, Nr. 4779, 1; LAB, C Rep. 341, Nr. 1737, 48.
122 HHStAW, Abt. 461, Nr. 18990, 26.
123 Ibid., 85, 123, 152.
124 Ibid., 167.
125 For more on the international scientific evolution of aversion therapy at
    the time, see Davison, "Cold War Pavlov."
126 Holger G., interview, 5 January 2017.
127 Hubert U., interview, 27 January 2017. In contrast, Kevin Murphy's
    interviews in Minneapolis indicate that American gay men remembered
    the 1950s and 1960s fondly and challenged the centrality of the 1969
    Stonewall riots as a turning point in their sexual lives. Murphy, "Gay Was
    Good," 308.
128 Though regular police surveillance of these spaces means the written
    record might over-represent the extent to which gay men relied on such
    public cruising spots to find sex, most of my oral sources remember
    cruising for sex during their youth, when §175 was still in force. On
    cruising, see too Rottmann, "Queer Home Berlin?," 181–5.
129 Volker K., interview, 18 December 2016.
130 Jugendamt Karlsruhe, 29 October 1963, GLAK, Abt. 309 Karlsruhe
    Nr. 1396.
131 GLAK, Abt. 309 Karlsruhe Nr. 4102, 3.
132 Georg R., interview, 7 January 2017.
133 Ibid.
134 Evans, "Bahnhof Boys," 621–2. The Zoo station would remain a popular
    cruising spot for both male and female sex workers for decades to come.
    See Hermann, Rieck, and Christiane F., *Wir Kinder vom Bahnhof Zoo*.
135 LAB, B Rep. 058, Nr. 13037, 2.
136 Hans-Carl Gressmann, "Bekämpfung homosexueller Umtriebe an und in
    öffentlichen Bedürfnisanstalten," *Kriminalistik*, no. 21 (1967): 552.
137 LAB, C Rep. 341, Nr. 4779, 8, 6.
138 Holger G., interview, 5 January 2017.
139 Falko D. to Hans Engelhard, 27 June 1983, BArch-Koblenz, B 141/85400.
    Gammerl similarly notes how the trauma of the 1950s and 1960s led some

men to keep their sexuality and their emotional lives separate. Gammerl, "Erinnerte Liebe," 331–8.

140 Whisnant, *Male Homosexuality in West Germany*, 136; Evans, *Life among the Ruins*, 179–80; Rottmann, "Queer Home Berlin?," 125–8.

141 von Mahlsdorf, *Ich bin meine eigene Frau*, 113.

142 Whisnant, *Male Homosexuality in West Germany*, 134ff; Rosenkranz and Lorenz, *Hamburg auf anderen Wegen*, 97ff.

143 E.g., HHStAW, Abt. 461, Nr. 30774, 1, 5; HHStAW, Abt. 461, Nr. 30970, 1; LAB, B Rep. 010, Nr. 2300.

144 HHStAW, Abt. 471, Nr. 115, 18.

145 E.g., twenty-three-year-old Fritz. H. attested that he first learned about gay "clubs" and "bars" from an older gay man. He asserted that "of such things I previously knew nothing." HHStAW, Abt. 631/A, Nr. 2280, 10. See Whisnant, *Male Homosexuality in West Germany*, 70.

146 H.W., "Eldorado der Unmoral: Westberlin – ein Schaufenster der 'freien' Ganovenwelt," *Neue Zeit*, 29 November 1966. See too Gammerl, *anders fühlen*, 87–93.

147 HHStAW, Abt. 461, Nr. 30970, 1.

148 Evans, *Life among the Ruins*, 179; Rottmann, "Queer Home Berlin?," 136–45.

149 "Groß-Razzia in Schöneberg," *Berliner Zeitung*, 29 October 1957, 8.

150 LAB, B Rep. 010, Nr. 2300, 6.

151 Georg R., interview, 7 January 2017. Gammerl questions the focus on large cities, examining gay and lesbian experiences in rural areas. Gammerl, *anders fühlen*, 203–16. On rural queerness in the United States, see Herring, "Out of the Closets, into the Woods."

152 BArch-Koblenz, B 141/17453, 170.

153 Poiger, *Jazz, Rock, and Rebels*, 83; Grotum, *Die Halbstarken*; Fenemore, *Sex, Thugs and Rock 'n' Roll*, 133; Layne, "*Halbstarke* and Rowdys," 437–40; Kurme, *Halbstarke*, 177–224; Whisnant, "Styles of Masculinity in the West German Gay Scene, 1950–1965," 367; Kalb, *Coming of Age*, 87–122.

154 LAB, B Rep. 010, Nr. 2300, 58.

155 Ibid., 59.

156 Ibid., 42. Evans similarly argues that the porous border made it possible before August 1961 for the East and West Berlin police to take a hand in the regulation of prostitution in the other half of the city. Evans, "Bahnhof Boys," 622.

157 "Anlage zum Schreiben vom 21. Dez. 1959," LAB, B Rep. 010, Nr. 2300. Andrea Rottmann presents evidence of a second such commission in the mid-1960s in "Queer Home Berlin?," 163–5.

158 BArch-Koblenz, B 141/85394, 79.

159 GLAK, Abt. 309 Karlsruhe, Nr. 1394, 165.

160 Ibid., 3ff.
161 Dobler, *Zwischen Duldungspolitik und Verbrechensbekämpfung*, 150–2; Beachy, *Gay Berlin*, 55; Whisnant, *Male Homosexuality in West Germany*, 29; BArch-Koblenz, B 141/85394, 79.
162 "Homosexuelle: Eine millione Delikte," 9.
163 Rudolf Eims, "Die bedenklichen Mittel einer Justiz!: Kronzeuge Blankenstein – unglaubwürdig: Das Sachverständigengutachten Professor Wietholds," *Der Kreis: Ein Monatsschrift* 19, no. 3 (1951): 2; Schiefelbein, "Wiederbeginn der juristischen Verfolgung homosexueller Männer in der Bundesrepublik Deutschland," 64.
164 "Homosexuelle: Eine Million Delikte," 9.
165 "Gesellschaft: Homosexualität: Späte Milde," *Der Spiegel*, 12 May 1969, 55; for more on the regulation of sexuality in Munich see Kalb, *Coming of Age*, 107–9.
166 Akantha, "Berlin tanzt!," 10.
167 Rosenberg, *Policing Paris*.
168 Weiner, *Enemies*, 131ff; Stockham, "'I Have Never Cut His Budget and I Never Expect To,'" 501–2; Charles, "From Subversion to Obscenity," 270–5.
169 Whisnant and Evans also point out how homophile commentators painted male prostitutes as criminals inclined to engage in blackmail or extortion. Whisnant, *Male Homosexuality in West Germany*, 119–21; Evans, *Life among the Ruins*, 122, 141; Evans, "Bahnhof Boys," 609.
170 "Kleine Berliner Chronik," *Berliner Zeitung*, 19 August 1955, 6.
171 HHStAW, Abt. 631/A, Nr. 2280, 1.
172 Ibid., 3.
173 Ibid., 33.
174 Beachy, *Gay Berlin*, 75ff.
175 Hans-Carl Gressmann, "Bekämpfung homosexueller Umtriebe an und in öffentlichen Bedürfnisanstalten," *Kriminalistik*, no. 21 (1967): 551.
176 "Preußenpark-Bande vor Gericht," *Neue Zeit*, 28 February 1959, 6.
177 "Gesellschaft: Homosexualität: Späte Milde," *Der Spiegel*, 12 May 1969, 57.
178 HHStAW, Abt. 471, Nr. 115, 2.
179 Ibid., 19.
180 BArch-Koblenz, B 141/4075, 32.
181 BArch-Koblenz, B 141/85394, 93.
182 Schissler, "Writing about 1950s West Germany," 1.
183 Monica Black similarly argues that the rise in magical and messianic thinking in the early Federal Republic was a product of the silence surrounding the Nazi past. Black, *A Demon-Haunted Land*, 13; Black, "Miracles in the Shadow of the Economic Miracle," 852–6.

3 Homosexuality and Socialism in East Germany

1 Klimmer, "Die Situation in der DDR," 275.
2 As Clayton Whisnant posits, "Other aspects of a gay scene – gay bars, parks, and public toilets – did exist, but in general activities remained more subdued than in West Germany." Paul Betts argues that, "Homosexuals for example were often singled out as dangerous citizens." Whisnant, *Male Homosexuality in West Germany*, 12; Betts, *Within Walls*, 27. See too McLellan, *Love in the Time of Communism*, 115; Stümke, *Homosexuelle in Deutschland*, 166–7.
3 Evans, "The Moral State," 360; Bock, "Producing the 'Socialist Personality'?," 223; Harsch, *Revenge of the Domestic*, 12–14; Heineman, *What Difference Does a Husband Make?*, 176–208; Herzog, *Sex after Fascism*, 200.
4 Frackman, "Persistent Ambivalence," 686. Interestingly, recent scholarship on homosexuality in West Germany also characterizes it as "ambivalent." Griffiths, *The Ambivalence of Gay Liberation*, 16–19; Gammerl, *anders fühlen*, 339.
5 Carsten I., interview, 11 November 2016.
6 Ibid.
7 SHStAD, 11455 Bezirksgericht Dresden, Nr. 3868, 1.
8 Peter Rausch, interview, 31 January 2017.
9 Rainer E., interview, 11 April 2017.
10 Turner, *Germany from Partition to Reunification*, 68.
11 Steiner, *The Plans That Failed*, 50.
12 von Mahlsdorf, *Ich bin meine eigene Frau*, 146–7; Dobler, "Schwules Leben in Berlin zwischen 1945 und 1969 im Ost-West-Vergleich," 162.
13 Harsch, "Between State Policy and Private Sphere," 96; Harsch, *Revenge of the Domestic*, 198–235; Merkel, "Another Kind of Woman," 6.
14 Borowski, *Parallelwelten*, 247; Borowski, "Erste Erkenntnisse zum lesbischen und schwulen Alltagslebel in der frühen DDR," 57–60.
15 BStU, MfS - AU, Nr. 1030/58, Bd. 1, 51.
16 Ibid., 10.
17 BStU, MfS - GH 90/78, Bd. A, 58, 253; BStU, MfS - AOP Nr. 2584/68, 97; von Mahlsdorf, *Ich bin meine eigene Frau*, 158; Rottmann, "Queer Home Berlin?," 129–31.
18 BStU, MfS - AOP Nr. 2584/68, 36, 97.
19 *Spartacus International Gay Guide*, 3rd ed. (Euro-Spartacus, 1973), 109ff.
20 BStU, MfS - GH 90/78, Bd. A, 43–6.
21 Ibid., 252.
22 BStU, MfS - GH 90/78, Bd. P, 46–7.
23 von Mahlsdorf, *Ich bin meine eigene Frau*, 155.
24 BStU, BVfS Leipzig Abt. II Nr. 798, 146
25 McLellan, "From Private Photography to Mass Circulation," 407.

26 LAB, C Rep. 330, Nr. 50, 2.
27 SHStAD, 11464 BDVP Dresden, Nr. 3.77, 15.
28 Ibid., 17.
29 Samuel Clowes Huneke, "Death Wish," 132–8. On suicidal ideation in West Germany, see Gammerl, *anders fühlen*, 53.
30 BStU, MfS - HA I, Nr. 14841, 260.
31 LAB, C Rep. 341, Nr. 800, 3–4.
32 Ibid., 7.
33 Herf, *Divided Memory*, 163.
34 Fulbrook, *Reckonings*, 240–5.
35 Marhoefer, *Sex and the Weimar Republic*, 128; Beachy, *Gay Berlin*, 237.
36 OLG Halle, "Beschluß v. 20.9.1948–1 Ws 53/48," 144.
37 Kammergericht Berlin, "Urteil vom 21. Februar 1950–1 Ss 165/49," 100.
38 "Gesetz zur Ergänzung des Strafgesetzbuches," §8.
39 Thinius, "Erfahrungen schwuler Männer in der DDR und in Deutschland Ost," n9; Schulz, *Paragraph 175 (abgewickelt)*, 52–3. There are references in the scholarship to a Berlin *Kammergericht* decision holding that consensual acts between adult men could not be prosecuted. The source for this assertion is often not cited, however, and I have not found evidence of such a ruling. See in particular Stümke, *Homosexuelle in Deutschland*, 166.
40 Berndl and Kruber, "Zur Statistik der Strafverfolgung homosexueller Männer in der SBZ und DDR bis 1959," 88; Berndl, "Zeiten der Bedrohung," 21–7; Erik Huneke, "Morality, Law, and the Socialist Sexual Self in the German Democratic Republic, 1945–1972," 208.
41 Dietz and Hesse, *Wörterbuch der Sexuologie und ihrer Grenzgebiete*, 138. See too Benjamin, *Das Strafrecht der sozialistischen Demokratie*, 13.
42 BStU, MfS - GH, Nr. 194/85, 12.
43 The East German *Statistisches Jahrbuch*, unlike its West German counterpart, did not publish statistics of §175 and §175(a) convictions. One estimate puts the total number of convictions at 4,000 between 1949 and 1969; Pretzel, *NS-Opfer unter Vorbehalt*, 185. Klaus Berndl and Vera Kruber's discovery provides complete statistics only for the years 1957–9. For more on the debates surrounding §175 repeal in the GDR see Erik Huneke, "Morality, Law, and the Socialist Sexual Self in the German Democratic Republic, 1945–1972," 179–225.
44 Berndl, "Zeiten der Bedrohung," 25.
45 "Moralhelden wollen prügeln," *Berliner Zeitung* 8/197 (24 August 1952), 4.
46 BStU, MfS - AU, Nr. 390/58, 45.
47 Ibid., 47.
48 Ibid.
49 "Control Council Directive No. 38"; Herf, *Divided Memory*, 73; Pendas, *Democracy, Nazi Trials, and Transitional Justice in Germany, 1945–1950*, 92–3.

50 BStU, MfS - AU, Nr. 390/58, 79.
51 Ibid., 81.
52 BStU, MfS, AU, Nr. 31/60, Bd. 2, 174, 134.
53 Ibid., 170.
54 Borowski, *Parallelwelten*, 84–100. See too Frackman, "Persistent Ambivalence," 676–83.
55 Berndl, "Zeiten der Bedrohung," 24–5.
56 LAB, C Rep 341, Nr. 4433, 1. Evans also discusses this case, arguing that it shows how penal institutions treated johns and call boys differently. Evans, *Life among the Ruins*, 137–9.
57 LAB, C Rep 341, Nr. 4433, 1, 13, 47.
58 Erik Huneke, "Morality, Law, and the Socialist Sexual Self in the German Democratic Republic, 1945–1972," 186; Frackman, "Persistent Ambivalence," 681; Schwartz, *Homosexuelle, Seilschaften, Verrat*, 274.
59 Kurt Freund, *Die Homosexualität beim Mann*.
60 Oberstes Gericht, "Urteil vom 28. März 1950–3 Tst. 9/50," 215.
61 On gender policy in East Germany see, *inter alia*, Heineman, *What Difference Does a Husband Make?*, 176–208; Herzog, *Sex after Fascism*, 184–219; Fulbrook, *The People's State*, 141–78; Harsch, *Revenge of the Domestic*.
62 Erik Huneke, "Morality, Law, and the Socialist Sexual Self in the German Democratic Republic, 1945–1972," 195–6.
63 Kleßmann, *Die doppelte Staatsgründung*, 268.
64 Qtd in Sandford, *From Hitler to Ulbricht*, 29.
65 Schroeder, *Der SED-Staat*, 412–16.
66 Turner, *Germany from Partition to Reunification*, 72–3, 77.
67 Herf, *Divided Memory*, 37.
68 Ibid., 13, 21.
69 Port, *Conflict and Stability in the German Democratic Republic*, 99ff.
70 Evans, "The Moral State," 360; Evans, "Bahnhof Boys," 636; Evans, "Decriminalization, Seduction, and 'Unnatural Desire,' in East Germany," 557.
71 Brock, "Producing the 'Socialist Personality'?," 223.
72 "Zehn Gebote für den neuen sozialistischen Menschen" (1958).
73 BStU, MfS, AU, Nr. 307/55, Bd. 2, 27; Evans, "Decriminalization, Seduction, and 'Unnatural Desire,'" 557.
74 BStU, MfS - AU, Nr. 307/55, Bd. 1, 65; BStU, MfS, AU, Nr. 307/55, Bd. 2, 81.
75 BStU, MfS, AU, Nr. 307/55, Bd. 2, 98.
76 Ibid., 144.
77 Grau, "Liberalisierung und Repression," 12; Erik Huneke, "Morality, Law, and the Socialist Sexual Self in the German Democratic Republic, 1945–1972," 197.

78 On Stalinism and homosexuality, see Dan Healey, *Homosexual Desire in Revolutionary Russia*, 207–50.

79 "'Onkel Tobias' – ein Unhold," *Neues Deutschland*, 18 August 1955, 8; "Homosexueller Minister a.D. im 'Klub der 300,'" *Berliner Zeitung*, 31 October 1954, 2; "Kronzeuge homosexuelle," *Berliner Zeitung*, 15 March 1952, 2.

80 "Tiergarten ein Verbrecherparadies: Enthüllungen der in Hamburg erscheinenden 'Bildzeitung,'" *Berliner Zeitung*, 23 October 1953; "Strichjungen, Mörder und Diebe," *Berliner Zeitung*, 8 July 1955.

81 "Westberliner Frauen als Freiwild: Westmächte unterbinden Razzien der Westberliner Polizei," *Berliner Zeitung*, 14 September 1951, 6.

82 "Mord vor den Augen der Polizei," *Neue Zeit*, 2 April 1954, 6; "Volkspolizei klärt Raubmord auf," *Berliner Zeitung*, 3 April 1954, 6; "Wo die Unterwelt Pläne schiedet: Die Tradition der Bülow-Klaus/Stupo schreitet nicht ein," *Berliner Zeitung*, 4 June 1954, 6.

83 "Ermordet aufgefunden," *Berliner Zeitung*, 2 April 1954, 8.

84 Evans, "Decriminalization, Seduction, and 'Unnatural Desire' in East Germany," 557.

85 Grau, "Return of the Past," 15.

86 Herzog, *Sex after Fascism*, 197.

87 BStU, MfS - GH 90/78, Bd. P, 63.

88 "Wenn's dem Esel zu wohl ist: Gefährliche 'Geschäfte' am Bahnhof Friedrichstraße / Beinahe Zuchthaus," *Berliner Zeitung*, 12 June 1957, 8; "Strichjungen, Mörder und Diebe," *Berliner Zeitung*, 8 July 1955, 6; "Kleine Berliner Chronik," *Berliner Zeitung*, 23 December 1955, 6; "'Politische Flüchtling' mordete," *Berliner Zeitung*, 1 July 1955, 6.

89 BStU, MfS - GH, Nr. 70/61, Bd. 1, 7. As in West German cases, men accused of having sex with other men often used their drunkenness as a defence. In the case of Fred V. and Werner W. discussed above, Werner told police he had consumed at least seven beers, eight schnapps, and six shots of other liquor. LAB, C Rep. 341, Nr. 4433, 6.

90 BStU, MfS - GH, Nr. 70/61, Bd. 1, 10.

91 Ibid., 11.

92 "Gesetz zur Ergänzung des Strafgesetzbuches," §20.

93 BStU, MfS - GH, Nr. 70/61, Bd. 2, 100.

94 BStU, MfS - GH, Nr. 70/61, Bd. 1, 13.

95 Ibid., 13, 83.

96 BStU, MfS - GH, Nr. 70/61, Bd. 2, 100.

97 BStU, MfS - GH, Nr. 647/59, Bd. 2, 223.

98 Evans, "The Moral State," 367–9.

99 Evans, "Decriminalization, Seduction, and 'Unnatural Desire' in East Germany," 564.

100 BStU, MfS, BdL/Dok. Nr. 403, 2.

101 Ibid., 7.

102 Evans, "Decriminalization, Seduction, and 'Unnatural Desire' in East Germany," 558.

103 BStU, MfS, AU, Nr. 307/55, Bd. 5, 137.

104 BStU, MfS, WR, Nr. 683, 48–50.

105 Marhoefer, "Lesbianism, Transvestitism, and the Nazi State," 1170.

106 Betts, *Within Walls*, 33; Evans, "Decriminalization, Seduction, and 'Unnatural Desire' in East Germany," 564.

107 Evans, "Decriminalization, Seduction, and 'Unnatural Desire' in East Germany," 555; Borowski, *Parallelwelten*, 86–91.

108 As noted earlier, much of the existing literature focuses on how, in McLellan's words, "the prosecution of male homosexuality was accompanied by widespread homophobia." McLellan, *Love in the Time of Communism*, 115.

109 Fulbrook, *Anatomy of a Dictatorship*, 129–50; Fulbrook, *The People's State*, ch. 7; Betts, *Within Walls*, 88–107; Harsch, *Revenge of the Domestic*; McLellan, *Love in the Time of Communism*; Port, "Love, Lust, and Lies under Communism," 502–3. Günter Gaus coined the concept of the "niche society" in 1983 in Gaus, *Wo Deutschland liegt*, 156–233.

110 Heineman, *What Difference Does a Husband Make?*, 90.

4 The Crooked Path of Emancipation in West Germany

1 "Das Gesetz fällt-bleibt die Ächtung?," *Der Spiegel*, 12 May 1969.

2 Whisnant, *Male Homosexuality in West Germany*, 166–203; Moeller, "'The Homosexual Man Is a "Man," the Homosexual Woman Is a "Woman"'"; Moeller, "Private Acts, Public Anxieties, and the Fight to Decriminalize Male Homosexuality in West Germany"; Moeller, *Protecting Motherhood*, 190–3; Schäfer, "*Widernatürliche Unzucht*," 79–188; Herzog, *Sex after Fascism*, 130–4.

3 Jackson, *Living in Arcadia*, 58–110; David Johnson, *The Lavender Scare*, 179–208; David Johnson, *Buying Gay*; Faderman, *The Gay Revolution*, 53–170; Cervini, *The Deviant's War*.

4 Pretzel and Weiß, "Überlegungen zum Erbe der zweiten deutschen Homosexuellenbewegung," 10–11; Evans, "Bahnhof Boys," 628–9.

5 Whisnant, *Male Homosexuality in West Germany*, 69; Griffiths, "Sex, Shame and West German Gay Liberation," 445–6. See too Hansen, "The Cold War and the Homophile, 1953–1963"; Rupp, "The Persistence of Transnational Organizing."

6 Whisnant, *Male Homosexuality in West Germany*, 65–79.

7 "Mitteilungen des Sekretariates," 5, ArchSM, Deutsche Gruppierungen und Organisationen, Wissenschaftlich-humanitäres Komitee, 1949–1960er.

8 Whisnant, *Male Homosexuality in West Germany*, 70–2; von Rönn, "Der Homosexualitätsentwürfe von Hans Giese und der lange Schatten von Hans Bürger-Prinz," 277–310.

9 Whisnant, *Male Homosexuality in West Germany*, 80–9; Rosenkranz and Lorenz, *Hamburg auf anderen Wegen*, 89.

10 Whisnant, *Male Homosexuality in West Germany*, 69–70.

11 Stümke, *Homosexuelle in Deutschland*, 137–42; Whisnant, *Male Homosexuality in West Germany*, 88–93; Lorenz, "Hamburg als Homosexuellenhauptstadt der 1950er Jahre," 128–35.

12 Whisnant, *Male Homosexuality in West Germany*, 65.

13 Whisnant also characterizes the arguments against §175 and §175(a) as both scientific and liberal. But he does so to highlight their connection to a larger "progressive project." In contradistinction, I do so in order to emphasize their limited reach and how they often recapitulated arguments from earlier decades. Whisnant, *Male Homosexuality in West Germany*, 169–70.

14 BArch-Koblenz, B 141/4075, 5.

15 Ibid., 43.

16 "Wir und der demokratische Staat," *Die Insel*, March 1952, 5.

17 BArch-Koblenz, B 141/4075, 50.

18 BArch-Koblenz, B 141/4071, 169.

19 Ibid., 170.

20 Ibid., 173.

21 Ibid., 169.

22 Ibid., 170. Benno Gammerl similarly argues that homophile campaigners stressed emotional intimacy over sexual desire in order to project a respectable image. Gammerl, "Affecting Legal Change," 113–14.

23 Hakkarainen, *A State of Peace in Europe*, 159.

24 BArch-Koblenz, B 141/4071, 172; "Grundgesetz für die Bundesrepublik Deutschland," Arts. 2 and 3.

25 BArch-Koblenz, B 141/4071, 176.

26 BArch-Koblenz, B 141/85394, 77.

27 Currah, "The State," 198. On the evolution of European statehood in the twentieth century, see Sheehan, "What It Means to Be a State," 18–20.

28 Gammerl and Whisnant both find some homophile writers who emphasized minority status, but the petitions and articles I assessed generally eschewed such language. Gammerl, *anders fühlen*, 66–8; Whisnant, *Male Homosexuality in West Germany*, 102–3.

29 "Mitteilungen des Wissenschaftlich-Humanitären Komitees e.V. in Frankfurt a.M., 1. Jahrgang, Nummer 1.," 3, ArchSM, Deutsche

Gruppierungen und Organisationen, Wissenschaftlich-humanitäres Komitee, 1949–1960er; Dieter Michael Specht, "In memoriam Hans Giese," *Him*, September 1970, 19.

30 Bundesverfassungsgericht, "Urteil des Ersten Senats vom 10. Mai 1957," 404–5; Becker, *Homosexualität und Jugendschutz*, 15; Gatzweiler, *Die Homosexualität des Mannes und die Strafrechtreform*, 15.

31 Whisnant, "Styles of Masculinity in the West German Gay Scene, 1950–1965," 383.

32 BArch-Koblenz, B 141/4071, 175.

33 Kempe, "Die Homophilen und die Gesellschaft," 1.

34 Baumann, *Paragraph 175*, 173–4.

35 "Gemacht wird's ja doch: In lila Nächten," *Der Spiegel*, 15 September 1949, 8.

36 Rosenkranz and Lorenz, *Hamburg auf anderen Wegen*, 89–90.

37 Landesgesundheitsamt to Magistrat von Groß Berlin, 23 February 1950, ArchSM, Deutsche Gruppierungen und Organisationen, Wissenschaftlich-humanitäres Komitee, 1949–1960er.

38 Abt. Personal und Verwaltung to Bezirksamt Zehlendorf, 11 December 1950, ArchSM, Deutsche Gruppierungen und Organisationen, Wissenschaftlich-humanitäres Komitee, 1949–1960er.

39 Akantha, "Wissenschaftlich-humanitäres Komitee auch in Berlin," *Der Kreis*, 1950, 32; Whisnant, *Male Homosexuality in West Germany*, 108.

40 Stümke, *Homosexuelle in Deutschland*, 137.

41 Whisnant, *Male Homosexuality in West Germany*, 82–7.

42 Heineman, *Before Porn Was Legal*, 27–60; Ritzheimer, *"Trash," Censorship, and National Identity in Early Twentieth-Century Germany*, 285; Whisnant, *Male Homosexuality in West Germany*, 105.

43 "Statistik und Bericht für das 1. Jahr der Tätigkeit der Bundesprüfstelle für jugendgefährdende Shcriften vom Mai 1954 bis einschl. 30. April 1955," *Der werbende Buch- und Zeitschriftenhandel*, September 1955, 293; "Zwei Jahre Bundesprüfstelle für jugendgefährdende Schriften," *Der werbende Buch- und Zeitschriftenhandel*, August 1956, 268; Johannes Werres, "Umwandelbar im Wandel der Zeiten: Die Bundesprüfstelle," *Him*, March 1972, 44.

44 Whisnant, *Male Homosexuality in West Germany*, 107; Lorenz, "Hamburg als Homosexuellenhauptstadt der 1950er Jahre," 133. See too Rosenkranz and Lorenz, *Hamburg auf anderen Wegen*, 81.

45 David Johnson, *Buying Gay*, 122–6; Jackson, *Living in Arcadia*; Kennedy, *The Ideal Gay Man: The Story of Der Kreis*.

46 Whisnant, *Male Homosexuality in West Germany*, 164.

47 Daub and Huneke, "Die unsichtbare Tradition," 88–93.

48 Whisnant, *Male Homosexuality in West Germany*, 108; Rosenkranz and Lorenz, *Hamburg auf anderen Wegen*, 89–91.

49 Loy Wenker, "§175 bleibt in Deutschland in Kraft," *Der Kreis: Ein Monatsschrift* 25, no. 6 (1957): 7.

50 "Die Lage der einsehl. Vereinigungen in Deutschland," 1960, 3, ArchSM, Deutsche Gruppierungen und Organisationen, Wissenschaftlich-humanitäres Komitee, 1949–1960er.

51 Moeller, "Private Acts," 546–7.

52 Bundesverfassungsgericht, "Urteil des Ersten Senats vom 10. Mai 1957," 413–19.

53 Ibid., 427.

54 Ibid., 428.

55 Ibid., 434.

56 Moeller, "'The Homosexual Man Is a "Man," the Homosexual Woman Is a Woman,'" 411.

57 Bundesverfassungsgericht, "Urteil des Ersten Senats vom 10. Mai 1957," 398.

58 Ibid., 404, 405.

59 Ibid., 404.

60 Jackson, *Living in Arcadia*, 10–11; David Johnson, *The Lavender Scare*, 179–208; Hobson, *Lavender and Red*, 18–41; Cervini, *The Deviant's War*, 65–6.

61 Cory, *The Homosexual in America*, 3ff.

62 Qtd in Cervini, *The Deviant's War*, 65.

63 Whisnant, *Male Homosexuality in West Germany*, 78.

64 Strote, *Lions and Lambs*, 147ff.

65 Ackermann, "Zur Frage der Strafwürdigkeit des homosexuellen Verhaltens des Mannes," 153.

66 Ibid., 153–4; Whisnant, *Male Homosexuality in West Germany*, 181–3.

67 Moeller, *Protecting Motherhood*, 47ff.

68 Bauer, Giese, Jäger, and Bürger-Prinz, eds, "Vorwort der Herausgeber," 7.

69 "Strafrechtsreform: Die Eigenart des Mannes," *Der Spiegel*, 19 June 1957, 23.

70 Schäfer, "Widernatürliche Unzucht," 161.

71 Ackermann, "Zur Frage der Strafwürdigkeit des homosexuellen Verhaltens des Mannes," 154.

72 Deutscher Bundestag, "Entwurf eines Strafgesetzbuches (StGB) E 1962," 44.

73 Ibid., 45.

74 Ibid., 47.

75 Ibid.

76 Ackermann, "Zur Frage der Strafwürdigkeit des homosexuellen Verhaltens des Mannes," 149; Deutscher Bundestag, "Entwurf eines Strafgesetzbuches (StGB) E 1962," 47.

77 Hans Peter Bull, "Gesetz aus einem Guß: Strafrechtsreform-warum und wie?," *Die Zeit*, 5 April 1963; Deutscher Bundestag, "Entwurf eines Strafgesetzbuches (StGB) E 1962," 377.

78 Deutscher Bundestag, "Entwurf eines Strafgesetzbuches (StGB) E 1962," 376, 377.

79 Ibid., 377.

80 Ibid.; Brühöfener, "Contested Masculinities," 299–300.

81 "Strafrechts-Reform: Schuld und Sühne," *Der Spiegel*, 7 May 1958, 14.

82 Bull, "Gesetz aus einem Guß: Strafrechtsreform-warum und wie?"

83 Herzog, "Sexuality, Memory, Morality," 257

84 Adorno, "Sexualtabus und Recht heute," 299.

85 "Bestseller: Belletristik, Sachbücher," *Der Spiegel*, 27 March 1963; "Bestseller: Belletristik, Sachbücher," *Der Spiegel*, 3 April 1963; "Bestseller: Belletristik, Sachbücher," *Der Spiegel*, 17 April 1963.

86 Bauer et al., "Vorwort der Herausgeber," 8.

87 Ibid., 10.

88 Ibid., 8.

89 "Strafrechtsreform: Vorerst gar nichts," *Der Spiegel*, 17 January 1966, 21.

90 Edward Ross Dickinson points out that a rapid decriminalization of "victimless sexual offenses" started in the 1960s. Dickinson, "Policing Sex in Germany," 240.

91 Herzog, "Between Coitus and Commodification," 270–3; Whisnant, *Male Homosexuality in West Germany*, 167.

92 Heineman, *Before Porn Was Legal*, 129.

93 Herzog, *Sex after Fascism*, 141.

94 Ibid., 129–34.

95 Fulbrook, *Reckonings*, 250.

96 Wittmann, *Beyond Justice*, 15.

97 Steinke, *Fritz Bauer oder Auschwitz vor Gericht*, 75–122.

98 Arendt, *Eichmann in Jerusalem*; see too Lipstadt, *The Eichmann Trial*.

99 The collaboration between Bauer and the Israeli government is described in Steinke, *Fritz Bauer oder Auschwitz vor Gericht*, 13–23.

100 Wittmann, *Beyond Justice*, 285–6.

101 Brown, *West Germany and the Global Sixties*, 95.

102 Pretzel, "Wiedergutmachung unter Vorbehalt und mit neuer Perspektive," 101–4.

103 Strote, *Lions and Lambs*, 224–31.

104 Schoeps, "Überlegungen zum Problem der Homosexualität," 113.

105 Ibid., 114.

106 Ibid., 86.

107 Harthauser, "Der Massenmord an Homosexuellen im Dritten Reich," 7.

108 Ibid., 8.

109 Wilde, *Das Schicksal der Verfemten*, 8.

110 E.g., Felix Rexhausen, "Wie es ist, ist es gut," *Der Spiegel*, no. 9 (22 February 1967): 127.

111 "Gesellschaft: Homosexualität: Späte Milde," 65, 55.

112 Franz M., "Eingabe," 15 February 1966, BArch-Koblenz, B 141/85395. Whisnant discusses *Quick*'s contribution to debate over E 62 in *Male Homosexuality in West Germany*, 188.

113 H. v. S., "Eingabe," 10 October 1967, BArch-Koblenz, B 141/85395.

114 Newsome, "Homosexuals after the Holocaust," 117–59; Jensen, "The Pink Triangle and Political Consciousness," 325–6; Griffiths, *The Ambivalence of Gay Liberation*, 124–39; Tremblay, "The Proudest Symbol We Could Put Forward?"; Schappach, "Geballte Faust, Doppelaxt, rosa Winkel."

115 Chitty, *Sexual Hegemony*, 149.

116 Rothberg defines multidirectional memory as "the interference, overlap, and mutual constitution of seemingly distinct collective memories that define the postwar era and the workings of memory more generally." Rothberg, "Between Auschwitz and Algeria," 162. See too Rothberg, "Work of Testimony in the Age of Decolonization," 1233–4. Similarly, Herzog has argued that "it was the project of struggling to liberalize sexual mores in West Germany in the 1960s that brought a new and different version of the Third Reich into public discussion." It is worth noting that, for gay men, the association went in reverse. Herzog, "Sexuality, Memory, Morality," 206.

117 Brown, *West Germany and the Global Sixties*, 239; Brown, "'1968' East and West: Divided Germany as a Case Study in Transnational History," 69–96; For more on the student movement and 1968, see von der Goltz, ed., *"Talkin' 'Bout My Generation"*; von der Goltz, *The Other '68ers*; von der Goltz, "Making Sense of East Germany's 1968," 53–69; Klimke and Scharloth, *1968 in Europe*; Klimke and Scharloth, *1968. Handbuch zur Kultur- und Mediengeschichte der Studentenbewegung*.

118 Herzog, *Sex after Fascism*, 141.

119 Ibid., 152–62.

120 Judt, *The Memory Chalet*, 122.

121 A rare student publication to mention homosexuality listed it among a litany of other marginalized sexualities discriminated against in the Federal Republic. "Sexualität und Herrschaft" (Kritische Universität, Summer 1958), 80, HA, German Subject Collection, XX741, Box 84, Folder FRG Student Protest Org. ASTA-Berlin.

122 HA, German Subject Collection, XX741, Box 82.

123 Judt, *The Memory Chalet*, 123.

124 Herzog, *Sex after Fascism*, 234–40; Brown, *West Germany and the Global Sixties*, 286–320; Chin, "Thinking Difference in Postwar Germany," 212.

125 Giese and Schmidt, *Studenten-Sexualität*, 207–9.
126 Collings, *Democracy's Guardians*, 112.
127 "Wir diskutieren Paragraph 175," *Twen*, no. 4 (1963): 42–52.
128 "175," *Twen*, no. 5 (1963): 70.
129 BArch-Koblenz, B 141/85394, 103. These petitions suggest that, even in the absence of a robust homophile movement, there was a growing "pressure 'from below'" for reform of §175 and §175(a). Whisnant, *Male Homosexuality in West Germany*, 167.
130 BArch-Koblenz, B 141/85394, 99.
131 "Aus den Protokollen des Juristentages: Was geht den Staat die 'Unzucht' an?," *Die Zeit*, 10 January 1969.
132 Ibid.
133 *Verhandlungen des siebenundvierzigsten deutschen Juristentages*, 145.
134 Italiaander, "Ein Rundbrief," 222; see too Whisnant, *Male Homosexuality in West Germany*, 196.
135 Italiaander, "Ein Rundbrief," 222.
136 "Erstes Gesetz zur Reform des Strafrechts (1. StrRG)," 653.
137 "Lex Homo," *Der Spiegel*, 3 February 1969, 18; Brühöfener, "Contested Masculinities," 3024; Schäfer, "Das Ringen um § 175 StGB während der Post-Adenauer-Ära," 203–5.
138 "Niederschrift über die Ressortbesprechung zu Fragen der Homosexualität am 14. Januar 1969 im Bundesministerium der Justiz," 29 January 1969, BArch-Koblenz, B 141/85386. See too Brühöfener, "Sex and the Soldier," 530–1; Whisnant, *Male Homosexuality in West Germany*, 199–201. On NATO and West Germany's remilitarization, see Sheehan, *Where Have All the Soldiers Gone?*, 160ff.
139 Deutscher Bundestag, "5. Wahlperiode – 230. Sitzung," 7 May 1969, 12788.
140 Qtd in "Lex Homo," *Der Spiegel*, 3 February 1969, 18.
141 "Gesellschaft: Homosexualität: Späte Milde," 55.
142 Ibid., 58.
143 Moeller, "Private Acts, Public Anxieties," 539.
144 Whisnant, *Male Homosexuality in West Germany*, 195.
145 Faderman, *The Gay Revolution*, 115–70.

5 Gay Spies in Cold War Germany

1 "Panik im RIAS: Verlagerung des NATO-Senders nach Luxemburg geplant," *Berliner Zeitung*, 11 November 1961, 1.
2 BStU, MfS - HA XX/9, Nr. 1684, 77.
3 Evans, "Decriminalization, Seduction, and 'Unnatural Desire' in East Germany," 572; Grau, "Erpressbar und Tendenziell Konspirativ," 23; Schwartz, *Homosexuelle, Seilschaften, Verrat*, 275–6.

4 Stapel, *Warme Brüder gegen Kalte Krieger*, 80.

5 Gieseke, *The History of the Stasi*, 158ff.

6 Bruce, *The Firm*, 99–100; Miller, *The Stasi Files Unveiled*, 38.

7 Gellately, "Denunciations in Twentieth-Century Germany," 955; Bruce, *The Firm*, 10.

8 Betts, *Within Walls*, 38. As Mark Fenemore points out, this desire to know everything often made the Stasi an ineffective agency, weighed down by the sheer volume of evidence it collected. Fenemore, *Fighting the Cold War in Post-Blockade, Pre-Wall Berlin*, 175.

9 David Johnson, *The Lavender Scare*, 120ff.

10 SHStAD, 11120 StAW LG DD, Nr. 2552, 4. For more about the Falcons, see Brown, *West Germany and the Global Sixties*, 69–70; Ruff, *The Wayward Flock*, 230.

11 SHStAD, 11120 StAW LG DD, Nr. 2552, 13.

12 SHStAD, 12916 Bezirksstaatsanwaltschaft Dresden, Nr. 309, 33.

13 Ibid., 20, 7.

14 Ibid., 7–9.

15 Ibid., 88, 131.

16 Ibid., 19.

17 Qtd in, McLellan, *Love in the Time of Communism*, 104; For more on the Stasi's "Romeo" agents, see Pfister, *Unternehmen Romeo*; Vilasi, *The History of the Stasi*, 165; Koehler, *Stasi*, 176–87.

18 Koehler, *Stasi*, 186–7.

19 BStU, MfS - AOP Nr. 1761/80, 7.

20 Fenemore estimates that there were between forty and ninety intelligence agencies operating in Berlin in the 1950s. Fenemore, *Fighting the Cold War in Post-Blockade, Pre-Wall Berlin*, 170.

21 Gaddis, "Intelligence, Espionage, and Cold War Origins," 191; McKnight, *Espionage and the Roots of the Cold War*, 6; Hopkins, "Continuing Debate and New Approaches in Cold War History," 930; Murphy, Kondrashev, and Bailey, *Battleground Berlin*; Sulick, *American Spies*, 149ff; Fenemore, *Fighting the Cold War in Post-Blockade, Pre-Wall Berlin*, 169–87.

22 BStU, MfS - AU, Nr. 1897/58, Bd. 2, 11.

23 Ibid., 10.

24 Ibid., 187.

25 BStU, MfS - GH 90/78, Bd. P, 16.

26 Ibid., 18, 15.

27 Ibid., 34.

28 Ibid., 41.

29 Ibid.

30 Ibid., 75, 80–113.

31 Ibid., 75.

32 Joachim's espionage experiences were probably quite similar to those of other agents in Berlin. As Fenemore notes, "The actual espionage operations [in Berlin] were often more prosaic and humdrum than their fictional counterparts." Fenemore, *Fighting the Cold War in Post-Blockade, Pre-Wall Berlin*, 186.
33 "Wie bei Edgar Wallace," *Der Spiegel*, 4 November 1953, 16.
34 SHStAD, 12916 Bezirksstaatsanwaltschaft Dresden, Nr. 309, 19.
35 BStU, MfS - GH 90/78, Bd. P, 34
36 Ibid., 48.
37 Ibid., 48–54.
38 Ibid., 54.
39 BStU, MfS - GH 90/78, Bd. A, 44.
40 Ibid., 94.
41 Ibid., 252–6.
42 Ibid., 101, 205, 251, 255, 259.
43 BStU, MfS - GH 90/78, Bd. P. 75.
44 BStU, MfS - GH 90/78, Bd. A, 125. This ring is also mentioned in BStU, MfS - AOP Nr. 2584/68, 44.
45 BStU, MfS - GH 90/78, Bd. A, 125.
46 David Johnson, *The Lavender Scare*, 109–11; Hammerich, "Joachim Krase (1925–1988)," 274; Trahair and Miller, *Encyclopedia of Cold War Espionage, Spies, and Secret Operations*, 112; Hepburn, *Intrigue*, 193.
47 BStU, MfS - GH 90/78, Bd. P, 11.
48 Ibid., 13.
49 Ibid., 12.
50 BStU, MfS - GH 90/78, Bd. A, 81.
51 BStU, MfS - GH 90/78, Bd. P, 58–61.
52 Ibid., 76.
53 "Die Stasi und die Homosexuellen," in Setz, *Homosexualität in der DDR*, 206. Kate Davison has also analysed this document, arguing that it reflects a Cold War consensus that there existed certain affinities between gay men's "emotional disposition" and the requirements of espionage. Davison, "The Sexual (Geo)Politics of Loyalty," 134.
54 BStU, MfS, BV Karl-Marx-Stadt, AIM, Nr. 1109/89, Teil I, Bd. 1, 50.
55 Ibid., 88.
56 BStU, MfS - HA XII Nr. 1643, 66.
57 Ibid., 7.
58 Ibid., 73.
59 BStU, MfS - HA II, Nr. 32736, 455.
60 BStU, MfS - AOP, Nr. 1761/80, 7.
61 Ibid., 8.
62 BStU, MfS - HA II, Nr. 32736, 19.

63 Ibid., 221.

64 Ibid., 455.

65 BStU, MfS - AOP, Nr. 1761/80, 7. About Sven-Hedin-Strasse 11, see Franz
Solms-Laubach, "Deutschlands geheimste Villa," *Bild*, 12 November 2012:
https://www.bild.de/politik/inland/bnd/bild-zu-besuch-in
-deutschlands-geheimster-villa-27153104.bild.html.

66 BStU, MfS - HA II, Nr. 32736, 220.

67 Ibid., 18.

68 Ibid., 454.

69 Ibid., 15.

70 Ibid., 456.

71 Ibid., 34, 455.

72 BStU, MfS - AOP, Nr. 1761/80, 212, 301.

73 Ibid., 207.

74 BStU, MfS - HA II, Nr. 32736, 15, 3.

75 Sheffer, *Burned Bridge*, 148.

76 Ibid., 261, 263; Fulbrook, *Anatomy of a Dictatorship*, 79; Port, *Conflict and
Stability in the German Democratic Republic*, 134–5.

77 BStU, MfS - HA II, Nr. 32736, 29.

78 Richard Tingel, "Agenten Unter Uns!," *Die Zeit*, 21 January 1954.

79 BArch-Koblenz, B 141/4071, 124.

80 Schwartz, *Homosexuelle, Seilschaften, Verrat*, 273; Shepherd, "Gay Sex Spy
Orgy," 213; Judt, *Reappraisals*, ch. 18; D'Emilio, "The Homosexual Menace,"
59–61; David Johnson, *The Lavender Scare*, 33ff.

81 Buck-Morss, *Dreamworld and Catastrophe*, 2–3; see too Clowes, *Russia on the
Edge*, 162–3.

6 Gay Citizenship and Power in West Germany

1 Scholars writing in English have only recently started to look at West
German homosexuality in the 1970s and 1980s. Timothy Scott Brown,
who places the groups considered here in a genealogy with 1960s
activism, notes how the movement splintered in ways "characteristic of
the historical moment." Much of Craig Griffiths's ground-breaking work
focuses on how these activists reproduced the respectability politics of their
homophile forebears. As noted below, German scholars writing about this
period include those, such as Patrick Henze, whose work focuses on the
exuberance as well as the conflict inherent in the movement, and those, such
as Michael Holy, who evince the view that West German efforts remained
a less-successful version of American queer activism. See Brown, *West
Germany and the Global Sixties*, 328; Griffiths, "Sex, Shame and West German
Gay Liberation"; Griffiths, *The Ambivalence of Gay Liberation*, 16–21; Henze,

"Die Lückenlose Kette"; Henze, *Schwule Emanzipation und ihre Konflikte*, 9–16; Holy, "Jenseits von Stonewall," 70. See too Magdalena Beljan's work, which problematizes the ways in which male homosexual identity was reproduced in the 1970s and 1980s. Beljan, *Rosa Zeiten?*, 83–172.

2 "Regierungserklärung von Bundeskanzler Willy Brandt," 2.

3 Chin, *The Guest Worker Question in Postwar Germany*, 89.

4 Sarotte, *Dealing with the Devil*, 129.

5 Koehler, *Stasi*, 151–63.

6 Eley, *Forging Democracy*, 418ff.

7 *Spartacus International Gay Guide*, 1972, 111.

8 Ibid., 113.

9 Ewing, "'Color Him Black,'" 383; "Flyer," January 1973, ArchSM, HAW, Nr. 12; Griffiths, *The Ambivalence of Gay Liberation*, 56.

10 For more on these magazines, see Griffiths, "Sex, Shame and West German Gay Liberation," 447–51; Ewing, "'Toward a Better World for Gays,'" 109–32. See too Beljan's work, which traces how contemporary understandings of gayness, including the significance of coming out, emerged from the discursive milieu that evolved after 1969. Beljan, *Rosa Zeiten?*, 83–122.

11 Martin Meeker asserts that personal ads are "a central, perhaps the central, thread that makes queer history a recognizable and unified phenomenon." Meeker, *Contacts Desired*, 2. The homophile publications of the 1950s experimented with personal ads, though some decided they posed too great a risk. Whisnant, *Male Homosexuality in West Germany*, 87–94.

12 "Freundschaftsanzeigen," *Du & Ich*, January 1973, 23.

13 "Annoncen," *Du & Ich*, February 1970, 48.

14 E.g., "Him Kontakt: Her," *him*, October 1976, 70.

15 "Freundschaftsanzeigen," *Du & Ich*, February 1973, 24.

16 "Offener Rundbrief an die Interessengruppen," 27 October 1970, ArchSM, Deutsche Gruppierungen und Organisationen, Interessenvereinigung Deutscher Homophiler e.V. (IDH); Griffiths, *The Ambivalence of Gay Liberation*, 58–61.

17 Heinz R. to Geschäftsstelle des Amtsgericht Charlottenburg, 12 January 1970, 1, LAB, B Rep. 042, Nr. 47034.

18 Hannes Sporer, "Homos, Opfer von Verbrechen: Über 80 Homophile wurden allein im Jahre 1969 in der Bundesrepublik emordet, hunderte beraubt, oder erpreßt und unzählige bestohlen," *him*, February 1971, 35.

19 "Razzia: Wer, wann, wo?," 1982, ArchSM, Berlin, Allgemeine Homosexuelle Aktion (AHA), Box 1.

20 Schäfer, *"Widernatürliche Unzucht,"* 231.

21 "Wahlprogramm der Christlich Demokratischen Union Deutschlands, 1969–1973"; "Regierungsprogramm der Sozialdemokratischen Partei

Deutschlands 1969"; "Wahlprogramm zur Bundestagswahl 1969 der Freien
Demokratischen Partei," 25 June 1969, Archive of Liberalism (*Archiv des
Liberalismus*, ADL), Druckschriftenbestand, Signatur D1–65 Archiviert als
PDF-Dokument, Signatur IN5–112; "Regierungsprogramm: Wir bauen
den Fortschritt auf Stabilität"; "Wahlaufruf zur Bundestagswahl 1972 der
Freien Demokratischen Partei," 1 October 1972, ADL, Flugblattsammlung,
Signatur E2–121 Archiviert als PDF-Dokument, Signatur IN5–196;
"Wahlprogramm der SPD."

22 Niels Kummer, "Ich bin schwul," *Stern*, 5 October 1978, 113.
23 Georg R., interview, 7 January 2017.
24 Rexhausen, *Lavendelschwert*.
25 "175," *Twen*, 1963, 72.
26 Redaktion, "Wir sind stärker als die F.D.P.," *Du & Ich*, March 1970.
27 Foucault, *The History of Sexuality*, 43.
28 E.g., Martin Dannecker, "Integration oder Emanzipation?," *Du & Ich*,
    February 1971, 36; "HAW Flyer," 1973, ArchSM, Berlin, Allgemeine
    Homosexuelle Aktion AHA, Box 1.
29 For more on the origins of the film, see Henze, "Perversions of Society,"
    89ff; Henze, *Schwule Emanzipation und ihre Konflikte*, 153–83. See too
    Stümke, *Homosexuelle in Deutschland*, 161–2; Brown, *West Germany and the
    Global Sixties*, 322–3; Griffiths, *The Ambivalence of Gay Liberation*, 71–9.
30 von Praunheim, "Nicht der Homosexuelle ist pervers, sondern die
    Situation in der er lebt oder 'Das Glück in der Toilette,'" 162.
31 von Praunheim and Dannecker, "Drehbuch," 54.
32 Ibid., 57.
33 Ibid., 25.
34 Wiebke Stelling, "Fernsehen propagiert Sittenzersetzung: 'Nicht der
    Homosexuelle ist pervers, sondern die Gesellschaft,'" *Deutsche Nachrichten*,
    2 February 1973, ArchSM, Rosa von Praunheim, 2–2.
35 Klaus Stelzer, *Rhein-Neckar-Zeitung*, 28 January 1973, ArchSM, Rosa von
    Praunheim, 2–2.
36 Marlis Haase, "Fragwürdiges Plädoyer für eine Minderheit: ARD bringt
    Praunheims Homosexuellen-Film," *Neue Rhein-Zeitung*, 13 January 1972,
    ArchSM, Rosa von Praunheim, 2–2. See too Wolfert, "'Sollen wir der
    Öffentlichkeit noch mehr Anlaß geben, gegen die "Schwulen" zu sein?,'"
    216–22.
37 Wolf Donner, "Credo einer neuen Klasse, Schwierigkeiten des Fernsehens
    mit den Homosexuellen," *Die Zeit*, January 1972, 9.
38 "In All Probability It's the Movie Maker Who Is Perverse," n.d., ArchSM,
    Rosa von Praunheim, 2–2.
39 Brown, *West Germany and the Global Sixties*, 370.
40 Littmann and Holy, "'Würden Sie das eventuell zurücknehmen?,'" 27.

41 "Nicht der Homosexuelle ist pervers: Rosa von Praunheims Film läuft heute im Gloria," *Sueddeutsche Zeitung*, 17 December 1971, ArchSM, Rosa von Praunheim, 2–2.

42 Holger G., interview, 5 January 2017.

43 Ralf G., interview, 12 February 2017.

44 "Grundsatzerklärung (7. Nov. 1971) | Organisationsstatut (20 Feb. 1972)," ArchSM, HAW, Nr. 1.

45 Ibid., 3–6.

46 von Praunheim, *Sex und Karriere*, 6.

47 Ralf Dose, interview, 23 January 2018; Newsome, "Homosexuals after the Holocaust," 117–19.

48 E.g., Haunss, "Von der Sexuellen Befreiung zur Normalität," 200. Many of these activists could be thought of as what Tiffany Florvil calls "quotidian intellectuals," authoring pamphlets, zines, and manifestos that form a rich source base for studying their movement. Florvil, *Mobilizing Black Germany*, 6.

49 Angelika Martin, "Sind wir Neger der Gesellschaft?," *Du & Ich*, April 1970; H.H. Genserti, "Neger, Schwule und Prostituierte: Immer mit dem Knüppel drauf," *him*, April 1971.

50 "Rotzschwul Grundlagenpapier," ArchSM, Deutsche Städte, Frankfurt, Rotzschwul.

51 Ewing, "The Color of Desire," 91–7.

52 "Weg mit §175," n.d., Personal Archive of Franz G.

53 Cory, *The Homosexual in America*, 83ff; Eisenbach, *Gay Power*, 12ff; Mann, "Homosexualität und Fascismus," 130–7; Bunzl, *Symptoms of Modernity*, 12–18.

54 Qtd in "Homosexuelle: Wind in Tuntenwohnungen," *Der Spiegel*, 30 April 1979, 248.

55 Ralf Dose, interview, 23 January 2018.

56 This change is an example of how, as Griffiths notes, the "Stonewall metanarrative" has privileged "the American national context over others." Griffiths, "Between Triumph and Myth," 55.

57 Lautmann, "Bewegung und Organisation," 496.

58 "Homosexuelle: Wind in Tuntenwohnungen," *Der Spiegel*, 30 April 1979, 248.

59 E.g., Gerd Hoffmeister, "Amerika, Amerika," *him*, January 1971, 5–6; Rosa von Praunheim, "Raus aus den Toiletten, rein in die Strassen! Ein Bericht aus New York über die Arbeit der homosexuellen Befreiungsfront," *him*, September 1971, 14–15. For more on the West German gay movement's transatlantic connections, see Newsome, "Homosexuals after the Holocaust," 133–41.

60 "Flyer," 20 October 1972, 1, ArchSM, HAW, Nr. 32.

61 "Schwule unterdrücken Schwule," n.d., 1, ArchSM, HAW, Nr. 12.

62 "Zu einem Brief vom D.M. Specht (Chefred. von 'him') an HSM Münst den Indizierungsantrag gegen das Magazin 'him' betreffed," October 1972, 3, ArchSM, HAW, Nr. 13b.

63 Hobson, *Lavender and Red*, 18.

64 Holy, "Jenseits von Stonewall," 41.

65 Franz G., interview, 29 May 2017.

66 "Podiumsgespräch mit AHA," *Neue Charlottenburger Rundschau*, April 1979, ArchSM, Berlin, AHA, Box 1; Franz G., interview, 29 May 2017.

67 Griffiths, "Sex, Shame, and West German Gay Liberation," 465–6.

68 Homosexueller Arbeitskreis Frankfurt (HAF) to Deutsche Aktionsgemeinschaft Homosexualität in Münster (DAH), 20 March 1973, ArchSM, Deutsche Städte, Frankfurt, HAF + Rotzschwul.

69 Ralf G., interview, 12 February 2017.

70 Ralf Dose, interview, 23 January 2018.

71 Ralf A., interview, 22 February 2017.

72 "Grundsatzerklärung (7. Nov. 1971) | Organisationsstatut (20 Feb. 1972)," 5, ArchSM, HAW, Nr. 1.

73 Holger G., interview, 5 January 2017.

74 Ralf Dose, interview, 23 January 2018; See too "Juristische Wertung der Homosexualität in der DDR," *HAW INFO*, December 1973, 31–5; Peter Larsen, "Rot und Rosa: Bemerkungen zur Situation der Schwulen in sozialistischen Ländern," *him*, November 1977.

75 For more on the role of *Tunten* in the 1970s movement, see Henze, *Schwule Emanzipation und ihre Konflikte*, 261–86; Griffiths, *The Ambivalence of Liberation*, 166–70.

76 Griffiths, "Konkurrierende Pfade der Emanzipation," 143ff; Griffiths, *The Ambivalence of Gay Liberation*, 166–72; Henze, *Schwule Emanzipation und ihre Konflikte*, 300–20; *Tuntenstreit*, 2–3.

77 "'Wider die Männerherrschaft in der HAW': Streitschrift der freifrau windfrieda von rechenberg," n.d., ArchSM, HAW, Nr. 16.

78 Manfred Herzer, "Es lebe der Feminismus," 28 October 1974, ArchSM, HAW, Nr. 16.

79 Ralf Dose, interview, 23 January 2018.

80 Kuckuc, "Gesellschaftspolitische Arbeit und Emanzipation von Lesbierinnen," 465; Kühn, "The Lesbian Action Centre, West Berlin," 311–14.

81 Kuckuc, "Gesellschaftspolitische Arbeit und Emanzipation von Lesbierinnen," 470.

82 Dorothea R., interview, 26 January 2018.

83 Hensel, Neef, and Pausch, "Von 'Knabenliebhabern' und 'Power-Pädos,'" 136–59.

84 Griffiths, "Sex, Shame and West German Gay Liberation," 459; Gammerl, "Affecting Legal Change," 115; Halperin, *How to Be Gay*, 52.

85　"Gefährliche Liebe oder: Was Sie über den Paragraphen 175 wissen sollten," *Du & Ich*, May 1978, 2.

86　"Protokoll vom HAW-Plenum," 30 July 1972, 2, ArchSM, HAW, Nr. 7a; Hensel, Neef, and Pausch, "Von 'Knabenliebhabern' und 'Power-Pädos'," 147–8.

87　"'Druck der bürgerlichen Moral': Frankfurts Homosexuelle wollen die Bevölkerung über ihre Situation informieren," *Frankfurter Rundschau*, 28 April 1973, ArchSM, Deutsche Städte, Frankfurt, Nr. 1. For more on *RotZSchwul*, see Plastargias, *RotZSchwul*.

88　Franz G., interview, 29 May 2017.

89　Torsten V., interview, 9 January 2017.

90　Holy, "Jenseits von Stonewall," 49; Rüdiger Lautmann, "Bewegung und Organisation: Versuche homosexueller Emanzipation," 498.

91　"Flyer," 1977, ArchSM, HAW, Nr. 12.

92　Niels Kummer, "Ich bin schwul," *Stern*, 5 October 1978, 113.

93　Moeller, "Private Acts, Public Anxieties, and the Fight to Decriminalize Male Homosexuality in West Germany," 548; Brown, *West Germany and the Global Sixties*, 327; Stümke, *Homosexuelle in Deutschland*, 162ff; Griffiths, "Sex, Shame and West German Gay Liberation," esp. 456; Henze, "'Die lückenlose Kette,'" 125.

94　Ralf Dose, interview, 23 January 2018.

95　LAB, B Rep. 211, Nr. 5414, 2.

96　Peter Rausch, 31 January 2017.

97　Ralf Dose, interview, 23 January 2018.

98　Niels Kummer, "Ich bin schwul," *Stern*, 5 October 1978.

99　"Wir haben abgetrieben!," *Stern*, 6 June 1971.

100　"Flyer," 1977, 1.

101　Dorothea R., interview, 26 January 2018; Roland R., interview, 26 January 2018.

102　Holy, "Einige Daten zur zweiten deutschen Homosexuellenbewegung (1969–1983)," 195.

103　Michael Rosenkranz, "'Gay Pride Week' in Hamburg: Wandlung einer Demonstration: Schwule Öffentlichkeitsarbeit & Polizeiprovokation," *Du & Ich*, August 1980, 10.

104　Griffiths, "Sex, Shame and West German Gay Liberation," 456.

105　Rose Schmid, "Außgießung des heiteren Geistes," *him*, September 1973, 6.

106　Holger G., interview, 5 January 2017.

107　Franz G., interview, 29 May 2017.

108　"Heiße Lava," *Der Spiegel*, 16 July 1979, 58.

109　Holy, "Jenseits von Stonewall," 70.

110　Hobson, *Lavender and Red*, 1–15.

111 "Freiburger Thesen zur Gesellschaftspolitik der Freien Demokratischen Partei," October 1971, 5, ADL, Druckschriftenbestand, Signatur D1–123 Archiviert als PDF-Dokument, Signatur IN5–94.

112 "Ein Schwuler kandidiert zur Bürgerschaftswahl," 1978, 8, ArchSM, Politische Gruppierungen, Bunte Liste. See too Rosenkranz and Lorenz, *Hamburg auf anderen Wegen*, 146–7.

113 "Homosexuelle: Hallo, Gerda," *Der Spiegel*, 20 August 1979, 40.

114 HSM (Münster), "Flyer," 12 July 1972, ArchSM, Schwulenbewegung, Deutsche Homophilen Organisation (DHO).

115 Fedor Fackeltanz, "Homopolitik – die notwendige Perversion," *him*, September 1972, 16.

116 Ibid., 18.

117 The German voting system allows each voter to cast two ballots. The first (*Erststimme*) allows residents of a voting district to elect a representative of that district. The winner is the candidate who receives the most votes, as in any other first-past-the-post system. The second ballot (*Zweitstimme*) allows voters to choose a party (as opposed to a candidate, as in the *Erststimme*). The total second-ballot votes for each party are aggregated at a national level, and each party that wins more than 5 per cent of the national vote on the second ballot is accorded an equivalent representation in the *Bundestag*.

118 Dannecker and Reiche, *Der gewöhnliche Homosexuelle*, 370–1.

119 Ibid., 370.

120 "Minderheiten-Problem," *Der Spiegel*, 9 October 1972, 19; Wolfert, "'Sollen wir der Öffentlichkeit noch mehr Anlaß geben, gegen die "Schwulen" zu sein?,'" 223–4.

121 Holy, "Einige Daten zur zweiten deutschen Homosexuellenbewegung (1969–1983)," 186.

122 Peter Föhrding, "Wie die Parteien um die Stimmen der Homosexuellen werben ...," *Du & Ich*, June 1980, 9.

123 Ibid.

124 Ibid., 10.

125 W. Selitsch, "Können wir den Parteien Trauen?," *Du & Ich*, June 1980, 12.

126 Klaus Brauer, "'Gay Pride Week' in Hamburg: Podiumsdiskussion mit Parteivertretern am 26.6.80," *Du & Ich*, August 1980, 12.

127 Ibid.

128 "Homosexuelle: Hallo, Gerda," *Der Spiegel*, 20 August 1979, 38.

129 "Lieber ein warmer Bruder als ein kalter Krieger: Arbeitskreis Homosexualität Dokumentation," 1980, 4, ArchSM, Politische Gruppierungen und Parteien, Jungdemokraten.

130 Ibid., 3.

131 Mewes, "A Brief History of the German Green Party," 35–6.
132 Merkl, "Adenauer's Heirs Reclaim Power," 59–75.
133 AHA, "Presse-Erklärung," 12 December 1979, ArchSM, Berlin, Allgemeine Homosexuelle Aktion (AHA), Box 1.
134 "AG Öffentlichkeit," n.d., ArchSM, Berlin, Allgemeine Homosexuelle Aktion (AHA), Box 1.
135 Wolfgang Selitsch, "Vorwort," *Du & Ich*, April 1980, 3.
136 Wolfgang Selitsch, "Sind 2 Millionen Homosexuellen wahlentscheidend?," *Du & Ich*, September 1980, 66.
137 Selitsch, "Vorwort," *Du & Ich*, April 1980, 3.
138 "Aktion '80 der deutschen Homophilen-Presse," *Don*, April 1980, 4.
139 "Die Grünen: Wahlplattform zur Bundestagswahl 1980," 12.
140 "Lieber ein warmer Bruder als ein kalter Krieger: Arbeitskreis Homosexualität Dokumentation," 1980, 4, ArchSM, Politische Gruppierungen und Parteien, Jungdemokraten," 13.
141 "Wahlprogramm zur Bundestagswahl 1980 der Freien Demokratischen Partei," 7 June 1980, 35, ADL, Druckschriftenbestand, Signatur D1–242, Archiviert als PDF-Dokument, Signatur IN5–93.
142 "Wir haben uns entschlossen, am 5. Oktober 1980 die F.D.P. zu wählen und bitten euch, das gleiche zu tun," *Du & Ich*, September 1980.
143 "Leserbriefe: Strauß/CSU," *Du & Ich*, October 1980, 7.
144 "Parteien auf dem Prüfstand," n.d., ArchSM, Berlin, Allgemeine Homosexuelle Aktion (AHA), Box 1.
145 Here "Indian" (*Indianer*) refers to Native Americans.
146 "Wortprotokoll der Veranstaltung am 12.07.80 in der Bonner Beethovenhalle," 233.
147 "Die Streichung des §175 StGB muß Bestandteil der Koalitionsvereinbarung der neuen Bundesregierung werden!," *Frankfurter Rundschau*, 13 October 1980.
148 BArch-Koblenz, B 141/85387, 36.
149 "Hans-Dietrich Genscher," *Der Spiegel*, 27 October 1980, 282; "Recht: Kiefer runter," *Der Spiegel*, 10 November 1980, 28–30.

7 When Gay Activists Met the Socialist State

1 "Protokoll über das Gespräch beim Ministerrat der Deutschen Demokratischen Republik am 20.9.1979 uber die Eingabe 'Sozialistische Freizeitgestaltung einer Minderheit' vom 22.10.1978, 23.2.1979, und 9.6.1979," ArchSM, DDR, HIB, Nr. 4.
2 Peter Rausch to *Volkskammer* der DDR Rechtsausschuß, 22 October 1978, ArchSM, DDR, HIB, Nr. 4.
3 Peter Rausch, interview, 31 January 2017.

4 This chapter builds in particular on McLellan's work, which examines the social, cultural, and transnational facets of gay East German activism in the 1970s. McLellan, "Glad to Be Gay behind the Wall"; McLellan, "From Private Photography to Mass Circulation"; McLellan, *Love in the Time of Communism*, 121–2. See too Tammer, "Schwul bis über die Mauer"; Evans, "Decriminalization, Seduction, and 'Unnatural Desire' in East Germany," 562–3.
5 Stelkens, "Machtwechsel in Ost-Berlin," 503ff.
6 Fulbrook, "The Concept of 'Normalisation' and the GDR in Comparative Perspective," 18.
7 Fulbrook, *The People's State*, 43ff; Schroeder, *Der SED-Staat*, 220.
8 Jarausch, "Care and Coercion," 42ff; Harsch, *Revenge of the Domestic*, 304–19.
9 Schroeder, *Der SED-Staat*, 202.
10 Major, *Behind the Berlin Wall*, 193.
11 Schroeder, *Der SED-Staat*, 223; Sheffer, *Burned Bridge*, 226.
12 Gieseke, *The History of the Stasi*, 59–65.
13 Sheffer, *Burned Bridge*, 263.
14 Schäfer, *"Widernatürliche Unzucht,"* 209.
15 Erik Huneke, "Morality, Law, and the Socialist Sexual Self in the German Democratic Republic, 1945–1972," 185ff.
16 Betts, *Within Walls*, 177ff.
17 Dr Ursula Sillge, interview, 11 February 2018.
18 Ibid.
19 "'Die Mauer war das Kondom der DDR': Aids und Homosexuelle in den neuen Bundesländern," *Der Spiegel*, 12 October 1992, 126.
20 Frank Schöne, "Homosexuelle in der DDR," June 1979, ArchSM, DDR, Nr. 22.
21 Lothar de Maizière, interview, 11 October 2016.
22 For more on everyday life and the emotional lives of lesbians in the GDR, see Bühner, "How to Remember Invisibility," 241–65; Borowski, *Parallelwelten*.
23 Sillge, *Un-Sichtbare Frauen*, 37.
24 Ibid., 49.
25 *Spartacus International Gay Guide*, 1973, 109–11.
26 Lothar de Maizière, interview, 11 October 2016.
27 BStU, BV Bln, AOG, Nr. 1144/86, 120.
28 Unless otherwise noted, the following information and quotations from Peter Rausch are drawn from my 31 January 2017 interview with him.
29 Peter Tatchell, "Ten Gay Days That Shook East Berlin: Eine Wahre Geschichte von Peter Tatchell," trans. Manfred Herzer, n.d., 1, Private Archive Peter Rausch.

30 Ibid., 8.
31 Ibid., n1.
32 Tammer, "Schwul bis über die Mauer," 71–7. McLellan too describes the event as a watershed in the creation of East Germany's gay community. McLellan, "Glad to Be Gay behind the Wall," 110–11.
33 BStU, MfS - HA XX, Nr. 5765, 152; BStU, MfS - BV Berlin AKG, Nr. 4675, 4.
34 BStU, MfS, HA VII, Nr. 3757, 154.
35 BStU, MfS, HA VII, Nr. 2743, 15.
36 In a public lecture from 1990, Rausch noted the group's early efforts to establish "a counselling and communication centre for homosexual men and women," but did not note the specific authors of the document. Peter Rausch, "Die vergessene Lesben- und Schwulengeschichte in Berlin-Ost (70er Jahre)," 8 December 1990, 4, ArchSM, DDR, HIB, Nr. 5.
37 BStU, MfS, HA VII, Nr. 2743, 16.
38 Ibid., 17–19.
39 Ibid., 20.
40 Ibid., 20. Other alternative groups in East Germany in the 1970s also used similar language to position themselves vis-à-vis the regime. See von der Goltz, "Attraction and Aversion," 549ff.
41 BStU, MfS, HA VII, Nr. 3757, 156.
42 BStU, MfS, HA VII, Nr. 2743, 23.
43 Schroeder, *Der SED-Staat*, 446; BStU, MfS, HA VII, Nr. 2743, 25.
44 BStU, MfS, HA VII, Nr. 2743, 35–8.
45 Ibid., 23.
46 Ibid., 23–4.
47 Ibid., 23.
48 Ibid., 35.
49 Ibid., 36.
50 Ibid., 38.
51 Ibid., 26.
52 McLellan similarly posits that the Stasi were "not concerned about same-sex activity per se." McLellan, *Love in the Time of Communism*, 132.
53 Peter Rausch, interview, 31 January 2017.
54 BStU, AIM, Nr. 10017/77, Bd. 1/I, 122–3.
55 Peter Rausch, interview, 31 January 2017.
56 Ibid.
57 BStU, BV Bln, AOG, Nr. 1144/86, 34–5.
58 BStU, MfS - BV Berlin AKG, Nr. 4675, 2.
59 Ibid., 2.
60 McLellan, "Glad to Be Gay behind the Wall," 112.
61 BStU, AIM, Nr. 10017/77, Bd. 1/II, 70.
62 BStU, MfS, HA VII, Nr. 3757, 135.

63 Peter Rausch, interview, 31 January 2017.

64 BStU, MfS - BV Berlin AKG, Nr. 4675, 2.

65 BStU, BV Bln, AOG, Nr. 1144/86, 74.

66 Ibid., 158.

67 Peter Rausch, interview, 31 January 2017.

68 von Mahlsdorf, *Ich bin meine eigene Frau*, 63. Mahlsdorf was also an IM, although scholars have not yet fully examined the extent of her collaboration with the Stasi. Giersdorf, "Why Does Charlotte von Mahlsdorf Curtsy?" 184–5; Evans, "Decriminalization, Seduction, and 'Unnatural Desire' in East Germany," 562.

69 von Mahlsdorf, *Ich bin meine eigene Frau*, 121–34.

70 In our interview, Rausch dated this meeting to 1973, and Mahlsdorf places it in 1974 in her autobiography. But circumstantial documentation suggests it took place in 1976. Peter Rausch, interview, 31 January 2017; von Mahlsdorf, *Ich bin meine eigene Frau*, 173.

71 von Mahlsdorf, *Ich bin meine eigene Frau*, 134–51.

72 Ibid., 173–4.

73 Peter Rausch, interview, 31 January 2017.

74 "Clubtagebuch," n.d., 3ff, ArchSM, DDR, HIB, Nr. 6.

75 BStU, AIM, Nr. 10017/77, Bd. 1/II, 11.

76 Dr Ursula Sillge, interview, 11 February 2018.

77 "'Ich war immer ein Mädchen': Homosexuelle in der DDR: Das Leben des Lothar Berfelde als Charlotte von Mahlsdorf," *Der Spiegel*, 9 November 1992, 300. See too McLellan, "Glad to Be Gay behind the Wall," 113–14, 121–2.

78 BStU, AIM, Nr. 10017/77, Bd. 1/II, 29; BStU, BV Bln, AOG, Nr. 1144/86, 18.

79 BStU, AIM, Nr. 10017/77, Bd. 1/II, 24.

80 BStU, AIM, Nr. 10017/77, Bd. 1/I, 142.

81 Peter Rausch, "Die vergessene Lesben- und Schwulengeschichte," 5.

82 Peter Rausch, interview, 31 January 2017.

83 Fulbrook, *The People's State*, 269–90; Betts, *Within Walls*, 173–92.

84 "Eingabe Betr.: Schließung des Espressos im Hotel 'Sofia' Berlin-Mitte Friedrichstraße," 12 April 1975, ArchSM, DDR, HIB, Nr. 4.

85 Michael Unger to DEWAG-Werbung, 9 January 1976, ArchSM, DDR, HIB, Nr. 4.

86 Siegfried Schnabl, "Plädoyer für eine Minderheit," *Das Magazin* 20, no. 12 (December 1973): 30.

87 Ibid., 29.

88 Peter Rausch to Siegfried Schnabl, 23 August 1976, ArchSM, DDR, HIB, Nr. 4.

89 Siegfried Schnabl and Peter Rausch, 9 September 1976, ArchSM, DDR, HIB, Nr. 4.

90   Bodo Amelang to VP-Inspektion Friedrichshain, 24 June 1978, ArchSM, Bestand Bodo Amelang, Nr. 1.
91   Volkspolizei Berlin to Bodo Amelang, 7 July 1978, ArchSM, Bestand Bodo Amelang, Nr. 1.
92   Betts, *Within Walls*, 170–2.
93   Ministerium der Justiz der DDR, *Zivilgesetzbuch der Deutschen Demokratischen Republik*, para. 266.
94   "Vertrag der Gemeinschaft von Bürgern Homosexuelle Interessengemeinschaft Berlin (HIB)," 15 January 1976, 1, Personal Archive of Peter Rausch.
95   BStU, MfS, HA VII, Nr. 2743, 81.
96   Ibid., 78.
97   Ibid., 77.
98   Ibid., 75–6.
99   BStU, BV Bln, AOG, Nr. 1144/86, 131.
100 Ibid., 103.
101 Weber, *Von der SBZ zur DDR, 1945–1968*, 216–17; Betts, *Within Walls*, 191–2.
102 "Verfassung der Deutschen Demokratischen Republik," secs. 1, 19.
103 Betts, *Within Walls*, 148–72; Richardson-Little, *The Human Rights Dictatorship*, 44–52.
104 Broszat, *The Hitler State*, 338.
105 Fulbrook, *Anatomy of a Dictatorship*, 53.
106 Gieseke, *The History of the Stasi*, 101; "K I (Arbeitsgebiet I der Kriminalpolizei)," *MFS-Lexikon*, accessed 14 July 2021, https://www.stasi-unterlagen-archiv.de/mfs-lexikon/detail/k-i-arbeitsgebiet-i-der-kriminalpolizei/.
107 BStU, MfS-HA VII, Nr. 3757, 162.
108 BStU, MfS-HA VII, Nr. 3757, 162; BStU, MfS, HA VII, Nr. 2743, 50.
109 BStU, AIM, Nr. 10017/77, Bd. 1/I, 143.
110 BStU, MfS, HA VII, Nr. 2743, 51.
111 Espindola, *Transitional Justice after German Reunification*, 1–5.
112 Miller, *The Stasi Files Unveiled*; Gieseke, *The History of the Stasi*, 89–92; Lewis, "En-Gendering Remembrance," 123.
113 BStU, BV Bln, AOG, Nr. 1144/86, 10.
114 Ibid.
115 Ibid.
116 BStU, MfS, HA VII, Nr. 3757, 152; BStU, BV Bln, AOG, Nr. 1144/86, 34; BStU, BV Bln, AOG, Nr. 1144/86, 104.
117 BStU, BV Bln, AOG, Nr. 1144/86, 101.
118 Ibid., 114, 171.
119 BStU, BV Bln, AOG, Nr. 1144/86, 35; BStU, MfS, HA VII, Nr. 3757, 150; BStU, AIM, Nr. 10017/77, Bd. 1/I, 123.

120 BStU, MfS - BV Berlin AKG, Nr. 4675, 2.
121 BStU, BV Bln, AOG, Nr. 1144/86, 133.
122 von der Goltz, "Attraction and Aversion," 550.
123 BStU, BV Bln, AOG, Nr. 1144/86, 35.
124 Ibid., 134.
125 BStU, MfS, HA VII, Nr. 2743, 67.
126 BStU, BV Bln, AOG, Nr. 1144/86, 130.
127 Ibid., 130.
128 Ibid., 12.
129 BStU, MfS, HA VII, Nr. 3757, 164.
130 BStU, MfS-HA XX, Nr. 11299, 130.
131 BStU, MfS, HA VII, Nr. 2743, 77.
132 BStU, AIM, Nr. 10017/77, Bd. 1/II, 28.
133 BStU, AIM, Nr. 10017/77, Bd. 1/I, 144–5.
134 Dr Ursula Sillge, interview, 11 February 2018.
135 Ibid.
136 BStU, BV Bln, AOG, Nr. 1144/86, 158.
137 Peter Rausch, interview, 31 January 2017.
138 Peter Rausch to *Volkskammer* der DDR Rechtsausschuß, 3.
139 Ibid., 5.
140 Sekretariat des *Volkskammers* der DDR to Peter Rausch, 4 July 1979, ArchSM, DDR, HIB, Nr. 4.
141 "Protokoll über das Gespräch beim Ministerrat," ArchSM, DDR, HIB, Nr. 4.

8 Homosexual Politics in 1980s West Germany

1 "Waterkantgate: 'Beschaffen Sie mir eine Wanze,'" *Der Spiegel*, 13 September 1987, 17.
2 Deutscher Bundestag, "Große Anfrage der Abgeornten Frau Oesterle-Schwerin, Frau Beer und die Fraktion Die Grünen: Die sexuelle Denunziation von tatsächlichen oder vermeintlichen 'Urningen' als Mittel der politischen Auseinandersetzung," Drucksache 11/3901, 24 January 1989, 5.
3 Witte, "Lesben und Schwule in den Kirchen," 137.
4 Andreas Salmen, "Diskussion um schwulen Dachverband: Muss den Gründen Sünde sein?," *Du & Ich*, May 1986, 58.
5 Albert Eckert, "Gemeinsam sind wir stärker: In Köln wurde der Bundesverband Homosexualität gegründet," *Du & Ich*, January 1987, 18.
6 Mielchen, "Wider die Norm," 119; Hensel, Neef, and Pausch, "Von 'Knabenliebhabern' und 'Power-Pädos,'" 149; Manfred Bruns, "Schwulenpolitik in der alten Bundesrepublik"; Holy, "Jenseits von

Stonewall," 75; Kraushaar, "Höhenflug und Absturz," 88; Henze, *Schwule Emanzipation und ihre Konflikte*, 345. Griffiths is one of the few historians to point out that these views are "exaggerated." Griffiths, *The Ambivalence of Gay Liberation*, 205.

7 Reichert, *Die Kapsel*, 35.
8 BArch-Koblenz, B 141/85387, 21.
9 AHA Berlin to Helmut Schmidt, 25 October 1980, BArch-Koblenz, B 141/85397; Arbeitskreis gegen die Diskriminierung Homosexueller Arbeitskreis von Sozialdemokraten to Helmut Schmidt, 26 October 1980, BArch-Koblenz, B 141/85397; "Vermerk," 28 November 1980, BArch-Koblenz, B 141/85399.
10 "Die Streichung des §175 StGB muß Bestandteil der Koalitionsvereinbarung der neuen Bundesregierung werden!," *Frankfurter Rundschau*, 13 October 1980.
11 Lorenz, "Hamburg als Homosexuellenhauptstadt der 1950er Jahre," 135.
12 "Recht: Kiefer runter," *Der Spiegel*, 10 November 1980, 28, 30.
13 Schmidt himself denied this characterization in 2010. Rainer Haubrich, "Helmut Schmidt im Interview: 'Homosexuelle Kanzler? Kein Problem,'" *Die Welt*, 9 May 2010: https://www.welt.de/politik/deutschland /article7534132/Homosexuelle-Kanzler-Kein-Problem.html; Sabine Sans, "Leserbriefe: Helmut Schmidt stellt klar," *Die Welt*, 11 April 2010: https:// www.welt.de/welt_print/debatte/article7131902/Helmut-Schmidt-stellt -klar.html.
14 "Recht: Kiefer runter," *Der Spiegel*, 10 November 1980, 30.
15 "Schwul mit zwölf," *Der Spiegel*, 15 June 1981, 52.
16 BArch-Koblenz, B 141/85387, 135.
17 Dittberner, *FDP – Partei der zweiten Wahl*, 19–20.
18 E.g., Duggan, "The New Homonormativity," 188–90.
19 Turner, *Germany from Partition to Reunification*, 175–6.
20 "Leserbriefe," *Du & Ich*, October 1980.
21 von der Goltz, *The Other '68ers*, 227-52; Wiliarty, *The CDU and the Politics of Gender in Germany*, 108–33; Granieri, "Politics in C Minor," 31.
22 Turner, *Germany from Partition to Reunification*, 176-9; "FDP: Der große Schub," *Der Spiegel*, 15 November 1982, 31.
23 "Justizminister: Bringt Ruhe," *Der Spiegel*, 11 October 1982, 26.
24 BArch-Koblenz, B 141/85391, 39–40.
25 Schwule Aktion Südwest, "Flyer," 1983, ArchSM, Schwulenbewegung, Schwule Aktion Südwest.
26 Karl-Georg Probst, "Wahlen '87: Auf dem Weg in die schwarze Republik?," *Du & Ich*, January 1987, 59.
27 Frieling, "Vorwort," 7.
28 "Gruppen," *Du & Ich*, February 1986, 20.

29 "Gruppen," *Du & Ich*, June 1986, 20.
30 "Gruppen," *Du & Ich*, February 1985.
31 Frieling, "Vorwort," 7.
32 *Spartacus International Guide for Gay Men*, 17th ed. (Spartacus, 1988), 294ff; *Spartacus International Guide for Gay Men*, 13th ed. (Spartacus, 1983), 252ff.
33 "Der Tuntenexpress rollt wieder! Im Tanzwagen nach Sylt," *Du & Ich*, July 1985, 17.
34 Florvil, *Mobilizing Black Germany*, 32–52, 60–1.
35 Sullivan and Middleton, *Queering the Museum*, 46–7.
36 Hans Halter, "Ich Bin En Tunt, Bin Kernjesund," *Der Spiegel*, 16 July 1984, 130.
37 "Anzeigen," *Du & Ich*, January 1985, Postleitraum 4.
38 Georg R., interview, 7 January 2017.
39 "Editorial," *Du & Ich*, January 1985, 3.
40 BArch-Koblenz, B 141/85400.
41 Hannes Sporer, "Homos, Opfer von Verbrechen: Über 80 Homophile wurden allein im Jahre 1969 in der Bundesrepublik emordet, hunderte beraubt, oder erpreßt und unzählige bestohlen," *him*, February 1971, 37.
42 Michael Rosenkranz, "Die 'Spiegelaffäre' der Schwulen: Über 2000 Homosexuelle erfasst!," *Du & Ich*, August 1980, 66.
43 "Affären: Dicker Hammer," *Der Spiegel*, 14 July 1980, 81; Michael Rosenkranz, "Die 'Spiegelaffäre' der Schwulen: Über 2000 Homosexuelle erfasst!," 66; "Homosexuelle in Hamburg: von der Polizei observiert, registriert, photographiert …: 'Rosa Listen' in der Hansestadt?," *Die Zeit*, 18 July 1980: https://www.zeit.de/1980/30/rosa-listen-in-der-hansestadt.
44 "Razzia: Wer, wann, wo?," 1982, ArchSM, Berlin, Allgemeine Homosexuelle Aktion (AHA), Box 1.
45 Elmar Drost, "Schulenrazzia in Hannover: 'Wie bei Adolf,'" *Du & Ich*, October 1984, 18; "'Razzia gegen Schwulenkneipe,' TAZ, 24.07.84," *Du & Ich*, September 1984, 3.
46 "Die Spitzel sind unter uns! Von der Praktiken der Polizei in der Homoszene," *Du & Ich*, October 1985, 18.
47 "Plötzlich stirbst du ein Stück weit," *Der Spiegel*, 28 January 1985, 179.
48 Deutscher Bundestag, "Beschlußempfehlung und Bericht das Verteidigungsausschusses," Drucksache 10/1604, 13 June 1984, 13. For a more detailed account of the Kießling Affair, see Brühöfener, "Defining the West German Soldier," 312–20.
49 Deutscher Bundestag, "Beschlußempfehlung und Bericht das Verteidigungsausschusses," Drucksache 10/1604, 13 June 1984, 14; "'Es geht nicht nur um meine Rehabilitierung': Spiegel-Interview mit dem entlassenen Vier-Sterne-General Günter Kießling," *Der Spiegel*, 16 January 1984.

50 Deutscher Bundestag, "Beschlußempfehlung und Bericht das Verteidigungsausschusses," Drucksache 10/1604, 13 June 1984, 16.
51 Ibid., 18–19.
52 Ibid., 22.
53 Ibid., 38, 74; Deutscher Bundestag, "Plenarprotokoll 10/47: Stenographischer Bericht: 47. Sitzung," 19 January 1984, 3375.
54 Taylor, *The Berlin Wall*, 385ff.
55 "Wörner: Der Lächerlichkeit preisgegeben," *Der Spiegel*, 30 January 1984, 20.
56 "Koalition: Wenn er will," *Der Spiegel*, 13 August 1984, 28–30.
57 Deutscher Bundestag, "Beschlußempfehlung und Bericht das Verteidigungsausschusses," Drucksache 10/1604, 13 June 1984, 70.
58 Bruehoefener, "Defining the West German Soldier," 321–30.
59 Franz M., "Eingabe," 21 February 1984, BArch-Koblenz, B 141/85400.
60 "Kiessling hat seine Ehre wieder – wer rehabilitiert die Homosexuellen?," *Du & Ich*, April 1984, 57.
61 Deutscher Bundestag, "Plenarprotokoll 10/47: Stenographischer Bericht: 47. Sitzung," 19 January 1984, 3374.
62 "Soldaten als potentielle Sexualpartner," *Der Spiegel*, 16 January 1984, 22.
63 Deutscher Bundestag, "Plenarprotokoll 10/52: Stenographischer Bericht: 52. Sitzung," 8 February 1984, 3695.
64 Deutscher Bundestag, "Beschlußempfehlung und Bericht das Verteidigungsausschusses," Drucksache 10/1604, 13 June 1984, 74.
65 Reuband, "Über Gesellschaftlichen Wandel, AIDS und die Beurteilung der Homosexualität als moralisches Vergehen," 66.
66 Vaid, *Virtual Equality*, 98–9, 115–16; Shilts, *And the Band Played On*, 495; Healey, *Russian Homophobia*, 9.
67 Großbölting, "Why Is There No Christian Right in Germany?" 210–26.
68 Freeman, "Governing the Voluntary Sector Response to AIDS," 32.
69 "Aids: Eine Epidemie, die erst beginnt," *Der Spiegel*, 6 June 1983, 150.
70 "Schwarzer Peter," *Du & Ich*, March 1986, 54.
71 Reichert, *Die Kapsel*, 99.
72 "Bayern: Entartung Ausdünnen," *Der Spiegel*, 16 March 1987, 131.
73 Ralf G., interview, 12 February 2017.
74 "AIDS: Hetze, Panik und Angstmache!," *Du & Ich*, January 1985, 8.
75 Volker K., interview, 18 December 2016.
76 Dorothea R., interview, 26 January 2018.
77 Gammerl notes that his interview partners recalled the disease in different ways. Gammerl, *anders fühlen*, 275.
78 See, for example, France, *How to Survive a Plague*, 253–4; Martel, *The Pink and the Black*, 216–44.
79 Reichert, *Die Kapsel*, 38; Bochow, "Reactions of the Gay Community to AIDS in East and West Berlin," 23–4.

80 von der Goltz, *The Other '68ers*, 136, 245ff.

81 W. Didzoleit and M. Schreiber, "Spiegel Gespräch: Ohne Druck passiert da nichts," *Der Spiegel*, 21 October 1985, 29; Borneman, "AIDS in the Two Berlins," 233.

82 Borneman, "AIDS in the Two Berlins," 229; Freeman, "Governing the Voluntary Sector Response to AIDS," 34.

83 Dorothea R., interview, 26 January 2018.

84 Freeman, "Governing the Voluntary Sector Response to AIDS," 34–5.

85 Ralf Dose, 23 January 2018.

86 While new HIV infections in 1985 accounted for approximately 0.05 per cent of the US population, 0.005 per cent of the UK population, and 0.0065 per cent of the West German population, by 1989 they represented 0.034 per cent of the US population, 0.004 per cent of the UK population, and 0.003 per cent of the West German population. Marcus and Starker, "HIV and AIDS," 3; Health Protection Agency, "HIV in the United Kingdom," 7; Centers for Disease Control and Prevention, "Estimates of New HIV Infections in the United States," 2. Tümmers also notes a shift towards safer-sex practices among gay men in West Germany. Tümmers, *AIDS*, 212.

87 Hans Halter, "Ich Bin En Tunt, Bin Kernjesund," *Der Spiegel*, 16 July 1984, 133.

88 France, *How to Survive a Plague*, 108.

89 Shilts, *And the Band Played On*, 210.

90 Ibid.; Reardon, "HIV's Patient Zero Exonerated."

91 McKay, "'Patient Zero,'" 161.

92 Rosa von Praunheim, "Bumsen unterm Safer-Sex Plakat," *Der Spiegel*, 14 May 1990, 245; James Jones, "Discourses on and of AIDS in West Germany, 1986–90," 456–7.

93 von Praunheim, "Bumsen unterm Safer-Sex-Plakat," *Der Spiegel*, 14 May 1990; Reichert, *Die Kapsel*, 44–5, 77–6.

94 Bochow, "Reactions of the Gay Community to AIDS in East and West Berlin," 29.

95 Reichert, *Die Kapsel*, 95.

96 For further discussion of *AIDS-Hilfe* posters, see Tümmers, *AIDS*, 184–6; Reichert, *Die Kapsel*, 77; Bochow, "Reactions of the Gay Community to AIDS in East and West Berlin," 28–9.

97 "Aids: Sex-Verbot für Zehntausende?," *Der Spiegel*, 12 January 1987, 161.

98 Tümmers describes how, under Süßmuth's successor, Ursula Lehr, the federal health ministry rejected a yet more ambitious plan on the part of the *Deutsche Aids-Hilfe* to create discussion circles that would spread information about safer-sex practices. Tümmers, *AIDS*, 186–9.

99 Seyfarth, *Schweine müssen nackt sein*; Zilles, "The 1970s in Retrospect and the HIV/AIDS Incision." As an example of the American AIDS memoir, see Monette, *Becoming a Man*.

100 Ralf Dose, interview, 23 January 2018.
101 Holy, "AIDS und Kießling," 117.
102 "Grüne Abgeordnete: Offen schwul im Parlament," *Du & Ich*, March 1986, 56–7; Deutscher Bundestag, "Plenarprotokoll 10/184: Stenographischer Bericht: 184. Sitzung," 12 December 1985, 14066.
103 Deutscher Bundestag, "Plenarprotokoll 10/184: Stenographischer Bericht: 184. Sitzung," 12 December 1985, 14066.
104 Deutscher Bundestag, "Große Anfrage der Abgeorneten Frau Oesterle-Schwerin, Frau Beer und der Fraktion Die Grünen: Die sexuelle Denunziation von tatsächlichen oder vermeintlichen 'Urningen' als Mittel der politischen Auseinandersetzung," Drucksache 11/3901, 24 January 1989; Deutscher Bundestag, "Große Anfrage der Abgeordneten Frau Oesterle-Schwerin, Frau Beer und der Fraktion Die Grünen: Rosa Listen," Drucksache 11/2586, 24 June 1988; Deutscher Bundestag, "Kleine Anfrage der Abgeordneten Rusche und der Fraktion Die Grünen: Diskriminierung von Homosexuellen im Berufsleben," Drucksache 10/6333, 4 November 1986; Deutscher Bundestag, "Antwort der Bundesregierung auf die Kleine Anfrage der Abgeordneten Frau Schoppe und der Fraktion Die Grünen," Drucksache 10/3161, 10 April 1985; Deutscher Bundestag, "Gesetzentwurf der Fraktion Die Grünen," Drucksache 10/2832, 4 February 1985.
105 Littmann and Holy, "'Würden Sie das eventuell zurücknehmen?,'" 36.
106 BArch-Koblenz, B 141/85392, Anlage 2.
107 Schelsky, *Die Strategie der "Systemüberwindung."*
108 Manfred H. Preusse, "Schwuler Alltag in der DDR," *Du & Ich*, October 1984; Thomas Grossmann, "Es bewegt sich was. Schwule in der DDR," *Du & Ich*, March 1985; "Homosexuelle in Osteuropa: DDR gibt sich liberal – in der Sowjetunion und im Rumänien verboten," *Tagesspiegel*, 17 April 1984; "Realier Sozialismus: DDR integriert Homosexuelle," *Du & Ich*, November 1987; "Tauwetter? DDR will Homosexuelle integrieren," 1986, ArchSM, DDR, Nr. 22; "DDR: Vorbehalte gegen homosexuelle," *Der Tagesspiegel*, 30 July 1987, ArchSM, DDR, Nr. 22; "Das Lächeln des André Gide: Geheuchelte Normalität? Die Homosexuellen in der DDR wollen kein Doppelleben führen," *Frankfurter Allgemeine Magazin*, 16 April 1987, ArchSM, DDR, Nr. 22; "Ihre Homosexualität halten sie vor der Partei geheim: Nur langsam öffnet sich die Gesellschaft der DDR für die Probleme der Betroffenen," *Frankfurter Rundschau*, 4 August 1987, ArchSM, DDR, Nr. 22; Michael Mara, "Integrationsangebote für eine Minderheit: Veränderte Haltung der DDR gegenüber den Homosexuellen," *Der Tagesspiegel*, 17 January 1988, ArchSM, DDR, Nr. 22; "Gespräch in der DDR über Homosexualität," *Frankfurter*

Allgemeine Zeitung, 4 February 1982, ArchSM, DDR, Nr. 22. See too Gammerl, *anders fühlen*, 295–6.

109 *Spartacus International Guide for Gay Men*, 13th ed., 252; *Spartacus International Guide for Gay Men*, 17th ed. (Spartacus, 1988), 287.
110 "Kennwort: DDR," *Du & Ich*, May 1985.
111 Norton G., interview, 17 September 2016.

9 Liberation and the Stasi in East Germany

1 Peter Rausch, interview, 16 February 2017.
2 Stümke, *Homosexuelle in Deutschland*, 168.
3 Stapel, *Warme Brüder gegen Kalte Krieger*, 83ff; Sillge, *Un-Sichtbare Frauen*, 92ff; Günter Grau, "Erpressbar und Tendenziell Konspirativ," 24; There is relatively little research on the East German gay movement of the 1980s or its relationship to the state. What does exist consists primarily of these monographs and a handful of essays. In English, works focus more on everyday experiences and less on either the policy changes or the relationships between activists and the state that are the focus of this chapter. McLellan, *Love in the Time of Communism*, 122–41; Evans, "Decriminalization, Seduction, and 'Unnatural Desire' in East Germany," 566–71; Sweet, "The Church, the Stasi, and Socialist Integration." Some of the policy changes are also discussed in Hillhouse, "Out of the Closet behind the Wall," and Bühner, "The Rise of a New Consciousness."
4 Stapel, *Warme Brüder gegen Kalte Krieger*, 10; BStU, MfS - HA XX ZMA 10050/11, Band I, 1.
5 BStU, MfS - HA XX ZMA 10050/11, Band I, 1.
6 BStU, MfS BV Halle, Abt. XX, Nr. 389, 10; Stapel, *Warmer Brüder gegen Kalte Krieger*, 11.
7 Schroeder, *Der SED-Staat*, 474; Fulbrook, *Anatomy of a Dictatorship*, 91.
8 Kocka, "Eine durchherrschte Gesellschaft," 547.
9 Fulbrook, *Anatomy of a Dictatorship*, 89.
10 Ibid., 110.
11 BStU, MfS - HA XX ZMA 10050/11, Band I, 1.
12 Ibid., 2.
13 BStU, Leipzig KDfS Leipzig-Stadt, Nr. 23855/03, 18.
14 BStU, MfS - HA XX ZMA 10050/11, Band I, 43; BStU, MfS - HA XX, Nr. 9962, 81.
15 ArchSM, DDR, Kirchliche Arbeitskreise Homosexualität, Nr. 5.
16 BStU, MfS - HA XX ZMA, Nr. 10050/3, Band 2/1, 55.
17 BStU, MfS - HA XX ZMA 10050/11, Band I, 108.
18 BStU, MfS, HA VII, Nr. 2743, 129.

19 Stapel, *Warme Brüder gegen Kalte Krieger*, 18.
20 BStU, MfS - HA X ZMA Nr. 10050/3, Band 2/1, 55; BStU, BVfS Leipzig KDfS Leipzig-Stadt, Nr. 3099/07, 18–19.
21 BStU, MfS, HA VII, Nr. 2743, 98; BStU, MfS - HA XX/9, Nr. 1684, 123–5; BStU, MfS - HA XX ZMA, Nr. 10050/3, Band 2/1, 2ff, 55; BStU, MfS - HA XX, Nr. 9962, 97; BStU, MfS - HA XX ZMA 10050/11, Band I, 44.
22 Sillge, *Un-Sichtbare Frauen*, 98–9.
23 Dr Ursula Sillge, interview, 11 February 2018.
24 BStU, MfS, HA VII, Nr. 2743, 5; BStU, MfS - HA XX ZMA, Nr. 10050/3, Band 3, 139.
25 Lothar de Maizière, interview, 11 October 2016. See too Hillhouse, "Out of the Closet behind the Wall," 593–4.
26 BStU, MfS BV Chemnitz, Abt. XX., Nr. 317, 7.
27 Ibid., 11, 12, 14.
28 Witte, "Lesben und Schwule in den Kirchen," 143–50; Jim Downs, *Stand by Me*, 41ff.
29 BStU, MfS - BV Halle, Abt. XX, Nr. 1846, 1.
30 Ralf Dose, interview, 23 January 2018.
31 BStU, MfS - HA XX ZMA, Nr. 10050/3, Band 2/1, 23.
32 BStU, MfS - HA XX ZMA, Nr. 10050/3, Band 4, 124.
33 BStU, MfS - HA XX, Nr. 5187, 46.
34 BStU, MfS - BV Halle, Abt. XX, Nr. 174, 39.
35 BStU, MfS - BV Halle, Abt. XX, Nr. 1846, 1.
36 BStU, BVfS Potsdam KD BRBG, Nr. 1076, Bd. 1, 69.
37 BStU, MfS - HA XX ZMA, Nr. 10050/3, Band 4, 8.
38 Lothar de Maizière, interview, 11 October 2016.
39 Ibid.
40 "Notizen," *Neue Zeit*, 10 October 1985, 8.
41 BStU, MfS - HA XX/9, Nr. 1952, 31.
42 BStU, BVfS Leipzig AKG, Nr. 608/01, 128; BStU, MfS - BV Chemnitz, Abt. XX, Nr. 1382, Bd. 1, 13.
43 Erik Huneke, "Sex, Sentiment, and Socialism," 231ff; BArch-Lichterfelde DQ/1/13733.
44 Dr Ursula Sillge, interview, 11 February 2018.
45 BStU, MfS - BV Halle, Abt. XX, Nr. 167, 108.
46 BStU, MfS - BV Chemnitz, Abt. XX, Nr. 1382, Bd. 1, 14.
47 Herf, *Divided Memory*, 177; Sharples, *Postwar Germany and the Holocaust*, 64f; Wüstenberg, *Civil Society and Memory in Postwar Germany*, 39.
48 BStU, MfS - BV Chemnitz, Abt. XX, Nr. 1382, Bd. 1, 14; BStU, MfS - BV Halle, Abt. XX, Nr. 167, 108.
49 BStU, BVfS Leipzig AKG, Nr. 608/01, 128; BStU, MfS - HA XX/9, Nr. 1683, 16.

50 Stedefelt, "Zur weiteren Veranlassung," 188. BStU, MfS - BV Chemnitz, Abt. XX, Nr. 1382, Bd. 1, 14.
51 BStU, MfS - HA XX ZMA, Nr. 10050/3, Band 3, 20.
52 BStU, MfS - HA XX ZMA, Nr. 10050/3, Band 2/1, 61.
53 Ibid., 67.
54 BStU, MfS - HA XX ZMA, Nr. 10050/3, Band 2/2, 195.
55 Ibid.
56 BStU, MfS - HA XX ZMA, Nr. 10050/3, Band 4, 105; Sillge, *Un-Sichtbare Frauen*, 85.
57 BStU, MfS - HA XX/9 Nr. 1684, 160.
58 Fulbrook, *The People's State*, 271ff; Port, "Love, Lust, and Lies under Communism," 503; DeBardeleben, "'The Future Has Already Begun,'" 155.
59 BStU, BVfS Leipzig AKG, Nr. 608/01, 128.
60 BStU, MfS - HA XX, Nr. 5191, 3.
61 BStU, MfS, HA VII, Nr. 2743, 8.
62 BStU, MfS - HA XX ZMA 10050/11, Band II, 81.
63 Ibid., 81.
64 Ibid., 83.
65 Ibid., 87.
66 Ibid., 90.
67 BStU, MfS - HA XX ZMA 10050/11, Band I, 95.
68 Ibid., 97.
69 BStU, MfS - HA XX/9 Nr. 1684, 125.
70 BStU, MfS - HA XX ZMA 10050/11, Band I, 129.
71 BStU, MfS - HA XX, Nr. 5190, 69.
72 BStU, MfS BV Erfurt BdL, Nr. 1136, 4.
73 BStU, MfS - HA XX ZMA 10050/11, Band I, 44.
74 Ibid., 103.
75 BStU, MfS, HA VII, Nr. 2743, 137.
76 E.g., BStU, MfS, HA VII, Nr. 2743, 9–10; BStU, MfS BV Mgd., Abt. XX, Nr. 4940, 231–2; BStU, MfS - HA XX/9, Nr. 1684, 115–90.
77 Eppelmann, "Opposition und Kirche in der DDR," 101–11; Ozawa-de Silva, "Peace, Pastors, and Politics," 511ff; Boyens, "Geteilter Friede," 440ff; Richardson-Little, *The Human Rights Dictatorship*, 176.
78 Fulbrook, *Anatomy of a Dictatorship*, 206–36.
79 Huff, "Über die Umweltpolitik der DDR," 523. See too Fleischman, *Communist Pigs*, 92–117.
80 Merrill Jones, "Origins of the East German Environmental Movement," 243ff.
81 Fulbrook, *Anatomy of a Dictatorship*, 201.
82 BStU, MfS - HA XX ZMA, Nr. 10050/3, Band 2/1, 1–2.
83 BStU, MfS - HA XX ZMA 10050/11, Band I, 7.
84 BStU, MfS BV Mgd., Abt. XX ZMA, Nr. 5349, Bd. I, 51.
85 BStU, BVfS Berlin Abt. VII, Nr. 1627, 116.

86 Ibid., 153.
87 Ibid., 116. Schwartz, Grau, and Evans all cite Fehr as evidence of enduring anti-gay animus in East Germany. Evans, "Decriminalization, Seduction, and 'Unnatural Desire' in East Germany," 567–8; Grau, "Erpressbar und Tendenziell Konspirativ," 22; Schwartz, *Homosexuelle, Seilschaft, Verrat*, 275–6.
88 BStU, MfS - HA XII, Nr. 6095, 103–4.
89 Bruce, *The Firm*, 10.
90 Schroeder, *Der SED-Staat*, 445.
91 BStU, MfS BV Halle, Abt. XVII, Nr. 3241, 2.
92 BStU, MfS BV Erfurst, BdL, Nr. 1136, 4.
93 BStU, BVfS Leipzig, Abt. XX, Nr. 306/03, 113.
94 Ibid., 113–14; Sweet, "The Church, the Stasi, and Socialist Integration," 357–8.
95 BStU, MfS - BV Berlin, AOPK, Nr. 110/87, 335.
96 BStU, BV Mgb., Abt. XX ZMA, Nr. 5349, Bd. I, 56.
97 Ibid., 57.
98 E.g., BStU, MfS - BV Chemnitz, Abt. XX, Nr. 1237, 3–35; BStU, MfS BV Chemnitz, Abt. XX., Nr. 317, 71.
99 Peter Rausch, interview, 16 February 2017.
100 BStU, MfS BV Halle, Abt. XX, Nr. 124, 24.
101 Peter Rausch, interview, 16 February 2017.
102 BStU, BVfS Leipzig, Abt. XX, Nr. 306/02, 37.
103 BStU, MfS, HA VII, Nr. 2743, 98.
104 BStU, MfS - BV Berlin, AKG, Nr. 1805, 6.
105 BStU, MfS, HA VII, Nr. 2743, 100.
106 BStU, MfS - BV Berlin, AKG, Nr. 1805, 11.
107 BStU, MfS, HA VII, Nr. 2743, 93.
108 BStU, MfS - BV Berlin, AKG, Nr. 1805, 36.
109 Ibid., 36.
110 Ibid., 24. These documents confirm the chronology outlined by Stasi officer Wolfgang Schmidt in an interview published in 2006. Stedefelt, "Zur weiteren Veranlassung," 185–91; McLellan, *Love in the Time of Communism*, 134.
111 BStU, MfS, HA VII, Nr. 2743, 156–7.
112 Ibid., 162.
113 Ibid., 164.
114 Ibid., 164.
115 Ibid., 165.
116 Ibid., 197.
117 Ibid., 196.
118 BStU, MfS - HA XX/9, Nr. 1684, 73.
119 Ibid., 77.

120 Ibid., 79.

121 The Stasi's novel attitude might be classified as a kind of "homoprotectionism," which Christine Keating defines as "an approach in which
political actors harness the power of the state to protect LGBTQ people
from persecution and domination. In the protectionist framework, the
state works to secure the allegiance of vulnerable groups by offering
protection to these groups." Keating, "Conclusion," 247.

122 BStU, BV Dresden, BdL/Dok 190, 4; BStU, MfS - BV Dresden KD
Dresden-Stadt, Nr. 90335, 4; BStU, MfS, HA VII, Nr. 2743, 11; BStU, MfS
- HA XX/9, Nr. 1684, 41, 64. See too Stapel, *Warme Brüder gegen Kalte
Krieger*, 53.

123 Sillge, *Un-Sichtbare Frauen*, 95; Thinius, "Aufbruch aus dem grauen
Versteck," 26; BStU, MfS BV Halle, Abt. XX, Nr. 124, 61.

124 "Positionspapier des Interdisziplinären Arbeitskreises Homosexualität
der Humboldt-Universität Berlin," in Sillge, *Un-Sichtbare Frauen*, 149. On
this report, see too McLellan, *Love in the Time of Communism*, 135–6; Evans,
"Decriminalization, Seduction, and 'Unnatural Desire' in East Germany,"
566; Hillhouse, "Out of the Closet behind the Wall," 590.

125 "Positionspapier," 151.

126 Ibid., 152.

127 Ibid., 152.

128 Ibid., 162–4.

129 BStU, MfS - HA XX ZMA, Nr. 10050/3, Band 3, 96.

130 "AIDS: 'Rätselhafte Krankheit: In den USA viele Todesfälle nach
Infektion,'" *Neue Zeit*, 24 August 1982; Eberhard Klages, "Einfluß von
Hormonen auf Gehirnentwicklung: Unionsfreund NPT Prof. Dr. G.
Dörner, Direktor des Instituts für experimentelle Endokrinologie Berlin,"
Neue Zeit, 23 February 1982; Eberhard Klages, "Hinlenkung auf feste
Partnerschaft: Erfahrungen aus Ehe- und Sexualberatungen für deviante
Gruppen," *Neue Zeit*, 2 February 1982.

131 "Evangelische Gottesdienste an diesem Wochenende," *Neue Zeit*, 14
December 1984; "Tips fürs Wochenende," *Neue Zeit*, 27 June 1986, 8;
"Tips zum Wochenende," *Neue Zeit*, 17 May 1985, 8.

132 "Wissenschaftliche Tagung über Homosexualität," *Neues Deutschland*,
29 June 1985; "Wissenschaftliche Tagung über Homosexualität," *Berliner
Zeitung*, 2 July 1985.

133 E.g., Prof. Dr Lykke Aresin, "Homosexuell sein – was bedeutet das?,"
Neues Leben, 1987; Jutta Resch-Treuwerth, "Unter vier Augen: Auf der
Suche nach einem Freund" *Junge Welt*, 2 March 1988, ArchSM, DDR,
Nr. 21; Dr Kurt Bach, "Wie helfen, ohne zu schaden?" *Für Dich*, 1984,
ArchSM, DDR, Nr. 21.

134 SAPMO-BArch Lichterfelde, DY/30/22491, 105.

135 BStU, MfS - HA XX/9, Nr. 1971, 48.

136 Fred Müller, "'Wir wollen kein offizielles Ghetto für Homosexuelle': Interview mit dem Ost-Berliner Psychologie-Professor und Bestsller-Autur Reiner Werner," *Thüringen Allgemeine*, 5 August 1987, ArchSM, DDR, Nr. 21.

137 BStU, MfS - HA XX/9, Nr. 1684, 261.

138 Dr Ursula Sillge, interview, 11 February 2018; Werner, *Homosexualität*, 133ff.

139 Eberhard Klages, "Sachkunde überwindet Berührungsängste: Reiner Werners neuestes Werk: 'Homosexualität,'" *Neue Zeit*, 13 June 1987, 8.

140 BStU, MfS - HA XX/9, Nr. 1684, 266.

141 SAPMO-BArch Lichterfelde DY/30/27357, 148.

142 Ibid., 153–4.

143 For more on *Coming Out* and its release, see Frackman, "Persistent Ambivalence," 683–5; Frackman, "The East German Film *Coming Out* (1989) as Melancholic Reflection and Hopeful Projection."

144 Wagner, *DEFA after East Germany*, 234.

145 BStU, MfS - HA XX, Nr. 21832, 35; BStU, MfS-HA VII, 2743, 202.

146 Carsten I., interview, 11 November 2016.

147 Dr Ursula Sillge, interview, 11 February 2018.

148 Ibid.

149 BStU, MfS BV Berlin, Abt. XX, Nr. 4329, 186; BStU, MfS BV Halle KD Halle VIII, Nr. 2495/87, 14.

150 Thinius, "Aufbruch aus dem grauen Versteck," 39.

151 Peter Rausch, interview, 16 February 2017.

152 SAPMO-BArch Lichterfelde DY/30/22491, 113.

153 Ibid., 116.

154 "'RosaLinde' heißt der erste Jugendklub für Homosexuelle in der DDR: Nach großen Schwierigkeiten mit Unterstützung der FDJ gegründet," *Der Tagesspiegel*, 8 June 1989, 4.

155 BStU, MfS BV Erfurt KD Weimar Nr. 899, 2–3; "Homosexuellenklub in Weimar nach Stalin-Opfer benannt," 4 February 1989, ArchSM, DDR, Nr. 13.

156 BStU, MfS - HA XX/9, Nr. 1684, 271.

157 BStU, BVfS Potsdam, AKG, Nr. 556, 4.

158 BStU, MfS - BV Chemnitz, Abt. XX, Nr. 1237, 84.

159 E.g., BStU, MfS - HA XX/9, Nr. 1684, 47.

160 BStU, MfS BV Chemnitz, Abt. XX., Nr. 317, 22.

161 Ibid., 23.

162 Ibid., 25, 26.

163 Hillhouse, "Out of the Closet behind the Wall," 589.

164 Tümmers criticizes the regime's prophylactic measures as both overly restrictive and uninterested in educating the general public. While undoubtedly correct in comparison with the Federal Republic's response,

it is difficult to be overly critical in comparison to those countries, such as the United States, whose governments refused even to acknowledge the virus as a problem. Tümmers, *AIDS*, 213–23; See too Folland, "Globalizing Socialist Health."

165 "DDR: Prinzip Hoffnung," *Der Spiegel*, 16 February 1987, 148.
166 E.g., BStU, MfS - HA XX, Nr. 16066, 1–2.
167 BStU, MfS BV Erfurt, BdL S, Nr. 111, 37.
168 Bochow, "Reactions of the Gay Community to AIDS in East and West Berlin," 32–4.
169 "'Die Mauer war das Kondom der DDR': Aids und Homosexuelle in den neuen Bundesländern," *Der Spiegel*, 12 October 1992. It is also worth noting that elements in the East German regime originated and spread the conspiracy theory that the American military had created HIV. Jeppsson, "How East Germany Fabricated the Myth of HIV Being Man-Made"; Tümmers, *AIDS*, 220–1.
170 Rainer E., interview, 11 April 2017.
171 BStU, MfS - HA XX/9, Nr. 948, 17.
172 BStU, MfS BV Halle KD Halle VII, Nr. 2495/87, 178.
173 BStU, MfS - HA I, Nr. 15318, 211.
174 Ibid., 212.
175 Ibid., 213.
176 Tom Smith discusses evidence that military leaders attempted to find ways around the new policy prohibiting dismissal on grounds of sexuality alone. Smith, *Comrades in Arms*, 211.
177 BStU, MfS - HA I, Nr. 15318, 212.
178 BStU, MfS - BV Karl-Marx-Stadt StvOp Nr. 64, 109.
179 BStU, MfS - ZAIG, Nr. 3668, 2.
180 BStU, MfS - BV Chemnitz, Abt. XX, Nr. 1237, 75.
181 Evans notes one estimate of more than 150 IMs set on gay organizations. Evans, "Decriminalization, Seduction, and 'Unnatural Desire' in East Germany," 567.
182 BStU, MfS - BV Chemnitz, Abt. XX, Nr. 1237, 73.
183 Ibid., 75.
184 Ibid., 55.
185 Paul Betts, *Within Walls*, 40.
186 BStU, MfS - HA XX/9, Nr. 1973, 59.
187 BStU, BV Mgb., Abt. XX ZMA, Nr. 5349, Bd. II, 64.
188 BStU, MfS, HA VII, Nr. 2743, 202.
189 BStU, MfS - HA XX, Nr. 4309, 76.
190 Sillge, *Un-Sichtbare Frauen*, 105.
191 Peter Rausch, interview, 16 February 2017.
192 BStU, MfS BV Berlin, Abt. XX, Nr. 4329, 245.
193 Stapel, *Warme Brüder gegen Kalte Krieger*, 40.

194 BStU, MfS - HA XX ZMA, Nr. 10050/3, Band 2/1, 67; BStU, MfS, HA VII, Nr. 2743, 142; Fulbrook, *Anatomy of a Dictatorship*, 219.

195 BStU, MfS - HA XX ZMA, Nr. 10050/3, Band 2/1, 43.

196 BStU, MfS - HA XX/9, Nr. 1684, 77.

197 BStU, MfS - BV Chemnitz, Abt. XX, Nr. 1237, 96; "Strafgesetzbuch der Deutschen Demokratischen Republik," §107.

198 BStU, MfS - HA XX, Nr. 18317, 4.

199 BStU, MfS - HA XX, Nr. 21841, 8-17.

200 BStU, MfS - HA XX/9, Nr. 1500, Teil I, 53.

201 Betts, *Within Walls*, 41–2.

202 SAPMO-BArch Lichterfelde DY/30/1275, 150. For more on homoeroticism and homosexuality in the NVA, particularly the ways in which literary culture has negotiated such memories, see Smith, *Comrades in Arms*, 200–30.

203 Peter Rausch, interview, 16 February 2017.

204 Stapel, *Warme Brüder gegen Kalte Krieger*, 81, 84.

205 Thinius, "Aufbruch aus dem grauen Versteck," 28–9; Lemke, "Gay and Lesbian Life in East German Society before and after 1989," 35–6.

206 Evans, "Decriminalization, Seduction, and 'Unnatural Desire' in East Germany," 567; Sweet, "The Church, the Stasi, and Socialist Integration," 364; McLellan, *Love in the Time of Communism*, 212.

207 BStU, MfS - HA XX/9, Nr. 1952, 31–2.

208 Ulrich Z., interview, 13 January 2017.

209 Carsten I., interview, 11 November 2016.

210 Fulbrook, *The People's State*, 10.

211 Healey, *Russian Homophobia*, 97–106; O'Dwyer, *Coming Out of Communism*, 1.

212 Szulc, *Transnational Homosexuals*, 109.

213 O'Dwyer, *Coming Out of Communism*, 87–8.

214 Ibid., 4.

215 Fulbrook, "The Limits of Totalitarianism," 52; Kershaw, *The Nazi Dictatorship*, 23ff; Samuel Clowes Huneke, "An End to Totalitarianism."

216 Fulbrook similarly argues of environmental activism in East Germany that "Stasi strategies had ultimately aided a process of political education, as more and more East Germans learnt the complex arts of self-organization and political pressure group work under dictatorial conditions." Fulbrook, *Anatomy of a Dictatorship*, 234.

Epilogue

1 Tocqueville, *The Old Regime and the Revolution*, 214.

2 Davies, "Toward a Theory of Revolution," 5–19; Koselleck, *Preussen Zwischen Reform und Revolution*, 143.

3 E.g., Pfaff, *Exit-Voice Dynamics and the Collapse of East Germany*, xi; Kupferberg, *The Break-up of Communism in East Germany and Eastern Europe*, 131; Saxonberg, *The Fall*, 13–23; Ash, *The Magic Lantern*, 140–2; Betts, *Within Walls*, 87; Judt, *Postwar*, 585ff.

4 Peter Rausch, interview, 16 February 2017. Raelynn Hillhouse also argues that the success of the gay and lesbian movement "foreshadowed the events of 1989." Hillhouse, "Out of the Closet behind the Wall," 596.

5 Sheffer, *Burned Bridge*, 235.

6 "Gesetz über die Wahlen zur Volkskammer der Deutschen Demokratischen Republik am 18. März 1990," §8-(2).

7 Grdesic, "Spatial Patterns of Thermidor," 24.

8 The Green Party program supported "recognition of homosexuality as an emancipated sexual variant," while the SPD program insisted, in less enthusiastic language, that gay men and lesbians had the right "in the framework defined solely by law to profess their lifestyle freely and openly." "Grüne Partei: Ökologisch, solidarisch, basisdemokratisch, gewaltfrei: Rahmenprogramm," n.d., 13, HA, German Subject Collection XX741, Box 46 (DDR 1990), "Election 1990 March 18 Grüne Partei"; "Parteitag in Leipzig 22. bis 25. Februar 1990: Grundsatzprogramm," n.d., 9, HA, German Subject Collection XX741, Box 46 (DDR 1990), "Election 1990 March 18 Sozialdemokratische Partei Deutschlands (SPD)."

9 Lothar de Maizière, interview, 11 October 2016.

10 "Programm Statut PDS," n.d., HA, German Subject Collection XX741, Box 46 (DDR 1990), "Election 1990 March 18 Partei des Demokratischen Sozialismus (PDS)."

11 "Electoral Poster," n.d., HA, German Subject Collection XX741, Box 46 (DDR 1990), "Election 1990 March 18 PDS."

12 "Zukunft für alle – arbeiten für soziale Gerechtigkeit und Frieden: Regierungsprogramm 1987–1990 der Sozialdemokratischen Partei Deutschlands," n.d.: http://library.fes.de/pdf-files/bibliothek/retro -scans/a87-04013.pdf.

13 Suleiman, "Bureaucracy and Democratic Consolidation," 159ff; Readings, *The University in Ruins*, 41; Yoder, *From East Germans to Germans?*, 247, n11.

14 Merkl, *German Unification in the European Context*, 189ff; Knuth, "Active Labor Market Policy and German Unification," 70.

15 Ireland, "Socialism, Unification Policy and the Rise of Racism in Eastern Germany," 541–68; Kurthen, Bermann, Erb, and Schubarth, "Xenophobia among East German Youth," 143–58; Betts, "Twilight of the Idols," 736.

16 von Mahlsdorf, *Ich bin meine eigene Frau*, 7.

17 Marc Fest, "Schwule wehren sich jetzt gewaltig," *Die Tageszeitung*, 28 September 1991, ArchSM, Gewalt gegen Homosexuelle.

18 "Schwulenverband beklagt zunehmende Gewalt," *Süddeutsche Zeitung*, n.d., ArchSM, Gewalt gegen Homosexuelle; "Schwule wollen sich gegen die steigende Gewalt wehren," *Spandauer Volksblatt*, 29 September 1991, ArchSM, Gewalt gegen Homosexuelle.

19 Deutscher Bundestag, "Homosexualität und die Rechtsangleichung von Bundesrepublik Deutschland und DDR," Drucksache 11/17544, 9 July 1990, 1–2.

20 Milder and Jarausch, "Renewing Democracy," 4.

21 "Wahlprogramm der Linken Liste/PDS zur Bundestagswahl 1990," 5. See too the PDS 1994 program. "Wahlprogramm der PDS 1994," n.d., 26, HA, German Subject Collection XX471, Box 46 (DDR 1990), "Election 1990 March 18 Partei des Demokratischen Sozialismus (PDS)."

22 "Sexualität Höhere Kulturstufe," *Der Spiegel*, 14 January 1991, 34.

23 McLellan, *Love in the Time of Communism*, 12, 53ff; Harsch, "Society, the State and Abortion in East Germany, 1950–1972"; Lothar de Maizière, interview, 11 October 2016.

24 "Sexualität: Höhere Kulturstufe," *Der Spiegel*, 14 January 1991, 34.

25 Ibid.

26 Lothar de Maizière, interview, 11 October 2016.

27 Deutscher Bundestag, "Plenarprotokoll 12/153: Stenographischer Bericht: 153. Sitzung," 23 April 1993, 13119.

28 Deutscher Bundestag, "Plenarprotokoll 12/216: Stenographischer Bericht: 216. Sitzung," 10 March 1994, 18699.

29 Lothar de Maizière, interview, 11 October 2016.

30 "Helden wie wir," *Die Zeit*, 29 April 1999.

31 "Schwuler Offizier darf bleiben," *Rhein-Zeitung*, 7 April 2000: http://archiv.rhein-zeitung.de/on/00/04/07/topnews/stecher.html.

32 Anthony Faiola, "Angela Merkel Congratulates Donald Trump – Kind Of," *Washington Post*, 9 November 2016, sec. WorldViews.

33 "Frau Merkel, das schaffen Sie!: Mehrheit der Deutschen will die Ehe für alle," FOCUS Online, accessed 12 July 2018: https://www.focus.de/politik/deutschland/75-prozent-stimmten-in-umfrage-dafuer-frau-merkel-das-schaffen-sie-mehrheit-der-deutschen-will-die-ehe-fuer-alle_id_6873290.html.

34 "More Germans Identify as LGBT than in Rest of Europe," 21 October 2016: https://www.thelocal.de/20161021/more-germans-identify-as-lgbt-than-in-rest-of-europe.

35 "Anonymes Beratungs- und Testangebot," Mann-O-Meter, accessed 12 July 2018: https://www.mann-o-meter.de/unsere-angebote-und-leistungen/anonymer-hiv-schnelltest/; "Anonymer HIV- und Syphilis-Test in der Berliner Aids-Hilfe," Berliner Aids-Hilfe e.V, 1 March 2013: https://www.berlin-aidshilfe.de/angebote/testcenter.

36 "Strut I The Home for Health & Wellness in the Castro, San Francisco," *Strut*, accessed 12 July 2018: https://www.strutsf.org/.

37 Schmidt Hickson, Weatherburn, Marcus, and the EMIS Network, "Comparison of the Performance of STI Screening Services for Gay and Bisexual Men across 40 European Cities," 579.

38 Sören Kittel, "Truvada: Die Pille zur HIV-Prävention wird bezahlbar," *Morgenpost*, 18 September 2017: https://www.morgenpost.de/ratgeber /article211964673/Die-Pille-zum-Schutz-vor-einer-HIV-Infektion-wird -bezahlbar.html.

39 Chin, "Thinking Difference in Postwar Germany," 221–2.

40 Haritaworn, "Queer Injuries," 71; Mohamed Amjahid, "Der lange Schatten des Regenbogens," *Der Tagesspiegel*, 30 October 2015, accessed 11 August 2020: https://www.tagesspiegel.de/gesellschaft/queerspiegel/rassismus -unter-queeren-der-lange-schatten-des-regenbogens/12504400.html. See, in particular, the public debate around Patsy L'Amour laLove's *Beißreflexe*, published in 2017.

41 "LSVD-Verbandstag 2018: Tätigkeitsbericht Des Bundesvorstandes," n.d., 26: https://www.lsvd.de/fileadmin/pics/Dokumente/Taetigkeitsberichte /LSVD_Taetigkeitsbericht_2017_2018.pdf.

42 Human Rights Campaign, "HRC Story," Human Rights Campaign, accessed 12 July 2018: http://www.hrc.org/hrc-story/about-us/.

43 E.g., Tania Witte, "Andersrum ist auch nicht besser: Homo AfDensis," *Die Zeit*, 26 April 2017: https://www.zeit.de/zeit-magazin/leben/2017-04 /alice-weidel-afd-spitzenkandidatin-homonationalismus; Samuel Clowes Huneke, "Queering the Vote."

Bibliography

Archives

ArchSM	Archive of the Gay Museum / *Archiv des Schwulen Museums*
BArch-Koblenz	Federal Archive in Koblenz / *Bundesarchiv – Koblenz*
BArch-Lichterfelde	Federal Archive in Berlin Lichterfelde / *Bundesarchiv – Berlin-Lichterfelde*
BStU	Stasi Archive / *Die Behörde des Bundesbeauftragten für die Stasi-Unterlagen*
GLAK	Karlsruhe General Regional Archive / *Generallandesarchiv Karlsruhe*
HA	The Hoover Institution Library and Archives
HHStAW	Hesse Main State Archive in Wiesbaden / *Hessische Hauptstaatsarchiv Wiesbaden*
LAB	Berlin Regional Archive / *Landesarchiv Berlin*
SAPMO-BArch	Foundation Archives of Parties and Mass Organizations of the GDR in the Federal Archives / *Stiftung Archiv der Parteien und Massenorganisationen der DDR im Bundesarchiv*
SHStAD	Saxony Main State Archive in Dresden / *Sächsisches Staatsarchiv – Hauptstaatsarchiv Dresden*

Oral Interviews[*]

Norton G., 17 September 2016
Lothar de Maizière, 11 October 2016

---

[*] Except in cases where the subject has given consent to be cited by name, the names of interview partners have been anonymized.

Carsten I., 11 November 2016
Samuel R., 15 November 2016
Volker K., 18 December 2016
Holger G., 5 January 2017
Erik A., 5 January 2017
Georg R., 7 January 2017
Torsten V., 9 January 2017
Ralf A., 11 January 2017 and 22 January 2017
Ulrich Z., 13 January 2017
Hubert U., 27 January 2017
Peter Rausch, 31 January 2017 and 16 February 2017
Ralf G., 12 February 2017
Michael Eggert, 16 February 2017
Franz G., 29 May 2017
Rainer E., 11 April 2017
Ralf Dose, 23 January 2018
Dorothea R., 26 January 2018
Roland R., 26 January 2018 (by email)
Dr Ursula Sillge, 11 February 2018

Online Archives

Archiv des Liberalismus (ADL). https://www.freiheit.org/archiv-des-liberalismus.
Dokumentations- und Informationssystem für Parlamentsmaterialien (DIP). https://
    dip.bundestag.de.

Cited Periodicals

Berliner Zeitung
Bild
Du & Ich
FOCUS Online
Hamburger Abendblatt
HAW INFO
him
Die Insel
Juristen Zeitung
Der Kreis
Kriminalistik
Das Magazin
Morgenpost
Neues Deutschland

Neue Zeit
The New Yorker
Rhein-Zeitung
Spartacus International Gay Guide
Der Spiegel
Statistisches Jahrbuch für die Bundesrepublik Deutschland
Statistisches Jahrbuch der Deutschen Demokratischen Republik
Stern
Stuttgarter-Zeitung
Twen
The Washington Post
Der werbende Buch- und Zeitschriftenhandel
Die Zeit

Legal Documents and Court Decisions

Allied Control Authority of Germany. *Enactments and Approved Papers.*
  Vols. I–IX. Legal Division, Office of Military Government for Germany
  (US). 1945–1948.
Bundesgerichtshof, "Urt. v. 13.03.151." No. 1 StR 1/51. 13 March 1951.
Bundesverfassungsgericht, "Urteil des Ersten Senats vom 10. Mai 1957." In
  Entscheidungen des Bundesverfassungsgerichts vol. 6, 389–443. J.C.B. Mohr
  (Paul Siebeck), 1957.
"Control Council Directive No. 38." 12 October 1946. http://ghdi.ghi-dc.org
  /sub_document.cfm?document_id=2307.
"Declaration Regarding the Defeat of Germany and the Assumption of
  Supreme Authority by Allied Powers." 5 June 1945. http://avalon.law.yale
  .edu/wwii/ger01.asp.
Deutscher Bundestag. "Entwurf eines Strafgesetzbuches (StGB) E 1962."
  Drucksache IV/650. 4 October 1962.
"Erstes Gesetz zur Reform des Strafrechts (1. StrRG)." *Bundesgesetzblatt* no. 52
  (1969): 645–82.
"Gesetz über die Wahlen zur Volkskammer der Deutschen Demokratischen
  Republik am 18. März 1990." 20 February 1990. https://deutsche-einheit
  -1990.de/wp-content/uploads/Gbl_DDR1990_I_9.pdf.
"Gesetz zur Ergänzung des Strafgesetzbuches." 11 December 1957. http://
  www.verfassungen.de/ddr/strafrechtsergaenzungsgesetz57.htm.
"Grundgesetz für die Bundesrepublik Deutschland." 23 May 1949. https://
  www.bundestag.de/grundgesetz.
Kammergericht Berlin. "Urteil vom 21. Februar 1950–1 Ss 165/49." *Neue Justiz:
  Zeitschrift für Recht und Rechtswissenschaft* (1950): 100–1.

Ministerium der Justiz der DDR. "Zivilgesetzbuch der Deutschen Demokratischen Republik." Staatsverlag der Deutschen Demokratischen Republik, 1977.

Oberstes Gericht. "Urteil vom 28. März 1950–3 Tst. 9/50." *Neue Justiz: Zeitschrift für Recht und Rechtswissenschaft* (1950): 215.

OLG Braunschweig. "Urteil v. 7.6.46 – Ss 5/46." *Süddeutsche Juristen-Zeitung* (August 1946): 119–20.

OLG Celle. "Urteil von 20.12.46, Ss 94/46." *Deutsche Rechts-Zeitschrift* 2, no. 4 (April 1947): 134.

OLG Halle. "Beschluß v. 20.9.1948–1 Ws 53/48." *Neue Justiz: Zeitschrift für Recht und Rechtswissenschaft* (1949): 143–5.

OLG Hamburg. "Urteil vom 22. Januar 1947." *Monatsschrift für Deutsches Recht* (1947): 75.

OLG Kiel, "Strafsenat v. 22.1.1947, Ss 208/46." *Deutsche Rechts-Zeitschrift* 2, no. 6 (June 1947): 198.

OLG Oldenburg. "Urteil v. 15.4.46." *Süddeutsche Juristen-Zeitung* 1, no. 4 (4 July 1946): 96–7.

OLG Stuttgart. "1 Ss 431/63." 21 June 1963.

Plischke, Elmer. "Denazification Law and Procedure." *The American Journal of International Law* 41, no. 4 (1947): 807–27. https://doi.org/10.2307/2193091.

"Strafgesetzbuch der Deutschen Demokratischen Republik." 12 January 1968. http://www.verfassungen.de/ddr/strafgesetzbuch68.htm.

"Verfassung der Deutschen Demokratischen Republik." 7 October 1974. http://www.documentarchiv.de/ddr/verfddr.html.

Weber. "Zur Auswirkung der Gesetzgebung der Besatzungsmächte auf das deutsche Strafgesetzbuch: Die Bedeutung der 'Allgemeinen Anweisung an Richter' Nr. 1." *Süddeutsche Juristen-Zeitung* 1, no. 8/9 (1946): 238–40.

Werner, Wolfhart. "Die Bedeutung der Ziffer 8 B der Allgemeinen Anweisungen der Militärregierung an Ricther Nr. 1 für die Anwendbarkeit strafrechtlicher Vorschriften, insbesondere des §175 a StGB." *Deutsche Rechts-Zeitschrift* 1, no. 3 (1946): 74–7.

Films

Anders als du und ich (§175). Dir. Veit Harlan. Arca-Filmproduktion GmbH, 1957.

Armee der Liebenden oder Aufstand der Perverse. Dir. Rosa von Praunheim. Rosa von Praunheim Filmproduktion, 1979.

Coming Out. Dir. Heiner Carow. DEFA, 1989.

Mein wunderbares Westberlin. Dir. Jochen Hick. 2017.

Nicht der Homosexuelle ist pervers, sondern die Situation, in der er lebt. Dir. Rosa von Praunheim. Bavaria Atelier, 1971.

Published Primary Sources

Ackermann, Heinrich. "Zur Frage der Strafwürdigkeit des homosexuellen Verhaltens des Mannes." In *Sexualität und Verbrechen: Beiträge zur Strafrechtsreform*, edited by Fritz Bauer, Hans Bürger-Prinz, Hans Giese, and Herbert Jäger, 149–60. Berlin: S. Fischer, 1963.

Adorno, Theodor. "Sexualtabus und Recht heute." In *Sexualität und Verbrechen: Beiträge zur Strafrechtsreform*, edited by Fritz Bauer, Hans Giese, Herbert Jäger, and Hans Bürger-Prinz, 299–317. Berlin: S. Fischer, 1963.

Bauer, Fritz, Hans Giese, Herbert Jäger, and Hans Bürger-Prinz. "Vorwort der Herausgeber." In *Sexualität und Verbrechen: Beiträge zur Strafrechtsreform*, edited by Fritz Bauer, Hans Giese, Herbert Jäger, and Hans Bürger-Prinz, 7–10. Berlin: S. Fischer, 1963.

Baumann, Jürgen. *Paragraph 175: Über die Möglichkeit, die Einfache, Nichtjugendgefährdende und Nichtöffentliche Homosexualität unter Erwachsenen straffrei zu lassen*. Munich: Luchterhand, 1968.

Bebel, August. *Woman and Socialism*. Trans. Meta L. Stern. New York: Socialist Literature, 1910.

Becker, Walter. *Homosexualität und Jugendschutz*. Hamm: Hoheneck, 1961.

Benjamin, Hilde. *Das Strafrecht der sozialistischen Demokratie*. Berlin: Deutscher Zentralverlag, 1958.

Blüher, Hans. *Die Rolle der Erotik in der männlichen Gesellschaft*. Munich: E. Diederichs, 1917.

Cory, Donald Webster. *The Homosexual in America: A Subjective Approach*. New York: Castle Books, 1960.

Dannecker, Martin, and Reimut Reiche. *Der gewöhnliche Homosexuelle: Eine soziologische Untersuchung über männliche Homosexuelle in der Bundesrepublik*. Berlin: S. Fischer, 1974.

Die Gefahren des Sexualismus und ihre Überwindung: (Referate, geh. auf d. Tagung d. Volkswartbundes am 19. Febr. 1952 in Köln). Köln-Klettenberg: Volkswartbund, 1952.

"Die Grünen: Wahlplattform zur Bundestagswahl 1980." https://www.boell.de/sites/default/files/assets/boell.de/images/download_de/publikationen/1980_Wahlplattform_Bundestagswahl.pdf?dimension1=division_agg.

Dietz, Karl, and Peter G. Hesse. *Wörterbuch der Sexuologie und ihrer Grenzgebiete*. Rudolstadt: Greifenverlag, 1964.

Eppelmann, Rainer. "Opposition und Kirche in der DDR." *German Studies Review* 17 (1994): 101–11.

Freud, Sigmund. *Drei Abhandlungen zur Sexualtheorie*. Third Edition. Leipzig: Franz Deuticke, 1915.

– "Historical Notes: A Letter from Freud." *The American Journal of Psychiatry* 107, no. 10 (April 1951): 786–7.

Freund, Kurt. *Die Homosexualität beim Mann*. Leipzig: S. Hirzel, 1965.

Frieling, Willi. "Vorwort." In *Schwule Regungen – schwule Bewegungen*, edited by Willi Freiling, 7–8. Berlin: Rosa Winkel, 1985.

Gatzweiler, Richard. *Das Dritte Geschlecht: Um die Strafbarkeit der Homosexualität*. Köln-Klettenberg: Volkswartbund, 1951.

– *Gleichberechtigung der Homosexuellen? Neue Angriffe gegen d. § 175 StGB*. Köln-Klettenberg: Volkswartbund, 1953.

– *Die Homosexualität des Mannes und das Strafgesetz*. Köln-Klettenberg: Volkswartbund, 1954.

– *Der Kampf um den §175 StGB geht weiter: Ein Situationsbericht*. Köln-Klettenberg: Volkswartbund, 1957.

– *Die Homosexualität des Mannes und die Strafrechtreform*. Köln-Klettenberg: Volkswartbund, 1961.

George, Stefan. *Die Gedichte*. Stuttgart: Klett-Cotta, 2003.

Giese, Hans. *Der Homosexuelle Mann in der Welt*. Stuttgart: Ferdinand Enke Verlag, 1964.

Giese, Hans, and Gunter Schmidt. *Studenten-Sexualität: Verhalten und Einstellung*. Reinbek bei Hamburg: Rowohlt, 1968.

Harthauser, Wolfgang. "Der Massenmord an Homosexuellen im Dritten Reich." In *Das Große Tabu. Zeugnisse und Dokumente zum Problem der Homosexualität*, edited by Willhart S. Schlegel, 7–37. Munich: Rütten & Loening, 1967.

Heger, Heinz. *Die Männer mit dem rosa Winkel: Der Bericht eines Homosexuellen über seine KZ-Haft von 1939–1945*. Gifkendorf: Merlin-Verlag, 1972.

Hermann, Kai, Hort Rieck, and Christiane F. *Wir Kinder vom Bahnhof Zoo*. Hamburg: Carlsen, 2017.

Hiller, Kurt. *Das Recht über sich selbst: Eine Strafrechtsphilosophische Studie*. Heidelberg: C. Winter, 1908.

Hirschfeld, Magnus. *Die Homosexualität des Mannes und des Weibes*. Berlin: L. Marcus, 1914.

Hitler, Adolf. "Reichstagsrede: Über die Entstehung und den Verlauf der SA-Revolte." 13 July 1934.

Holy, Michael. "AIDS und Kießling." In *Schwule Regungen – schwule Bewegungen*, edited by Willi Frieling, 117–20. Berlin: Rosa Winkel, 1985.

– "Einige Daten zur Zweiten deutschen Homosexuellenbewegung (1969–1983)." In *Schwule Regungen – schwule Bewegungen*, edited by Willi Frieling, 183–200. Berlin: Rosa Winkel, 1985.

Isherwood, Christopher. *Christopher and His Kind*. New York: Vintage Classic, 2012.

Italiaander, Rolf. "Ein Rundbrief." In *Weder Krankheit noch Verbrechen: Pläydoyer für eine Minderheit,* edited by Rolf Italiaander, 221–6. Hamburg: Gala Verlag, 1969.

Italiaander, Rolf, ed. *Weder Krankheit noch Verbrechen: Plädoyer für eine Minderheit.* Hamburg: Gala, 1969.

Jäger, Herbert. "Strafrechtspolitik und Wissenschaft." In *Sexualität und Verbrechen: Beiträge zur Strafrechtsreform,* edited by Fritz Bauer, Hans Bürger-Prinz, Hans Giese, and Herbert Jäger, 273–98. Berlin: S. Fischer, 1963.

Kempe, G.Th. "Die Homophilen und die Gesellschaft." In *Studien zur männlichen Homosexualität,* edited by H. Bürger-Prinz and H. Giese, 1–21. Stuttgart: Ferdinand Enke, 1954.

Kertbeny, Károly Mária. *§143 des Presussischen Trafgesetzbuches vom 14. April 1851 und seine Aufrechterhaltung als §152 im Entwurfe eines Strafgesetzbuches für den Norddeutschen Bund. Offene, fachwissenschaftliche Zuschrift an Seine Excellenz Herrn Dr. Leonhardt, königl. preußischen Staats- und Justizminister.* Leipzig: M. Spohr, 1905.

Klare, Rudolf. "Homosexualität und Strafrecht." Martin-Luther-Universität Halle, 1937.

Klimmer, Rudolf. "Die Situation in der DDR." In *Weder Krankheit noch Verbrechen: Pläydoyer für eine Minderheit,* edited by Rolf Italiaander. Hamburg: Gala Verlag, 1969.

Kuckuc, Ina. "Gesellschaftspolitische Arbeit und Emanzipation von Lesbierinnen." In *Seminar: Gesellschaft und Homosexualität,* edited by Rüdiger Lautmann, 465–73. Frankfurt am Main: Suhrkamp, 1977.

Lautmann, Rüdiger. "Bewegung und Organisation: Versuche homosexueller Emanzipation." In *Seminar: Gesellschaft und Homosexualität,* edited by Rüdiger Lautmann, 492–531. Frankfurt am Main: Suhrkamp, 1977.

– "Das Verbrechen der widernatürlichen Unzucht: Seine Grundlegung in der preußischen Gesetzesrevision des 19. Jahrhunderts." *Kritische Justiz* 25, no. 3 (1992): 294–314.

Lautmann, Rüdiger, ed. *Seminar: Gesellschaft und Homosexualität.* Frankfurt am Main: Suhrkamp, 1977.

Littmann, Corny, and Michael Holy. "'Würden Sie das eventuell zurücknehmen?': Gespräch über die 'Homosexuelle Aktion Hamburg.'" In *Schwule Regungen – schwule Bewegungen,* edited by Willi Frieling, 25–36. Berlin: Rosa Winkel, 1985.

Mann, Klaus. *Der Vulkan.* Munich: Nymphenburger, 1968.

– "Homosexualität und Fascismus." In Klaus Mann. *Heute und Morgen: Schriften zur Zeit,* edited by Martin Grego-Dellin, 130–7. Nymphenburger, 1969.

Monette, Paul. *Becoming a Man: Half a Life Story.* San Francisco: Harper, 1991.

Obama, Barack. "Inaugural Address." Speech, Washington, DC, 21 January 2013. The White House: President Barack Obama. https://obamawhitehouse.archives.gov/the-press-office/2013/01/21/inaugural-address-president-barack-obama%20.

"Regierungserklärung von Bundeskanzler Willy Brandt." Speech, Bonn, 28 October 1969. https://www.willy-brandt.de/fileadmin/brandt/Downloads/Regierungserklaerung_Willy_Brandt_1969.pdf.

"Regierungsprogramm der Sozialdemokratischen Partei Deutschlands 1969." 17 April 1969. http://library.fes.de/pdf-files/bibliothek/retro-scans/fa-06999.pdf.

"Regierungsprogramm: Wir bauen den Fortschritt auf Stabilität." CDU-Bundesgeschäftsstelle, 1972. https://www.kas.de/c/document_library/get_file?uuid=fe891947-82a1-6b72-d541-3687f62e89c0&groupId=252038.

"Report of the Committee on Homosexual Offences and Prostitution." Richmond: Her Majesty's Stationary Office, 1957.

Reuband, Karl Heinz. "Über Gesellschaftlichen Wandel, AIDS und die Beurteilung der Homosexualität als moralisches Vergehen: Eine Trendanalyse von Bevölkerungsumfragen der Jahre 1970 bis 1987." *Zeitschrift Für Soziologie* 18, no. 1 (1989): 65–73.

Rexhausen, Felix. *Lavendelschwert: Dokumente einer seltsamen Revolution.* Frankfurt am Main: Bärmeier & Nikel, 1965.

Schelsky, Helmut. *Die Strategie der "Systemüberwindung": Der lange March durch die Institutionen.* Berlin: Notgemeinsch f.e. Freie Universität, 1971.

Schewe, Dieter. "Die Kontinuität der Sozialgesetzgebung in den letzten 50 Jahren in Deutschland." *Sozialer Fortschritt* 49, no. 1 (2000): 1–6.

Schoeps, Hans-Joachim. "Überlegungen zum Problem der Homosexualität." In *Der homosexuelle Nächste: Ein Symposium,* 74–114. Berlin: Furche-Verlag, 1963.

Seyfarth, Napoleon. *Schweine müssen nackt sein: Ein Leben mit dem Tod.* Berlin: Diá, 1991.

Sillge, Ursula. *Un-Sichtbare Frauen: Lesben und ihre Emanzipation in der DDR.* Berlin: Ch. Links, 1991.

Stapel, Eduard. *Warme Brüder gegen Kalte Krieger: Schwulenbewegung in der DDR im Visier der Staatssicherheit.* Magdeburg: Landesbeauftragte für die Unterlagen des Staatssicherheitsdienstes der ehemaligen DDR Sachsen-Anhalt, 1999.

Stedefelt, Eike. "Zur weiteren Veranlassung: Ein Interview mit dem MfS-Offizier Wolfgang Schmidt." In *Homosexualität in der DDR: Materialien und Meinungen,* edited by Wolfram Setz, 185–202. Hamburg: Männerschwarm, 2006.

Tuntenstreit: Theoriediskussion der Homosexuellen Aktion Westberlin. Berlin: Rosa Winkel, 1975.

Verhandlungen des siebenundvierzigsten deutschen Juristentages. Vol. 1 (Gutachten). Munich: Beck, 1970.

Volkswartbund. *Homosexualität als akute öffentliche Gefahr.* Köln-Klettenberg: Volkswartbund, 1950.

von Mahlsdorf, Charlotte. *Ich bin meine eigene Frau.* Munich: dtv, 1995.

von Praunheim, Rosa. "Nicht der Homosexuelle ist pervers, sondern die Situation in der er lebt oder, Das Glück in der Toilette.'" In Rosa von Praunheim, *Sex und Karriere,* 162–5. Munich: Rogner & Bernhard, 1991.

– *Sex und Karriere.* Munich: Rogner & Bernhard, 1991.

von Praunheim, Rosa, and Martin Dannecker. "Drehbuch." In Rosa von Praunheim. *Nicht der Homosexuelle ist pervers, sondern die Situation, in der er lebt.* 2007.

"Wahlprogramm der Christlich Demokratischen Union Deutschlands, 1969–1973." Bundesgeschäftsstelle der CDU, 1969. https://www.kas.de/c/document_library/get_file?uuid=99347a53-b10c-810d-0c02-155e13beb4f2&groupId=252038.

"Wahlprogramm der Linken Liste/PDS zur Bundestagswahl 1990." https://www.rosalux.de/fileadmin/rls_uploads/pdfs/ADS/Bundestagswahl_1990_-_Programm.pdf.

"Wahlprogramm der SPD: Mit Willy Brandt für Frieden, Sicherheit und bessere Qualität des Lebens." 13 October 1972. http://library.fes.de/pdf-files/bibliothek/bestand/a83-02241.pdf.

Weber, Ulrich, Martin Heidenhain, and Hendrik Gröttup. "Der 47. Deutsche Juristentag." *Juristische Zeitung* 23, no. 22 (1968): 755–9.

Werner, Reiner. *Homosexualität: Herausforderung an Wissen und Toleranz.* Berlin: VEB Verlag Volk und Gesundheit, 1988.

Wilde, Harry. *Das Schicksal der Verfemten: Die Verfolgung der Homosexuellen im "Dritten Reich" und ihre Stellung in der heutigen Gesellschaft.* Tübingen: Katzmann Verlag, 1969.

Witte, Hajo. "Lesben und Schwule in den Kirchen." In *Schwule Regungen – schwule Bewegungen,* edited by Willi Frieling, 137–50. Berlin: Rosa Winkel, 1985.

"Wortprotokoll der Veranstaltung am 12.07.80 in der Bonner Beethovenalle." In *...alle Schwestern werden Brüder...,* edited by Dieter Bachnick and Rainer Schädlich, 222–42. Berlin: Trifolium, 1986.

Secondary Literature

Adam, Barry D. "Structural Foundations of the Gay World." *Comparative Studies in Society and History* 27, no. 4 (1985): 658–71.

Adam, Barry D., Jan Willem Duyvendak, and André Krouwel, eds. *The Global Emergence of Gay and Lesbian Politics: National Imprints of a Worldwide Movement*. Philadelphia, PA: Temple University Press, 1999.

Alexander, Rustam. "Soviet Legal and Criminological Debates on the Decriminalization of Homosexuality (1965–75)." *Slavic Review* 77, no. 1 (Spring 2018): 30–52.

Antidiskriminierungsstelle des Bundes. "Studie zu Einstellungen gegenüber Lesben, Schwulen und Bisexuellen: Mehr als 80 Prozent der Menschen in Deutschland für 'Ehe für alle.'" News release, 12 January 2017. Antidiskriminierungsstelle des Bundes. Accessed 17 December 2020. https://www.antidiskriminierungsstelle.de/SharedDocs/Aktuelles /DE/2017/20170112_Umfrage_LSB.html.

Arendt, Hannah. *Eichmann in Jerusalem: A Report on the Banality of Evil*. New York: Penguin, 2006.

Art, David. *The Politics of the Nazi Past in Germany and Austria*. Cambridge: Cambridge University Press, 2005.

Ash, Timothy Garton. *The File: A Personal History*. New York: Vintage, 1998.

– *The Magic Lantern: The Revolution of '89 Witnessed in Warsaw, Budapest, Berlin, and Prague*. New York: Vintage, 1999.

Ashkenasi, Abraham. *Modern German Nationalism*. Rochester, VT: Schenkman. 1976.

Baer, Hester. *Dismantling the Dream Factory: Gender, German Cinema, and the Postwar Quest for a New Film Language*. New York: Berghahn, 2009.

Balser, Kristof, Mario Kramp, Jürgen Müller, and Joanna Götzmann. *Himmel und Hölle. Das Leben der Kölner Homosexuellen 1945–1969*. Köln: Emons Verlag, 1997.

Bauer, Heike. *The Hirschfeld Archives: Violence, Death, and Modern Queer Culture*. Philadelphia, PA: Temple University Press, 2017.

Beachy, Robert. "The German Invention of Homosexuality." *The Journal of Modern History* 82, no. 4 (1 December 2010): 801–38.

– *Gay Berlin: Birthplace of a Modern Identity*. New York: Knopf, 2014.

Beljan, Magdalena. *Rosa Zeiten? Eine Geschichte der Subjektivierung männlicher Homosexualität in den 1970er und 1980er Jahren der BRD*. Bielefeld: Transcript, 2014.

Belkin, Aaron, and Margot Canaday. "Assessing the Integration of Gays and Lesbians into the South African National Defence Force." *Scientia Militaria: South African Journal of Military Studies* 38, no. 2 (2010): 1–21.

Berndl, Klaus. "Zeiten der Bedrohung: Männliche Homosexuelle in Ost-Berlin und der DDR in den 1950er Jahren." In *Konformitäten und Konfrontationen: Homosexuelle in der DDR*, edited by Rainer Marbach and Volker Weiß, 19–50. Hamburg: Männerschwarm, 2017.

Berndl, Klaus, and Vera Kruber. "Zur Statistik der Strafverfolgung homosexueller Männer in der SBZ und DDR bis 1959." *Invertito: Jahrbuch für die Geschichte der Homosexualitäten* 12 (2010): 58–124.

Bernstein, Herbert. "West Germany: Free Press and National Security. Reflections on the Spiegel Case." *The American Journal of Comparative Law* 15, no. 3 (1966): 547–61.

Bérubé, Allan. *Coming Out under Fire: The History of Gay Men and Women in World War II.* Chapel Hill, NC: University of North Carolina Press, 2010.

Betts, Paul. "The Twilight of the Idols: East German Memory and Material Culture." *Journal of Modern History* 72, no. 3 (2000): 731–65.

– *Within Walls: Private Life in the German Democratic Republic.* Oxford: Oxford University Press, 2010.

Biess, Frank. "Moral Panic in Postwar Germany: The Abduction of Young Germans into the Foreign Legion and French Colonialism in the 1950s." *The Journal of Modern History* 84, no. 4 (December 2012): 789–832.

– *Republik der Angst: Eine Andere Geschichte der Bundesrepublik.* Reinbek bei Hamburg: Rowohlt, 2019.

Biess, Frank, and Astrid Eckert. "Introduction: Why Do We Need New Narratives for the History of the Federal Republic?" *Central European History* 52, Special Issue 1 (March 2019): 1–18.

Black, Monica. "Miracles in the Shadow of the Economic Miracle: The 'Supernatural '50s' in West Germany." *The Journal of Modern History* 84, no. 4 (2012): 833–60.

– *A Demon-Haunted Land: Witches, Wonder Doctors, and the Ghosts of the Past in Post-WWII Germany.* New York: Metropolitan Books, 2020.

Bochow, Michael. "Reactions of the Gay Community to AIDS in East and West Berlin." In *Aspects of AIDS and AIDS-Hilfe in Germany,* 19–46. Deutsche AIDS-Hilfe e.V., 1993.

Bock, Angela. "Producing the 'Socialist Personality'? Socialisation, Education, and the Emergence of New Patterns of Behaviour." In *Power and Society in the GDR, 1961–1979: The 'Normalisation of Rule'?*, edited by Mary Fulbrook, 220–52. New York: Berghahn Books, 2009.

Borneman, John. "AIDS in the Two Berlins." *October* 43 (1987): 223–36.

Borowski, Maria. "Erste Erkenntnisee zum lesbischen und schwulen Alltagslebel in der frühen DDR." In *Konformitäten und Konfrontationen: Homosexuelle in der DDR,* edited by Rainer Marbach and Volker Weiß, 51–63. Hamburg: Männerschwarm, 2017.

– *Parallelwelten: Lesbisch-Schwules Leben in der frühen DDR.* Berlin: Metropol, 2017.

Bosia, Michael J., and Meredith L. Weiss. "Political Homophobia in Comparative Perspective." In *Global Homophobia: States, Movements, and the Politics of Oppression*, edited by Meredith L. Weiss and Michael J. Bosia, 1–29. Champaign, IL: University of Illinois Press, 2013.

Boyd, Nan Alamilla. "Talking about Sex: Cheryl Gonzales and Rikki Streicher Tell Their Stories." In *Bodies of Evidence: The Practice of Queer Oral History*, edited by Nan Alamilla Boyd and Horacio N. Roque Ramirez, 95–112. Oxford: Oxford University Press, 2012.

Boyens, Armin. "Geteilter Friede: Anmerkungen Zur Friedensbewegung in den 80er Jahren." *Kirchliche Zeitgeschichte* 8, no. 2 (1995): 440–509.

Brock, Angela. "Producing the 'Socialist Personality'?: Socialisation, Education, and the Emergence of New Patterns of Behaviour." In *Power and Society in the GDR, 1961–1979: The 'Normalisation of Rule'?*, edited by Mary Fulbrook, 220–52. New York: Berghahn Books, 2009.

Broszat, Martin. *The Hitler State: The Foundation and Development of the Internal Structure of the Third Reich*. Translated by John W. Hinden. London: Longman, 1981.

Brown, Timothy Scott. "'1968' East and West: Divided Germany as a Case Study in Transnational History." *The American Historical Review* 114, no. 1 (2009): 69–96.

– *West Germany and the Global Sixties: The Anti-Authoritarian Revolt, 1962–1978.* Cambridge: Cambridge University Press, 2013.

Bruce, Gary. *The Firm: The Inside Story of the Stasi*. Oxford: Oxford University Press, 2010.

Brühöfener/Bruehoefener, Friederike. "Defining the West German Soldier: Military, Masculinity and Society in West Germany, 1945–1989." University of North Carolina, Chapel Hill, 2014.

– "Sex and the Soldier: The Discourse about the Moral Conduct of 'Bundeswehr' Soldiers and Officers in the Adenauer Era." *Central European History* 48, no. 4 (December 2015): 523–40.

– "Contested Masculinities: Debates about Homosexuality in the West German Bundeswehr in the 1960s and 1970s." In *Gendering Post-1945 German History: Entanglements*, edited by Karen Hagemann, Donna Harsch, and Friederike Brühöfener, 295–314. New York: Berghahn Books, 2019.

Bruns, Claudia. "The Politics of Masculinity in the (Homo-)Sexual Discourse (1880 to 1920)." *German History* 23, No. 3 (July 2005): 306–20.

– *Politik des Eros: Der Männerbund in Wissenschaft, Politik und Jugendkultur.* Köln: Böhlau, 2008.

Bruns, Manfred. "Schwulenpolitik in der alten Bundesrepublik." *LSVD Lesben- und Schwulenverband*. Accessed 16 May 2017. https://www.lsvd.de /homosexualitaet/rueckblicke/schwulenpolitik-in-der-brd.html.

Buck-Morss, Susan. *Dreamworld and Catastrophe: The Passing of Mass Utopia in East and West*. Cambridge, MA: MIT Press, 2002.

Bühner, Maria. "How to Remember Invisibility: Documentary Projects on Lesbians in the German Democratic Republic as Archives of Feelings." In *Sexual Culture in Germany in the 1970s: A Golden Age for Queers?*, edited by Janin Afken and Benedikt Wolf, 241–65. New York: Palgrave Macmillan, 2019.

– "The Rise of a New Consciousness: Lesbian Activism in East Germany in the 1980s." In *The Politics of Authenticity: Countercultures and Radical Movements across the Iron Curtain, 1968–1989*, edited by Joachim C. Häberlen, Mark Keck-Szajbel, and Kate Mahoney, 151–73. New York: Berghahn, 2018.

Bunzl, Matti. *Symptoms of Modernity: Jews and Queers in Late-Twentieth-Century Vienna*. Berkeley, CA: University of California Press, 2004.

Burleigh, Michael, and Wolfgang Wippermann. *The Racial State: Germany 1933–1945*. Cambridge: Cambridge University Press, 1991.

Canaday, Margot. *The Straight State: Sexuality and Citizenship in Twentieth-Century America*. Princeton, NJ: Princeton University Press, 2011.

Canning, Kathleen. "Class vs. Citizenship: Keywords in German Gender History." *Central European History* 37, no. 2 (2004): 225–44.

– "Claiming Citizenship: Suffrage and Subjectivity in Germany after World War I." In *Weimar Publics/Weimar Subjects: Rethinking the Political Culture of Germany in the 1920s*, edited by Kathleen Canning, Kerstin Barndt, and Kristin McGuire, 116–37. New York: Berghahn Books, 2010.

Centers for Disease Control and Prevention. "Estimates of New HIV Infections in the United States." August 2008. https://www.cdc.gov /nchhstp/newsroom/docs/fact-sheet-on-hiv-estimates.pdf.

Cervini, Eric. *The Deviant's War: The Homosexual vs. The United States of America*. New York: Farrar, Straus and Giroux, 2020.

Charles, Douglas M. "From Subversion to Obscenity: The FBI's Investigations of the Early Homophile Movement in the United States, 1953–1958." *Journal of the History of Sexuality* 19, no. 2 (May 2010): 262–87.

Chasin, Alexandra. *Selling Out: The Gay and Lesbian Movement Goes to Market*. New York: Palgrave Macmillan, 2000.

Chauncey, George. *Why Marriage: The History Shaping Today's Debate over Gay Equality*. New York: Basic Books, 2009.

Chin, Rita. *The Guest Worker Question in Postwar Germany*. Cambridge: Cambridge University Press, 2007.

– "Thinking Difference in Postwar Germany: Some Epistemological Obstacles around 'Race.'" In *Migration, Memory, and Diversity*, edited by Cornelia Wilhelm, 206–29. New York: Berghahn Books, 2016.

Chitty, Christopher. *Sexual Hegemony: Statecraft, Sodomy, and Capital in the Rise of the World System*. Durham, NC: Duke University Press, 2020.

Clech, Arthur. "Between the Labor Camp and the Clinic: *Tema* or the Shared Forms of Late Soviet Homosexual Subjectivities." *Slavic Review* 77, no. 1 (Spring 2018): 6–29.

Clowes, Edith W. *Russia on the Edge: Imagined Geographies and Post-Soviet Identity.* Ithaca, NY: Cornell University Press, 2011.

Collings, Justin. *Democracy's Guardians: A History of the German Federal Constitutional Court, 1951–2001.* Oxford: Oxford University Press, 2015.

Conrad, Kathryn A. *Locked in the Family Cell: Gender, Sexuality, and Political Agency in Irish National Discourse.* Madison, WI: University of Wisconsin Press, 2004.

Cook, Matt. *London and the Culture of Homosexuality 1885–1914.* Cambridge: Cambridge University Press, 2003.

Crahan, Margaret E., et al. *The Oxford Companion to Politics of the World.* Oxford: Oxford University Press, 2001.

Currah, Paisley. "The State." *Transgender Studies Quarterly* 1, no. 1–2 (2014): 197–200.

D'Amico, Francine. "Race-ing and Gendering the Military Closet." In *Gay Rights, Military Wrongs: Political Perspectives on Lesbians and Gays in the Military*, edited by Craig A. Rimmerman, 3–46. New York: Routledge, 1996.

Daub, Adrian. "From Maximin to Stonewall: Sexuality and the Afterlives of the George Circle." *The Germanic Review: Literature, Culture, Theory* 87 (2012): 19–34.

Daub, Adrian, and Samuel Huneke. "Die unsichtbare Tradition: Wo war die schwule Literatur Nachkriegsdeutschlands." *Merkur: Deutsche Zeitschrift für europäisches Denken* 70, no. 808 (September 2016): 88–93.

Davies, James C. "Toward a Theory of Revolution," *American Sociological Review* 27, no. 1 (1962): 5–19.

Davison, Kate. "The Sexual (Geo)Politics of Loyalty: Homosexuality and Emotion in Cold War Security Policy." In *From Sodomy Laws to Same-Sex Marriage: International Perspectives since 1789*, edited by Mark Seymour and Sean Brady, 123–40. London: Bloomsbury, 2019.

– "Cold War Pavlov: Homosexual Aversion Therapy in the 1960s." *History of the Human Sciences* (6 May 2020): 1–31.

DeBardeleben, Joan. "'The Future Has Already Begun': Environmental Damage and Protection in the GDR." *International Journal of Sociology* 18, no. 4 (1988): 144–64.

D'Emilio, John. "Capitalism and Gay Identity." In *Powers of Desire: The Politics of Sexuality*, edited by Ann Snitow, Christine Stansell, and Sharan Thompson, 100–13. New York: Monthly Review Press, 1983.

– "The Homosexual Menace: The Politics of Sexuality in Cold War America." In John D'Emilio, *Making Trouble: Essays on Gay History, Politics, and the University*, 57–73. New York: Routledge, 2013.

Dickinson, Edward Ross. "Policing Sex in Germany, 1882–1982: A Preliminary Statistical Analysis." *Journal of the History of Sexuality* 16, no. 2 (2007): 204–50.

– "Not So Scary after All? Reform in Imperial and Weimar Germany." *Central European History* 43, no. 1 (2010): 149–72.

– *Sex, Freedom, and Power in Imperial Germany, 1880–1914.* Cambridge: Cambridge University Press, 2016.

Diefendorf, Jeffry. *In the Wake of War: The Reconstruction of German Cities after World War II.* Oxford: Oxford University Press, 1993.

Dittberner, Jürgen. *FDP – Partei der zweiten Wahl: Ein Beitrag zur Geschichte der liberalen Partei und ihrer Funktionen im Parteiensystem der Bundesrepublik.* Berlin: Springer-Verlag, 2013.

Dobler, Jens. *Zwischen Duldungspolitik und Verbrechensbekämpfung: Homosexuellenverfolgung durch die Berliner Polizei von 1848 bis 1933.* Frankfurt am Main: Verlag für Polizeiwissenschaft, 2008.

– "Schwules Leben in Berlin zwischen 1945 und 1969 im Ost-West-Vergleich." In *Ohnmacht und Aufbegehren: Homosexuelle Männer in der frühen Bundesrepublik*, edited by Andreas Pretzel and Volker Weiß, 152–63. Hamburg: Männerschwarm, 2010.

– "Unzucht und Kuppelei: Lesbenverfolgung im Nationalsozialismus." In *Homophobie und Devianz: Weibliche und männliche Homosexualität im Nationalsozialismus*, edited by Insa Eschebach, 53–62. Berlin: Metropol, 2012.

Dose, Ralf. *Magnus Hirschfeld: The Origins of the Gay Liberation Movement.* Translated by Edward H. Willis. New York: Monthly Review Press, 2014.

Downs, Jim. *Stand by Me: The Forgotten History of Gay Liberation.* New York: Basic Books, 2016.

Duberman, Martin. *Has the Gay Movement Failed?* Berkeley, CA: University of California Press, 2018.

Duggan, Lisa. "The New Homonormativity: The Sexual Politics of Neoliberalism." In *Materializing Democracy: Toward a Revitalized Cultural Politics*, edited by Russ Castronovo and Dana D. Nelson, 175–94. Durham, NC: Duke University Press, 2002.

Duncan, Derek. *Reading and Writing Italian Homosexuality: A Case of Possible Difference.* Burlington, VT: Ashgate, 2006.

Dupont, Wannes. "The Two-Faced Fifties: Homosexuality and Penal Policy in the International Forensic Community, 1945–1965." *Journal of the History of Sexuality* 28, no. 3 (September 2019): 357–95.

Eckert, Astrid. *West Germany and the Iron Curtain: Environment, Economy, and Culture in the Borderlands.* Oxford: Oxford University Press, 2019.

Eisenbach, David. *Gay Power: An American Revolution.* Boston: Da Capo Press, 2007.

Eley, Geoff. *Forging Democracy: The History of the Left in Europe, 1850–2000.* Oxford: Oxford University Press, 2002.

Epstein, Catherine. "East Germany and Its History since 1989." *The Journal of Modern History* 75, no. 3 (2003): 634–61.

Eskridge, William, Jr. *Equality Practice: Civil Unions and the Future of Gay Rights.* New York: Routledge, 2002.

Espindola, Juan. *Transitional Justice after German Reunification: Exposing Unofficial Collaborators.* Cambridge: Cambridge University Press, 2015.

Evans, Jennifer V. "Bahnhof Boys: Policing Male Prostitution in Post-Nazi Berlin." *Journal of the History of Sexuality* 12, no. 4 (2003): 605–36.

– "The Moral State: Men, Mining, and Masculinity in the Early GDR." *German History* 23, no. 3 (1 July 2005): 367–9.

– "Decriminalization, Seduction, and 'Unnatural Desire' in East Germany." *Feminist Studies* 36, no. 3 (1 October 2010): 553–77.

– *Life among the Ruins: Cityscape and Sexuality in Cold War Berlin.* New York: Palgrave Macmillan, 2011.

– "Introduction: Why Queer German History?" *German History* 34, no. 3 (2016): 371–84.

Ewing, Christopher. "'Color Him Black': Erotic Representations and the Politics of Race in West German Homosexual Magazines, 1949–1974." *Sexuality and Culture* 21 (2017): 382–403.

– "'Toward a Better World for Gays': Race, Tourism, and the Internationalization of the West German Gay Rights Movement, 1969–1983." *GHI Forum* 61 (Fall 2017): 109–32.

– "The Color of Desire: Contradictions of Race, Sex, and Gay Rights in the Federal Republic of Germany." The Graduate Center, City University of New York, 2018.

Faderman, Lillian. *The Gay Revolution: The Story of the Struggle.* New York: Simon and Schuster, 2015.

Fenemore, Mark. *Sex, Thugs and Rock 'n' Roll: Teenage Rebels in Cold War East Germany.* New York: Berghahn Books, 2009.

– *Fighting the Cold War in Post-Blockade, Pre-Wall Berlin: Behind Enemy Lines.* New York: Routledge, 2019.

Fleischmann, Thomas. *Communist Pigs: An Animal History of East Germany's Rise and Fall.* Seattle, WA: University of Washington Press, 2020.

Florvil, Tiffany N. *Mobilizing Black Germany: Afro-German Women and the Making of a Transnational Movement.* Champaign, IL: University of Illinois Press, 2020.

Folland, Johanna. "Globalizing Socialist Health: Africa, East Germany, and the AIDS Crisis." University of Michigan, 2019.

Fone, Byrne. *Homophobia: A History.* New York: Henry Holt, 2001.

Foucault, Michel. *The History of Sexuality, Vol. 1: An Introduction.* Translated by Robert Hurley. New York: Vintage, 1990.

– *"Society Must Be Defended": Lectures at the Collège de France, 1975–1976.* Translated by Francois Ewald. New York: St Martin's Press, 2003.

Frackman, Kyle. "The East German Film *Coming Out* (1989) as Melancholic Reflection and Hopeful Projection." *German Life and Letters* 71, no. 4 (2018): 452–72.

– "Persistent Ambivalence: Theorizing Queer East German Studies." *Journal of Homosexuality* (9 April 2018): 669–89.

France, David. *How to Survive a Plague: The Story of How Activists and Scientists Tamed AIDS*. New York: Vintage Books, 2017.

Freedman, Estelle B. *Redefining Rape: Sexual Violence in the Era of Suffrage and Segregation*. Cambridge, MA: Harvard University Press, 2015.

Freeman, Elizabeth. "Introduction." *GLQ: A Journal of Lesbian and Gay Studies* 13, no. 2–3 (2007): 159–76.

Freeman, Richard. "Governing the Voluntary Sector Response to AIDS: A Comparative Study of the UK and Germany." *Voluntas: International Journal of Voluntary and Nonprofit Organizations* 3, no. 1 (1992): 29–47.

Frei, Norbert. *Adenauer's Germany and the Nazi Past: The Politics of Amnesty and Integration*. Translated by Joel Golb. New York: Columbia University Press, 2002.

Freud, Sigmund. *Civilization and Its Discontents*. Translated by Joan Riviere. Eastford, CT: Martinto Publishing, 2011.

Freund, Alexander. "Oral History as Process-generated Data." *Historical Social Research* 34, no. 1 (2009): 24–48.

Fulbrook, Mary. "The Limits of Totalitarianism: God, State and Society in the GDR." *Transactions of the Royal Historical Society* 7 (1997): 25–52.

– *Anatomy of a Dictatorship: Inside the GDR, 1949–1989*. Oxford: Oxford University Press, 1998.

– *The People's State*. New Haven, CT: Yale University Press, 2008.

– "The Concept of 'Normalisation' and the GDR in Comparative Perspective." In *Power and Society in the GDR, 1961–1979: The "Normalisation of Rule"?*, edited by Mary Fulbrook, 1–32. New York: Berghahn Books, 2013.

– *Reckonings: Legacies of Nazi Persecution and the Quest for Justice*. Oxford: Oxford University Press, 2019.

Gaddis, John Lewis. "Intelligence, Espionage, and Cold War Origins." *Diplomatic History* 13, no. 2 (1989): 191–212.

Gade, Paul A., David R. Segal, and Edgar M. Johnson. "The Experience of Foreign Militaries." In *Out in Force: Sexual Orientation and the Military*, edited by Gregory M. Herek, Jared B. Jobe, and Ralph M Carney, 106–30. Chicago: University of Chicago Press, 1996.

Gammerl, Benno. "Erinnerte Liebe. Was kann eine Oral History zur Geschichte der Gefühle und der Homosexualitäten beitragen?" *Geschichte und Gesellschaft* 35, no. 2 (April–June 2009): 314–45.

– "Affecting Legal Change: How Laws Impacted Same-Sex Feelings and Relationships in West Germany since the 1950s." In *From Sodomy Laws to Same-Sex Marriage: International Perspectives since 1789*, edited by Mark Seymour and Sean Brady, 109–21. London: Bloomsbury Academic, 2019.

– *anders fühlen: Schwules und lesbisches Leben in der Bundesrepublik: Eine Emotionsgeschichte*. Munich: Hanser, 2021.

Gaus, Günter. *Wo Deutschland liegt: Eine Ortsbestimmung*. Hamburg: Hoffmann & Campe, 1983.

Gassert, Philipp, and Alan E. Steinweis. *Coping with the Nazi Past: West German Debates on Nazism and Generational Conflict, 1955–1975*. New York: Berghahn Books, 2007.

Gellately, Robert. "Denunciations in Twentieth-Century Germany: Aspects of Self-Policing in the Third Reich and the German Democratic Republic." *The Journal of Modern History* 68 (December 1996): 931–67.

Gentile, Patrizia. "Queering Subversives in Cold War Canada." In *Gender, Sexuality, and the Cold War: A Global Perspective*, edited by Philip E. Muehlenbeck, 53–67. Nashville, TN: Vanderbilt University Press, 2017.

Ghodsee, Kristen R. *Why Women Have Better Sex under Socialism: And Other Arguments for Economic Independence*. New York: Public Affairs, 2018.

Giersdorf, Jens Richard. "Why Does Charlotte von Mahlsdorf Curtsy? Representations of National Queerness in a Transvestite Hero." *GLQ* 12, no. 2 (2006): 171–96.

Gieseke, Jens. *The History of the Stasi: East Germany's Secret Police, 1945–1990*. New York: Berghahn Books, 2014.

Giles, Geoffrey. "'The Most Unkindest Cut of All': Castration, Homosexuality and Nazi Justice." *Journal of Contemporary History* 27, no. 1 (January 1992): 41–61.

– "The Institutionalization of Homosexual Panic in the Third Reich." In *Social Outsiders in Nazi Germany*, edited by Robert Gellately and Nathan Stolzfus, 223–55. Princeton, NJ: Princeton University Press, 2001.

– "The Denial of Homosexuality: Same-Sex Incidents in Himmler's SS and Police." *Journal of the History of Sexuality* 11, no. 1/2 (2002): 256–90.

Gilroy, Paul. *Postcolonial Melancholia*. New York: Columbia University Press, 2005.

Glass, James. *Life Unworthy of Life: Racial Phobia and Mass Murder in Hitler's Germany*. New York: Basic Books, 1999.

Glienke, Stephan Alexander, Volker Paulmann, and Joachim Perels, eds. *Erfolgsgeschichte Bundesrepublik?: Die Nachkriegsgesellschaft im langen Schatten des Nationalsozialismus*. Göttingen: Wallstein Verlag, 2008.

Gordon, Mel. *Voluptuous Panic: The Erotic World of Weimar Berlin*. Minneapolis, MN: Feral House, 2008.

Granieri, Ronald J. "Politics in C Minor: The CDU/CSU between Germany and Europe since the Secular Sixties." *Central European History* 42, no. 1 (2009): 1–32.

Grau, Günter. "Erpressbar und Tendenziell Konspirative: Die 'Bearbeitung' von Lesben und Schwulen durch das MfS." *Weibblick* 16 (1994): 21–4.

– "Return of the Past." *Journal of Homosexuality* 37, no. 4 (August 19, 1999): 1–21.

– "Liberalisierung und Repression: Zur Strafrechtsdiskussion zum §175 in der DDR." *Zeitschrift für Sexualforschung* 15 (2002): 323–40.

Grau, Günter, and Rüdiger Lautmann. *Lexikon zur Homosexuellenverfolgung 1933–1945: Institutionen-Kompetenzen-Betätigungsfelder.* Münster: LIT Verlag, 2011.

Grau, Günter, and Claudia Schoppmann, eds. *Hidden Holocaust? Gay and Lesbian Persecution in Germany 1933–1945.* New York: Routledge, 1995.

Grdesic, Marko. "Spatial Patterns of Thermidor: Protest and Voting in East Germany's Revolution, 1989–1990." *German Politics and Society* 34, no. 2 (2016): 17–35.

Griffiths, Craig. "Between Triumph and Myth: Gay Heroes and Navigating the schwule Erfolgsgeschichte." *helden. heroes. héros.* (2014): 54–60.

– "Konkurrierende Pfade der Emanzipation: Der Tuntenstreit (1973–1975) und die Frage des 'respektablen Auftretens.'" In *Rosa Radikale: Die Schwulenbewegung der 1970er Jahre,* edited by Andreas Pretzel and Volker Weiß, 143–59. Hamburg: Männerschwarm Verlag, 2012.

– "Sex, Shame and West German Gay Liberation." *German History* 34, no. 3 (2016): 445–67.

– *The Ambivalence of Gay Liberation: Male Homosexual Politics in 1970s West Germany.* Oxford: Oxford University Press, 2021.

Großbölting, Thomas. "Why Is There No Christian Right in Germany? German Conservative Christians and the Invention of a Silent Majority in the 1970s." In *Inventing the Silent Majority in Western Europe and the United States: Conservatism in the 1960s and 1970s,* edited by Anna von der Goltz and Britta Waldschmidt-Nelson, 210–26. Cambridge: Cambridge University Press, 2017.

Grossmann, Atina. *Jews, Germans, and Allies: Close Encounters in Occupied Germany.* Princeton, NJ: Princeton University Press, 2007.

Grotum, Thomas. *Die Halbstarken: Zur Geschichte einer Jugendkultur der 50er Jahre.* Frankfurt am Main: Campus, 1994.

Haeberle, Erwin J. "Swastika, Pink Triangle and Yellow Star: The Destruction of Sexology and the Persecution of Homosexuals in Nazi Germany." *The Journal of Sex Research* 17, no. 3 (1 August 1981): 270–87.

Hájková, Anna. *Menschen ohne Geschichte sind Staub: Homophobie und Holocaust.* Göttingen: Wallstein, 2021.

Hakkarainen, Petri. *A State of Peace in Europe: West Germany and the CSCE, 1966–1975.* New York: Berghahn Books, 2011.

Hall, Claire M. "An Army of Spies? The Gestapo Spy Network 1933–1945." *Journal of Contemporary History* 44, no. 2 (April 2009): 247–65.

Halperin, David. *How to Be Gay*. Cambridge, MA: Harvard University Press, 2012.

Hammerich, Helmut R. "Joachim Krase (1925–1988): Ein 'unscheinbarer grauer Oberst': Der MAD-Vize als IM der Stasi." In *Spione und Nachrichtenhändler: Geheimdienst-Karrieren in Deutschland 1939–1989*, edited by Helmut Müller-Enbergs and Armin Wagner, 272–301. Berlin: Ch. Links Verlag, 2016.

Hancock, Eleanor. "'Only the Real, the True, the Masculine Held Its Value': Ernst Röhm, Masculinity, and Male Homosexuality." *Journal of the History of Sexuality* 8, no. 4 (1998): 616–41.

– "The Purge of the SA Reconsidered: 'An Old Putschist Trick'?" *Central European History* 44, no. 4 (2011): 669–83.

Hansen, Will. "The Cold War and the Homophile, 1953–1963." *Australasian Journal of American Studies* 38, no. 1 (July 2019): 79–96.

Haritaworn, Jin. "Queer Injuries: The Racial Politics of 'Homophobic Hate Crime' in Germany." *Social Justice* 37, no. 1 (2010–11): 69–89.

Harsch, Donna. "Society, the State, and Abortion in East Germany, 1950–1972." *The American Historical Review* 102, no. 1 (1997): 53–84.

– *Revenge of the Domestic: Women, the Family, and Communism in the German Democratic Republic*. Princeton, NJ: Princeton University Press, 2006.

– "Between State Policy and Private Sphere: Women in the GDR in the 1960s and 1970s." *Clio: Women, Gender, History* 41 (2015): 85–105.

Haunss, Sebastian. "Von der Sexuellen Befreiung zur Normalität: Das Ende der zweiten deutschen Schwulenbewegung." In *Rosa Radikale: Die Schwulenbewegung der 1970er Jahre*, edited by Andreas Pretzel and Volker Weiß, 199–212. Hamburg: Männerschwarm Verlag, 2012.

Haus, Sebastian. "Risky Sex – Risky Language. HIV/AIDS and the West German Gay Scene in the 1980s." *Historical Social Research / Historische Sozialforschung* 41, no. 1 (155) (2016): 111–34.

Haynes, John Earl, and Harvey Klehr. *Early Cold War Spies: The Espionage Trials That Shaped American Politics*. Cambridge: Cambridge University Press, 2006.

Healey, Dan. *Homosexual Desire in Revolutionary Russia: The Regulation of Sexual and Gender Dissent*. Chicago: University of Chicago Press, 2001.

– *Russian Homophobia from Stalin to Sochi*. London: Bloomsbury Academic, 2017.

Health Protection Agency. "HIV in the United Kingdom: 2012 Report." November 2012. https://webarchive.nationalarchives.gov.uk/2014071411 3035/http://www.hpa.org.uk/webc/HPAwebFile/HPAweb_C/1317137 200016.

Heineman, Elizabeth. *What Difference Does a Husband Make? Women and Marital Status in Nazi and Postwar Germany*. Berkeley, CA: University of California Press, 2003.

– *Before Porn Was Legal: The Erotica Empire of Beate Uhse*. Chicago: University of Chicago Press, 2011.

Hekma, Gert, Harry Oosterhuis, and James Steakley. "Leftist Sexual Politics and Homosexuality: A Historical Overview." *Journal of Homosexuality* 29, no. 2/3 (1995): 1–40.

Hensel, Alexander, Tobias Neef, and Robert Pausch. "Von 'Knabenliebhabern' und 'Power-Pädos': Zur Entstehung und Entwicklung der westdeutschen Pädophilen-Bewegung." In *Die Grünen und die Pädosexualität: Eine bundesdeutsche Geschichte*, edited by Franz Walter, Stephan Klecha, and Alexander Hensel, 136–59. Göttingen: Vandenhoeck & Ruprecht, 2015.

Henze, Patrick (Patsy L'Amour laLove). "'Die Lückenlose Kette Zwischen Politik und Schwul-sein Aufzeigen': Aktivismus und Debatten in der Homosexuellen Aktion Westberlin Zwischen 1971 und 1973." In *Rosa Radikale: Die Schwulenbewegung der 1970er Jahre*, edited by Andreas Pretzel and Volker Weiß, 124–42. Hamburg: Männerschwarm Verlag, 2012.

– "Perversions of Society: Rosa von Praunheim and Martin Dannecker's Film *It Is Not the Homosexual Who Is Perverse but the Society in Which He Lives* (1971) as the Initiation of the Golden Age of the Radical Left Gay Movement in West Germany." In *Sexual Culture in Germany in the 1970s: A Golden Age for Queers?*, edited by Janin Afken and Benedikt Wolf, 89–118. New York: Palgrave Macmillan, 2019.

– *Schwule Emanzipation und ihre Konflikte: Zur westdeutschen Schwulenbewegung der 1970er*. Berlin: Quer Verlag, 2019.

Hepburn, Allan. *Intrigue: Espionage and Culture*. New Haven, CT: Yale University Press, 2014.

Herf, Jeffrey. *Divided Memory: The Nazi Past in the Two Germanys*. Cambridge, MA: Harvard University Press, 2013.

Herring, Scott. "Out of the Closets, into the Woods: 'RFD,' 'Country Women,' and the Post-Stonewall Emergence of Queer Anti-Urbanism." *American Quarterly* 59, no. 2 (2007): 341–72.

Herzog, Dagmar. "Sexuality, Memory, Morality." *History and Memory* 17, no. 1–2 (2005): 238–66.

– "Between Coitus and Commodification: Young West German Women and the Impact of the Pill." In *Between Marx and Coca-Cola: Youth Cultures in Changing European Societies, 1960–1980*, edited by Axel Schildt and Detlef Siegfried, 261–86. New York: Berghahn Books, 2006.

– *Sex after Fascism: Memory and Morality in Twentieth-Century Germany*. Princeton, NJ: Princeton University Press, 2007.

– "Syncopated Sex: Transforming European Sexual Cultures." *The American Historical Review* 114, no. 5 (2009): 1287–308.

Hillhouse, Raelynn J. "Out of the Closet behind the Wall: Sexual Politics and Social Change in the GDR." *Slavic Review* 49, no. 4 (1990): 585–96.

Hirshman, Linda. *Victory: The Triumphant Gay Revolution.* New York: Harper, 2012.

Hobson, Emily K. *Lavender and Red: Liberation and Solidarity in the Gay and Lesbian Left.* Berkeley, CA: University of California Press, 2016.

Hochscherf, Tobias, Christoph Laucht, and Andrew Plowman. "Introduction." In *Divided, but Not Disconnected: German Experiences of the Cold War,* edited by Tobias Hochscherf, Christoph Laucht, and Andrew Plowman, 1–10. New York: Berghahn Books, 2010.

Hodges, Andrew. *Alan Turing: The Enigma.* Princeton, NJ: Princeton University Press, 2014.

Hoffschildt, Rainer. "140.000 Verurteilungen nach, '§175.'" *Invertito: Jahrbuch für die Geschichte der Homosexualitäten* 4 (2002): 140–9.

Holy, Michael. "Jenseits von Stonewall – Rückblicke auf die Schwulenbewegung in der BRD 1969–1980." In *Rosa Radikale: Die Schwulenbewegung der 1970er Jahre,* edited by Andreas Pretzel and Volker Weiß, 39–79. Hamburg: Männerschwarm Verlag, 2012.

Hopkins, Michael F. "Continuing Debate and New Approaches in Cold War History." *The Historical Journal* 50, no. 4 (2007): 913–34.

Houlbrook, Matt. *Queer London: Perils and Pleasures in the Sexual Metropolis, 1918–1957.* Chicago: University of Chicago Press, 2006.

House, Jim, and Neil MacMaster. *Paris 1961: Algerians, State Terror, and Memory.* Oxford: Oxford University Press, 2006.

Huff, Tobias. "Über die Umweltpolitik der DDR: Konzepte, Strukturen, Versagen." *Geschichte und Gesellschaft* 40, no. 4 (2014): 523–54.

Hull, Isabel. *The Entourage of Kaiser Wilhelm II, 1888–1918.* Cambridge: Cambridge University Press, 2004.

Huneke, Erik. "Sex, Sentiment, and Socialism: Relationship Counseling in the GDR in the Wake of the 1965 Family Law Code." In *After the History of Sexuality: German Genealogies with and beyond Foucault,* edited by Scott Spector, Dagmar Herzog, and Helmut Puff, 231–47. New York: Berghahn Books, 2012.

– "Morality, Law, and the Socialist Sexual Self in the German Democratic Republic, 1945–1972." University of Michigan, 2013.

Huneke, Samuel Clowes. "The Reception of Homosexuality in Klaus Mann's Weimar Era Works." *Monatshefte für deutschsprachige Literatur und Kultur* 105, no. 1 (March 2013): 86–100.

– "The Duplicity of Tolerance: Lesbian Experiences in Nazi Berlin." *Journal of Contemporary History* 54, no.1 (3 April 2017): 30–59.

– "Queering the Vote." *Los Angeles Review of Books,* 27 January 2019. https://lareviewofbooks.org/article/queering-the-vote/.

– "Death Wish: Suicide and Stereotype in the Gay Discourses of Imperial and Weimar Germany." *New German Critique* 46, no. 1 (February 2019): 127–67.

– "An End to Totalitarianism." *Boston Review*, 16 April 2020. http:// bostonreview.net/politics/samuel-clowes-huneke-end-totalitarianism.

– "Die Grenzen der Homophobie: Lesbischsein unter nationalsozialistischer Herrschaft." In *Homosexuelle in Deutschland 1933–1945: Beiträge zu Alltag, Stigmatisierung und Verfolgung*, edited by Alexander Zinn, 117–30. Göttingen: V&R Unipress, 2020.

– "Heterogeneous Persecution: Lesbianism and the Nazi State." *Central European History* 54, no. 2 (June 2021): 297–325.

Ireland, Patrick R. "Socialism, Unification Policy and the Rise of Racism in Eastern Germany." *International Migration Review* 31, no. 3 (1 October 1997): 541–68.

Jackson, Julian. *Living in Arcadia: Homosexuality, Politics, and Morality in France from the Liberation to AIDS*. Chicago: University of Chicago Press, 2005.

Jarausch, Konrad. "Care and Coercion: The GDR as Welfare Dictatorship." In *Dictatorship as Experience: Towards a Socio-cultural History of the GDR*, edited by Konrad Jarausch, 42–72. New York: Berghahn Books, 1999.

Jellonnek, Burkhard. *Homosexuelle unter dem Hakenkreuz*. Paderborn: Ferdinand Schöningh, 1990.

Jensen, Erik N. "The Pink Triangle and Political Consciousness: Gays, Lesbians, and the Memory of Nazi Persecution." *Journal of the History of Sexuality* 11, no. 1/2 (2002): 319–49.

Jeppsson, Anders. "How East Germany Fabricated the Myth of HIV Being Man-Made." *Journal of the International Association of Providers of AIDS Care* 16, no. 6 (2017): 519–22.

Jesse, Eckhard. *Diktaturen in Deutschland: Diagnosen und Analysen*. Baden-Baden: Nomos, 2008.

Johnson, David K. *The Lavender Scare: The Cold War Persecution of Gays and Lesbians in the Federal Government*. Chicago: University of Chicago Press, 2009.

– "America's Cold War Empire: Exporting the Lavender Scare." In *Global Homophobia: States, Movements, and the Politics of Oppression*, edited by Meredith L. Weiss and Michael J. Bosia, 55–74. Champaign, IL: University of Illinois Press, 2013.

– *Buying Gay: How Physique Entrepreneurs Sparked a Movement*. New York: Columbia University Press, 2019.

Johnson, Eric. *Nazi Terror: The Gestapo, Jews, and Ordinary Germans*. New York: Basic Books, 1999.

Jones, James W. "Discourses on and of AIDS in West Germany, 1986–90." *Journal of the History of Sexuality* 2, no. 3 (1992): 439–68.

Jones, Merrill E. "Origins of the East German Environmental Movement." *German Studies Review* 16, no. 2 (1993): 235–64.

Judaken, Jonathan. "Introduction." *The American Historical Review* 123, no. 4 (October 2018): 1122–38.

Judt, Tony. *Postwar: A History of Europe since 1945*. New York: Penguin Books, 2006.

– *Reappraisals: Reflections on the Forgotten Twentieth Century*. New York: Penguin, 2008.

– *The Memory Chalet*. New York: Penguin Books, 2011.

Kalb, Martin. *Coming of Age: Constructing and Controlling Youth in Munich, 1942–1973*. New York: Berghahn Books, 2020.

Keating, Christine (Cricket). "Conclusion: On the Interplay of State Homophobia and Homoprotectionism." In *Global Homophobia: States, Movements, and the Politics of Oppression*, edited by Meredith L. Weiss and Michael J. Bosia, 246–54. Champaign, IL: University of Illinois Press, 2013.

Keilson-Lauritz, Marita. *Von der Liebe die Freundschaft heisst: Zur Homoerotik im Werk Stefan Georges*. Berlin: Rosa Winkel, 1987.

– *Die Geschichte der eigenen Geschichte: Literatur und Literaturkritik in den Anfängen der Schwulenbewegung am Beispiel des Jahrbuchs für sexuelle Zwischenstufen und der Zeitschrift Der Eigene*. Berlin: Rosa Winkel, 1997.

– *Kentaurenliebe: Seitenwege der Männerliebe im 20. Jahrhundert: Essays 1995–2010*. Hamburg: Männerschwarm, 2013.

Kennedy, Hubert. *The Ideal Gay Man: The Story of Der Kreis*. New York: Harrington Park Press, 1999.

Kershaw, Ian. *The Nazi Dictatorship: Problems and Perspectives of Interpretation*. London: Bloomsbury, 2015.

Kinsman, Gary, and Patrizia Gentile. *The Canadian War on Queers: National Security as Sexual Regulation*. Vancouver: University of British Columbia Press, 2010.

Kleßmann, Christoph. *Die doppelte Staatsgründung: Deutsche Geschichte, 1945–1955*. Bonn: Bundeszentrale für politische Bildung, 1991.

– *Zwei Staaten, eine Nation: Deutsche Geschichte, 1955–1970*. Bonn: Bundeszentrale für politische Bildung, 1997.

Klimke, M., and J. Scharloth. *1968 in Europe: A History of Protest and Activism, 1956–1977*. Berlin: Springer, 2008.

– *1968. Handbuch zur Kultur- und Mediengeschichte der Studentenbewegung*. Berlin: Springer, 2016.

Knuth, Matthias. "Active Labor Market Policy and German Reunification: The Role of Employment and Training Companies." In *Negotiating the New Germany: Can Social Partnership Survive?*, edited by Lowell Turner, 69–86. Ithaca, NY: ILR Press, 1997.

Kocka, Jürgen. "Eine Durchherrschte Gesellschaft." In *Sozialgeschichte der DDR*, edited by Hartmut Kaelble, Jürgen Kocka, and Hartmut Zwahr, 547–53. Stuttgart: Klett-Cotta, 1994.

Koehler, John O. *Stasi: The Untold Story of the East German Secret Police.* London: Hachette UK, 2008.

Kokula, Ilse. "Zur Situation lesbischer Frauen während des NS-Zeit." *Beiträge zur feministischen Theorie und Praxis* 12, no. 25/26 (1989): 29–36.

Koonz, Claudia. *Mothers in the Fatherland: Women, the Family and Nazi Politics.* New York: Routledge, 2013.

Koselleck, Reinhart. *Preussen Zwischen Reform und Revolution: Allgemeines Landrecht Verwaltung und Soziale Bowegung von 1791 bis 1848.* Stuttgart: Klett-Cotta, 1967.

Kraushaar, Elmar. "Höhenflug und Absturz: Von Homolulu am Main nach Bonn in die Beethoven-Halle." In *Rosa Radikale: Die Schwulenbewegung der 1970er Jahre,* edited by Andreas Pretzel and Volker Weiß, 80–90. Berlin: Rosa Winkel, 2012.

Kühn, Monika. "The Lesbian Action Centre, West Berlin: The Formation of Group Solidarity." In *German Feminism,* edited by Edith Hoshino Altbach, Jeannette Clausen, Dagmar Schultz, and Naomi Stephan, 311–14. Albany, NY: State University of New York Press, 1984.

Kupferberg, Feiwel. *The Break-up of Communism in East Germany and Eastern Europe.* Berlin: Springer, 2016.

Kurme, Sebastian. *Halbstarke: Jugendprotest in den 1950er Jahren in Deutschland und den USA.* Frankfurt am Main: Campus, 2006.

Kurthen, Hermann, Werner Bermann, Rainer Erb, and Wilfried Schubarth. "Xenophobia among East German Youth." In *Antisemitism and Xenophobia in Germany after Unification,* 143–58. Oxford: Oxford University Press, 1997.

Lautmann, Rüdiger, Winfried Grikschat, and Egbert Schmidt. "Der rosa Winkel in den nationalsozialistischen Konzentrationslagern." In *Seminar: Gesellschaft und Homosexualität,* edited by Rüdiger Lautmann, 325–65. Frankfurt am Main: Suhrkamp, 1977.

Layne, Priscilla. "*Halbstarke* and Rowdys: Consumerism, Youth Rebellion, and Gender in the Postwar Cinema of the Two Germanys." *Central European History* 53 (2020): 432–52.

Leavy, Patricia. *Oral History: Understanding Qualitative Research.* Oxford: Oxford University Press, 2011.

Leidinger, Christiane. "Lesbische Existenz 1945–1969: Aspekte der Erforschung gesellschaftlicher Ausgrenzung und Diskriminierung lesbischer Frauen mit Schwerpunkt auf Lebenssituationen, Diskriminierungs- und Emanzipationserfahrungen in der frühen Bundesrepublik." Berlin: Landesstelle für Gleichbehandlung gegen Diskriminierung, 2015.

Lemke, Jürgen. "Gay and Lesbian Life in East German Society before and after 1989." Translated by Judith Orban. *The Oral History Review* 21, no. 2 (1993): 31–40.

Leng, Kirsten. *Sexual Politics and Feminist Science: Women Sexologists in Germany, 1900–1933*. Ithaca, NY: Signale, 2018.

Lewis, Alison. "En-Gendering Remembrance: Memory, Gender and Informers for the Stasi." *New German Critique* no. 86 (2002): 103–34.

Lipstadt, Deborah E. *The Eichmann Trial*. Schocken, 2011.

Lorenz, Gottfried. "Hamburg als Homosexuellenhauptstadt der 1950er Jahre: Die Homophilen-Szene und ihre Unterstützer für die Abschaffung des §175 STGB." In *Ohnmacht und Aufbegehren: Homosexuelle Männer in der frühen Bundesrepublik*, edited by Andreas Pretzel and Volker Weiß, 117–51. Hamburg: Männerschwarm, 2010.

Lorenz, Gottfried, and Ulf Bollmann. "Die Rechtsprechung nach §§175 und 175a StGB in der Freien und Hansestadt Hamburg im Spiegel der Haupt- und Vorverfahrensregister der Staatsanwaltschaft der Jahre 1948 bis 1969." In *Queer | Gender | Historiographie: Aktuelle Tendenzen und Projekte*, edited by Norbert Finzsch and Marcus Velke, 253–79. Münster: LIT Verlag, 2016.

Love, Heather. *Feeling Backward: Loss and the Politics of Queer History*. Cambridge, MA: Harvard University Press, 2009.

Lownie, Andrew. *Stalin's Englishman: Guy Burgess, the Cold War, and the Cambridge Spy Ring*. New York: St Martin's Press, 2016.

Lüdtke, Alf. "Organizational Order or Eigensinn? Workers' Privacy and Workers' Politics in Imperial Germany." In *Rites of Power: Symbolism, Ritual, and Politics since the Middle Ages*, edited by Sean Wilentz, 303–34. Philadelphia, PA: University of Pennsylvania Press, 1985.

– *Eigen-Sinn: Fabrikalltag, Arbeitererfahrungen und Politik vom Kaiserreich bis in den Faschismus*. Hamburg: Ergebnisse, 1993.

Lybeck, Marti. *Desiring Emancipation: New Women and Homosexuality in Germany, 1890–1933*. Albany, NY: State University of New York Press, 2014.

Maier, Sascha. "Homosexualität in der Nachkriegszeit: Kastriert, der Liebe wegen." *Stuttgarter-Zeitung*, 25 January 2017.

Major, Patrick. *Behind the Berlin Wall: East Germany and the Frontiers of Power*. Oxford: Oxford University Press, 2009.

Marcus, Ulrich, and Anne Starker. "HIV and AIDS." *Federal Health Reporting*. July 2006. https://www.gbe-bund.de/pdf/hiv_aids_english.pdf.

Marhoefer, Laurie. "Degeneration, Sexual Freedom, and the Politics of the Weimar Republic, 1918–1933." *German Studies Review* 34, no. 3 (2011): 529–49.

– *Sex and the Weimar Republic: German Homosexual Emancipation and the Rise of the Nazis*. Toronto: University of Toronto Press, 2015.

– "Lesbianism, Transvestitism, and the Nazi State: A Microhistory of a Gestapo Investigation, 1939–1943." *American Historical Review* 121, no. 4 (October 2016): 1167–95.

Martel, Frédéric. *The Pink and the Black: Homosexuals in France since 1968*. Translated by Jane Marie Todd. Palo Alto, CA: Stanford University Press, 2000.

McCloskey, Deirdre Nansen. *Why Liberalism Works: How True Liberal Values Produce a Freer, More Equal, Prosperous World for All*. New Haven, CT: Yale University Press, 2019.

McKay, Richard. "'Patient Zero': The Absence of a Patient's View of the Early North American AIDS Epidemic." *Bulletin of the History of Medicine* 88, no. 1 (Spring 2014): 161–94.

McKnight, David. *Espionage and the Roots of the Cold War: The Conspiratorial Heritage*. New York: Routledge, 2001.

McLellan, Josie. *Love in the Time of Communism: Intimacy and Sexuality in the GDR*. Cambridge: Cambridge University Press, 2011.

– "Glad to Be Gay behind the Wall: Gay and Lesbian Activism in 1970s East Germany." *History Workshop Journal*, no. 74 (2012): 105–30.

– "From Private Photography to Mass Circulation: The Queering of East German Visual Culture, 1968–1989." *Central European History* 48, no. 3 (September 2015): 405–23.

Meeker, Martin. *Contacts Desired: Gay and Lesbian Communications and Community, 1940s-1970s*. Chicago: University of Chicago Press, 2006.

Merkel, Ina. "Another Kind of Woman." Translated by Diane Forman Kent. *German Politics & Society* no. 24/25 (Winter 1991/1992): 1–9.

Merkl, Peter H. "Adenauer's Heirs Reclaim Power: The CDU and CSU in 1980–83." In *Germany at the Polls: The Bundestag Elections of the 1980s*, edited by Karl H. Cerny, 58–87. Durham, NC: Duke University Press, 1990.

– *German Unification in the European Context*. University Park, PA: Penn State Press, 2010.

Mewes, Horst. "A Brief History of the German Green Party." In *The German Greens: Paradox between Movement and Party*, edited by Margit Mayer and John Ely, 29–48. Philadelphia, PA: Temple University Press, 1998.

Micheler, Stefan. "'… und verbleibt weiter in Sicherungsverwahrung' – Kontinuitäten der Verfolgung Männer begehrender Männer in Hamburg 1945–1949." In *Ohnmacht und Aufbegehren: Homosexuelle Männer in der frühen Bundesrepublik*, edited by Andreas Pretzel and Volker Weiß, 62–90. Hamburg: Männerschwarm Verlag, 2010.

Mielchen, Stefan. "Wider die Norm: Die Lebensformenpolitik des Bundesverbandes Homosexualität 1986–1997." In *Zwischen Autonomie und Integration: Schwule Politik und Schwulenbewegung in den 1980er und 1990er Jahren*, edited by Andreas Pretzel and Volker Weiß, 118–35. Hamburg: Männerschwarm, 2013.

Milder, Stephen, and Konrad H. Jarausch. "Renewing Democracy: The Rise of Green Politics in West Germany." *German Politics & Society* 33, no. 4 (Winter 2015): 3–24.

Miller, Barbara. *The Stasi Files Unveiled: Guilt and Compliance in a Unified Germany*. New Brunswick, NJ: Transaction Publishers, 1999.

Moeller, Robert G. "'The Homosexual Man Is a "Man," the Homosexual Woman Is a "Woman"': Sex, Society, and the Law in Postwar West Germany." *Journal of the History of Sexuality* 4, no. 3 (1994): 395–429.

– *Protecting Motherhood: Women and the Family in the Politics of Postwar West Germany.* Berkeley, CA: University of California Press, 1996.

– *War Stories: The Search for a Usable Past in the Federal Republic of Germany.* Berkeley, CA: University of California Press, 2001.

– "Private Acts, Public Anxieties, and the Fight to Decriminalize Male Homosexuality in West Germany." *Feminist Studies* 36, no. 3 (2010): 528–52.

Moore, Robert I. *The Formation of a Persecuting Society: Authority and Deviance in Western Europe, 950–1250.* Hoboken, NJ: Wiley-Blackwell, 1987.

Müller, Jürgen. *Ausgrenzung der Homosexuellen aus der 'Volksgemeinschaft': Die Verfolgung von Homosexuellen in Köln, 1933–1945.* Köln: Emons, 2003.

Murphy, David E., Sergei A Kondrashev, and George Bailey. *Battleground Berlin: CIA vs. KGB in the Cold War.* New Haven, CT: Yale University Press, 1999.

Murphy, Kevin. "Gay Was Good: Progress, Homonormativity, and Oral History." In *Queer Twin Cities*, edited by Kevin P. Murphy, Jennifer L. Pierce, and Larry Knopp, 305–18. Minneapolis, MN: University of Minnesota Press, 2010.

Myers, JoAnne. *Historical Dictionary of the Lesbian and Gay Liberation Movements.* Lanham, MD: Scarecrow Press, 2013.

Newsome, W. Jake. "Homosexuals after the Holocaust: Sexual Citizenship and the Politics of Memory in Germany and the United States, 1945–2008." State University of New York, 2016.

Norton, Robert Edward. *Secret Germany: Stefan George and His Circle.* Ithaca, NY: Cornell University Press, 2002.

O'Dwyer, Conor. *Coming Out of Communism: The Emergence of LGBT Activism in Eastern Europe.* New York: New York University Press, 2018.

Olick, Jeffrey K. *The Sins of the Fathers: Germany, Memory, Method.* Chicago: University of Chicago Press, 2016.

Oosterhuis, Harry. "Eros and Male Bonding in Society: Introduction." In: *Homosexuality and Male Bonding in Pre-Nazi Germany: Original Transcripts from* Der Eigene, *the First Gay Journal in the World*, edited by Harry Oosterhuis, translated by Hubert Kennedy, 119–26. Philadelphia, PA: Haworth Press, 1991.

– "Political Issues and the Rise of Nazism: Introduction." In *Homosexuality and Male Bonding in Pre-Nazi Germany: Original Transcripts from* Der Eigene, *the First Gay Journal in the World*, edited by Harry Oosterhuis, translated by Hubert Kennedy, 183–92. Philadelphia, PA: Haworth Press, 1991.

– "Medicine, Male Bonding and Homosexuality in Nazi Germany." *Journal of Contemporary History* 32, no. 2 (1 April 1997): 187–205.

– *Stepchildren of Nature: Krafft-Ebing, Psychiatry, and the Making of Sexual Identity.* Chicago: University of Chicago Press, 2000.

– "Sexual Modernity in the Works of Richard von Krafft-Ebing and Albert Moll. *Medical History* 56, no. 2 (April 2012): 133–55.

Ozawa-de Silva, Brenda. "Peace, Pastors, and Politics: Tactics of Resistance in East Germany." *Journal of Church and States* 47, no. 3 (2005): 503–29.

Pendas, Devin O. *Democracy, Nazi Trials, and Transitional Justice in Germany, 1945–1950.* Cambridge: Cambridge University Press, 2020.

Pfaff, Steven. *Exit-Voice Dynamics and the Collapse of East Germany: The Crisis of Leninism and the Revolution of 1989.* Durham, NC: Duke University Press, 2006.

Pfister, Elisabeth. *Unternehmen Romeo.* Berlin: Aufbau-Verlag, 1999.

Plant, Richard. *The Pink Triangle: The Nazi War against Homosexuals.* New York: Macmillan, 2011.

Plastargias, Jannis. *RotZSchwul: Der Beginn einer Bewegung.* Berlin: Querverlag, 2015.

Plötz, Kirsten. "Verfolgung und Diskriminierung der weiblichen Homosexualität in Rheinland-Pfalz 1947 bis 1973." In *Aufarbeitung der strafrechtlichen Verfolgung und Rehabilitierung homosexueller Menschen,* edited by Kirsten Plötz und Günter Grau, 217–336. Mainz: Ministrium für Familie, Frauen, Jugend, Integration und Verbraucherschutz Rheinland-Pfalz, 2016.

Poiger, Uta G. *Jazz, Rock, and Rebels: Cold War Politics and American Culture in a Divided Germany.* Berkeley, CA: University of California Press, 2000.

Pond, Frank D. "A Comparative Survey and Analysis of Military Policies with Regard to Service by Gay Persons." In *Policy Concerning Homosexuality in the Armed Forces* (S. Hrg. 103–845), 951–1062. US Senate, 103rd Cong. (1993).

Port, Andrew I. *Conflict and Stability in the German Democratic Republic.* Cambridge: Cambridge University Press, 2007.

– "Love, Lust, and Lies under Communism: Family Values and Adulterous Liaisons in Early East Germany." *Central European History* 44, no. 3 (2011): 478–505.

Portelli, Alessandro. "The Peculiarities of Oral History." *History Workshop* no. 12 (Autumn 1981): 96–107.

Pretzel, Andreas. *NS-Opfer unter Vorbehalt: Homosexuelle Männer in Berlin nach 1945.* Münster: LIT Verlag, 2002.

– "Wiedergutmachung unter Vorbehalt und mit neuer Perspektive: Was Homosexuellen NS-Opfer verweigert wurde und was wir noch tun können." In *Ohnmacht und Aufbegehren: Homosexuelle Männer in der frühen Bundesrepublik,* edited by Andreas Pretzel and Volker Weiß, 91–116. Hamburg: Männerschwarm, 2010.

Pretzel, Andreas, and Volker Weiß. "Überlegungen zum Erbe der zweiten deutschen Homosexuellenbewegung." In *Ohnmacht und*

Aufbegehren: Homosexuelle Männer in der frühen Bundesrepublik, edited by Andreas Pretzel and Volker Weiß, 9–26. Hamburg: Männerschwarm, 2010.

Proctor, Robert. *Racial Hygiene: Medicine under the Nazis*. Cambridge, MA: Harvard University Press, 2002.

Rasberry, Vaughn. *Race and the Totalitarian Century: Geopolitics in the Black Literary Imagination*. Cambridge, MA: Harvard University Press, 2016.

Readings, Bill. *The University in Ruins*. Cambridge, MA: Harvard University Press, 1996.

Reardon, Sara. "HIV's Patient Zero Exonerated." *Nature* (26 October 2016).

Reichert, Martin. *Die Kapsel: Aids in der Bundesrepublik*. Berlin: Suhrkamp, 2018.

Richardson, Diane. "Sexuality and Citizenship." *Sociology* 32, no. 1 (1998): 83–100.

Richardson-Little, Ned. *The Human Rights Dictatorship: Socialism, Global Solidarity and Revolution in East Germany*. Cambridge: Cambridge University Press, 2020.

– "Citizenship and Sexuality: What Do We Mean by 'Citizenship'?" *Counterpoints* 367 (2012): 219–28.

Ritzheimer, Kara L. *"Trash," Censorship, and National Identity in Early Twentieth-Century Germany*. Cambridge: Cambridge University Press, 2016.

Rosenberg, Clifford D. *Policing Paris: The Origins of Modern Immigration Control between the Wars*. Ithaca, NY: Cornell University Press, 2006.

Rosenkranz, Bernhard, and Gottfried Lorenz. *Hamburg auf anderen Wegen: Die Geschichte des schwulen Lebens in der Hansestadt*. Hamburg: Lambda, 2012.

Ross, Corey. *The East German Dictatorship: Problems and Perspectives in the Interpretation of the GDR*. London: Bloomsbury Academic, 2002.

Ross, Kristin. *Fast Cars, Clean Bodies: Decolonization and the Reordering of French Culture*. Cambridge, MA: MIT Press, 1996.

Rothberg, Michael. "The Work of Testimony in the Age of Decolonization: 'Chronicle of a Summer,' Cinema Verité, and the Emergence of the Holocaust Survivor." *PMLA* 119, no. 5 (October 2004): 1231–46.

– "Between Auschwitz and Algeria: Multidirectional Memory and the Counterpublic Witness." *Critical Inquiry* 33, no. 1 (Autumn 2006): 158–84.

Rottmann, Andrea. "Queer Home Berlin?: Making Queer Selves and Spaces in the Divided City, 1945–1970." University of Michigan, 2019.

Rueschemeyer, Marilyn, and Hanna Schissler. "Women in the Two Germanys." *German Studies Review* 13 (1990): 71–85.

Ruff, Mark Edward. *The Wayward Flock: Catholic Youth in Postwar West Germany, 1945–1965*. Chapel Hill, NC: University of North Carolina Press, 2005.

Rupp, Leila J. "The Persistence of Transnational Organizing: The Case of the Homophile Movement." *The American Historical Review* 116, no. 4 (2011): 1014–39.

Rydström, Jens. "Introduction: Same-Sex Sexuality and the Law in Scandinavia 1842–1999." In *Criminally Queer: Homosexuality and Criminal*

Law in Scandinavia, 1842–1999, edited by Jens Rydström and Kati Mustola, 13–40. Amsterdam: Aksant, 2007.

– *Odd Couples: A History of Gay Marriage in Scandinavia*. Amsterdam: Amsterdam University Press, 2011.

Samper Vendrell, Javier. *The Seduction of Youth: Print Culture and Homosexual Rights in the Weimar Republic*. Toronto: University of Toronto Press, 2020.

Sandford, Gregory. *From Hitler to Ulbricht: The Communist Reconstruction of East Germany, 1945–1956*. Princeton, NJ: Princeton University Press, 2017.

Sandfort, Theo. "Pedophilia and the Gay Movement." *Journal of Homosexuality* 13, no. 2/3 (1987): 89–110.

Sarotte, M.E. *Dealing with the Devil: East Germany, Détente, and Ostpolitik, 1969–1973*. Chapel Hill, NC: University of North Carolina Press, 2003.

Saxonberg, Steven. *The Fall: A Comparative Study of the End of Communism in Czechoslovakia, East Germany, Hungary and Poland*. New York: Routledge, 2013.

Schäfer, Christian. *"Widernatürliche Unzucht" (§§ 175, 175a, 175b, 182 a.F. StGB): Reformdiskussion und Gesetzgebung seit 1945*. Berlin: Berliner Wissenschafts-Verlag, 2006.

– "Das Ringen um §175 StGB während der Post-Adenauer-Ära – Der überfällige Wandel einer Sitten- zu einer Jugendschutzvorschrift." In *Ohnmacht und Aufbegehren: Homosexuelle Männer in der frühen Bundesrepublik*, edited by Andreas Pretzel and Volker Weiß, 189–210. Hamburg: Männerschwarm, 2010.

Schappach, Beate. "Geballte Faust, Doppelaxt, rosa Winkel: Gruppenkonstituierende Symbole der Frauen-, Lesben- und Schwulenbewegung." In *Linksalternative Milieus und Neue Soziale Bewegungen in den 1970er Jahren*, edited by Cordia Baumann, Sebastian Gehrig, and Nicolas Büchse, 259–86. Heidelberg: C. Winter, 2011.

Schiefelbein, Dieter. "Wiederbeginn der juristischen Verfolgung homosexueller Männer in der Bundesrepublik Deutschland: Die Homosexuellen-Prozesse in Frankfurt am Main 1950/51." *Zeitschrift für Sexualforschung* 5, no. 1 (1992): 59–73.

Schissler, Hanna. "Writing about 1950s West Germany." In *The Miracle Years: A Cultural History of West Germany, 1949–1968*, edited by Hanna Schissler, 1–15. Princeton, NJ: Princeton University Press, 2001.

Schmidt, Axel J., Ford Hickson, Peter Weatherburn, Ulrich Marcus, and The EMIS Network. "Comparison of the Performance of STI Screening Services for Gay and Bisexual Men across 40 European Cities: Results from the European MSM Internet Survey." *Sexually Transmitted Infections* (June 2013): 575–82.

Schoppmann, Claudia. *Nationalsozialistische Sexualpolitik und weibliche Homosexualität*. Pfaffenweiler: Centaurus-Verlagsgesellschaft, 1991.

– "The Position of Lesbian Women in the Nazi Period." In *Hidden Holocaust? Gay and Lesbian Persecution in Germany 1933–1945*, edited by Günter Grau, 8–15. London: Cassell, 1993.

– *Days of Masquerade*. New York: Columbia University Press, 1996.

– "National Socialist Policies towards Female Homosexuality." Translated by Elizabeth Harvey. In *Gender Relations in German History: Power, Agency and Experience from the Sixteenth to the Twentieth Century*, edited by Lynn Abrams and Elizabeth Harvey, 177–87. London: UCL Press, 1996.

– *Verbotene Verhältnisse: Frauenliebe 1938–1945*. Berlin: Quer Verlag, 1999.

– "Zwischen strafrechtlicher Verfolgung und gesellschaftlicher Ächtung: Lesbische Frauen im, 'Dritten Reich.'" In *Homophobie und Devianz: Weibliche und männliche Homosexualität im Nationalsozialismus*, edited by Insa Eschebach, 35–52. Berlin: Metropol, 2012.

Schroeder, Klaus. *Der SED-Staat: Partei, Staat und Gesellschaft*. Munich: Hanser, 1998.

Schulz, Christian. *Paragraph 175 (abgewickelt): Homosexualität und Strafrecht im Nachkriegsdeutschland: Rechtsprechung, juristische Diskussion und Reformen seit 1945*. Hamburg: Männerschwarm, 1994.

Schwartz, Michael. *Homosexuelle, Seilschaften, Verrat: Ein transnationales Stereotyp im 20. Jahrhundert*. Berlin: De Gruyter Oldenbourg, 2019.

Scott, Joan Wallach. "The Evidence of Experience." *Critical Inquiry* 17, no. 4 (1 July 1991): 773–97.

Scott, J. Wilbur, and Sandra Carson Stanley, eds. *Gays and Lesbians in the Military: Issues, Concerns, and Contrasts*. New York: Aldine de Gruyter, 1994.

Sedgwick, Eve Kosofsky. *Epistemology of the Closet*. Berkeley, CA: University of California Press, 2008.

Sender, Katherine. *Business, Not Politics: The Making of the Gay Market*. New York: Columbia University Press, 2004.

Setz, Wolfram, ed. *Homosexualität in der DDR: Materialien und Meinungen*. Hamburg: Männerschwarm Verlag, 2006.

Sharples, Caroline. *Postwar Germany and the Holocaust*. London: Bloomsbury, 2015.

Sheehan, James J. "What It Means to Be a State: States and Violence in Twentieth-Century Europe." *Journal of Modern European History* 1, no. 1 (2003): 11–23.

– "The Problem of Sovereignty in European History." *The American Historical Review* 111, no. 1 (February 2006): 1–15.

– *Where Have All the Soldiers Gone?: The Transformation of Modern Europe*. Boston: Houghton Mifflin Harcourt, 2008.

Sheffer, Edith. *Burned Bridge: How East and West Germans Made the Iron Curtain*. New York: Oxford University Press, 2014.

– *Asperger's Children: The Origins of Autism in Nazi Vienna*. New York: Norton, 2018.

Shepard, Todd. *The Invention of Decolonization: The Algerian War and the Remaking of France.* Ithaca, NY: Cornell University Press, 2008.

– *Sex, France, and Arab Men, 1962–1979.* Chicago: University of Chicago Press, 2018.

Shepherd, Simon. "Gay Sex Spy Orgy: The State's Need for Queers." In *Coming On Strong: Gay Politics and Culture,* edited by Simon Shephard and Mick Wallis, 213–30. Crows Nest: Unwin Hyman, 1989.

Shilts, Randy. *And the Band Played On: Politics, People, and the AIDS Epidemic.* New York: St Martin's Press, 2007.

Sigusch, Volkmar. "The Sexologist Albert Moll – between Sigmund Freud and Magnus Hirschfeld." *Medical History* 56, no. 2 (2012): 184–200.

Smith, Tom. *Comrades in Arms: Military Masculinities in East German Culture.* New York: Berghahn Books, 2020.

Steiner, André. *The Plans That Failed: An Economic History of East Germany, 1945–1989.* New York: Berghahn Books, 2010.

Steinke, Ronen. *Fritz Bauer oder Auschwitz vor Gericht.* Munich: Piper, 2015.

Stelkens, Jochen. "Machtwechsel in Ost-Berlin. Der Sturz Walter Ulbrichts 1971." *Vierteljahreshefte für Zeitgeschichte* 45, no. 4 (1997): 503–33.

Stewart-Winter, Timothy. *Queer Clout: Chicago and the Rise of Gay Politics.* Philadelphia, PA: University of Pennsylvania Press, 2016.

Stockham, Aaron J. "'I Have Never Cut His Budget and I Never Expect To': The House Appropriations Committee's Role in Increasing the Federal Bureau of Investigation's Cold War Power." *The Historian* 75, no. 3 (Fall 2013): 499–516.

Stokes, Lauren. "The Permanent Refugee Crisis in the Federal Republic of Germany, 1949–." *Central European History* 52, Special Issue 1 (March 2019): 19–44.

– "The Protagonists of Democratization in the Federal Republic." *German History* (29 June 2021): 1–13.

Stone, Dan. *The Liberation of the Camps: The End of the Holocaust and Its Aftermath.* New Haven, CT: Yale University Press, 2015.

Strote, Noah Benezra. *Lions and Lambs: Conflict in Weimar and the Creation of Post-Nazi Germany.* New Haven, CT: Yale University Press, 2017.

Stümke, Hans-Georg. *Homosexuelle in Deutschland: Eine politische Geschichte.* Munich: CH Beck, 1989.

Stümke, Hans-Georg, and Rudi Finkler. *Rosa Winkel, rosa Listen: Homosexuelle und 'Gesundes Volksempfinden' von Auschwitz bis heute.* Reinbek bei Hamburg: Rowohlt, 1981.

Suleiman, Ezra. "Bureaucracy and Democratic Consolidation: Lessons from Eastern Europe." In *Transitions to Democracy,* edited by Lisa Anderson, 141–67. New York: Columbia University Press, 1999.

Sulick, Michael J. *American Spies: Espionage against the United States from the Cold War to the Present.* Washington, DC: Georgetown University Press, 2013.

Sullivan, Nikki, and Craig Middleton. *Queering the Museum*. New York: Routledge, 2020.

Sutton, Katie. *The Masculine Woman in Weimar Germany*. New York: Berghahn Books, 2011.

– "A Tale of Origins: The Emergence of Sexual Citizens in German Modernity." *Journal of the History of Sexuality* 27, no. 1 (2018): 186–207.

– *Sex between Body and Mind: Psychoanalysis and Sexology in the German-speaking World, 1890s-1930s*. Ann Arbor, MI: University of Michigan Press, 2019.

Sweet, Dennis. "The Church, the Stasi, and Socialist Integration: Three Stages of Lesbian and Gay Emancipation in the Former German Democratic Republic." *Journal of Homosexuality* 29, no. 2/3 and 4 (1995): 351–68.

Szulc, Lukasz. *Transnational Homosexuals in Communist Poland: Cross-border Flows in Gay and Lesbian Magazines*. New York: Palgrave Macmillan, 2018.

Tammer, Teresa. "Schwul bis über die Mauer: Die Westkontakte der Ost-Berliner Schwulenbewegung in den 1970er und 1980er Jahren." In *Konformitäten und Konfrontationen: Homosexuelle in der DDR*, edited by Rainer Marbach and Volker Weiß, 70–90. Hamburg: Männerschwarm, 2017.

Taylor, Frederick. *The Berlin Wall: A World Divided, 1961–1989*. Harper Perennial, 2006.

Thinius, Bert. "Ausbruch auf dem grauen Versteck. Ankunft im bunten Ghetto?" In *Schwuler Osten: Homosexuelle Männer in der DDR*, edited by Kurt Starke, 11–90. Berlin: Ch. Links, 1994.

– "Erfahrungen schwuler Männer in der DDR und in Deutschland Ost." In *Homosexualität in der DDR: Materialien und Meinungen*, edited by Wolfram Setz, 9–88. Hamburg: Männerschwarm Verlag, 2006.

Tocqueville, Alexis de. *The Old Regime and the Revolution*. Translated by John Bonner. New York: Harper, 1856.

Trahair, Richard C.S., and Robert Miller. *Encyclopedia of Cold War Espionage, Spies, and Secret Operations*. New York: Enigma Books, 2012.

Tremblay, Sébastien. "'The Proudest Symbol We Could Put Forward?': The Pink Triangle as a Transatlantic Symbol of Gay and Lesbian Identities from the 1970s to the 1990s." Freie Universität Berlin, 2020.

Tümmers, Henning. *AIDS: Autopsie einer Bedrohung im geteilten Deutschland*. Göttingen: Wallstein, 2017.

Turner, Henry Ashby, Jr. *Germany from Partition to Reunification*. New Haven, CT: Yale University Press, 1992.

Vaid, Urvashi. *Virtual Equality: The Mainstreaming of Gay and Lesbian Liberation*. New York: Anchor Books, 1996.

Vilasi, Antonella Colonna. *The History of the Stasi*. Bloomington, IN: AuthorHouse, 2015.

Vogt, Timothy R. *Denazification in Soviet-Occupied Germany: Brandenburg, 1945–1948*. Cambridge, MA: Harvard University Press, 2000.

von der Goltz, Anna, ed. *"Talkin' 'Bout My Generation": Conflicts of Generation Building and Europe's "1968."* Göttingen: Wallenstein Verlag, 2011.

– "Making Sense of East Germany's 1968: Multiple Trajectories and Contrasting Memories." *Memory Studies* 6, no. 1 (1 January 2013): 53–69.

– "Attraction and Aversion in Germany's '1968': Encountering the Western Revolt in East Berlin." *Journal of Contemporary History* 50, no. 3 (2015): 536–59.

– *The Other '68ers: Student Protest and Christian Democracy in West Germany.* Oxford: Oxford University Press, 2021.

von Hodenberg, Christina. "Writing Women's Agency into the History of the Federal Republic: '1968,' Historians, and Gender." *Central European History* 52, Special Issue 1 (March 2019): 87–106.

von Rönn, Peter. "Der Homosexualitätsentwürfe von Hans Giese und der lange Schatten von Hans Bürger-Prinz." *Zeitschrift für Sexualforschung* 13, no. 4 (December 2000): 277–310.

Wachsmann, Nikolaus. *Hitler's Prisons: Legal Terror in Nazi Germany.* New Haven, CT: Yale University Press, 2015.

Wackerfuss, Andrew. *Stormtrooper Families: Homosexuality and Community in the Early Nazi Movement.* New York: Harrington Park Press, 2015.

Wagner, Brigitta B. *DEFA after East Germany.* Rochester, NY: Camden House, 2014.

Warner, Michael. *The Trouble with Normal: Sex, Politics, and the Ethics of Queer Life.* Cambridge, MA: Harvard University Press, 1999.

Weber, Hermann. *Von der SBZ zur DDR, 1945–1968.* Hannover: Verlag für Literatur und Zeitgeschichte, 1966.

Wehler, Hans-Ulrich. "Ein deutsches Säkulum?" *Berliner Zeitung* (8 August 1996): 18.

Weiner, Tim. *Enemies: A History of the FBI.* New York: Random House, 2012.

Weitz, Eric. "The Ever-present Other: Communism in the Making of West Germany." In *The Miracle Years: A Cultural History of West Germany, 1949–1968,* edited by Hanna Schissler, 219–32. Princeton, NJ: Princeton University Press, 2001.

– *Weimar Germany: Promise and Tragedy.* Princeton, NJ: Princeton University Press, 2007.

Whisnant, Clayton. "Styles of Masculinity in the West German Gay Scene, 1950–1965." *Central European History* 39, no. 3 (2006): 359–93.

– "Gay German History: Future Directions?" *Journal of the History of Sexuality* 17, no. 1 (2008): 1–10.

– *Male Homosexuality in West Germany: Between Persecution and Freedom, 1945–1969.* New York: Palgrave Macmillan, 2012.

– *Queer Identities and Politics in Germany: A History, 1880–1945.* New York: Harrington Park Press, 2016.

Wiliarty, Sarah. *The CDU and the Politics of Gender in Germany: Bringing Women to the Party.* Cambridge: Cambridge University Press, 2010.

Wittmann, Rebecca. *Beyond Justice: The Auschwitz Trial.* Cambridge, MA: Harvard University Press, 2012.

Wolfert, Raimund. "'Sollen wir der Öffentlichkeit noch mehr Anlaß geben, gegen die "Schwulen" zu sein?': Zur Position der Internationalen Homophilen Welt-Orbganisation (IHWO)." In *Ohnmacht und Aufbegehren: Homosexuelle Männer in der frühen Bundesrepublik,* edited by Andreas Pretzel and Volker Weiß, 210–30. Hamburg: Männerschwarm, 2010.

Wolff, Frank. *Die Mauergesellschaft: Kalter Krieg, Menschenrechte und die deutsch-deutsche Migration 1961–1989.* Berlin: Suhrkamp, 2019.

Wolin, Sheldon S. *Democracy Incorporated: Managed Democracy and the Specter of Inverted Totalitarianism.* Princeton, NJ: Princeton University Press, 2017.

Woods, Gregory. *Homintern: How Gay Culture Liberated the Modern World.* New Haven, CT: Yale University Press, 2016.

Wüstenberg, Jenny. *Civil Society and Memory in Postwar Germany.* Cambridge: Cambridge University Press, 2017.

Yoder, Jennifer A. *From East Germans to Germans?: The New Postcommunist Elites.* Durham, NC: Duke University Press, 1999.

Zinn, Alexander. *"Aus dem Volkskörper entfernt"? Homosexuelle Männer im Nationalsozialismus.* Frankfurt am Main: Campus, 2018.

zur Nieden, Susanne. "Aufstieg und Fall des virilen Männerhelden: Der Skandal um Ernst Röhm und seine Ermordung." In *Homosexualität und Staatsräson: Männlichkeit, Homophobie und Politik in Deutschland 1900–1945,* edited by Susanne zur Neiden, 147–92. Frankfurt am Main: Campus, 2005.

Index

Page numbers in *italics* indicate illustrations or graphics

SED (Socialist Unity Party): about,
68, 72; discussions with, 203, 211;
gay/lesbian members of, 78, 227;
and opposition to criminalizing
homosexuality, 117; and SEW, 130.
See also PDS (Party of Democratic
Socialism)
Sedgwick, Eve Kosofsky, 26, 29
seduction of youth: in East Germany,
71; and police, 44–5. *See also* age
of consent; Paragraph (§)175;
Paragraph (§)175(a)
Sex Welle, 95, 99
sex workers: and criminal code,
28, 32, 37, 45, 60–1, 63–5, 71, 91;
cruising spots, 56–7; at gay bars,
174; and the Stasi, 107, 111
sexology, 23, 24, 26, 91
sexual acts, 31, 52
sexual citizenship: about, 11–12;
and activism, 98, 126–7, 141, 147,
228; between East/West Germany,
19–20; and gay liberation, 232–3;
and private/public divide, 14
sexual education, 138, 194
sexual violence, 61, 67, 74
sexuality, 26, 80, 131
*Sexuality and Crime (Sexualität und
Verbrechen)* (book), 94–5
Sheffer, Edith, 226, 247n27
Shilts, Randy, 181
Siegessäule (magazine), 177
Sillge, Ursula: about, 144; on lesbians/
lesbianism, 145, 192, 206–7; medical
experiences of, 194; organizing, 162,
163, 202, 211; Sunday Club, 235; on
Werner's book, 209
Smith, Tom, 301n176
Social-Liberal Coalition (SPD-FDP),
119, 166
socialism: about, 68–9, 72, 129–30,
147–8; and homosexual action
groups, 129–32; life under, 143–4;

as a threat, 42, 51; and views of
homosexuality, 27–8, 74, 223
socialist personality, 73
Soviet Union: activity in Germany,
65, 68; and gay intelligence,
34, 259n86; historical events,
72, 174; persecution of gay
men, 74; recriminalization of
homosexuality, 28; treaties signed
with, 119
Spartacus International Gay Guide
(guidebook), 120, *121*, 187–8
SPD (Social Democratic Party):
and the Christian Democrats,
100; and elections, 41, 231; and
Engholm, 165–6; and the KPD, 27,
72; and Paragraph (§)175, 138; and
Stecher, 232
Der Spiegel (periodical): AIDS
coverage, 177, *178*, 180, 213; on gay
activist demonstrations, 134; on
homosexuality, 97, 99; on Night of
Long Knives, 47; and Paragraph
(§)175, 39, 81, *82*, 167, 168, 230;
Süßmuth interviewed in, 179
Stapel, Eduard: about, 190, 191; on the
Stasi, 105, 218, 219–20
Stasi, the (Ministry for State
Security): about, 15–16, 105, 107,
199; and Americans, 107; and
church groups, 20, 191, 216, 218–19;
citizens as informants, 158–9;
departments, 203–5; fear of gay
people, 19, 104–5, 110, 115–16,
199–201, 286n52; and gay activism,
299n121; and gay IMs, 108–12,
114–15, 116, 117; and gay working
circles, 198–201, 204, 215–16, 219,
220; and HIB, 156–63, 203; and
homosexuality, 77–8, 105, 215;
Inoffizielle Mitarbeiter (IMs), 105;
and lesbians, 116, 200–1;
memoranda, 203–6; perceptions of

GERMAN AND EUROPEAN STUDIES

General Editor: Jennifer L. Jenkins

Milton Keynes UK
Ingram Content Group UK Ltd.
UKHW012228190424
441406UK00003B/265

9 781487 542146